Evolutionary Computation, Metaheuristics, Nature-Inspired Algorithms, and Symmetry

Evolutionary Computation, Metaheuristics, Nature-Inspired Algorithms, and Symmetry

Guest Editors

Yirui Wang
Shangce Gao
Yang Yu

MDPI

Basel • Beijing • Wuhan • Barcelona • Belgrade • Novi Sad • Cluj • Manchester

Guest Editors
Yirui Wang
Faculty of Electrical
Engineering and Computer
Science
Ningbo University
Ningbo
China

Shangce Gao
Faculty of Engineering
University of Toyama
Toyama
Japan

Yang Yu
College of Automation &
College of Artificial
Intelligence
Nanjing University of Posts
and Telecommunications
Nanjing
China

Editorial Office
MDPI AG
Grosspeteranlage 5
4052 Basel, Switzerland

This is a reprint of the Special Issue, published open access by the journal *Symmetry* (ISSN 2073-8994), freely accessible at: https://www.mdpi.com/journal/symmetry/special_issues/24GBAD8UEM.

For citation purposes, cite each article independently as indicated on the article page online and as indicated below:

Lastname, A.A.; Lastname, B.B. Article Title. *Journal Name* **Year**, *Volume Number*, Page Range.

ISBN 978-3-7258-5833-0 (Hbk)
ISBN 978-3-7258-5834-7 (PDF)
https://doi.org/10.3390/books978-3-7258-5834-7

Contents

About the Editors

Yirui Wang

Yirui Wang received his Ph.D. degree from the Faculty of Engineering, University of Toyama, Toyama, Japan, in 2020. He is currently an Associate Professor with the Faculty of Electrical Engineering and Computer Science, Ningbo University, Zhejiang, China. His research interests include computational intelligence, swarm intelligent algorithms, combinatorial optimization, and computer vision.

Shangce Gao

Shangce Gao received his Ph.D. degree in Innovative Life Science from the University of Toyama, Toyama, Japan, in 2011. He is currently a Professor with the Faculty of Engineering, University of Toyama, Japan. His current research interests include nature-inspired technologies, machine learning, and neural networks for real-world applications. He serves as an Associate Editor for many international journals such as *IEEE Transactions on Neural Networks and Learning Systems*, and *IEEE/CAA Journal of Automatica Sinica.*

Yang Yu

Yang Yu received his M.S. and Ph.D. degrees from the University of Toyama, Toyama, Japan, in 2017 and 2020, respectively. He is currently a Lecturer within the College of Automation & College of Artificial Intelligence, Nanjing University of Posts and Telecommunications. His main research interests are evolutionary computing, optimization problems, and artificial neural networks.

symmetry

MDPI

Article

GAPSO: Cloud-Edge-End Collaborative Task Offloading Based on Genetic Particle Swarm Optimization

Wu Wen [1], Yibin Huang [1], Zhong Xiao [2,*], Lizhuang Tan [3] and Peiying Zhang [4]

1 School of Computer Science and Cyber Engineering, Guangzhou University, Guangzhou 510006, China; wenwu@gzhu.edu.cn (W.W.); gd.hyb@e.gzhu.edu.cn (Y.H.)
2 School of Mechanical and Electrical Engineering, Guangzhou University, Guangzhou 510006, China
3 Key Laboratory of Computing Power Network and Information Security, Ministry of Education, Qilu University of Technology (Shandong Academy of Sciences), Jinan 250014, China; tanlzh@sdas.org
4 Qingdao Institute of Software, College of Computer Science and Technology, China University of Petroleum (East China), Qingdao 266580, China; zhangpeiying@upc.edu.cn
* Correspondence: gzxiaozhong@gzhu.edu.cn

Abstract

In the 6G era, the proliferation of smart devices has led to explosive growth in data volume. The traditional cloud computing can no longer meet the demand for efficient processing of large amounts of data. Edge computing can solve the energy loss problems caused by transmission delay and multi-level forwarding in cloud computing by processing data close to the data source. In this paper, we propose a cloud–edge–end collaborative task offloading strategy with task response time and execution energy consumption as the optimization targets under a limited resource environment. The tasks generated by smart devices can be processed using three kinds of computing nodes, including user devices, edge servers, and cloud servers. The computing nodes are constrained by bandwidth and computing resources. For the target optimization problem, a genetic particle swarm optimization algorithm considering three layers of computing nodes is designed. The task offloading optimization is performed by introducing (1) opposition-based learning algorithm, (2) adaptive inertia weights, and (3) adjustive acceleration coefficients. All metaheuristic algorithms adopt a symmetric training method to ensure fairness and consistency in evaluation. Through experimental simulation, compared with the classic evolutionary algorithm, our algorithm reduces the objective function value by about 6–12% and has higher algorithm convergence speed, accuracy, and stability.

Keywords: cloud–edge–end collaborative network; task offloading; method symmetry; genetic algorithm; particle swarm optimization; metaheuristic algorithm

1. Introduction

With the rapid advancement of intelligent technology, mobile devices have become extremely popular in daily life. For example, in the Internet of Vehicles field, mobile devices equipped on vehicles are widely used for image processing, video streaming, and augmented reality/virtual reality [1]. In the smart healthcare domain, smart devices and sensors are widely used to remotely collect and monitor patient status in order to collect patient health data [2,3]. In the industrial field, Industry 5.0 is the next stage of industrial development. It has become a trend to integrate modern technologies such as artificial intelligence, robotics, and the Internet of Things into manufacturing and production processes [4]. Numerous sensors and mobile devices continuously collect and generate massive amounts of data. However, mobile devices themselves have significant limitations in processing large-scale data. Their computing power and storage capacity are difficult to cope with such a huge data torrent. At the same time, the centralized processing method of traditional cloud computing is not friendly to delay-sensitive tasks [5]. Long delays will occur during data transmission, which cannot meet the immediacy requirements of scenarios such as autonomous driving and real-time industrial control. Edge computing (EC) sinks computing resources to the edge of the network. Mobile devices can offload tasks to edge servers to achieve task processing with lower transmission delays, while expanding computing resources and improving user service quality.

The continuous generation of large-scale data has led to an increasing demand for computing resources and user experience. In this context, cloud computing and mobile edge computing each play an indispensable and important role. Cloud computing provides powerful centralized computing and storage resources, which are suitable for processing tasks that require large amounts of computing and data storage [6,7]. Edge computing, due to its proximity to the data source, can provide low-latency computing services, which is particularly suitable for tasks with high real-time requirements. On the other hand, user devices themselves also have certain computing resources. For simple tasks and scenarios with high privacy protection requirements, local computing can be used for data processing. However, a single form of edge computing or cloud computing cannot meet the needs of complex scenarios and cannot balance energy consumption and time delay [8]. The cloud–edge–end collaborative computing model that integrates cloud computing, edge computing, and local computing can give full play to their respective advantages and build an efficient and flexible data processing architecture.

Task offloading is a key link in the cloud–edge–end collaborative environment, which involves the decision-making process of transferring tasks from mobile devices to edge servers or cloud servers [9]. This process requires a comprehensive consideration of the characteristics of the task itself, the performance parameters of the user device, the resource status of the edge server, and the relevant properties of the cloud server. By formulating a reasonable task offloading strategy, cloud–edge–end collaborative computing can achieve full utilization of resources and efficient processing of tasks, thereby meeting the diverse needs of users for service quality in different scenarios.

In this paper, we use the Genetic Particle Swarm Optimization (GAPSO) algorithm to solve the task offloading problem in the cloud–edge–end collaborative network environment. This algorithm helps to reduce task response time and energy consumption under the constraints of limited computing resources and edge server bandwidth. The main contributions of this paper are as follows:

(1) This paper proposes a task processing framework for a cloud–edge–end collaborative environment. User devices can choose between three computing modes: local computing, edge computing, and cloud computing. Compared with the traditional mode, the cloud–edge–end collaborative environment can better utilize limited computing resources and improve data processing efficiency.

(2) This paper implements a task transmission method that fully considers the bandwidth resources of edge servers. The transmission process of tasks from user devices (UDs) to edge servers (ESs) and ES to cloud servers (CSs) is more in line with the actual situation.

(3) This paper designs a GAPSO algorithm, which improves the diversity of initial particles through the Opposition-Based Learning (OBL) algorithm, introduces adaptive

inertia weights and adjustive acceleration coefficients, and uses a genetic algorithm (GA) to optimize the local optimal solution of particles.

(4) This paper uses a symmetrical training method to conduct multiple experiments. The experimental results show that the GAPSO algorithm can achieve higher convergence accuracy, stability, and convergence speed.

In this paper, the entire experiment is constructed using a symmetric design method. All metaheuristic algorithms are applied under the same training conditions, including the same cloud–edge–end collaborative architecture and environmental parameter configuration. At the same time, the optimization target metric, number of training iterations, and experimental evaluation indicators are also kept consistent. This structured framework not only enhances the reliability of comparative analysis but also highlights the importance of symmetric experiments in the study of cloud–edge–end collaborative applications.

The rest of this paper is organized as follows. Related work is reviewed in Section 2. Section 3 presents the system model and problem formulation of this paper. The proposed GAPSO algorithm is introduced in Section 4. Section 5 provides our experimental results. Finally, in Section 6, we summarize our work.

2. Related Work

2.1. *Task Offloading for Edge Computing*

Edge computing task offloading refers to offloading tasks to edge servers close to data sources or user devices. Edge computing is usually deployed close to end devices, such as base stations or routers. Compared with cloud computing, edge computing can significantly reduce network latency and bandwidth usage [10,11] and is suitable for applications with high real-time requirements and large data volumes, such as intelligent transportation [12], smart healthcare [13], autonomous driving [14], unmanned aerial vehicles (UAVs) [15], and the Metaverse [16]. Zhou [17] considered the joint task offloading and resource allocation problem of multiple MEC server collaboration and proposed a two-level algorithm. The upper-level algorithm combines the advantages of algorithms such as PSO and GA to globally search for advanced offloading solutions. The lower-level algorithm is used to effectively utilize server resources and generate resource allocation plans with fairness guarantees. Sun [18] considers splitting multiple computationally intensive tasks into multiple subtasks simultaneously. A joint task segmentation and parallel scheduling scheme based on the dominant actor–critic (A2C) algorithm is proposed to minimize the total task execution delay. Chen [19] proposed a two-stage evolutionary search scheme (TESA), where the first stage optimizes computing resource selection, and the second stage jointly optimizes task offloading decisions and resource allocation based on a subset of the first stage, thereby significantly reducing latency. Zhu [20] considered the impact of user offloading decisions, uplink power allocation, and MEC computing resource allocation on system performance. An edge computing task offloading strategy based on improved genetic algorithm (IGA) is proposed.

2.2. *Task Offloading for Cloud–Edge Collaboration*

Cloud–edge collaborative task offloading refers to the collaborative processing between cloud computing and edge computing. Tasks can be allocated between the cloud and edge based on their characteristics and requirements. The advantage of cloud–edge collaboration is that it can take into account the powerful computing power of cloud computing and the low latency characteristics of edge computing, thereby optimizing resource utilization and service quality [21,22]. Zhang [23] proposed a task offloading strategy based on a time delay penalty mechanism and a bipartite graph matching method to optimize the task allocation between edge devices and the cloud. The aim is to minimize system energy consumption. Gao [24] established a dynamic queue model and used the drift and penalty function framework to transform the problem into a constrained optimization problem. Finally, a task offloading algorithm based on Lyapunov optimization was proposed. Lei [25] considered that the performance of geographically distributed edge servers varies over time and developed a dynamic offloading strategy based on a probabilistic evolutionary game theory model.

2.3. Task Offloading for Cloud–Edge–End Collaboration

Cloud–edge–end collaborative task offloading further extends the concept of cloud–edge collaboration by incorporating the computing capabilities of end devices (such as smartphones, sensors, and IoT devices). In this model, tasks can be flexibly allocated between end devices, edge servers, and cloud servers. This collaborative approach maximizes the use of computing resources at all levels and provides a more flexible and efficient computing solution. Liu [26] decomposed the task offloading and resource allocation problem into two sub-problems. First, the optimal solution of the task partitioning ratio was obtained using a mathematical analytical method, and then the Lagrangian dual (LD) method was used to optimize the task offloading and resource allocation strategies to minimize the task processing delay. Zhu [27] proposed a speed-aware and customized task offloading and resource allocation scheme aimed at optimizing service latency in mobile edge computing systems. By utilizing the Advantage Actor Critic (A2C) algorithm, computing nodes are dynamically selected to improve user service quality. Qu [28] takes the total task execution delay and key task execution delay as the optimization goals and proposes an emergency offloading strategy for smart factories based on cloud–edge collaboration through the Fast Chemical Reaction Optimization (Fast-CRO) algorithm. The algorithm can quickly make emergency unloading decisions for the system. Wu [29] proposed an online task scheduling algorithm based on deep reinforcement learning for mobile edge computing networks with variable task arrival intensity to achieve online task offloading and optimize overall task latency. Ji [30] performed intelligent tasks through a cloud–edge collaborative computing network. A hybrid framework that combines a model-free deep reinforcement learning algorithm and a model-based optimization algorithm was proposed to jointly optimize communication resources and computing resources, achieving near-optimal energy performance. Zhou [31] proposed an edge server placement algorithm ISC-QL to determine the optimal placement location of edge servers in the Internet of Vehicles system, which achieved optimization of load balancing, average latency, and average energy consumption.

In summary, researchers have conducted a lot of research on the task offloading problem of cloud computing and edge computing. The relevant work is shown in Table 1, but there are relatively few studies that consider the collaborative integration of cloud, edge, and end for the task offloading environment. The above research content does not clarify the impact of edge bandwidth resources on the system data transmission environment. At the same time, there is a lack of stable and efficient algorithms to solve the task offloading problem of cloud–edge–end collaboration, which is crucial for optimizing the execution of large-scale tasks in a multi-user environment.

Table 1. Summary of related works versus our survey.

Reference	Task Offloading Environment			Optimization Objective		Algorithm
	Cloud	Edge	End	Completion Time	Energy Consumption	
[17]	✗	✓	✗	✓	✗	APGTO + FGRA two-level algorithm.
[18]	✗	✓	✗	✓	✗	Advantage Actor Critic (A2C) algorithm.
[19]	✗	✓	✓	✓	✗	Two-stage evolutionary search scheme (TESA).
[20]	✗	✓	✓	✓	✓	Improved genetic algorithm (IGA).
[23]	✓	✓	✗	✗	✓	Dichotomy search algorithm.
[24]	✓	✓	✗	✗	✓	Lyapunov optimization method.
[25]	✓	✓	✗	✓	✗	Evolutionary Game Algorithm.
[26]	✓	✓	✓	✓	✗	Mathematical analytical method and Lagrangian dual (LD) method.
[27]	✓	✓	✓	✓	✗	Speed aware and customized TORA scheme based on A2C algorithm.
[28]	✓	✓	✓	✓	✗	Fast Chemical Reaction Optimization (Fast-CRO) algorithm.
[29]	✓	✓	✓	✓	✗	Online task scheduling (Online-TS) algorithm.
[30]	✓	✓	✓	✗	✓	Deep reinforcement learning based hybrid (DRLH) framework.
[31]	✓	✓	✓	✓	✓	Edge Server Placement Algorithm ISC-QL.
Ours	✓	✓	✓	✓	✓	Genetic particle swarm optimization (GAPSO) algorithm.

3. System Model and Problem Formulation

As shown in Figure 1, we consider a three-layer network framework for cloud–edge–end collaboration, which mainly includes the cloud computing layer, edge computing layer, and user device layer. It consists of 1 CS, S ESs, and N UDs, with a total of $1 + S + N$ nodes. The coordinates of each node are composed of (X, Y, Z) three-dimensional coordinates. Each node has its own CPU clock frequency f, f_C represents the CPU clock frequency of the CS, f_{E_j} represents the CPU clock frequency of the j_{th} ES $(j \in S)$, and f_{U_i} represents the CPU clock frequency of the i_{th} UD $(i \in N)$. We assume that each i_{th} UD has M_i tasks to execute, and each task has a unique characteristic attribute d_k $(k \in M_i)$ to represent the computing data size of the task. Each task can be executed on its own user device, all edge servers, and cloud servers, and the offloading node is unique. Therefore, each task has $(S + 2)$ execution modes. For tasks with a small computing data size, they can be executed on the user device, while for tasks with a large computing data size, they can be transferred to the edge server or cloud server for execution, that is, the processing power of the user device itself is taken into account, while the high computing resources of the cloud server are also taken into account.

Since users are generally concerned about task completion efficiency, while service providers focus on the energy consumption of service provision, we focus on optimizing the average response time and average energy consumption of all tasks. In the three-layer network architecture, response time must account for the influence of transmission delay factors in both edge computing and cloud computing modes. For the cloud computing mode, the edge server is selected as a transit node. Given that cloud servers feature abundant bandwidth resources, edge servers act as transit nodes for both edge computing and cloud computing modes; thus, we focus on the bandwidth resource constraints of edge servers. W_j represents the bandwidth resource of the j_{th} ES.

In order to make full use of bandwidth resources and computing resources in the three-layer computing environment, resource exclusivity will be adopted. When there is a task transmission, the remaining tasks will wait for the release of bandwidth resources. Similarly, when there is a task execution, the remaining tasks will wait for the release of computing resources. Table 2 summarizes the key symbols used in this paper. Next, we introduce the response time model and energy consumption model, respectively [32–35], and analyze the three-layer computing mode corresponding to each model.

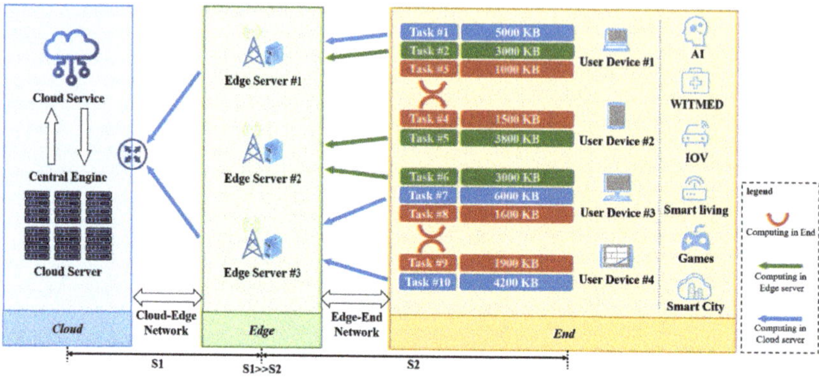

Figure 1. Cloud–edge–end collaborative computing model.

Table 2. Commonly used terms in cloud–edge–end model.

Notation	Description
N	The number of UD
S	The number of ES
M_i	The amount of tasks generated by i_{th} UD
M	Total number of tasks
d_k	The data size of k_{th} task
c	The number of CPU clock cycles required per bit
κ	The effective switching capacitance of the chip
W_j	The communication bandwidth of j_{th} ES
N_0	Power of noise
σ	Path loss index
f_{U_i}	The CPU clock frequency of i_{th} UD
f_{E_j}	The CPU clock frequency of j_{th} ES
f_C	The CPU clock frequency of the CS
p_U	The transmit power of UD
p_E	The transmit power of ES
q_E	Energy consumption per bit in ES
q_C	Energy consumption per bit in CS
D_{U_i,E_j}	The distance between i_{th} UE and j_{th} ES
g_{U_i,E_j}	Channel gain between i_{th} UE and j_{th} ES
$D_{E_j,C}$	The distance between j_{th} ES and CS
$g_{E_j,C}$	Channel gain between j_{th} ES and CS
r_{U_i,E_j}	The communication rate between i_{th} UD and j_{th} ES
$r_{E_j,C}$	The communication rate between j_{th} ES and CS
T_{res_k}	The response time of k_{th} task
EG_k	The energy consumption of k_{th} task

3.1. Response Time Model

Task response time refers to the complete time interval from task submission to the return of task processing results, and its components include task waiting time, task transmission time, and task processing time. In this subsection, we will calculate and analyze the response time of tasks in different computing modes.

(1) Local computing mode: The local computing mode means that the tasks generated by the user device are directly executed on the user device. The local computing mode is not affected by the transmission delay factor. The task response time is the sum of the execution waiting time and the execution time. When i_{th} UD is idle, the response time T_{res_k} of k_{th} task $(k \in Mi)$ in i_{th} UD is the local execution time of the task, and the task execution waiting time is 0. Otherwise, the response time T_{res_k} of k_{th} task needs to take into account the waiting time of the task. The task response time of the local computing mode is defined as follows:

$$T_{res_k} = T_{ew_k} + \frac{d_k c}{f_{U_i}} \tag{1}$$

where T_{ew_k} represents the execution waiting time of k_{th} task.

(2) Edge computing mode: The edge computing mode refers to the transmission of tasks generated by user devices to edge servers for execution. The edge computing mode needs to consider the transmission delay of tasks between user devices and edge servers. Since the result data after the task is executed is small, the transmission delay of the result data transmitted back to the user device is ignored here. The transmission time of k_{th} task is the transmission delay of k_{th} task from i_{th} UD to j_{th} ES. The task response time is the sum of the transmission waiting time, transmission time, execution waiting time, and execution time. When the edge server bandwidth resources are not occupied, the transmission waiting time of k_{th} task is 0. When j_{th} ES is idle, T_{ew_k} of k_{th} task is 0. The transmission rate r_{U_i,E_j} [36] between i_{th} UD and j_{th} ES is defined as follows:

$$D_{U_i,E_j} = \sqrt{(X_{E_j} - X_{U_i})^2 + (Y_{E_j} - Y_{U_i})^2 + (Z_{E_j} - Z_{U_i})^2} \tag{2}$$

$$g_{U_i,E_j} = (D_{U_i,E_j})^{-\sigma} \tag{3}$$

$$r_{U_i,E_j} = W_j \log_2 (1 + \frac{p_U g_{U_i,E_j}}{N_0 W_j}) \tag{4}$$

The task response time of the edge computing model is defined as follows:

$$T_{to_k} = T_{tw_k} + \frac{d_k}{r_{U_i,E_j}} \tag{5}$$

$$T_{res_k} = T_{to_k} + T_{ew_k} + \frac{d_k c}{f_{E_j}} \tag{6}$$

where T_{tw_k} represents the transmission waiting time of k_{th} task, and T_{to_k} represents the transmission end time of k_{th} task.

(3) Cloud computing mode: The cloud computing model refers to the task generated by the user device being transmitted to the cloud server for execution. The task is transmitted to the cloud server, with the edge server as the transit transmission node. The selection method of the transit edge node is determined by comprehensively considering the amount of tasks to be transmitted, bandwidth resources of the edge node, and the distance between the user UD and the CS to which the task is transited using the edge node. And the occupation of the edge bandwidth resources by the task transmission is not released until it is transmitted to the cloud server. Since the result data after the task is executed is small, the transmission delay of the result data

from the cloud server back to the edge server and from the edge server back to the user device is also ignored here. The transmission time of k_{th} task is the sum of the transmission delays of k_{th} task from i_{th} UD to j_{th} ES and j_{th} ES to CS. The task response time is the sum of the transmission waiting time, transmission time, execution waiting time, and execution time. Similarly, when the edge server bandwidth resources are not occupied, T_{tw_k} of k_{th} task is 0. When CS is idle, T_{ew_k} of k_{th} task is 0. The transmission rate $r_{E_j,C}$ between j_{th} ES and CS is defined as follows:

$$D_{E_j,C} = \sqrt{(X_C - X_{E_j})^2 + (Y_C - Y_{E_j})^2 + (Z_C - Z_{E_j})^2} \tag{7}$$

$$g_{E_j,C} = (D_{E_j,C})^{-\sigma} \tag{8}$$

$$r_{E_j,C} = W_j \log_2 (1 + \frac{p_E g_{E_j,C}}{N_0 W_j}) \tag{9}$$

The task response time of the cloud computing model is defined as follows:

$$T_{to_k} = T_{tw_k} + \frac{d_k}{r_{U_i,E_j}} + \frac{d_k}{r_{E_j,C}} \tag{10}$$

$$T_{res_k} = T_{to_k} + T_{ew_k} + \frac{d_k c}{f_C} \tag{11}$$

3.2. Energy Consumption Model

Energy consumption refers to the total energy consumed by the system in the process of processing tasks, and its components mainly include task execution energy consumption and task transmission energy consumption. In this subsection, we will specifically calculate and analyze the energy consumption of tasks in different computing modes.

(1) Local computing mode: Since the local computing mode does not perform task transmission, there is no energy consumption generated by task transmission. Therefore, the energy consumption EG_k of k_{th} task is the execution energy consumption of k_{th} task. The energy consumption of the local computing mode is defined as follows:

$$EG_k = \kappa (f_{U_i})^{v-1} d_k c \tag{12}$$

where v is a positive constant.

(2) Edge computing mode: Since the edge computing mode requires the transmission of tasks between user devices and edge servers, the transmission energy consumption of tasks needs to be considered. Since the result data after the task is executed is small, the transmission energy consumption of the result data transmitted from the edge server back to the user device is ignored here. The transmission energy consumption only considers the transmission energy consumption of k_{th} task from i_{th} UD to j_{th} ES. The energy consumption of k_{th} task is the sum of the transmission energy consumption and the execution energy consumption. The energy consumption of the edge computing mode is defined as follows:

$$EG_k = p_U \frac{d_k}{r_{U_i,E_j}} + d_k q_{E_j} \tag{13}$$

(3) Cloud computing mode: Since the cloud computing model requires edge servers as transit nodes, it is necessary to consider the transmission energy consumption of tasks from user devices to edge servers and from edge servers to cloud servers. Since the result data after the task is executed is small, the transmission energy consumption of the result data from the cloud server back to the edge server and from the edge server back to the user device is also ignored here. The energy consumption of the cloud computing model is defined as follows:

$$EG_k = p_U \frac{d_k}{r_{U_i,E_j}} + p_E \frac{d_k}{r_{E_j,C}} + d_k q_C \tag{14}$$

3.3. Problem Formulation

The purpose of this paper is to optimize the task offloading problem in the cloud–edge collaborative network environment while taking into account the full utilization of the edge server bandwidth resources and the CPU resources of the three-layer computing nodes. Formulas (1), (6), and (11) describe the task response time of the three computing modes, respectively. Since each user is mainly concerned about the efficiency of completing his or her own tasks, we use the average response time of the task as a measure of user service quality. The average response time of M tasks is defined as follows:

$$T_{res_{avg}} = \sum_{k=1}^{M} \left(\frac{T_{res_k}}{M} \right) \tag{15}$$

Formulas (12)–(14) describe the energy consumption corresponding to the three computing modes, respectively. Since service providers are mainly concerned with the energy consumption caused by providing services, we use the average energy consumption of tasks as a measure to evaluate service energy consumption. The average energy consumption of M tasks is defined as follows:

$$EG_{avg} = \sum_{k=1}^{M} \left(\frac{EG_k}{M} \right) \tag{16}$$

The target optimization problem is defined as follows:

$$\min_{\omega_1,\omega_2} \left(\omega_1 T_{res_{avg}} + \omega_2 EG_{avg} \right) \tag{17}$$

where w_1 and w_2 represent the weights of average response time and average energy consumption in the target optimization problem, respectively.

4. Task Offloading Based on GAPSO

4.1. Standard Particle Swarm Optimization (SPSO) Algorithm and Coding

(1) SPSO: The particle swarm optimization algorithm is a swarm intelligence optimization technology that simulates the foraging behavior of bird flocks. It finds the optimal solution by simulating information sharing between individuals in a bird flock [37]. In the algorithm, each solution is regarded as a particle flying in the solution space. The particle adjusts its flight direction and velocity according to the individual's historical best position (individual extremum) and the group's historical best position (global extremum). Each particle has only two attributes: speed and position. The speed indicates the particle's moving speed, and the position indicates the particle's moving direction [38]. Specifically, since there are M tasks in total, the spatial dimension

is M, and there are L particles in the population, then the solution space can be expressed as $X = (X^1, X^2, X^3, \ldots, X^L)$, where the lth particle consists of two M-dimensional vectors, X^l and V^l. $X^l = (x_1^l, x_2^l, x_3^l, \ldots, x_M^l)^\top$ represents the position of the particle, and $X^{l(h)}$ represents the position after h rounds of iteration. At the same time, the speed of each particle is expressed as $V^l = (v_1^l, v_2^l, v_3^l, \ldots, v_M^l)^\top$. As the iteration proceeds, the position and speed of the particle will change according to the individual historical optimal solution p_{best} and the global optimal solution g_{best}, as shown in Formulas (18) and (19). The solution can be obtained by iterative execution until the end.

$$V^{l(h+1)} = \omega V^{l(h)} + c_1 r_1 (p_{best} - X^{l(h)}) + c_2 r_2 (g_{best} - X^{l(h)}) \tag{18}$$

$$X^{l(h+1)} = X^{l(h)} + V^{l(h+1)} \tag{19}$$

where r_1 and r_2 are random numbers in the range $[0, 1]$.

(2) Coding: The position and speed of particles in the PSO algorithm are two important properties, since each task has $O = S + 2$ execution modes. The position and speed of particles are expressed by Formulas (20) and (21). Among them, $x_{mo} = 0$ means that task m is not executed at node o, and $x_{mo} = 1$ means that task m is executed at node o. The particle position is constrained by Formula (22). And v_{mo} is a random number between $(-5, 5)$. After the calculation of Formula (18), $V^{l(h+1)}$ will be calculated by Formula (23), and each v_{mo} value will be converted into a probability between $(0, 1)$. Formula (19) indicates that roulette is used to select execution nodes to avoid falling into local optimality. In the particle position matrix of this paper, the higher the number of rows, the lower the corresponding task transmission and execution priority. Formula (24) is used as the particle fitness.

$$X = \begin{bmatrix} x_{11} & x_{12} & \cdots & x_{1O} \\ x_{21} & x_{22} & \cdots & x_{2O} \\ x_{31} & x_{32} & \cdots & x_{3O} \\ \cdots & \cdots & \cdots & \cdots \\ x_{M1} & x_{M2} & \cdots & x_{MO} \end{bmatrix} \tag{20}$$

$$V = \begin{bmatrix} v_{11} & v_{12} & \cdots & v_{1O} \\ v_{21} & v_{22} & \cdots & v_{2O} \\ v_{31} & v_{32} & \cdots & v_{3O} \\ \cdots & \cdots & \cdots & \cdots \\ v_{M1} & v_{M2} & \cdots & v_{MO} \end{bmatrix} \tag{21}$$

$$\Sigma_{o=1}^{O} x_{mo} = 1 \tag{22}$$

$$\phi(v) = \frac{1}{1 + e^v} \tag{23}$$

$$-\left(\omega_1 T_{res_{avg}} + \omega_2 EG_{avg}\right) \tag{24}$$

where $m = 1, 2, \ldots, M$. $o = 1, 2, \ldots, O$.

4.2. Adaptive Inertia Weight w

The inertia weight w plays a balancing role between the global search capability and local search capability of the SPSO algorithm. It determines the extent to which the current velocity of the particle is affected by the previous velocity and has a significant impact on the accuracy and convergence speed of the algorithm. In the early stage of algorithm iteration, setting a larger w can increase the movement speed of particles, thus enhancing the global search capability. As the iterative process proceeds, gradually reducing w can reduce the moving speed of particles, prompting the particle swarm to focus on local search. We adopt a linear strategy to adjust w to adaptively adjust the local and global search ability of particles. The specific adjustment method is shown in Formula (25).

$$\omega = \omega_{max} - (\omega_{max} - \omega_{min}) * \frac{h}{h_{max}} \tag{25}$$

where h and h_{max} represent the current iteration number and the maximum iteration number, respectively, and w_{max} and w_{min} are the maximum and minimum values of the predefined inertia weight, respectively.

4.3. Adaptive Acceleration Coefficients c_1, c_2

The acceleration coefficient c_1 determines the particle's dependence on the local optimum, which helps to explore the local environment and maintain population diversity. The acceleration coefficient c_2 determines the particle's dependence on the global optimum, which helps the algorithm converge quickly. We use a nonlinear strategy to dynamically adjust c_1 and c_2. Specifically, let c_1 gradually decrease from 2.5, while c_2 gradually increases from 0.5. In the early stages of iteration, particles rely more on personal experience, increase search diversity, quickly approach the global optimal solution, and avoid falling into the local optimum. As the iteration deepens, particles gradually turn to rely on group experience, enhance local search capabilities, fine-tune the optimal solution, and accelerate convergence. The specific adjustment method is shown in Formulas (26) and (27).

$$c_1 = (c_{min} - c_{max}) * \sqrt{\frac{h}{h_{max}}} + c_{max} \tag{26}$$

$$c_2 = (c_{max} - c_{min}) * \sqrt{\frac{h}{h_{max}}} + c_{min} \tag{27}$$

where c_{max} and c_{min} are the maximum and minimum values of the predefined acceleration coefficients, respectively.

4.4. OBL Algorithm Initialization Population

The OBL algorithm is a search strategy for optimization problems that enhances population diversity by introducing the concept of opposition. This approach effectively improves the algorithm's search capability and the quality of the initial population. It increases the diversity of the search by generating a corresponding opposition solution for each initial solution, which helps to explore the solution space more comprehensively. Compared with simply introducing random solutions, it is more likely to approach the global optimum, thereby accelerating the convergence of the algorithm. At the same time, it also helps to avoid falling into the local optimum and improve the global search performance of the algorithm. The detailed process of initializing the particle swarm is shown in Algorithm 1.

4.5. Crossover and Mutation

Crossover in genetic algorithms is a process that simulates biological reproduction. It allows two parent individuals to exchange some of their genetic information to produce offspring. The purpose of crossover is to combine the excellent characteristics of parent individuals to create new individuals that may have higher fitness. Mutation is a process that simulates gene mutation. It introduces new genetic diversity by randomly changing one or more gene bits in the genetic code of an individual with a certain probability. Mutation operations can sometimes guide particles out of the local optimum and find the global optimal solution.

This paper uses crossover and mutation operations in GA to update the local optimal solution of particles, that is, to update the position matrix of particles. This paper uses two-point crossover to generate new individuals. And all gene bits of new individuals are mutated probabilistically. Since each column in the position matrix represents an execution mode, the S column is edge server computing, and the two columns are local computing and cloud server computing. Therefore, when a gene bit mutates, first, the three computing methods are selected with equal probability, and then the specific execution mode is selected with equal probability, that is, the probability of mutation to local computing and cloud server computing is $\frac{1}{3}$, and the probability of mutation to any edge server computing is $\frac{1}{3S}$. The crossover and mutation operations are shown in Figures 2 and 3. Algorithm 2 details the process of GA updating the local optimal solution.

Algorithm 1 Initialize the population-based OBL

Input: L (population size), M (number of tasks), O (number of execution modes)

for $l = 1$ to L **do**
    for $m = 1$ to M **do**
        $mode = randint(1, O + 1);$
        $mode^T = O + 1 - mode;$
        for $o = 1$ to O **do**
            if then$o = mode$
                $x^l_{mo} = 1;$
            else
                $x^l_{mo} = 0;$
            end if
            if $o = mode^T$ **then**
                $x^{l'}_{mo} = 1;$
            else
                $x^{l'}_{mo} = 0;$
            end if
            $v^l_{mo} = randfloat(-5, 5);$
            $v^{l'}_{mo} = randfloat(-5, 5);$
        end for
    end for
    $P = P \cup (X^l, V^l);$
    $P' = P' \cup (X^{l'}, V^{l'});$
end for
In the population $P \cup P'$, the task response time and energy consumption of each particle are calculated using Equations (1), (6), (11)–(14) according to the position of each particle. And obtain the fitness of all particles according to (15), (16), (24) and sort them;
Select the top L particles as the initial population P;
return P

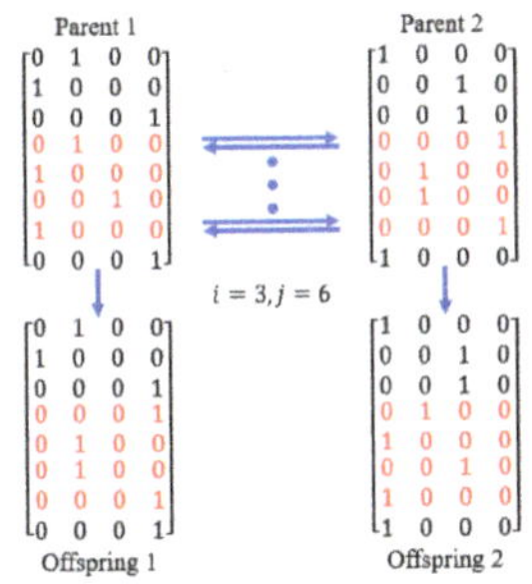

Figure 2. Crossover operation of the position matrix.

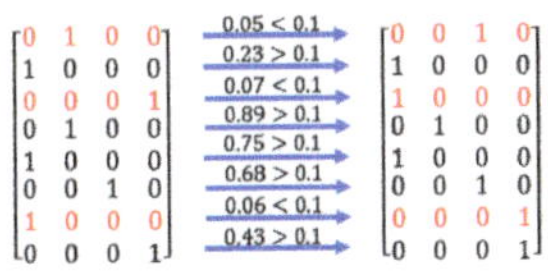

Figure 3. Mutation operation on the location matrix.

Algorithm 2 Update local optimal solution based GA

Input: p (current particle), X_{pbest} (position matrix of the local optimal solution of the current particle), X_{gbest} (position matrix of the global optimal solution of the population), p_m (mutation probability)

$X_1, X_2 = Crossover(X_p, X_{pbest})$;
$X_3, X_4 = Crossover(X_p, X_{gbest})$;
for $i = 1$ to 4 **do**
  $X_i^{'} = Mutation(X_i)$;
end for
Calculate the fitness corresponding to the position matrices $X_1^{'}$, $X_2^{'}$, $X_3^{'}$, and $X_4^{'}$ respectively;
Compare the fitness corresponding to the position matrices X_{pbest}, X_p, $X_1^{'}$, $X_2^{'}$, $X_3^{'}$, $X_4^{'}$, select the position matrix with the best fitness as the position matrix of the local optimal solution for the current particle, and update the particle's local optimal position X_{pbest};

4.6. GAPSO Algorithm

This paper adopts the GAPSO algorithm to solve the problem of task offloading in cloud–edge–end collaboration. Task offloading is optimized by introducing the OBL algorithm, adaptive inertia weight, and adaptive acceleration coefficient. In this algorithm, the OBL algorithm is first used to initialize the particle swarm. The OBL algorithm introduces the concept of opposition in the particle initialization process, constructs opposing particles, and avoids the initial solution being confined to a limited range, so as to improve the quality and diversity of the initial population. Then the population is updated iteratively. The inertia weight and acceleration coefficient are updated at the beginning of each iteration, responding to the evolution state of the particle swarm in real time, dynamically optimizing the balance between exploration and development, and avoiding premature convergence or slow convergence. During the iteration process, the GA algorithm is used to implement particle crossover and mutation operations, update the local optimal solutions of all particles, and guide the particles to jump out of the local optimal solution with a certain possibility. Until the end condition is met, the optimal task offloading solution is output. The detailed process is shown in Algorithm 3.

Algorithm 3 The algorithm steps of GAPSO

Initialization parameters: w_{max}, w_{min}, c_{max}, c_{min}
Output: The offloading solution for all tasks corresponding to the global optimal solution
Use Algorithm 1 to initialize the population P;
Initialize the local optimal solution of each particle and the global optimal solution of the population;
$h = 0$;
while $(h < h_{max})$ **or** (the fitness function value does not change within a certain number of iterations) **do**
    Use Equations (25)–(27) to update the inertia weight ω and acceleration coefficients c_1, c_2;
    for $l = 1$ to L **do**
        Particle $P^l = (X^l, V^l)$, use Equation (18) to update the speed V^l, and use Equations (19) and (23) to update the position X^l;
        Through the position X^l, calculate the response time and energy consumption of all tasks, and update the fitness of the current particle P^l;
        Use Algorithm 2 to update the local optimal solution of the current particle;
    end for
    Update the global optimal solution of the population;
    $h = h + 1$;
end while

5. Experiments and Analysis

5.1. Experimental Settings

In this section, we will consider a network topology environment covered by one CS, multiple ESs, and multiple UDs. The positions of CS, ESs, and UDs are determined by three-dimensional spatial coordinates (X, Y, Z). The position of CS is fixed. The positions of ESs and UDs are randomly distributed in the spatial area, and the distance between them is ensured to exceed a certain limit distance to avoid overcrowding. Each UD will generate a random number of tasks, each with a unique attribute, task data size, in the range of $[3000, 5000]$ KB.

We use the Windows 11 operating system to build the experimental simulation environment on the Python 3.11.5 platform. The relevant parameters used in the simulation experiment are summarized in Table 3 [39,40]. The following algorithms are used to compare the performance with the algorithm proposed in this paper: GA, SPSO, adaptive inertia weight and chaotic learning factor particle swarm optimization (AICLPSO) [41], and chaotic adaptive particle swarm optimization algorithm (CAPSO) [42]. This experiment is based on a symmetric architecture. All algorithms are run under the same conditions, including the same cloud–edge–end topology environment, environment parameter configuration, number of iterations, and evaluation criteria. This symmetric design ensures fairness in the comparison between algorithms and helps improve the reliability of the results. At the same time, this balanced experimental structure not only helps to enhance the effectiveness of the research but also fits in with the consistency emphasized by symmetry.

In view of the research problem in this paper, the parameter settings of each algorithm are shown in Table 4. Considering the influence of randomness, each algorithm is repeated 10 times.

Table 3. Experimental parameter setting.

Parameters	Value
M_i	Unif (8, 10)
d_k (KB)	Unif (3000, 5000)
c (cycles/bit)	500
κ	10^{-28}
v	3
σ	4
W_j (MHZ)	randint (10, 15)
N_0 (dBm/HZ)	−174
f_{U_i} (GHZ)	Unif (0.5, 1.0)
f_{E_j} (GHZ)	Unif (5.0, 10.0)
f_C (GHZ)	40
p_U (mW)	100
p_E (mW)	200
q_E (J/bit)	Unif ($10^{-8}, 2 \times 10^{-8}$)
q_C (J/bit)	Unif ($3 \times 10^{-8}, 4 \times 10^{-8}$)

Table 4. Information on algorithm parameters settings.

Algorithm	Parameter Settings
GA	$p_m = 0.1, p_c = 0.8$
SPSO	$\omega = 0.9, c_1 = c_2 = 2$
AICLPSO	$\omega_1 = 0.75, \omega_2 = 0.35, c_{i1} = c_{i2} = n = h = 2, g = m = 1,$ $s = f = 0.4, a = 0, r = 0.5, \rho = 2.593, x_0 = 0.6$
CAPSO	$\omega_{max} = 0.9, \omega_{min} = 0.4, c_{max} = 2.5, c_{min} = 0.5, \xi = 0.2, a = 4$
GAPSO	$\omega_{max} = 0.9, \omega_{min} = 0.4, c_{max} = 2.5, c_{min} = 0.5, p_m = 0.2$

5.2. Performance Evaluation

Based on actual needs, users are usually more concerned about the efficiency of task execution, while service providers regard energy consumption in the service process as a core concern. Based on this realistic scenario, in order to achieve a balanced optimization of the interests of both users and service providers, this section uses the average response time and average energy consumption with equal weights as comprehensive evaluation indicators. In this section, in order to intuitively show the significant advantages of the cloud–edge–end environment, we rely on the offloading algorithm proposed in this article. For the four environments of cloud–edge–end (CEE) collaboration, cloud–edge (CE1) collaboration, cloud–end (CE2) collaboration, and edge–end (EE) collaboration, we focus on comparing and analyzing their optimal average response time and total energy consumption performance under the task number gradient of 200, 225, 250, 275, and 300. At the same time, under the same cloud–edge–end collaboration experimental environment configuration, we will further compare the optimization performance differences between the proposed algorithm and other algorithms.

(1) Parameter sensitivity analysis: Figure 4a,b are experiments conducted while keeping c_{max} and c_{min} unchanged. In Figure 4a, ω_{max} is kept unchanged. It can be seen from the figure that the curve converges earlier when ω_{min} is 0.2. This is because the low inertia weight in the middle and late stages of the iteration causes the particles to ignore the historical speed and completely rely on the current optimal position, resulting in too fast convergence. When ω_{min} is 0.6, the curve converges more slowly and the final effect is poor. This is because the particle speed is insufficiently attenuated, and a

strong exploration inertia is always maintained, resulting in the inability to converge well in the over-exploration search space. In Figure 4b, ω_{min} is kept unchanged. It can be seen from the figure that the curve converges the worst when ω_{max} is 0.7. This is because when ω_{max} is small, the inertial component of the particle speed is weak, so the particles rely on the attraction of c_1 and c_2 earlier, which accelerates the development to the current optimal position, resulting in insufficient exploration, and the particles are easy to quickly gather in the local optimal area. When ω_{max} is 1.1, the effect of faster exploration of the optimal solution is shown in the early stage of the iteration. This is because the inertial component of the particle velocity is higher and more dependent on the historical velocity, which reduces the attraction of c_1 and c_2, thereby promoting a wider exploration of the search space, so there is a greater probability of finding a better solution in the early stage, but it will not be able to converge to the optimal solution quickly in the later stage. Figure 4c,d are experiments carried out while keeping ω_{max} and ω_{min} unchanged. In Figure 4c, c_{max} is kept unchanged. It can be seen from the figure that the convergence effect is the worst when c_{min} is 0.2. This may be because the particles in the later stage mainly rely on inertial motion, lack traction to the optimal solution, and cannot jump out of the suboptimal solution. When c_{min} is 0.8, the convergence effect is poor. This is because the c_1 and c_2 coefficients are too high in the middle and late stages, forcing the particles to develop to the current optimal position too early and fall into the local optimal solution. In Figure 4d, c_{min} is kept unchanged. It can be seen from the figure that when c_{max} is 2.2, the convergence is slow and the convergence effect is the worst. This is because the maximum step size is limited in the early stage, the exploration ability is insufficient, and it is impossible to jump out of the local optimum. When c_{max} is set to 2.6, the initial optimization is faster, but the convergence effect is poor. This is because the higher the c_{max} value, the greater the exploration advantage in the early stage. However, this will also make the particle movement step too large, which makes it easy to miss the optimal solution. Therefore, in order to achieve a balance between exploration and development and ensure robust convergence, ω_{max} is set to 0.9, ω_{min} is set to 0.4, c_{max} is set to 2.5, and c_{min} is set to 0.5.

(2) Comparison of average response time, total energy consumption, and number of tasks: Figures 5 and 6 show the changing trends of the average response time for completing each task and the total energy consumption for completing all tasks in different environments. In the four operating environments, as the number of tasks increases, the amount of tasks waiting to be processed in different execution modes increases due to the total amount of computing resources, resulting in an upward trend in the average response time and total energy consumption of tasks. In Figure 5, under the same number of tasks, CEE has a maximum acceleration effect of 49.64% in response time compared with CE2, a maximum acceleration effect of 27.26% compared with EE, and a maximum acceleration effect of 4.31% compared with CE1, showing a significant advantage overall. In Figure 6, under the same number of tasks, CEE has a maximum energy saving of 24.83% compared with CE2 and a maximum energy saving of 22.89% compared with CE1, showing a significant advantage. Compared with EE, CEE takes the cloud computing model into consideration. Since the distance from CS to ES is significantly increased compared to the distance from ES to UD, a large amount of transmission energy is required to offload tasks to CS for processing, resulting in more total energy consumption for CEE than EE. These two figures show that the emergence of edge computing will greatly reduce the response time and energy

consumption of completing tasks. At the same time, it can also show that cloud–edge–end collaboration has significant advantages and broad development prospects.

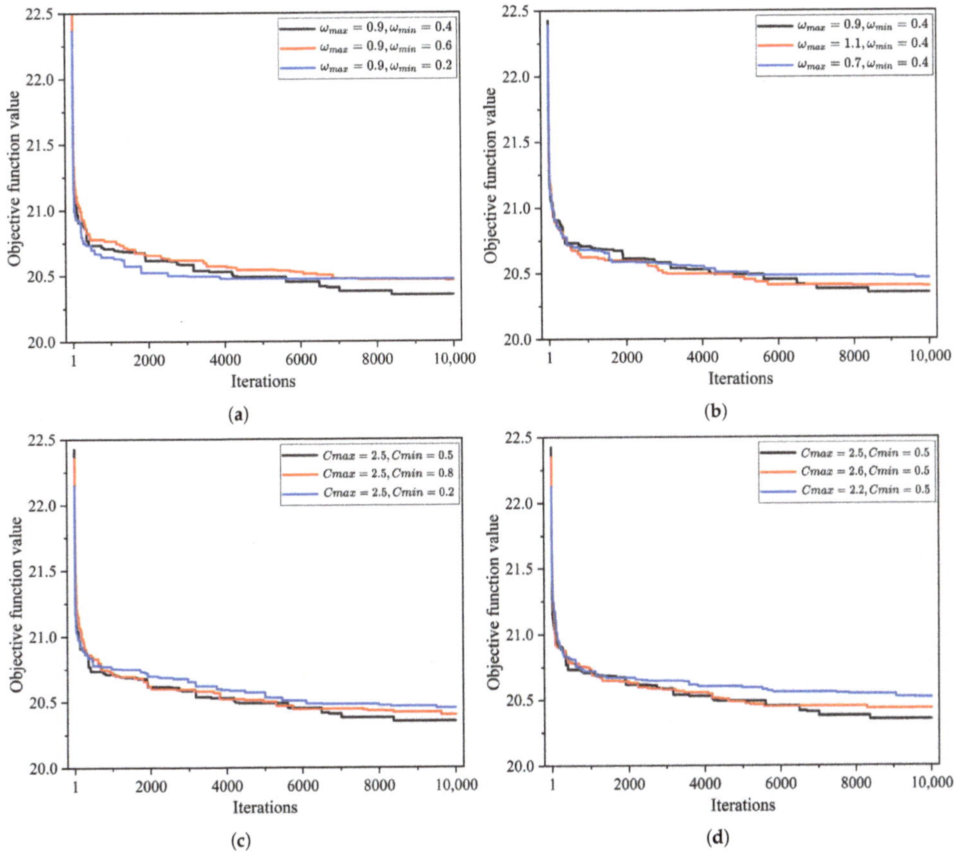

Figure 4. (**a**) ω_{min} variable. (**b**) ω_{max} variable. (**c**) c_{min} variable. (**d**) c_{max} variable.

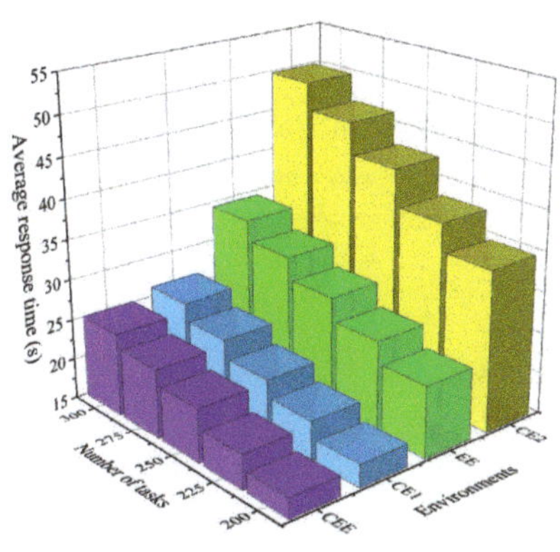

Figure 5. Average response times for different environments and number of tasks.

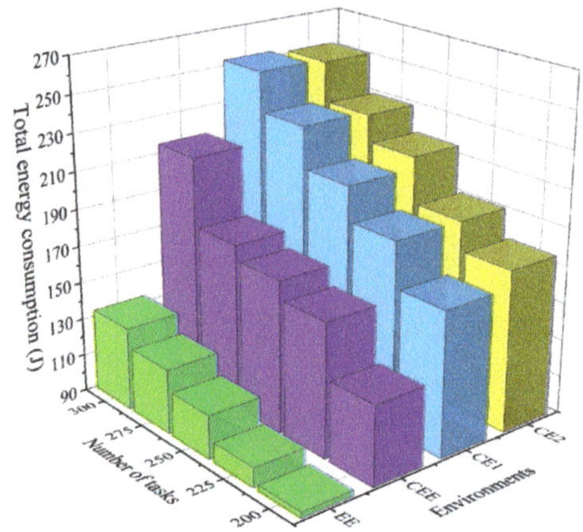

Figure 6. Total energy consumption for different environments and number of tasks.

(3) Algorithm performance: Under the cloud–edge–end collaborative processing framework proposed in this paper, the time complexity of the GAPSO, GA, SPSO, AICLPSO, and CAPSO algorithms is consistent with $O(n^3 \log n)$. The average change in the objective function value obtained by repeating 10 experiments for each algorithm to process the same task data in the same cloud–edge–end collaborative environment is shown in Figure 7. From the change in the curve, the GAPSO algorithm proposed in this paper shows obvious optimization effect. In the early stage of iteration, the GAPSO algorithm can obtain better initial solutions than the GA, SPSO, and AICLPSO algorithms, which highlights that the introduction of the OBL algorithm in the GAPSO algorithm can increase the diversity of the initial population and overcome the obstacle of falling into the local optimum to a certain extent. In the later stage of iteration, the GAPSO algorithm achieves better convergence accuracy than the other four algorithms and can reduce the objective function value by about 6–12%, indicating that the algorithm can find a better task allocation solution. The objective function value does not change after 1200 consecutive iterations, which is used as the basis for judging the convergence of the algorithm. From the convergence points marked in the figure, it can be seen that the GAPSO algorithm converges faster than the GA and SPSO algorithms. As can be seen from Table 5, GAPSO has obvious advantages over other algorithms in terms of mean, variance, and standard deviation, indicating that the algorithm has high stability. In general, the GAPSO algorithm we proposed has higher convergence accuracy and stronger stability. It can effectively avoid falling into local optimal solutions and is easier to search for global optimal solutions.

Table 5. Test results of each algorithm.

Algorithm	Count	Mean	Variance	Standard Deviation
GA	10	23.2442	0.0667	0.2582
SPSO	10	21.9417	0.0193	0.1391
AICLPSO	10	22.3194	0.0464	0.2153
CAPSO	10	21.8245	0.0602	0.2453
GAPSO	10	20.3197	0.0134	0.1156

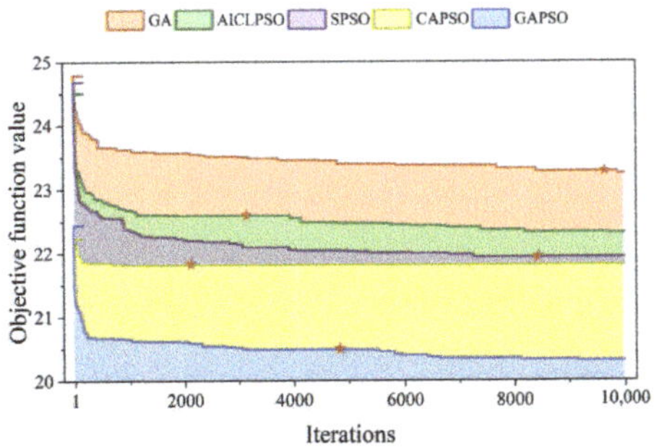

Figure 7. Change in the average objective function value of each algorithm.

6. Conclusions

This paper focuses on the problem of task offloading in the cloud–edge–end collaborative environment and constructs a cloud–edge–end collaborative task processing framework. The framework supports flexible allocation of tasks between user devices, edge servers, and cloud servers, can give full play to the advantages of nodes at each layer, and effectively reduce the computing pressure of user devices. At the same time, in order to reduce the average response time and execution energy consumption of task completion, this paper introduces an opposition-based learning algorithm, adaptive inertia weight, and adaptive acceleration coefficient to propose a GAPSO algorithm. The proposed algorithm is compared with other traditional algorithms and heuristic algorithms using method symmetric design. Experimental results verify that the proposed algorithm can obtain a better initialization solution set and task offloading scheme, reducing the objective function value by about 6–12%, while showing excellent convergence speed, accuracy, and stability. At the algorithm level, there are many research algorithms for the cloud–edge–device collaborative environment. However, algorithms with high adaptability to actual application scenarios are still scarce. At the practical application level, cloud–edge–end collaboration has gradually penetrated into key areas such as industrial Internet of Things, intelligent transportation, smart cities, and telemedicine. However, the heterogeneity and dynamic nature of resources in different hardware devices, as well as the privacy and security issues of user devices during collaborative task processing, have not been effectively resolved. Therefore, for cloud–edge–end collaborative applications, the development of highly adaptable algorithms, the research on resource computing power, and the privacy and security of data transmission are still issues worth studying in the future.

Author Contributions: Conceptualization, W.W., Y.H. and P.Z.; Methodology, W.W., Z.X. and L.T.; Software, W.W. and Y.H.; Investigation, Y.H., Z.X. and L.T.; Writing—original draft, W.W., Y.H. and Z.X.; Visualization: Y.H. and L.T.; Validation, W.W. and Y.H.; Formal analysis, P.Z. All authors have read and agreed to the published version of this manuscript.

Funding: This work is partially supported by the Tertiary Education Scientific research project of Guangzhou Municipal Education Bureau under Grant 2024312246, the Guangdong Province Natural Science Foundation of Major Basic Research and Cultivation Project under Grant 2024A1515011976, the Shandong Provincial Natural Science Foundation under Grant ZR2023LZH017, ZR2022LZH015, ZR2023QF025 and ZR2024MF066, the National Natural Science Foundation of China under Grant 52477138, 62471493 and 62402257, and the China University Research Innovation Fund under Grant 2023IT207.

Data Availability Statement: The original contributions presented in this study are included in the article. Further inquiries can be directed to the corresponding author.

Conflicts of Interest: The authors declare no potential conflicts of interests.

References

1. Gao, H.; Wang, X.; Wei, W.; Al-Dulaimi, A.; Xu, Y. Com-DDPG: Task offloading based on multiagent reinforcement learning for information-communication-enhanced mobile edge computing in the internet of vehicles. *IEEE Trans. Veh. Technol.* **2023**, *73*, 348–361. [CrossRef]
2. Quy, V.K.; Hau, N.V.; Anh, D.V.; Ngoc, L.A. Smart healthcare IoT applications based on fog computing: Architecture, applications and challenges. *Complex Intell. Syst.* **2022**, *8*, 3805–3815. [CrossRef]
3. Mahajan, H.B.; Junnarkar, A.A. Smart healthcare system using integrated and lightweight ECC with private blockchain for multimedia medical data processing. *Multimed. Tools Appl.* **2023**, *82*, 44335–44358. [CrossRef] [PubMed]
4. Sharma, M.; Tomar, A.; Hazra, A. Edge computing for industry 5.0: Fundamental, applications and research challenges. *IEEE Internet Things J.* **2024**, *11*, 19070–19093. [CrossRef]
5. Tang, S.; Chen, L.; He, K.; Xia, J.; Fan, L.; Nallanathan, A. Computational intelligence and deep learning for next-generation edge-enabled industrial IoT. *IEEE Trans. Netw. Sci. Eng.* **2022**, *10*, 2881–2893. [CrossRef]
6. Islam, A.; Debnath, A.; Ghose, M.; Chakraborty, S. A survey on task offloading in multi-access edge computing. *J. Syst. Archit.* **2021**, *118*, 102225. [CrossRef]
7. Liu, B.; Xu, X.; Qi, L.; Ni, Q.; Dou, W. Task scheduling with precedence and placement constraints for resource utilization improvement in multi-user MEC environment. *J. Syst. Archit.* **2021**, *114*, 101970. [CrossRef]
8. Wang, X.; Xing, X.; Li, P.; Zhang, S. Optimization Scheme of Single-Objective Task Offloading with Multi-user Participation in Cloud-Edge-End Environment. In Proceedings of the 2022 IEEE Smartworld, Ubiquitous Intelligence & Computing, Scalable Computing & Communications, Digital Twin, Privacy Computing, Metaverse, Autonomous & Trusted Vehicles (SmartWorld/UIC/ScalCom/DigitalTwin/PriComp/Meta), Haikou, China, 15–18 December 2022; pp. 1166–1171.
9. Saeik, F.; Avgeris, M.; Spatharakis, D.; Santi, N.; Dechouniotis, D.; Violos, J.; Leivadeas, A.; Athanasopoulos, N.; Mitton, N.; Papavassiliou, S. Task offloading in Edge and Cloud Computing: A survey on mathematical, artificial intelligence and control theory solutions. *Comput. Netw.* **2021**, *195*, 108177. [CrossRef]
10. Zhang, Y.; Yu, H.; Zhou, W.; Man, M. Application and research of IoT architecture for End-Net-Cloud Edge computing. *Electronics* **2022**, *12*, 1. [CrossRef]
11. Pan, L.; Liu, X.; Jia, Z.; Xu, J.; Li, X. A multi-objective clustering evolutionary algorithm for multi-workflow computation offloading in mobile edge computing. *IEEE Trans. Cloud Comput.* **2021**, *11*, 1334–1351. [CrossRef]
12. Gong, T.; Zhu, L.; Yu, F.R.; Tang, T. Edge intelligence in intelligent transportation systems: A survey. *IEEE Trans. Intell. Transp. Syst.* **2023**, *24*, 8919–8944. [CrossRef]
13. Zhang, Y.; Chen, G.; Wen, T.; Yuan, Q.; Wang, B.; Hu, B. A cloud-edge collaborative framework and its applications. In Proceedings of the 2021 IEEE International Conference on Emergency Science and Information Technology (ICESIT), Chongqing, China, 22–24 November 2021; pp. 443–447.
14. McEnroe, P.; Wang, S.; Liyanage, M. A survey on the convergence of edge computing and AI for UAVs: Opportunities and challenges. *IEEE Internet Things J.* **2022**, *9*, 15435–15459. [CrossRef]
15. Liu, Y.; Deng, Q.; Zeng, Z.; Liu, A.; Li, Z. A hybrid optimization framework for age of information minimization in UAV-assisted MCS. *IEEE Trans. Serv. Comput.* **2025**, *18*, 527–542. [CrossRef]
16. Chen, M.; Liu, A.; Xiong, N.N.; Song, H.; Leung, V.C. SGPL: An intelligent game-based secure collaborative communication scheme for metaverse over 5G and beyond networks. *IEEE J. Sel. Areas Commun.* **2023**, *42*, 767–782. [CrossRef]
17. Zhou, J.; Zhang, X. Fairness-aware task offloading and resource allocation in cooperative mobile-edge computing. *IEEE Internet Things J.* **2021**, *9*, 3812–3824. [CrossRef]
18. Sun, Y.; Zhang, X. A2C learning for tasks segmentation with cooperative computing in edge computing networks. In Proceedings of the GLOBECOM 2022—2022 IEEE Global Communications Conference, Rio de Janeiro, Brazil, 4–8 December 2022; pp. 2236–2241.
19. Chen, Q.; Yang, C.; Lan, S.; Zhu, L.; Zhang, Y. Two-Stage Evolutionary Search for Efficient Task Offloading in Edge Computing Power Networks. *IEEE Internet Things J.* **2024**, *11*, 30787–30799. [CrossRef]
20. Zhu, A.; Wen, Y. Computing offloading strategy using improved genetic algorithm in mobile edge computing system. *J. Grid Comput.* **2021**, *19*, 38. [CrossRef]
21. Chen, H.; Qin, W.; Wang, L. Task partitioning and offloading in IoT cloud-edge collaborative computing framework: A survey. *J. Cloud Comput.* **2022**, *11*, 86. [CrossRef]

22. Hu, S.; Xiao, Y. Design of cloud computing task offloading algorithm based on dynamic multi-objective evolution. *Future Gener. Comput. Syst.* **2021**, *122*, 144–148. [CrossRef]
23. Zhang, X.; Zhang, H.; Zhou, X.; Yuan, D. Energy minimization task offloading mechanism with edge-cloud collaboration in IoT networks. In Proceedings of the 2021 IEEE 93rd Vehicular Technology Conference (VTC2021-Spring), Helsinki, Finland, 25–28 April 2021; pp. 1–7.
24. Gao, J.; Chang, R.; Yang, Z.; Huang, Q.; Zhao, Y.; Wu, Y. A task offloading algorithm for cloud-edge collaborative system based on Lyapunov optimization. *Clust. Comput.* **2023**, *26*, 337–348. [CrossRef]
25. Lei, Y.; Zheng, W.; Ma, Y.; Xia, Y.; Xia, Q. A novel probabilistic-performance-aware and evolutionary game-theoretic approach to task offloading in the hybrid cloud-edge environment. In Proceedings of the Collaborative Computing: Networking, Applications and Worksharing: 16th EAI International Conference, CollaborateCom 2020, Shanghai, China, 16–18 October 2020; Proceedings, Part I 16; Springer: Berlin/Heidelberg, Germany, 2021; pp. 255–270.
26. Liu, F.; Huang, J.; Wang, X. Joint task offloading and resource allocation for device-edge-cloud collaboration with subtask dependencies. *IEEE Trans. Cloud Comput.* **2023**, *11*, 3027–3039. [CrossRef]
27. Zhu, D.; Li, T.; Tian, H.; Yang, Y.; Liu, Y.; Liu, H.; Geng, L.; Sun, J. Speed-aware and customized task offloading and resource allocation in mobile edge computing. *IEEE Commun. Lett.* **2021**, *25*, 2683–2687. [CrossRef]
28. Qu, X.; Wang, H. Emergency task offloading strategy based on cloud-edge-end collaboration for smart factories. *Comput. Netw.* **2023**, *234*, 109915. [CrossRef]
29. Wu, H.; Geng, J.; Bai, X.; Jin, S. Deep reinforcement learning-based online task offloading in mobile edge computing networks. *Inf. Sci.* **2024**, *654*, 119849. [CrossRef]
30. Ji, Z.; Qin, Z. Computational offloading in semantic-aware cloud-edge-end collaborative networks. *IEEE J. Sel. Top. Signal Process.* **2024**, *18*, 1235–1248. [CrossRef]
31. Zhou, Z.; Abawajy, J. Reinforcement learning-based edge server placement in the intelligent internet of vehicles environment. *IEEE Trans. Intell. Transp. Syst.* **2025**. [CrossRef]
32. Cai, J.; Liu, W.; Huang, Z.; Yu, F.R. Task decomposition and hierarchical scheduling for collaborative cloud-edge-end computing. *IEEE Trans. Serv. Comput.* **2024**, *17*, 4368–4382. [CrossRef]
33. Wang, J.; Feng, D.; Zhang, S.; Liu, A.; Xia, X.G. Joint computation offloading and resource allocation for MEC-enabled IoT systems with imperfect CSI. *IEEE Internet Things J.* **2020**, *8*, 3462–3475. [CrossRef]
34. An, X.; Fan, R.; Hu, H.; Zhang, N.; Atapattu, S.; Tsiftsis, T.A. Joint task offloading and resource allocation for IoT edge computing with sequential task dependency. *IEEE Internet Things J.* **2022**, *9*, 16546–16561. [CrossRef]
35. Fan, W.; Liu, X.; Yuan, H.; Li, N.; Liu, Y. Time-slotted task offloading and resource allocation for cloud-edge-end cooperative computing networks. *IEEE Trans. Mob. Comput.* **2024**, *23*, 8225–8241. [CrossRef]
36. Tong, Z.; Deng, X.; Mei, J.; Liu, B.; Li, K. Response time and energy consumption co-offloading with SLRTA algorithm in cloud–edge collaborative computing. *Future Gener. Comput. Syst.* **2022**, *129*, 64–76. [CrossRef]
37. Alqarni, M.A.; Mousa, M.H.; Hussein, M.K. Task offloading using GPU-based particle swarm optimization for high-performance vehicular edge computing. *J. King Saud Univ.-Comput. Inf. Sci.* **2022**, *34*, 10356–10364. [CrossRef]
38. Ma, S.; Song, S.; Yang, L.; Zhao, J.; Yang, F.; Zhai, L. Dependent tasks offloading based on particle swarm optimization algorithm in multi-access edge computing. *Appl. Soft Comput.* **2021**, *112*, 107790. [CrossRef]
39. Wang, Y.; Ru, Z.Y.; Wang, K.; Huang, P.Q. Joint deployment and task scheduling optimization for large-scale mobile users in multi-UAV-enabled mobile edge computing. *IEEE Trans. Cybern.* **2019**, *50*, 3984–3997. [CrossRef]
40. Tong, Z.; Deng, X.; Ye, F.; Basodi, S.; Xiao, X.; Pan, Y. Adaptive computation offloading and resource allocation strategy in a mobile edge computing environment. *Inf. Sci.* **2020**, *537*, 116–131. [CrossRef]
41. Yuan, C.; Su, Y.; Chen, R.; Zhao, W.; Li, W.; Li, Y.; Sang, L. Multimedia task scheduling based on improved PSO in cloud environment. In Proceedings of the 2023 IEEE International Symposium on Broadband Multimedia Systems and Broadcasting (BMSB), Beijing, China, 14–16 June 2023; pp. 1–6.
42. Duan, Y.; Chen, N.; Chang, L.; Ni, Y.; Kumar, S.S.; Zhang, P. CAPSO: Chaos adaptive particle swarm optimization algorithm. *IEEE Access* **2022**, *10*, 29393–29405. [CrossRef]

symmetry

MDPI

Article

Adaptive Network-Based Fuzzy Inference System Training Using Nine Different Metaheuristic Optimization Algorithms for Time-Series Analysis of Brent Oil Price and Detailed Performance Analysis

Ebubekir Kaya [1,2,*], Ahmet Kaya [3] and Ceren Baştemur Kaya [4]

1 Department of Computer Engineering, Engineering Architecture Faculty, Nevşehir Hacı Bektaş Veli University, Nevşehir 50100, Türkiye
2 CEKA Software R&D Co., Ltd., Nevşehir 50100, Türkiye
3 Departments of Mathematics, Faculty of Arts and Sciences, Nevşehir Hacı Bektaş Veli University, Nevşehir 50100, Türkiye; ahmetkaya@nevsehir.edu.tr
4 Department of Computer Technologies, Nevşehir Vocational School, Nevşehir Hacı Bektaş Veli University, Nevşehir 50100, Türkiye; ceren@nevsehir.edu.tr
* Correspondence: ebubekir@nevsehir.edu.tr or ebubekirkaya@yandex.com

Abstract: Brent oil holds a significant position in the global energy market, as oil prices in many regions are indexed to it. Therefore, forecasting the future price of Brent oil is of great importance. In recent years, artificial intelligence techniques have been widely applied in modeling and prediction tasks. In this study, an Adaptive Neuro-Fuzzy Inference System (ANFIS), a well-established AI approach, was employed for the time-series forecasting of Brent oil prices. To ensure effective learning and improve prediction accuracy, ANFIS was trained using nine different metaheuristic algorithms: Artificial Bee Colony (ABC), Selfish Herd Optimizer (SHO), Biogeography-Based Optimization (BBO), Multi-Verse Optimizer (MVO), Teaching–Learning-Based Optimization (TLBO), Cuckoo Search (CS), Moth Flame Optimization (MFO), Marine Predator Algorithm (MPA), and Flower Pollination Algorithm (FPA). Symmetric training procedures were applied across all algorithms to ensure fair and consistent evaluation. The analyses were conducted on the lowest and highest daily, weekly, and monthly Brent oil prices. Mean squared error (MSE) was used as the primary performance metric. The results showed that all algorithms achieved effective prediction performance. Among them, BBO and TLBO demonstrated superior accuracy and stability, particularly in handling the complexities of Brent oil forecasting. This study contributes to the literature by combining ANFIS and metaheuristics within a symmetric framework of experimentation and evaluation.

Keywords: artificial intelligence; ANFIS; Brent oil; metaheuristic optimization; methodological symmetry; time-series analysis; swarm intelligence; optimization algorithms; nature-inspired algorithms

1. Introduction

For many years, crude oil has been one of the most significant energy and financial assets in the world and continues to be so. Roughly one-third of the world's energy is derived from crude oil, which may be refined into a variety of fuels to satisfy varied consumer needs [1]. It is also a common raw material for petroleum-based items in daily life. Since fluctuations in the price of crude oil have a domino effect on the global economy, forecasting its price is crucial for planning long-term strategies. Because of its very volatile and turbulent structure—which is especially influenced by politics—accurate prediction-making is crucial [1,2]. In order to make our predictions, we must first discuss artificial intelligence, an area of study that has seen significant growth in popularity recently and has been employed widely. The primary methods of artificial intelligence include heuristic optimization algorithms, fuzzy logic, artificial neural networks, and neuro-fuzzy systems. Numerous issues in the actual world have been resolved with them [3–5]. Fuzzy sets and inference systems are the most preferred approach for solving ambiguous and imprecise situations [6]. However, it is crucial to keep in mind that they are unable to make rules on their own or carry out the learning process [7]. Nonetheless, self-organization, self-interaction, and environmental learning are all possible with artificial neural networks (ANNs) [8]. The Adaptive Network-Based Fuzzy Inference System (ANFIS) [9], which integrates the characteristics of artificial neural networks and fuzzy inference systems, is one of the most well-known neuro-fuzzy systems. It combines the best features of both systems: fuzzy, which performs well in mapping via membership functions and alpha cuts, and ANN, which is great at self-organizing [5,8]. Hence, it provides a reliable approach to problem modeling and identification.

2. Literature Review

During the past few decades, forecasting the price of crude oil has made extensive use of conventional statistical and econometric methods [10,11]. Amano made one of the first study proposals about oil market forecasting [12]. The author predicted the oil market using a small-scale econometric model. In order to forecast crude oil prices in the 1980s, Huntington used an advanced econometric model [13]. Furthermore, a probabilistic model was used by Abramson and Finizza to forecast oil prices [14]. When the price series being studied is linear or nearly linear, the models mentioned above can produce accurate forecast results. However, there is a significant amount of nonlinearity and irregularity in real-world crude oil price series [10,11,15].

To deal with the limitations of classic models, some nonlinear and advanced artificial intelligence (AI) models have been applied to predict crude oil [15]. Wang, Yu, and Lai integrated an ANN model with a knowledge database that includes historical events and their influence on oil prices. According to the authors, performance for a hybrid ANN approach was 81%, and it was 61% for a pure ANN system [16]. Mirmirani and Li applied genetic algorithms for predicting the price of crude oil and compared their findings with the VAR model [17].

Using intrinsic mode function inputs and an adaptive linear ANN learning paradigm, Yu, Wang, and Keung forecasted the West Texas Intermediate (WTI) crude oil and Brent petrol spot prices for the years 1986–2006 [10]. Kulkarni and Haidar provided an excellent description of building an ANN model [2]. They employed a multilayer feedforward neural network to estimate the direction of the crude oil spot price up to three days ahead of time, using data spanning from 1996 to 2007. For one, two, and three days in the future, respectively, their forecast accuracy was 78%, 66%, and 53%.

Gori et al. trained and tested an ANFIS method that was able to estimate oil prices for the years 1999 to 2003 by using data on oil prices from July 1973 to January 1999 [18]. Chiroma et al. applied a novel approach, a co-active neuro-fuzzy inference system (CANFIS), to predict crude oil price by using monthly data of WTI [19]. They developed this approach in place of ANFIS and frequently used techniques to increase forecast accuracy. Mombeini and Yazdani suggested a hybrid model based on ARIMA (AutoRegressive Integrated

Moving Average) and ANFIS to study the fluctuation and volatility of prices of West Texas Intermediate (WTI) crude oil markets to create a more exact and accurate model. Several statistical studies utilizing the MAPE, R2, and PI tests were carried out in order to reach this purpose [20]. The objective of Abdollahi and Ebrahimi in their study was to present a strong hybrid model for accurate Brent oil price forecasts [21]. The suggested hybrid model includes ANFIS, Autoregressive Fractionally Integrated Moving Average (ARFIMA), and Markov-switching models. To effectively capture the linear and nonlinear characteristics, these three techniques were combined. The technique put out by AbdElaziz et al. depends on using a modified salp swarm algorithm (SSA) to improve the ANFIS's performance [22]. They compared the outcome with nine further modified ANFIS approaches. Anshori et al. examined a case study and optimized the initial ANFIS parameters using the Cuckoo Search technique to estimate global crude oil prices [23]. Eliwa et al. [24] used 30-year gasoline prices to anticipate prices using the ANFIS model. By supporting this model with VAR (Vector Autoregression) and ARIMA models, they were able to obtain high accuracy and significant correlation.

Recently, deep learning and hybrid models, such as LSTM (Long Short-Term Memory), GRU (Gated Recurrent Unit), SVM (Support Vector Machine), RF (Random Forest), XGBoost (eXtreme Gradient Boosting), and other hybrid approaches, have begun to appear as novel methodologies in time-series analyses. Awijen et al. [25] presented a comparative research study on the use of machine learning and deep learning to anticipate oil prices during crises. In the study, processes were performed primarily utilizing RNN (recurrent neural network), LSTM, and SVM algorithms. Jabeur et al. [26] predicted the fall in oil prices using some machine learning techniques with neural network models. They found that among the methods applied, such as RF, LightGBM (Light Gradient-Boosting Machine), XGBoost, and CatBoost, RF and LightGBM offered the best results. Jiang et al. [27] compared the LSTM model to other methods such as AR (Autoregression), SVR, RNN (recurrent neural network), and GRU and determined that the LSTM model produced better outcomes for China's crude oil forecast. In order to predict and test the prices of Brent and WTI crude oil at various time-series frequencies, Hasan et al. [28] present a model they call LKDSR, which combines machine learning techniques like k-nearest neighbor regression, linear regression, regression tree, support vector regression, and ridge regression. Furthermore, Sezer et al.'s study [29], a comprehensive literature review on the use of deep learning for forecasting financial time series, is valuable.

Iftikhar et al. [30] conducted a comprehensive analysis for Brent oil price forecasting by evaluating hybrid combinations of linear and nonlinear time-series models using the Hodrick–Prescott filter. Using European Brent crude oil spot data, Zhao et al. [31] constructed a three-layer LSTM model to predict prices, with highly positive outcomes. Dong et al. [32] used VMD to eliminate noise from the data and PSR (Phase Space Reconstruction) to rebuild the price of crude oil. Lastly, they used CNN-BILSTM (a hybrid bidirectional LSTM and CNN architecture) to make multi-step predictions. By using SVM, ARIMA, and LSTM techniques to analyze crude oil prices, Naeem et al. [33] developed a hybrid model for crude oil price prediction. In order to improve the forecasting accuracy of crude oil prices and properly analyze the linear and nonlinear features of crude oil, Xu et al. [34] developed hybrid approaches. For this purpose, they used models such as ARIMAX, GRU, LSTM, and MLP (Multilayer Perceptron). Sen et al. [35] investigated the prediction of crude oil prices using ANN, LSTM, and GRU models. They optimized the hyperparameters of LSTM and GRU using the PSO (Particle Swarm Optimization) method. Jin et al. [36] forecasted daily and monthly prices for Henry Hub natural gas, New York Harbor No. 2 heating oil, and WTI and Brent crude oil using nonlinear autoregressive neural network models. Various model configurations, training methods, hidden neurons, delays, and data segmentations are taken into account while evaluating the performance.

ANFIS was chosen due to its ability to combine the strengths of both neural networks and fuzzy logic, making it highly suitable for modeling complex, nonlinear systems such as time-series prediction problems. Additionally, ANFIS allows flexible adaptation through learning, while also maintaining interpretability through fuzzy rules.

When compared with hybrid models, ANFIS produces successful results when the proper parameters are introduced for time-series analysis. While hybrid models require more computations and make the model more complicated, they cannot produce a noticeable effect. As a result, thanks to ANFIS, we achieve successful results in a simpler way without the need for further processing.

In this study, metaheuristic algorithms were employed in the training process of ANFIS. Achieving effective results with ANFIS largely depends on the quality of the training process. A review of the literature shows that metaheuristic algorithms are commonly used for training ANFIS and have led to successful outcomes in various applications. Therefore, in the context of Brent oil price prediction, metaheuristic optimization was selected as the training strategy for ANFIS. Specifically, nine widely used and literature-supported metaheuristic algorithms—known for their strong performance in ANFIS training—were implemented in this study.

In this study, the entire experimental setup was constructed with a methodologically symmetric design. All metaheuristic algorithms were applied under the same training conditions, including identical datasets, ANFIS configurations, input–output pairings, and evaluation metrics. This symmetry in training and evaluation ensured fairness, consistency, and repeatability across the experiments. Such a structured and balanced framework contributes not only to the reliability of the comparative analysis but also reflects the core principles of symmetric design in artificial intelligence research.

3. Materials and Methods

3.1. Selfish Herd Optimizer

Each individual in a herd groups up with other conspecifics in an attempt to enhance its chance of avoiding predator attacks; however, it does not consider how this behavior may influence the chances of survival of other individuals [37]. SHO is an optimization algorithm based on the simulation of selfish herd behavior observed in individuals in animal herds at risk of predation. In this algorithm, there are two different kinds of search agents: packs of predators (P) and members of a selfish herd (H) known as the prey. The survival value of each individual in the population is obtained by the following formula:

$$\mathrm{SV_i} = \frac{\mathrm{f_i} - \mathrm{f_{best}}}{\mathrm{f_{best}} - \mathrm{f_{worst}}} \tag{1}$$

where $\mathrm{f_i}$ denotes the fitness value of i, which is the individual's position, and $\mathrm{f_{best}}$ and $\mathrm{f_{worst}}$ are the best and worst fitness values reached after running the SHO [37]. The two movements that make up the herd movement operator are the leader movement and the following and deserting movement of the herd. The leader movement and the herd's following and deserting movements are the two movements that make up the herd movement operator. The next iteration updates the herd leader's position using the following formula:

$$h_L^{t+1} = \begin{cases} h_L^t + c^t, & if\ S_{h_L^t} = 1 \\ h_L^t + s^t, & if\ S_{h_L^t} < 1 \end{cases} \tag{2}$$

where c^t and s^t are movement vectors that depend on the selfish repulsion experiment and selfish attraction experiment, respectively [37].

Furthermore, members of an aggregation other than the leader are classified into two groups: herd followers (HFs) and herd defectors (HDs). Each herd member's updated location is computed using the following equation [37]:

$$h_i^{t+1} = \begin{cases} h_i^t + f_i^t, & if\ h_i^t \in H_F^t \\ h_i^t + d_i^t, & if\ h_i^t \in H_D^t \end{cases} \tag{3}$$

where f_i^t is the herd following vector and d_i^t is the herd deserting vector. Then, SHO considers the location of a specific herd member while modeling the movement of each predator p_i within the attacking predator P, as seen below:

$$p_i^{t+1} = p_i^t + 2q\left(h_r^t - p_i^t\right) \tag{4}$$

where q is a random number in the interval $[0,1]$ [37].

Lastly, two phases are applied: the predation phase, which determines the predation probability for each individual in the threatened herd, and the renewal phase, which replenishes the population in the event that hunting causes it to decline by creating new individuals through mating operations. In the end, the iteration terminates if the stopping condition is satisfied.

3.2. Biogeography-Based Optimization

This optimization technique was developed by Dan Smith in 2008 and is based on the migration and dispersal of live organisms in an ecosystem [38]. The method treats each solution conceptually as an island, and these islands are optimized using the migration and emigration behavior of species. The migration of species, the emergence of new species, and the extinction of existing ones are all explained by this mathematical modeling [39]. BBO analyzes whether migration and change will occur, respectively, using its two functioning mechanisms: migration and mutation.

For the habitat suitability index (HSI) corresponding to the fitness value, if the solution vector suitability index variables (SIVs) are suitable for the considered habitat, it is called a high his; otherwise, it is called a low HSI. Here, the SIV is the independent variable of the habitat, and the HSI is the dependent variable. The ratio λ is used to probabilistically decide whether to migrate each SIV in the solution. In the migration part, if the given SIV value for the ith solution is chosen to migrate, the ratio μ is used to probabilistically decide whether to migrate a randomly selected SIV variable for the ith solution [39]. If a solution has a low probability, its existence is unexpected. As a result, it is likely to evolve into a different solution. In contrast, a solution with a high probability is less likely to transform into another solution. As a result, the probability of a solution is determined using the following equation:

$$\mathrm{m_S} = \mathrm{m_{max}}\left(\frac{1 - \mathrm{P_s}}{\mathrm{P_{max}}}\right) \tag{5}$$

where S is a solution and the parameter m_{max} is user-defined [39].

3.3. Multi-Verse Optimizer

The Big Bang theory states that the universe began with this explosion. According to the theory, there were several explosions, each of which created a new universe. The Multi-Verse Optimization (MVO) technique is inspired by the three major sources in this theory: white holes, black holes, and wormholes [40,41]. The MVO algorithm is divided into two parts: exploration (using white and black holes) and exploitation (using wormholes). The exploration section provides the most promising places for finding the best local optima. Wormholes are utilized in the second stage, called exploitation, to search local areas for the global best. MVO uses a roulette wheel selection process to obtain universe matrix input values across different universes [40,41]. If we suppose that wormhole tunnels bridge one universe with the best universe yet created to accommodate local changes in each universe, then this mechanism has the following formula [40]:

$$X_i^j = \begin{cases} \begin{cases} X_j + TDR \times ((ub_j - lb_j) \times r4 + lb_j) \; if \; r3 < 0.5 \\ X_j - TDR \times ((ub_j - lb_j) \times r4 + lb_j) if \; r3 \geq 0.5 \end{cases} & if \; r2 < WEP \\ x_i^j & if \; r2 \geq WEP \end{cases} \tag{6}$$

where X_j denotes the jth parameter of the best universe, x_i^j is the jth parameter of the ith universe, TDR and WEP are two coefficients, lb_j and ub_j are the lower and upper bounds, and r2, r3, and r4 are random values between 0 and 1. The travel distance ratio (TDR), which determines the distance rate (variation) at which an object can be transported, and the wormhole existence probability (WEP), which indicates the likelihood that wormholes exist in universes, are two coefficients with the following formulas [40]:

$$WEP = min + l \times \left(\frac{max - min}{L}\right) \tag{7}$$

$$TDR = 1 - \frac{l^{\frac{1}{p}}}{L^{\frac{1}{p}}} \tag{8}$$

3.4. Teaching–Learning-Based Optimization

This is an algorithm constructed around classical learning theory, which was inspired by the ability of students to acquire knowledge and the ability of teachers to teach. It is divided into two phases: learning from the teacher (teacher phase) and learning through student engagement (learner phase) [42].

The teacher phase begins with identifying the teacher who provides the best solution in the population. The probability of success at this stage is distributed according to a Gaussian distribution. Although it is not realistically practical, a competent teacher is expected to raise the level of the students to that of their own. The truth is that the teacher attempts to increase the average class results depending on their own strengths. Therefore, at this stage, the current answer is modified according to the following expression [42]:

$$x^{new,i} = x^{old,i} + r^i \left(M^{new} - T^F M^i\right) \tag{9}$$

where r^i is a random value from 0 to 1, T^F is a teaching factor, M^i is the mean, and M^{new} is the new mean. Here, T^F might be either 1 or 2.

In the learner phase, students connect with one another and share information in order to raise their knowledge levels. Interacting with a more informed student leads to increased knowledge by learning new things from them. If the new student provides a better answer than the previous student as a result of their learning, the following changes are made [42]:

$$\begin{pmatrix} If \; f(x^i) < f(x^j), \; then \; x^{old,i} + r^i(x^i - x^j) \\ If \; f(x^j) < f(x^i), \; then \; x^{old,i} + r^i(x^j - x^i) \end{pmatrix} \tag{10}$$

3.5. Cuckoo Search

Some cuckoo species engage in parasitic behavior, placing their own eggs in the foreign nest and tossing the eggs of the nest owner bird to increase the survival probability of their own eggs. This behavior served as the inspiration for the CS algorithm. In the algorithm, each egg is considered a solution. The initial population is the number of randomly generated eggs in the nest where the egg is placed. From just one egg chosen by the cuckoo to be placed in this nest, a new solution is produced as follows [43]:

$$x_i^{t+1} = x_i^t + \alpha \oplus Levy(\lambda) \tag{11}$$

where $\alpha > 0$ denotes the step size.

The best nests with high-quality eggs are kept for future generations, whereas P_a values of the rest are reproduced. Here, $P_a \in [0,1]$ represents the probability that the cuckoo egg will be detected by the host bird [43].

3.6. Moth Flame Optimization

This algorithm was inspired by the motions of moths around a light source. The developed MFO technique treats possible solutions as moths and problem variables as their location in space. Because the MFO method is population-based, each moth represents a potential solution, and each location is represented as a decision matrix [44]. Another key component of this method is flames, which are represented by a matrix similar to the moth matrix. In this technique, both moths and flames represent solutions; the only difference is how they are handled and transformed at each iteration. While moths are the basic search components that move around the search space using the spiral flight mechanism, flames indicate the best locations obtained by the moths up to the relevant iteration [44]. The algorithm defines the main update mechanism as a logarithmic spiral, with the moth as the starting point and the flame position as the end point, as follows:

$$\mathrm{S}(\mathrm{M_i}, \mathrm{F_j}) = \mathrm{D_i e^{bt} cos}(2\pi \mathrm{t}) + \mathrm{F_j} \tag{12}$$

where $\mathrm{D_i}$ is the distance of the ith moth for the jth flame, constant b defines the form of the logarithmic spiral, and t is a random value between -1 and 1 [44].

3.7. Marine Predator Algorithm

Inspired by the predator–prey relationship between marine predators and their prey, this algorithm was developed to depend on the probability of encounters between marine predators and their prey [45,46]. The initial solution starts with random variables in the search space and continues by defining the best solution values for prey and predator in two same-sized matrices named prey and elite [45]. In the first phase, the prey moves rapidly and conducts an exploratory phase to look for its food using Brownian motion. On the other hand, the predator monitors the prey's movements while remaining motionless. Then, the prey matrices are updated according to the following formulas [45]:

$$\begin{pmatrix} \overrightarrow{\mathrm{stepsize_i}} = \vec{\mathrm{R}}_\mathrm{B} \otimes \left(\overrightarrow{\mathrm{Elite_i}} - \vec{\mathrm{R}}_\mathrm{B} \otimes \overrightarrow{\mathrm{Prey_i}}\right) \\ \overrightarrow{\mathrm{Prey_i}} = \overrightarrow{\mathrm{Prey_i}} + P \cdot \vec{\mathrm{R}} \otimes \overrightarrow{\mathrm{stepsize_i}} \end{pmatrix} \tag{13}$$

where $\mathrm{I} = 1, 2, \ldots, \mathrm{n}$, constant $\mathrm{P} = 0.5$, and $\mathrm{R} \in [0,1]$.

In Phase 2, the prey and predator move at the same speed; the predator uses Brownian motion, and the prey uses Levy motion. The following formulas are used to update the prey matrices [45]:

$$\left(\begin{array}{c}\overrightarrow{\mathrm{stepsize}_i} = \vec{\mathrm{R}}_{\mathrm{L}} \otimes \left(\overrightarrow{\mathrm{Elite}_i} - \vec{\mathrm{R}}_{\mathrm{L}} \otimes \overrightarrow{\mathrm{Prey}_i}\right) \\ \overrightarrow{\mathrm{Prey}_i} = \overrightarrow{\mathrm{Prey}_i} + P \cdot \vec{\mathrm{R}} \otimes \overrightarrow{\mathrm{stepsize}_i}\end{array}\right) \tag{14}$$

where $i = 1, 2, \ldots, n/2$.

$$\left(\begin{array}{c}\overrightarrow{\mathrm{stepsize}_i} = \vec{\mathrm{R}}_{\mathrm{B}} \otimes \left(\vec{\mathrm{R}}_{\mathrm{B}} \otimes \overrightarrow{\mathrm{Elite}_i} - \overrightarrow{\mathrm{Prey}_i}\right) \\ \overrightarrow{\mathrm{Prey}_i} = \overrightarrow{\mathrm{Elite}_i} + P \cdot CF \otimes \overrightarrow{\mathrm{stepsize}_i}\end{array}\right) \tag{15}$$

Here, $i = n/2, \ldots, n$, and $CF = \left(1 - \frac{Iter}{Max-Iter}\right)^{2\frac{Iter}{Max-Iter}}$.

In the third phase, the algorithm employs the predator's Levy motion for the duration of the iteration, assuming that the predator moves faster than the prey. After that, the prey matrices are updated using the subsequent formulas [45]:

$$\left(\begin{array}{c}\overrightarrow{\mathrm{stepsize}_i} = \vec{\mathrm{R}}_{\mathrm{L}} \otimes \left(\overrightarrow{\mathrm{R}_{\mathrm{L}}} \otimes \overrightarrow{\mathrm{Elite}_i} - \overrightarrow{\mathrm{Prey}_i}\right) \\ \overrightarrow{\mathrm{Prey}_i} = \overrightarrow{\mathrm{Elite}_i} + P \cdot CF \otimes \overrightarrow{\mathrm{stepsize}_i}\end{array}\right) \tag{16}$$

The procedure continues until the algorithm's stopping condition is satisfied or the maximum number of iterations is reached.

3.8. Flower Pollination Algorithm

The basis of the FPA was inspired by the reproductive process of flowering plants. There are two main ways that flowers are pollinated: biotic and abiotic. While biotic methods—that is, by organisms like flies, insects, bees, butterflies, etc.—pollinate the majority of flowering plants, abiotic methods—that is, by inanimate objects like the wind—pollinate some flowering plants. Pollen can travel over great distances thanks to insects' long-range flight capabilities. This characteristic helps to ensure the best reproduction during the flower pollination process. The following equation illustrates how this circumstance can be expressed mathematically [47]:

$$\mathrm{x}_i^{t+1} = \mathrm{x}_i^t + \gamma \mathrm{L}(\mathrm{g}_* - \mathrm{x}_i^t) \tag{17}$$

where the current best solution is represented by g_*, the step size is adjusted by γ, the solution vector is represented by x_i^{t+1}, and the Levy distribution $\mathrm{L} > 0$ denotes the strength of pollination.

The rule for local pollination is as follows [47]:

$$\mathrm{x}_i^{t+1} = \mathrm{x}_i^t + \gamma \mathrm{L}\left(\mathrm{x}_j^t - \mathrm{x}_k^t\right) \tag{18}$$

where x_j^t and x_k^t denote pollen types found in different flowers of the same plant species.

3.9. Artificial Bee Colony Algorithm

This is a metaheuristic optimization technique inspired by the foraging behavior of bees. The algorithm includes three types of bees: the onlooker bee, which waits in the dance area to select a food source; the employed bee, which searches for nectar by visiting known food sources and sharing the source information with the onlooker bee; and the scout bee, which searches for food at random around the hive [48,49]. The colony of ABC has an equal number of worker and spectator bees, and each food source has a single worker bee. Stated differently, the quantity of food sources surrounding the hive and the size of worker bees are chosen equally. The ABC algorithm begins with a random solution that is spread over the population that was initially created in the first step. If the nectar content of the new source is greater than that of the prior one, the bee forgets the former location and memorizes the new one. To find a potential solution, employed bees look for a better location in the nearby food source as described below [49]:

$$v_{ij} = x_{ij} + \phi_{ij}\left(x_{ij} - x_{kj}\right) \tag{19}$$

where ϕ_{ij} represents a random number from -1 to 1. In the second step, the employed bees share knowledge, while the onlooker bees choose the food source and compute the amount of nectar. The third stage involves sending the determined scout bees to potential food sources. These three steps continue until the stopping criteria are satisfied, after which the algorithm is terminated.

3.10. *Adaptive Network-Based Fuzzy Inference System (ANFIS)*

ANFIS is a hybrid artificial intelligence method consisting of the combination of artificial neural networks and fuzzy inference systems, which uses different methods in parameter calculations. An effective structure was created by combining the learning ability of artificial neural networks with the IF–THEN rule between the input and output of fuzzy logic in ANFIS. The structure of ANFIS is divided into five layers, as seen in Figure 1, and they are explained below [9,50].

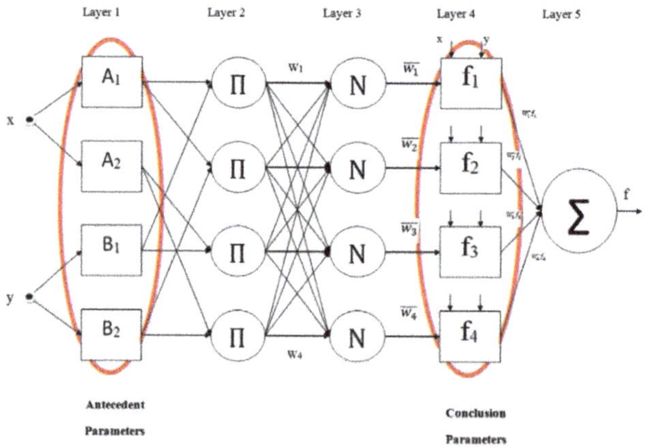

Figure 1. The general ANFIS structure consists of two inputs and one output [48].

Layer 1. This layer, known as the fuzzification layer, employs membership functions to generate fuzzy sets from inputs. The values of the prior parameters allow the shape of the membership functions to be determined. Also, membership functions' shapes can be defined by the parameters in their structure.

Layer 2. The rule layer calculates the product of membership functions from the preceding layer to generate firing strength (w_i) values as follows:

$$O_i^2 = w_i = \mu_{a_i}(x)\mu_{b_i}(yx) \tag{20}$$

where i = 1 and 2. The outputs of this layer are used as input weight functions for the following node.

Layer 3. This layer is known as the normalization layer, and the normalized firing strengths are calculated from the firing strengths obtained in previous layers using the following formula:

$$O_i^3 = \overline{w_i} = \frac{w_i}{w_1 + w_2} \tag{21}$$

where i = 1 and 2.

Layer 4. In the defuzzification layer, the output obtained in the normalization layer is multiplied by a linear equation (first order), and the output values are calculated as follows:

$$O_i^4 = \overline{w_i} x f_i = \overline{w_i} x(p_i t + q_i u + v_i) \tag{22}$$

Here, the parameter set $\{p, q, r\}$ is known as the result parameter.

Layer 5. The summation layer sums the results of each rule in the defuzzification layer to generate the ANFIS output, as shown below:

$$O_i^5 = \sum_i \overline{w_i} x f_i \tag{23}$$

To summarize, ANFIS training includes determining structural parameters using an optimization approach, and successful training is necessary for producing successful outcomes with ANFIS.

4. Simulation Results and Discussion

Within the scope of this study, ANFIS training was carried out using nine different metaheuristic algorithms to estimate the daily, weekly, and monthly minimum and maximum values of Brent oil price, and the obtained results were analyzed in detail. The algorithms used in ANFIS training were SHO, BBO, MVO, TLBO, CS, MFO, MPA, FPA, and ABC.

The Brent oil data used in this study were taken from the investing.com website as daily, weekly, and monthly datasets. The daily dataset covered the period between 3 January 2022, and 29 December 2023. Here, it is crucial to note that daily databases did not include data for weekends and holidays. The weekly dataset contained data from 1 January 2014 to 31 December 2023, and the monthly dataset spanned from 1 January 2014 to 1 January 2024. We collected 515 data points for the daily dataset and 522 data points for the weekly dataset to achieve more fitting analysis results. In contrast, since the monthly data collection contained fewer data over a larger range, 121 data points were collected to guarantee consistency. It is also worth noting that these daily, weekly, and monthly data were acquired separately for the lowest and highest values in the specified date ranges.

In this study, six prediction problems, as outlined in Table 1, are addressed. Specifically, the aim is to estimate the minimum and maximum values that Brent oil prices can reach on a daily, weekly, and monthly basis. The data used in these estimations are structured as time series. The time-series data were transformed into input–output pairs suitable for the training of ANFIS. The main goal of this transformation is to predict future values by using past data. However, in time-series problems, it is not always clear how many past values should be used to achieve the best prediction accuracy. To reduce this uncertainty, separate datasets were prepared for daily, weekly, and monthly predictions, each consisting of two, three, and four inputs, respectively, along with one output. Through these multiple configurations, the effect of the number of inputs on prediction performance was systematically investigated.

The ANFIS structures used in the study are illustrated in Figure 2. Figure 2a shows the block diagram of an ANFIS model with two inputs, while Figure 2b presents the training process and error calculation steps for a three-input model. Figure 2c displays the system structure when four inputs are used. In all these models, the output represents the subsequent time step value in the series.

Table 1. List of problems regarding the forecasting of Brent oil.

Problem	Definition
D_{Min}	Predicting the lowest daily price of Brent oil
D_{Max}	Predicting the highest daily price of Brent oil
W_{Min}	Predicting the lowest weekly price of Brent oil
W_{Max}	Predicting the highest weekly price of Brent oil
M_{Min}	Predicting the lowest monthly price of Brent oil
M_{Max}	Predicting the highest monthly price of Brent oil

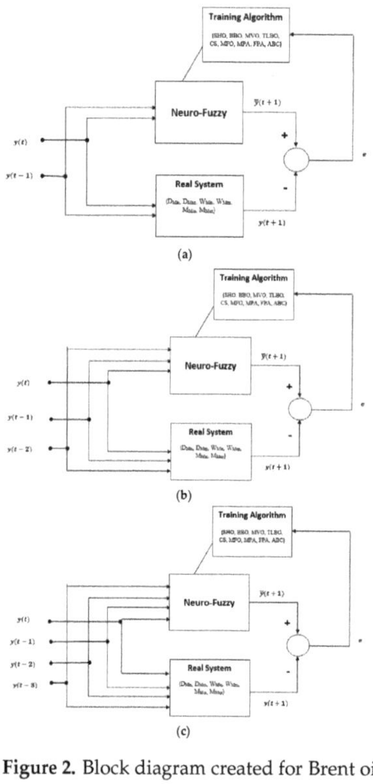

Figure 2. Block diagram created for Brent oil price prediction using (**a**) two (**b**) three (**c**) four input systems.

In the preprocessing phase, normalization plays an important role, especially when the dataset is large or contains high variability. For this reason, all input and output values were normalized to the [0, 1] range. All results and evaluations were made based on these normalized values.

Another critical factor that influences the performance of ANFIS is the type and number of membership functions (MFs). According to the literature, generalized bell-shaped membership functions (gbellmf) are effective in modeling normalized time-series data. Therefore, gbellmf was selected in this study to remain consistent with existing studies and to avoid unnecessary experimentation.

Additionally, the number of membership functions significantly affects learning performance. In this work, systems with different input counts were trained using two, three, and four membership functions, respectively, in order to analyze their impact on prediction accuracy. Since the number of parameters to be optimized increases with more inputs, the number of MFs was adjusted accordingly. For example, in the model with four inputs, only two MFs were used to reduce the complexity of the learning process.

Notably, 80% of the obtained dataset is used in the training process, and 20% is utilized in the testing process. All error values in the study are calculated as mean squared error (MSE). To compare the results obtained with each algorithm fairly, the population size and maximum generation number were evaluated similarly. In other words, the population size and maximum generation number were set as 20 and 2500, respectively.

Table 2 presents a summary of the overall workflow followed in this study. The process begins with data collection, where time-series data relevant to Brent oil prices are obtained. This is followed by the normalization and feature setup stage, where raw data are scaled to a uniform range and input–output pairs are prepared for model training. In the next step, the ANFIS structure is defined, including the selection of membership function types and their quantities. The model is then subjected to training and testing, allowing performance evaluation based on different configurations. Finally, the results are assessed through various evaluation metrics to determine prediction accuracy and overall model effectiveness.

Table 2. Step-by-step workflow of the proposed ANFIS model.

Step	Description
1	Data Collection
2	Normalization and Feature Setup
3	ANFIS Structure Definition
4	Training and Testing
5	Evaluation Metrics

4.1. *Analysis for Predicting the Lowest and Highest Daily Prices of Brent Oil*

The results obtained in estimating the daily minimum value of Brent oil price are presented in Table 3. When the results obtained for all applications of all algorithms are examined, it is seen that the average training error values do not exceed the 10^{-3} level. The mean training error values were found to be in the range of 1.7×10^{-3} to 2.6×10^{-3}. The best mean training error value, 1.7×10^{-3}, was achieved with TLBO, BBO, and MPA. The worst mean training error value was found with SHO. The results of other algorithms, except SHO, are 1.9×10^{-3} or better. Due to the structure of the problem, increasing the number of membership functions did not clearly improve or worsen the mean training error values. Minor behavioral differences were observed between the algorithms. The best training error value was found as 1.5×10^{-3} on the four-input system with BBO. Low standard deviation values were achieved for the training process. Except for a few applications, the value was at the 10^{-5} level. The best mean test error value was found to be 1.6×10^{-3}, and this value was obtained from many algorithms and many applications. The training algorithms could not make the mean test error value better than 1.6×10^{-3}. In addition, the best mean training error and the best mean test error values are parallel to each other. The best test error value was 1.4×10^{-3}. This value can be obtained with different algorithms. Good standard deviation values were also achieved for the test, except for a few applications. The comparison graph for the real output and the predicted output, taking into account the best training error value obtained with BBO, is presented in Figure 3.

Table 3. Comparison of the results obtained for the solution of the D_{Min} problem.

Algorithm	Number of Inputs	Number of MFs	Results					
			Train			Test		
			Mean	Best	Standard Deviation	Mean	Best	Standard Deviation
ABC	2	2	1.9×10^{-3}	1.8×10^{-3}	4.2×10^{-5}	**1.6×10^{-3}**	**1.4×10^{-3}**	1.1×10^{-4}
		3	1.9×10^{-3}	1.8×10^{-3}	3.5×10^{-5}	**1.6×10^{-3}**	1.5×10^{-3}	1.0×10^{-4}
		4	1.8×10^{-3}	1.7×10^{-3}	4.6×10^{-5}	**1.6×10^{-3}**	1.5×10^{-3}	1.2×10^{-4}
	3	2	1.9×10^{-3}	1.7×10^{-3}	6.3×10^{-5}	**1.6×10^{-3}**	**1.4×10^{-3}**	1.0×10^{-4}
		3	1.9×10^{-3}	1.7×10^{-3}	5.0×10^{-5}	**1.6×10^{-3}**	1.5×10^{-3}	1.1×10^{-4}
	4	2	1.9×10^{-3}	1.8×10^{-3}	5.4×10^{-5}	1.7×10^{-3}	1.5×10^{-3}	1.4×10^{-4}
FPA	2	2	1.9×10^{-3}	1.7×10^{-3}	3.5×10^{-5}	**1.6×10^{-3}**	1.5×10^{-3}	9.5×10^{-5}
		3	1.9×10^{-3}	1.8×10^{-3}	2.1×10^{-5}	**1.6×10^{-3}**	**1.4×10^{-3}**	1.2×10^{-4}
		4	1.9×10^{-3}	1.8×10^{-3}	2.3×10^{-5}	**1.6×10^{-3}**	1.5×10^{-3}	9.0×10^{-5}
	3	2	1.9×10^{-3}	1.8×10^{-3}	3.1×10^{-5}	**1.6×10^{-3}**	1.5×10^{-3}	7.1×10^{-5}
		3	1.9×10^{-3}	1.8×10^{-3}	4.1×10^{-5}	**1.6×10^{-3}**	1.5×10^{-3}	1.1×10^{-4}
	4	2	1.9×10^{-3}	1.8×10^{-3}	4.7×10^{-5}	**1.6×10^{-3}**	1.5×10^{-3}	7.9×10^{-5}
BBO	2	2	1.8×10^{-3}	1.6×10^{-3}	8.8×10^{-5}	**1.6×10^{-3}**	**1.4×10^{-3}**	1.3×10^{-4}
		3	**1.7×10^{-3}**	1.6×10^{-3}	6.1×10^{-5}	1.7×10^{-3}	1.6×10^{-3}	9.9×10^{-5}
		4	**1.7×10^{-3}**	1.6×10^{-3}	8.3×10^{-5}	**1.6×10^{-3}**	1.5×10^{-3}	7.5×10^{-5}
	3	2	**1.7×10^{-3}**	1.6×10^{-3}	5.5×10^{-5}	**1.6×10^{-3}**	1.5×10^{-3}	3.1×10^{-5}
		3	**1.7×10^{-3}**	1.6×10^{-3}	7.2×10^{-5}	**1.6×10^{-3}**	1.5×10^{-3}	5.7×10^{-5}
	4	2	**1.7×10^{-3}**	**1.5×10^{-3}**	1.1×10^{-4}	**1.6×10^{-3}**	1.5×10^{-3}	3.9×10^{-3}
MFO	2	2	1.8×10^{-3}	1.7×10^{-3}	7.4×10^{-5}	**1.6×10^{-3}**	1.5×10^{-3}	3.9×10^{-5}
		3	1.8×10^{-3}	1.6×10^{-3}	7.8×10^{-5}	**1.6×10^{-3}**	1.5×10^{-3}	4.8×10^{-5}
		4	1.8×10^{-3}	1.6×10^{-3}	7.8×10^{-5}	**1.6×10^{-3}**	1.5×10^{-3}	5.6×10^{-5}
	3	2	1.8×10^{-3}	1.7×10^{-3}	8.3×10^{-5}	**1.6×10^{-3}**	1.5×10^{-3}	6.7×10^{-5}
		3	1.8×10^{-3}	1.6×10^{-3}	7.5×10^{-5}	**1.6×10^{-3}**	1.5×10^{-3}	6.2×10^{-5}
	4	2	1.8×10^{-3}	1.7×10^{-3}	6.7×10^{-5}	**1.6×10^{-3}**	1.5×10^{-3}	6.0×10^{-5}
CS	2	2	1.8×10^{-3}	1.7×10^{-3}	3.8×10^{-5}	**1.6×10^{-3}**	1.5×10^{-3}	1.7×10^{-4}
		3	1.8×10^{-3}	1.8×10^{-3}	2.7×10^{-5}	**1.6×10^{-3}**	**1.4×10^{-3}**	7.7×10^{-5}
		4	1.8×10^{-3}	1.8×10^{-3}	2.7×10^{-5}	**1.6×10^{-3}**	**1.4×10^{-3}**	1.1×10^{-4}
	3	2	1.9×10^{-3}	1.8×10^{-3}	2.7×10^{-5}	**1.6×10^{-3}**	**1.4×10^{-3}**	9.3×10^{-5}
		3	1.9×10^{-3}	1.8×10^{-3}	2.1×10^{-5}	**1.6×10^{-3}**	1.5×10^{-3}	7.6×10^{-5}
	4	2	1.9×10^{-3}	1.8×10^{-3}	3.5×10^{-5}	**1.6×10^{-3}**	1.5×10^{-3}	9.8×10^{-5}
MPA	2	2	**1.7×10^{-3}**	1.6×10^{-3}	7.4×10^{-5}	**1.6×10^{-3}**	1.5×10^{-3}	5.8×10^{-5}
		3	**1.7×10^{-3}**	1.6×10^{-3}	8.5×10^{-5}	**1.6×10^{-3}**	**1.4×10^{-3}**	6.6×10^{-5}
		4	**1.7×10^{-3}**	1.6×10^{-3}	6.8×10^{-5}	**1.6×10^{-3}**	1.5×10^{-3}	7.1×10^{-5}
	3	2	**1.7×10^{-3}**	1.6×10^{-3}	8.1×10^{-5}	**1.6×10^{-3}**	1.5×10^{-3}	5.6×10^{-5}
		3	1.8×10^{-3}	1.6×10^{-3}	6.9×10^{-5}	**1.6×10^{-3}**	1.5×10^{-3}	4.6×10^{-5}
	4	2	1.8×10^{-3}	1.6×10^{-3}	6.7×10^{-5}	**1.6×10^{-3}**	**1.4×10^{-3}**	8.6×10^{-5}
MVO	2	2	1.8×10^{-3}	1.7×10^{-3}	5.9×10^{-5}	**1.6×10^{-3}**	1.5×10^{-3}	7.0×10^{-5}
		3	1.8×10^{-3}	1.7×10^{-3}	6.0×10^{-5}	**1.6×10^{-3}**	1.5×10^{-3}	7.9×10^{-5}
		4	1.8×10^{-3}	1.7×10^{-3}	6.4×10^{-5}	**1.6×10^{-3}**	1.5×10^{-3}	4.8×10^{-5}
	3	2	1.8×10^{-3}	1.7×10^{-3}	5.2×10^{-5}	**1.6×10^{-3}**	1.5×10^{-3}	7.9×10^{-5}
		3	1.8×10^{-3}	1.6×10^{-3}	6.0×10^{-5}	**1.6×10^{-3}**	**1.4×10^{-3}**	7.3×10^{-5}
	4	2	1.8×10^{-3}	1.7×10^{-3}	5.4×10^{-5}	**1.6×10^{-3}**	1.5×10^{-3}	5.3×10^{-5}
SHO	2	2	1.9×10^{-3}	1.8×10^{-3}	1.1×10^{-4}	**1.6×10^{-3}**	1.5×10^{-3}	1.4×10^{-4}
		3	1.9×10^{-3}	1.8×10^{-3}	1.1×10^{-4}	1.7×10^{-3}	1.5×10^{-3}	1.6×10^{-4}
		4	1.9×10^{-3}	1.8×10^{-3}	9.0×10^{-5}	1.7×10^{-3}	1.5×10^{-3}	1.0×10^{-4}
	3	2	1.9×10^{-3}	1.8×10^{-3}	1.3×10^{-4}	**1.6×10^{-3}**	**1.4×10^{-3}**	1.5×10^{-4}
		3	2.1×10^{-3}	1.9×10^{-3}	1.4×10^{-4}	1.9×10^{-3}	1.5×10^{-3}	3.1×10^{-4}
	4	2	2.6×10^{-3}	1.9×10^{-3}	2.0×10^{-3}	2.3×10^{-3}	**1.4×10^{-3}**	2.1×10^{-3}
TLBO	2	2	1.8×10^{-3}	1.6×10^{-3}	8.6×10^{-5}	**1.6×10^{-3}**	1.5×10^{-3}	8.7×10^{-5}
		3	1.8×10^{-3}	1.6×10^{-3}	8.8×10^{-5}	**1.6×10^{-3}**	1.5×10^{-3}	2.9×10^{-4}
		4	**1.7×10^{-3}**	1.6×10^{-3}	9.1×10^{-5}	**1.6×10^{-3}**	1.5×10^{-3}	1.0×10^{-4}
	3	2	1.8×10^{-3}	1.7×10^{-3}	7.4×10^{-5}	**1.6×10^{-3}**	1.5×10^{-3}	6.1×10^{-5}
		3	**1.7×10^{-3}**	1.6×10^{-3}	7.4×10^{-5}	**1.6×10^{-3}**	1.5×10^{-3}	4.9×10^{-5}
	4	2	1.8×10^{-3}	1.6×10^{-3}	8.8×10^{-5}	**1.6×10^{-3}**	1.5×10^{-3}	5.6×10^{-5}

Best results are given in bold.

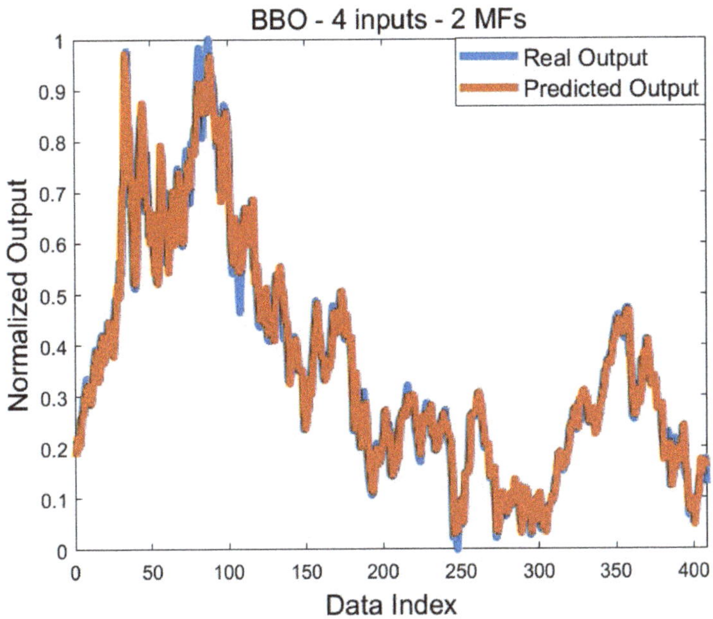

Figure 3. Comparison of graphs of real and predicted outputs plotted according to the best training error obtained for $D_{Min.}$

Table 4 presents a comparison of the estimates for the highest daily price of Brent oil. Changing the number of membership functions affected the results differently depending on the training algorithms. When the training results are evaluated, it is seen that the change in the number of membership functions does not change the mean error values obtained with ABC, CS, and MVO. In all applications of these algorithms, the 1.1×10^{-3} value was reached as the mean error value. The increase in the number of membership functions improved the mean training error in BBO and TLBO. The opposite situation was observed in MPA. The best mean training error value was obtained on a two-input system using MPA. This value is 9.3×10^{-4}. After MPA, the best mean training error value belongs to BBO. The best training error value was found to be 7.7×10^{-4} on the four-input system using TLBO. For at least one implementation of algorithms other than CS, the best training errors are at a level of 10^{-4}. Effective standard deviation values were obtained, especially because the training error values found by the algorithms were close to each other. When we look at the mean test error values, we see that the algorithms mostly obtain results that are close to each other. The mean test error values are in the range of 1.0×10^{-3} to 1.6×10^{-3}. The best mean error value was found to be 1.0×10^{-3} with BBO, MFO, and TLBO. According to all test results, the mean error value is frequently obtained as 1.1×10^{-3}. In fact, these results are parallel to the training results. As with the mean test error value, the best test error value also belongs to BBO. It is 8.3×10^{-4}. In addition to that, effective standard deviation values were obtained in the test results. Figure 4 presents the comparison of graphs of real and predicted outputs plotted according to the best training error obtained for the highest daily Brent oil price. It is seen that a very successful prediction was made, and the predicted output mostly coincides with the actual output.

Table 4. Comparison of the results obtained for the solution of the D_{Max} problem.

Algorithm	Number of Inputs	Number of MFs	Results					
			Train			Test		
			Mean	Best	Standard Deviation	Mean	Best	Standard Deviation
ABC	2	2	1.1×10^{-3}	1.0×10^{-3}	5.1×10^{-5}	1.2×10^{-3}	9.3×10^{-4}	1.0×10^{-4}
		3	1.1×10^{-3}	9.3×10^{-4}	5.6×10^{-5}	1.1×10^{-3}	9.6×10^{-4}	7.1×10^{-5}
		4	1.1×10^{-3}	1.0×10^{-3}	2.7×10^{-5}	1.1×10^{-3}	9.2×10^{-4}	9.2×10^{-5}
	3	2	1.1×10^{-3}	9.5×10^{-4}	6.1×10^{-5}	1.1×10^{-3}	8.8×10^{-4}	1.1×10^{-4}
		3	1.1×10^{-3}	1.0×10^{-3}	4.2×10^{-5}	1.1×10^{-3}	8.9×10^{-4}	1.8×10^{-4}
	4	2	1.1×10^{-3}	1.0×10^{-3}	4.1×10^{-5}	1.1×10^{-3}	1.0×10^{-3}	9.1×10^{-4}
FPA	2	2	1.1×10^{-3}	9.9×10^{-4}	3.7×10^{-5}	1.2×10^{-3}	1.0×10^{-3}	9.5×10^{-5}
		3	1.1×10^{-3}	1.1×10^{-3}	2.4×10^{-5}	1.1×10^{-3}	9.2×10^{-4}	8.9×10^{-5}
		4	1.1×10^{-3}	1.1×10^{-3}	1.7×10^{-5}	1.1×10^{-3}	9.4×10^{-4}	8.2×10^{-5}
	3	2	1.1×10^{-3}	9.1×10^{-4}	4.8×10^{-5}	1.1×10^{-3}	9.7×10^{-4}	1.9×10^{-4}
		3	1.2×10^{-3}	1.1×10^{-3}	2.3×10^{-5}	1.2×10^{-3}	1.0×10^{-3}	1.4×10^{-4}
	4	2	1.2×10^{-3}	1.1×10^{-3}	4.2×10^{-5}	1.51×10^{-3}	9.7×10^{-4}	3.2×10^{-4}
BBO	2	2	1.0×10^{-3}	8.6×10^{-4}	8.9×10^{-5}	1.1×10^{-3}	8.4×10^{-4}	9.6×10^{-5}
		3	9.5×10^{-4}	8.4×10^{-4}	9.9×10^{-5}	$\mathbf{1.0 \times 10^{-3}}$	8.9×10^{-4}	8.1×10^{-5}
		4	9.4×10^{-4}	8.1×10^{-4}	1.1×10^{-4}	$\mathbf{1.0 \times 10^{-3}}$	$\mathbf{8.3 \times 10^{-4}}$	9.8×10^{-5}
	3	2	1.1×10^{-3}	8.2×10^{-4}	9.1×10^{-5}	1.1×10^{-3}	8.8×10^{-4}	1.7×10^{-4}
		3	9.8×10^{-4}	8.1×10^{-4}	1.0×10^{-4}	1.1×10^{-3}	8.7×10^{-4}	1.7×10^{-4}
	4	2	9.6×10^{-4}	8.1×10^{-4}	9.7×10^{-5}	1.3×10^{-3}	9.8×10^{-4}	2.0×10^{-4}
MFO	2	2	1.1×10^{-3}	8.7×10^{-4}	7.1×10^{-5}	1.1×10^{-3}	1.0×10^{-3}	5.0×10^{-5}
		3	1.0×10^{-3}	8.5×10^{-4}	1.0×10^{-4}	1.1×10^{-3}	1.0×10^{-3}	4.9×10^{-5}
		4	1.0×10^{-3}	8.1×10^{-4}	1.1×10^{-4}	1.1×10^{-3}	9.1×10^{-4}	5.7×10^{-5}
	3	2	1.1×10^{-3}	9.3×10^{-4}	4.2×10^{-5}	1.1×10^{-3}	9.4×10^{-4}	8.4×10^{-5}
		3	1.1×10^{-3}	8.5×10^{-4}	6.3×10^{-5}	$\mathbf{1.0 \times 10^{-3}}$	9.2×10^{-4}	7.3×10^{-5}
	4	2	1.0×10^{-3}	8.4×10^{-4}	7.5×10^{-5}	1.4×10^{-3}	1.0×10^{-3}	2.4×10^{-4}
CS	2	2	1.1×10^{-3}	1.0×10^{-3}	2.4×10^{-5}	1.4×10^{-3}	9.2×10^{-4}	1.0×10^{-4}
		3	1.1×10^{-3}	1.0×10^{-3}	2.1×10^{-5}	1.2×10^{-3}	1.0×10^{-3}	9.6×10^{-5}
		4	1.1×10^{-3}	1.0×10^{-3}	2.5×10^{-5}	1.2×10^{-3}	1.0×10^{-3}	1.1×10^{-4}
	3	2	1.1×10^{-3}	1.0×10^{-3}	3.5×10^{-5}	1.2×10^{-3}	9.2×10^{-4}	1.3×10^{-4}
		3	1.1×10^{-3}	1.0×10^{-3}	3.1×10^{-5}	1.2×10^{-3}	9.6×10^{-4}	2.2×10^{-4}
	4	2	1.1×10^{-3}	1.0×10^{-3}	2.7×10^{-5}	1.3×10^{-3}	9.3×10^{-4}	2.2×10^{-4}
MPA	2	2	$\mathbf{9.3 \times 10^{-4}}$	8.2×10^{-4}	1.0×10^{-4}	1.1×10^{-3}	8.9×10^{-4}	7.1×10^{-5}
		3	9.7×10^{-4}	8.3×10^{-4}	1.1×10^{-4}	1.1×10^{-3}	9.2×10^{-4}	7.4×10^{-5}
		4	1.0×10^{-3}	8.4×10^{-4}	1.0×10^{-4}	1.1×10^{-3}	1.0×10^{-3}	1.1×10^{-4}
	3	2	9.8×10^{-4}	8.5×10^{-4}	8.9×10^{-5}	1.1×10^{-3}	9.7×10^{-4}	7.1×10^{-5}
		3	1.0×10^{-3}	8.4×10^{-4}	8.4×10^{-5}	1.1×10^{-3}	9.9×10^{-4}	7.6×10^{-5}
	4	2	9.8×10^{-4}	8.6×10^{-4}	7.1×10^{-5}	1.3×10^{-3}	1.0×10^{-3}	2.0×10^{-4}
MVO	2	2	1.1×10^{-3}	9.1×10^{-4}	4.8×10^{-5}	1.1×10^{-3}	9.9×10^{-4}	5.1×10^{-5}
		3	1.1×10^{-3}	9.5×10^{-4}	5.7×10^{-5}	1.1×10^{-3}	9.7×10^{-4}	7.0×10^{-5}
		4	1.1×10^{-3}	9.7×10^{-4}	4.3×10^{-5}	1.1×10^{-3}	9.9×10^{-4}	8.2×10^{-5}
	3	2	1.1×10^{-3}	9.1×10^{-4}	5.4×10^{-5}	1.1×10^{-3}	9.0×10^{-4}	1.0×10^{-4}
		3	1.1×10^{-3}	9.2×10^{-4}	5.3×10^{-5}	1.1×10^{-3}	9.2×10^{-4}	1.2×10^{-4}
	4	2	1.1×10^{-3}	9.1×10^{-4}	5.5×10^{-5}	1.3×10^{-3}	9.1×10^{-4}	2.2×10^{-4}
SHO	2	2	1.1×10^{-3}	9.2×10^{-4}	8.7×10^{-5}	1.2×10^{-3}	9.0×10^{-4}	1.6×10^{-4}
		3	1.1×10^{-3}	8.8×10^{-4}	1.2×10^{-4}	1.2×10^{-3}	8.5×10^{-4}	1.6×10^{-4}
		4	1.1×10^{-3}	1.0×10^{-3}	8.4×10^{-5}	1.2×10^{-3}	9.2×10^{-4}	1.7×10^{-4}
	3	2	1.1×10^{-3}	1.0×10^{-3}	5.2×10^{-5}	1.3×10^{-3}	9.0×10^{-4}	3.6×10^{-4}
		3	1.0×10^{-3}	1.1×10^{-3}	2.0×10^{-4}	1.6×10^{-3}	1.0×10^{-3}	5.5×10^{-4}
	4	2	1.3×10^{-3}	1.0×10^{-3}	1.4×10^{-4}	1.6×10^{-3}	9.9×10^{-4}	3.3×10^{-4}
TLBO	2	2	1.1×10^{-3}	8.3×10^{-4}	6.8×10^{-5}	1.1×10^{-3}	1.0×10^{-3}	4.3×10^{-5}
		3	1.0×10^{-3}	8.5×10^{-4}	1.2×10^{-4}	1.1×10^{-3}	9.8×10^{-4}	6.3×10^{-5}
		4	9.7×10^{-4}	8.3×10^{-4}	1.1×10^{-4}	1.1×10^{-3}	9.9×10^{-4}	5.4×10^{-5}
	3	2	1.0×10^{-3}	8.2×10^{-4}	1.0×10^{-4}	1.1×10^{-3}	9.5×10^{-4}	4.2×10^{-5}
		3	9.9×10^{-4}	8.2×10^{-4}	1.2×10^{-4}	$\mathbf{1.0 \times 10^{-3}}$	9.1×10^{-4}	1.1×10^{-4}
	4	2	9.6×10^{-4}	$\mathbf{7.7 \times 10^{-4}}$	8.3×10^{-5}	1.4×10^{-3}	9.3×10^{-4}	3.1×10^{-4}

Best results are given in bold.

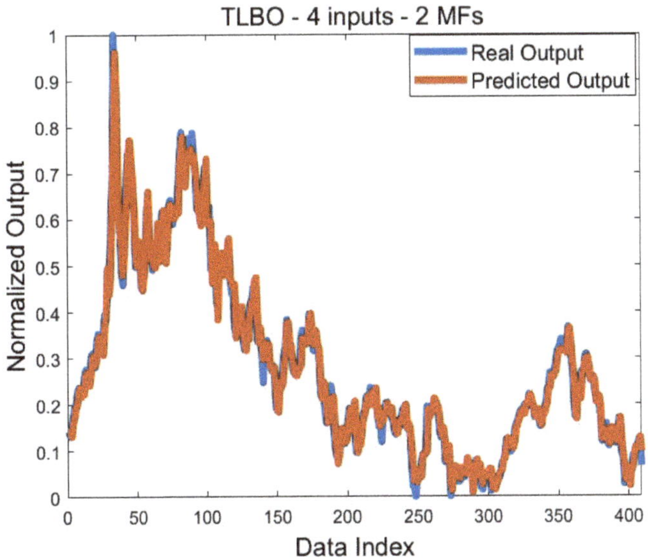

Figure 4. Comparison of graphs of real and predicted outputs plotted according to the best training error obtained for D_{Max}.

4.2. Analysis for Predicting the Lowest and Highest Weekly Prices of Brent Oil

Table 5 shows the results obtained with the training algorithms for predicting the lowest weekly price. Although it varies according to the training algorithms, the increase in the number of membership functions usually does not significantly affect the mean training error values. Except for a few applications of SHO, the mean training error value at a level of 10^{-4} was achieved. The best mean training error value was found to be 7.1×10^{-4} with BBO, MPA, and TLBO. The worst mean training error value for this problem was obtained on the four-input system using SHO. In other words, the mean training error value in all applications is in the range of 7.1×10^{-4} to 1.1×10^{-3}. In addition, the best training error value was found to be 6.6×10^{-4} using TLBO and BBO. When we look at the training results, generally, successful results were obtained in all algorithms. It is seen that these results are supported by low standard deviation values. Standard deviations were found especially at the 10^{-4}, 10^{-5}, and 10^{-6} levels. No algorithm was able to find a better result than 1.0×10^{-3} in the mean test error values. In this respect, it is a fact that test error values lag behind training error values. The best mean test error was found using FPA, BBO, MFO, CS, MPA, MVO, and TLBO. The worst mean error value was reached with SHO. In other words, it is possible to say that the mean test error values were obtained in the range of 1.0×10^{-3} to 1.5×10^{-3}. The best test error value was found to be 9.4×10^{-4}. The effective standard deviation value was reached in the testing process as well as in the training process. Figure 5 shows the comparison graph of the predicted output and the real output for the mean error value of 7.1×10^{-4}. Since this result was obtained with several algorithms, the graph was drawn by considering only the result found with TLBO. The large overlap of both graphs is an indication that the training process was successful.

Table 5. Comparison of the results obtained for the solution of the W_{Min} problem.

Algorithm	Number of Inputs	Number of MFs	Results					
			Train			Test		
			Mean	Best	Standard Deviation	Mean	Best	Standard Deviation
ABC	2	2	7.8×10^{-4}	7.2×10^{-4}	3.2×10^{-5}	1.1×10^{-3}	9.8×10^{-4}	8.0×10^{-5}
		3	7.8×10^{-4}	7.2×10^{-4}	3.6×10^{-5}	1.1×10^{-3}	**9.4×10^{-4}**	6.4×10^{-5}
		4	7.8×10^{-4}	7.4×10^{-4}	2.2×10^{-5}	1.1×10^{-3}	1.0×10^{-3}	6.7×10^{-5}
	3	2	8.1×10^{-4}	7.1×10^{-4}	5.1×10^{-5}	1.1×10^{-3}	9.7×10^{-4}	7.2×10^{-5}
		3	8.2×10^{-4}	7.5×10^{-4}	3.8×10^{-5}	1.1×10^{-3}	9.9×10^{-4}	7.7×10^{-5}
	4	2	8.6×10^{-4}	7.9×10^{-4}	5.0×10^{-5}	1.2×10^{-3}	1.0×10^{-3}	7.8×10^{-5}
FPA	2	2	7.5×10^{-4}	7.3×10^{-4}	1.2×10^{-5}	**1.0×10^{-3}**	**9.4×10^{-4}**	4.4×10^{-5}
		3	7.7×10^{-4}	7.3×10^{-4}	2.1×10^{-5}	1.1×10^{-3}	8.7×10^{-4}	7.8×10^{-5}
		4	7.7×10^{-4}	7.4×10^{-4}	1.4×10^{-5}	1.1×10^{-3}	9.9×10^{-4}	5.7×10^{-5}
	3	2	7.9×10^{-4}	7.4×10^{-4}	3.0×10^{-5}	1.1×10^{-3}	1.0×10^{-3}	6.1×10^{-5}
		3	8.1×10^{-4}	7.6×10^{-4}	2.7×10^{-5}	1.1×10^{-3}	9.5×10^{-4}	6.1×10^{-5}
	4	2	8.4×10^{-4}	7.7×10^{-4}	4.4×10^{-5}	1.1×10^{-3}	1.0×10^{-3}	8.9×10^{-5}
BBO	2	2	7.2×10^{-4}	7.1×10^{-4}	6.8×10^{-6}	**1.0×10^{-3}**	9.7×10^{-4}	2.8×10^{-5}
		3	7.2×10^{-4}	7.0×10^{-4}	4.3×10^{-6}	**1.0×10^{-3}**	9.6×10^{-4}	4.4×10^{-5}
		4	**7.1×10^{-4}**	**6.6×10^{-4}**	1.4×10^{-5}	**1.0×10^{-3}**	9.9×10^{-4}	3.0×10^{-5}
	3	2	7.2×10^{-4}	7.0×10^{-4}	9.1×10^{-6}	1.1×10^{-3}	9.5×10^{-4}	5.7×10^{-5}
		3	**7.1×10^{-4}**	7.0×10^{-4}	7.8×10^{-6}	1.1×10^{-3}	9.9×10^{-4}	5.0×10^{-5}
	4	2	7.2×10^{-4}	**6.6×10^{-4}**	1.6×10^{-5}	1.1×10^{-3}	9.6×10^{-4}	5.6×10^{-5}
MFO	2	2	7.4×10^{-4}	7.2×10^{-4}	4.5×10^{-6}	**1.0×10^{-3}**	9.9×10^{-4}	2.4×10^{-5}
		3	7.3×10^{-4}	7.2×10^{-4}	4.1×10^{-6}	**1.0×10^{-3}**	9.9×10^{-4}	2.2×10^{-5}
		4	7.2×10^{-4}	7.1×10^{-4}	8.6×10^{-6}	**1.0×10^{-3}**	9.9×10^{-4}	3.1×10^{-5}
	3	2	7.3×10^{-4}	7.0×10^{-4}	9.6×10^{-6}	**1.0×10^{-3}**	9.8×10^{-4}	2.1×10^{-5}
		3	7.3×10^{-4}	7.1×10^{-4}	1.1×10^{-5}	1.1×10^{-3}	9.8×10^{-4}	5.1×10^{-5}
	4	2	7.4×10^{-4}	7.2×10^{-4}	1.6×10^{-5}	1.1×10^{-3}	1.0×10^{-3}	8.7×10^{-5}
CS	2	2	7.4×10^{-4}	7.3×10^{-4}	5.3×10^{-6}	**1.0×10^{-3}**	**9.4×10^{-4}**	3.6×10^{-5}
		3	7.4×10^{-4}	7.3×10^{-4}	8.4×10^{-6}	**1.0×10^{-3}**	9.6×10^{-4}	4.7×10^{-5}
		4	7.5×10^{-4}	7.3×10^{-4}	1.3×10^{-5}	**1.0×10^{-3}**	9.6×10^{-4}	4.7×10^{-5}
	3	2	7.6×10^{-4}	7.4×10^{-4}	1.5×10^{-5}	1.1×10^{-3}	9.7×10^{-4}	9.9×10^{-5}
		3	7.8×10^{-4}	7.5×10^{-4}	1.5×10^{-5}	1.1×10^{-3}	1.0×10^{-3}	6.1×10^{-5}
	4	2	8.0×10^{-4}	7.6×10^{-4}	2.7×10^{-5}	1.1×10^{-3}	9.9×10^{-4}	7.9×10^{-5}
MPA	2	2	7.2×10^{-4}	7.1×10^{-4}	6.2×10^{-6}	**1.0×10^{-3}**	9.9×10^{-4}	1.5×10^{-5}
		3	7.2×10^{-4}	7.0×10^{-4}	7.0×10^{-6}	**1.0×10^{-3}**	9.8×10^{-4}	1.9×10^{-5}
		4	7.2×10^{-4}	7.1×10^{-4}	5.8×10^{-6}	**1.0×10^{-3}**	9.7×10^{-4}	2.3×10^{-5}
	3	2	**7.1×10^{-4}**	6.7×10^{-4}	1.1×10^{-5}	1.1×10^{-3}	9.7×10^{-4}	4.7×10^{-5}
		3	**7.1×10^{-4}**	6.8×10^{-4}	1.2×10^{-5}	1.1×10^{-3}	9.6×10^{-4}	1.3×10^{-4}
	4	2	**7.1×10^{-4}**	6.9×10^{-4}	6.9×10^{-6}	1.1×10^{-3}	1.0×10^{-3}	2.8×10^{-5}
MVO	2	2	7.3×10^{-4}	7.2×10^{-4}	4.1×10^{-6}	**1.0×10^{-3}**	9.9×10^{-4}	2.6×10^{-5}
		3	7.3×10^{-4}	7.2×10^{-4}	5.8×10^{-6}	**1.0×10^{-3}**	9.9×10^{-4}	1.9×10^{-5}
		4	7.3×10^{-4}	7.1×10^{-4}	9.2×10^{-6}	**1.0×10^{-3}**	9.8×10^{-4}	2.8×10^{-5}
	3	2	7.3×10^{-4}	7.1×10^{-4}	9.8×10^{-6}	1.1×10^{-3}	9.7×10^{-4}	4.3×10^{-5}
		3	7.3×10^{-4}	7.2×10^{-4}	1.4×10^{-5}	1.1×10^{-3}	**9.4×10^{-4}**	9.5×10^{-5}
	4	2	7.4×10^{-4}	7.2×10^{-4}	2.4×10^{-5}	1.1×10^{-3}	9.5×10^{-4}	5.5×10^{-5}
SHO	2	2	7.5×10^{-4}	7.2×10^{-4}	3.9×10^{-5}	1.1×10^{-3}	9.6×10^{-4}	7.0×10^{-5}
		3	7.9×10^{-4}	7.3×10^{-4}	6.2×10^{-5}	1.1×10^{-3}	9.9×10^{-4}	1.6×10^{-4}
		4	8.1×10^{-4}	7.4×10^{-4}	6.3×10^{-5}	1.1×10^{-3}	9.9×10^{-4}	9.8×10^{-5}
	3	2	8.2×10^{-4}	7.1×10^{-4}	1.4×10^{-4}	1.1×10^{-3}	9.9×10^{-4}	1.8×10^{-4}
		3	1.0×10^{-3}	7.7×10^{-4}	1.8×10^{-4}	1.1×10^{-3}	1.0×10^{-3}	2.6×10^{-4}
	4	2	1.1×10^{-3}	7.5×10^{-4}	3.1×10^{-4}	1.5×10^{-3}	1.1×10^{-3}	5.1×10^{-4}
TLBO	2	2	7.2×10^{-4}	7.0×10^{-4}	8.8×10^{-6}	**1.0×10^{-3}**	9.9×10^{-4}	1.6×10^{-5}
		3	7.2×10^{-4}	6.9×10^{-4}	1.1×10^{-5}	**1.0×10^{-3}**	9.8×10^{-4}	2.7×10^{-5}
		4	7.2×10^{-4}	6.9×10^{-4}	1.2×10^{-5}	**1.0×10^{-3}**	9.7×10^{-4}	2.6×10^{-5}
	3	2	7.2×10^{-4}	6.8×10^{-4}	1.4×10^{-5}	1.1×10^{-3}	1.0×10^{-3}	3.1×10^{-5}
		3	**7.1×10^{-4}**	**6.6×10^{-4}**	1.5×10^{-5}	1.1×10^{-3}	9.9×10^{-4}	4.7×10^{-5}
	4	2	7.2×10^{-4}	6.7×10^{-4}	1.5×10^{-5}	1.1×10^{-3}	9.9×10^{-4}	5.4×10^{-5}

Best results are given in bold.

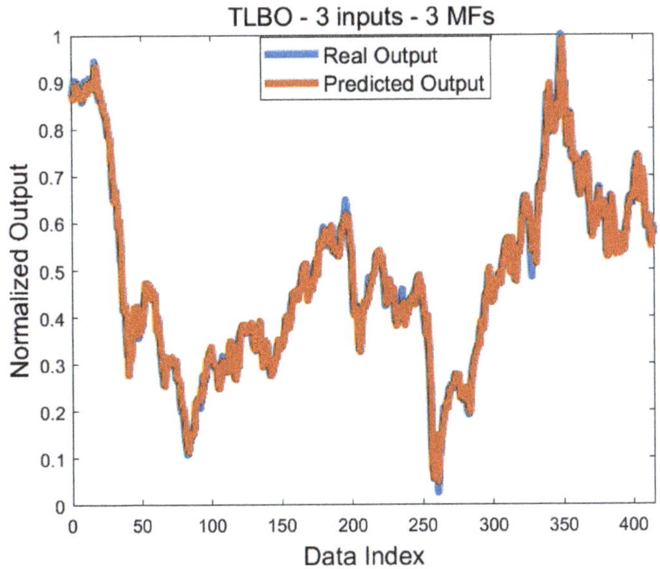

Figure 5. Comparison of graphs of real and predicted outputs plotted according to the best training error obtained for W_{Min}.

Table 6 shows the results obtained for predicting the highest weekly price. Increasing the number of membership functions of the inputs in ABC, BBO, and MFO also improved the solutions. Mixed behaviors were observed in other algorithms. The best mean training error was obtained by using BBO algorithms and MPAs on the two-input system. This value is 6.0×10^{-4}. The worst mean training error value was found to be 1.0×10^{-3} with SHO. Other application results are between the best and worst mean values specified. The best training error value was found using MFO, and its value was 5.4×10^{-4}. Effective standard deviation values were reached in the training process. Except for a few applications, standard deviation was found at the 10^{-5} level. During the testing process, especially in FPA and TLBO, increasing the number of membership functions used in the inputs improved the mean test error value. A similar situation was observed in three-input systems in ABC, BBO, and MVO. In other applications, stable behavior was not exhibited. The best mean error value was found on four-input systems with TLBO and MVO. This value is 5.8×10^{-4}. In addition, the best error value was found to be 4.6×10^{-4}. This value was obtained with four different training algorithms. Successful standard deviation values were achieved in the testing process as well as in the training process. It is seen that the standard deviation values obtained in all applications are in the 10^{-4} or 10^{-5} level. Figure 6 shows a comparison graph of the predicted output and the real output based on the best training result. It is seen that the graphs overlap except for a few output values. This shows that the training process carried out to solve the relevant problem was successful.

Table 6. Comparison of the results obtained for the solution of the W_{Max} problem.

Algorithm	Number of Inputs	Number of MFs	Results					
			Train			Test		
			Mean	Best	Standard Deviation	Mean	Best	Standard Deviation
ABC	2	2	7.5×10^{-4}	6.3×10^{-4}	5.2×10^{-5}	7.0×10^{-4}	5.1×10^{-4}	2.7×10^{-4}
		3	7.4×10^{-4}	6.6×10^{-4}	4.2×10^{-5}	7.0×10^{-4}	4.7×10^{-4}	1.4×10^{-4}
		4	7.2×10^{-4}	6.3×10^{-4}	4.1×10^{-5}	8.1×10^{-4}	5.4×10^{-4}	7.6×10^{-4}
	3	2	7.8×10^{-4}	6.2×10^{-4}	6.4×10^{-5}	7.3×10^{-4}	5.0×10^{-4}	2.2×10^{-4}
		3	7.7×10^{-4}	6.5×10^{-4}	4.6×10^{-5}	6.9×10^{-4}	5.5×10^{-4}	5.1×10^{-5}
	4	2	8.2×10^{-4}	7.1×10^{-4}	4.8×10^{-5}	6.8×10^{-4}	5.2×10^{-4}	1.2×10^{-4}
FPA	2	2	7.2×10^{-4}	6.1×10^{-4}	3.8×10^{-5}	6.4×10^{-4}	4.7×10^{-4}	1.2×10^{-4}
		3	7.4×10^{-4}	6.7×10^{-4}	3.2×10^{-5}	6.3×10^{-4}	5.0×10^{-4}	8.9×10^{-5}
		4	7.4×10^{-4}	6.8×10^{-4}	3.1×10^{-5}	6.1×10^{-4}	5.0×10^{-4}	7.8×10^{-5}
	3	2	7.7×10^{-4}	6.7×10^{-4}	3.7×10^{-5}	6.5×10^{-4}	5.0×10^{-4}	1.2×10^{-4}
		3	8.0×10^{-4}	7.1×10^{-4}	3.3×10^{-5}	6.3×10^{-4}	5.3×10^{-4}	6.9×10^{-5}
	4	2	8.4×10^{-4}	7.7×10^{-4}	4.0×10^{-5}	6.8×10^{-4}	5.4×10^{-4}	8.31×10^{-5}
BBO	2	2	6.3×10^{-4}	5.7×10^{-4}	3.5×10^{-5}	6.7×10^{-4}	$\mathbf{4.6 \times 10^{-4}}$	1.1×10^{-4}
		3	6.1×10^{-4}	5.5×10^{-4}	3.7×10^{-5}	7.4×10^{-4}	4.8×10^{-4}	2.3×10^{-4}
		4	$\mathbf{6.0 \times 10^{-4}}$	5.6×10^{-4}	2.7×10^{-5}	7.1×10^{-4}	4.7×10^{-4}	2.5×10^{-4}
	3	2	6.4×10^{-4}	5.5×10^{-4}	5.7×10^{-5}	6.9×10^{-4}	5.1×10^{-4}	2.1×10^{-4}
		3	6.3×10^{-4}	5.6×10^{-4}	5.2×10^{-5}	6.4×10^{-4}	5.0×10^{-4}	7.7×10^{-4}
	4	2	6.6×10^{-4}	5.6×10^{-4}	6.6×10^{-5}	6.6×10^{-4}	4.8×10^{-4}	1.6×10^{-4}
MFO	2	2	7.1×10^{-4}	6.1×10^{-4}	9.3×10^{-5}	6.7×10^{-4}	5.1×10^{-4}	1.1×10^{-4}
		3	6.6×10^{-4}	5.5×10^{-4}	5.6×10^{-5}	6.9×10^{-4}	$\mathbf{4.6 \times 10^{-4}}$	1.2×10^{-4}
		4	6.4×10^{-4}	$\mathbf{5.4 \times 10^{-4}}$	4.6×10^{-5}	6.5×10^{-4}	5.1×10^{-4}	9.4×10^{-5}
	3	2	6.9×10^{-4}	5.8×10^{-4}	6.0×10^{-5}	6.6×10^{-4}	5.1×10^{-4}	9.4×10^{-5}
		3	6.6×10^{-4}	6.0×10^{-4}	3.9×10^{-5}	6.9×10^{-4}	4.8×10^{-4}	2.0×10^{-4}
	4	2	7.0×10^{-4}	5.5×10^{-4}	6.0×10^{-5}	6.1×10^{-4}	4.8×10^{-4}	8.2×10^{-5}
CS	2	2	6.6×10^{-4}	6.4×10^{-4}	2.7×10^{-5}	6.3×10^{-4}	4.8×10^{-4}	1.1×10^{-4}
		3	7.0×10^{-4}	6.7×10^{-4}	1.7×10^{-5}	6.0×10^{-4}	4.9×10^{-4}	5.5×10^{-5}
		4	7.0×10^{-4}	6.7×10^{-4}	2.0×10^{-5}	6.0×10^{-4}	5.1×10^{-4}	2.6×10^{-5}
	3	2	7.2×10^{-4}	7.0×10^{-4}	1.9×10^{-5}	6.3×10^{-4}	5.2×10^{-4}	3.9×10^{-5}
		3	7.4×10^{-4}	7.0×10^{-4}	3.1×10^{-5}	6.4×10^{-4}	5.3×10^{-4}	1.6×10^{-5}
	4	2	7.1×10^{-4}	7.0×10^{-4}	1.6×10^{-5}	6.6×10^{-4}	5.4×10^{-4}	3.3×10^{-5}
MPA	2	2	6.1×10^{-4}	5.7×10^{-4}	2.6×10^{-5}	6.9×10^{-4}	4.7×10^{-4}	9.2×10^{-5}
		3	$\mathbf{6.0 \times 10^{-4}}$	5.7×10^{-4}	2.0×10^{-5}	6.5×10^{-4}	4.7×10^{-4}	1.2×10^{-4}
		4	6.2×10^{-4}	5.8×10^{-4}	3.8×10^{-5}	6.8×10^{-4}	$\mathbf{4.6 \times 10^{-4}}$	1.7×10^{-4}
	3	2	6.4×10^{-4}	5.8×10^{-4}	4.5×10^{-5}	6.4×10^{-4}	5.0×10^{-4}	6.4×10^{-5}
		3	6.3×10^{-4}	5.8×10^{-4}	2.8×10^{-5}	6.7×10^{-4}	5.4×10^{-4}	1.2×10^{-4}
	4	2	6.5×10^{-4}	5.7×10^{-4}	5.7×10^{-5}	6.3×10^{-4}	5.2×10^{-4}	6.1×10^{-5}
MVO	2	2	6.6×10^{-4}	6.0×10^{-4}	4.4×10^{-5}	6.8×10^{-4}	5.3×10^{-4}	1.1×10^{-4}
		3	6.5×10^{-4}	6.0×10^{-4}	4.0×10^{-5}	7.1×10^{-4}	5.1×10^{-4}	1.7×10^{-4}
		4	6.5×10^{-4}	6.1×10^{-4}	3.9×10^{-5}	6.4×10^{-4}	4.9×10^{-4}	1.1×10^{-4}
	3	2	6.8×10^{-4}	6.0×10^{-4}	5.1×10^{-5}	6.4×10^{-4}	5.3×10^{-4}	1.7×10^{-4}
		3	6.8×10^{-4}	6.1×10^{-4}	5.0×10^{-5}	6.3×10^{-4}	4.7×10^{-4}	8.9×10^{-5}
	4	2	7.2×10^{-4}	6.2×10^{-4}	6.5×10^{-5}	$\mathbf{5.8 \times 10^{-4}}$	$\mathbf{4.6 \times 10^{-4}}$	6.2×10^{-5}
SHO	2	2	7.2×10^{-4}	6.1×10^{-4}	8.1×10^{-5}	6.6×10^{-4}	5.2×10^{-4}	1.1×10^{-4}
		3	7.5×10^{-4}	6.2×10^{-4}	7.8×10^{-5}	6.4×10^{-4}	4.7×10^{-4}	7.7×10^{-5}
		4	7.8×10^{-4}	6.3×10^{-4}	7.1×10^{-5}	6.8×10^{-4}	5.6×10^{-4}	9.3×10^{-5}
	3	2	8.6×10^{-4}	6.7×10^{-4}	1.8×10^{-4}	7.1×10^{-4}	4.9×10^{-4}	2.3×10^{-4}
		3	1.0×10^{-3}	7.5×10^{-4}	2.9×10^{-4}	7.2×10^{-4}	5.6×10^{-4}	3.1×10^{-4}
	4	2	9.5×10^{-4}	6.4×10^{-4}	1.7×10^{-4}	8.6×10^{-4}	4.9×10^{-4}	2.5×10^{-4}
TLBO	2	2	6.3×10^{-4}	5.8×10^{-4}	2.7×10^{-5}	7.4×10^{-4}	5.3×10^{-4}	8.0×10^{-5}
		3	6.1×10^{-4}	5.6×10^{-4}	3.3×10^{-5}	7.0×10^{-4}	4.8×10^{-4}	1.2×10^{-4}
		4	6.2×10^{-4}	5.5×10^{-4}	4.5×10^{-5}	6.4×10^{-4}	4.7×10^{-4}	1.2×10^{-4}
	3	2	6.3×10^{-4}	5.7×10^{-4}	5.1×10^{-5}	7.3×10^{-4}	5.1×10^{-4}	8.9×10^{-5}
		3	6.2×10^{-4}	5.5×10^{-4}	3.8×10^{-5}	6.7×10^{-4}	5.0×10^{-4}	1.3×10^{-4}
	4	2	6.6×10^{-4}	5.5×10^{-4}	7.1×10^{-5}	$\mathbf{5.8 \times 10^{-4}}$	4.8×10^{-4}	6.4×10^{-5}

Best results are given in bold.

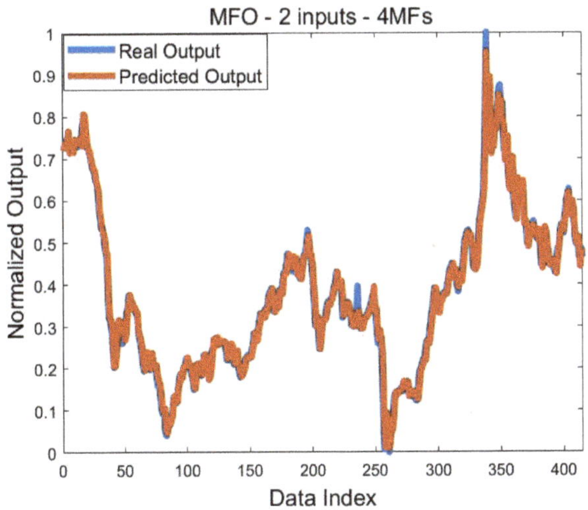

Figure 6. Comparison of graphs of real and predicted outputs plotted according to the best training error obtained for W_{Max}.

4.3. Analysis for Predicting the Lowest and Highest Monthly Prices of Brent Oil

Table 7 shows the results of estimating the lowest monthly price of Brent oil. According to the mean error values of the training process, the increase in the number of membership functions in ABC, BBO, MFO, and TLBO algorithms generally partially improved the results. In the FPA and some results of CS, it is seen that the increase in the number of membership functions does not affect the result. Effective results were obtained in MPA with low membership numbers. In CS, better results were obtained in two-input systems. The effect of the number of membership functions is limited. In SHO, increasing the number of membership functions worsened the mean error. The best training mean error value was found to be 2.9×10^{-3} with BBO. A 3.0×10^{-3} mean error value was achieved with MPA and TLBO algorithms. The worst mean value among all algorithms was found with SHO on the four-input system. This value is 4.3×10^{-3}. The best training error value was found to be 2.1×10^{-3} with the BBO algorithm. After BBO, the best training error value belongs to TLBO. The value of TLBO is 2.2×10^{-3}. Standard deviation values were reached at 10^{-4} and 10^{-5} levels for the training process. It is particularly noteworthy that the standard deviation values obtained in the training results of CS are at the 10^{-5} level. When all algorithms are considered, it is seen that average test error values are reached in the 4.7×10^{-3} to 6.3×10^{-3} range. The best mean test error value was found with MFO on a three-input system. This value is 4.7×10^{-3}. Especially in BBO, MFO, MPA, MVO, SHO, and TLBO, it was observed that the mean test error values worsened as the number of membership functions increased. The best test error value was obtained as 4.0×10^{-3} using SHO. It is seen that in other algorithms, error values of 4.3×10^{-3}, 4.4×10^{-3}, 4.5×10^{-3}, and 4.6×10^{-3} are mostly obtained. In the testing process, effective standard deviation values were generally achieved. In the test condition, standard deviation values were found at the 10−4 level except for some applications of MFO, CS, and SHO. As stated before, the best training error was obtained on BBO as 2.9×10^{-3}. Figure 7 compares the graphs of the predicted output and the real output for this result. It is seen that the real output and the predicted output are consistent with each other except for a few points.

Table 7. Comparison of the results obtained for the solution of the M_{Min} problem.

Algorithm	Number of Inputs	Number of MFs	Results					
			Train			Test		
			Mean	Best	Standard Deviation	Mean	Best	Standard Deviation
ABC	2	2	3.5×10^{-3}	2.9×10^{-3}	1.7×10^{-4}	5.2×10^{-3}	4.5×10^{-3}	8.2×10^{-4}
		3	3.4×10^{-3}	2.9×10^{-3}	1.6×10^{-4}	5.3×10^{-3}	4.4×10^{-3}	6.1×10^{-4}
		4	3.3×10^{-3}	3.0×10^{-3}	9.4×10^{-5}	5.3×10^{-3}	4.5×10^{-3}	5.4×10^{-4}
	3	2	3.5×10^{-3}	3.0×10^{-3}	1.5×10^{-4}	5.4×10^{-3}	4.3×10^{-3}	9.2×10^{-4}
		3	3.4×10^{-3}	3.0×10^{-3}	1.4×10^{-4}	5.4×10^{-3}	4.5×10^{-3}	6.8×10^{-4}
	4	2	3.4×10^{-3}	3.2×10^{-3}	1.1×10^{-4}	5.6×10^{-3}	4.5×10^{-3}	6.6×10^{-4}
FPA	2	2	3.5×10^{-3}	3.4×10^{-3}	5.5×10^{-5}	4.8×10^{-3}	4.5×10^{-3}	2.6×10^{-4}
		3	3.5×10^{-3}	3.4×10^{-3}	6.8×10^{-5}	5.1×10^{-3}	4.5×10^{-3}	5.7×10^{-4}
		4	3.5×10^{-3}	3.3×10^{-3}	7.7×10^{-5}	5.0×10^{-3}	4.5×10^{-3}	4.9×10^{-4}
	3	2	3.6×10^{-3}	3.4×10^{-3}	9.4×10^{-5}	5.0×10^{-3}	4.4×10^{-3}	3.3×10^{-4}
		3	3.6×10^{-3}	3.4×10^{-3}	1.0×10^{-4}	5.3×10^{-3}	4.5×10^{-3}	5.3×10^{-4}
	4	2	3.7×10^{-3}	3.4×10^{-3}	1.8×10^{-4}	5.4×10^{-3}	4.5×10^{-3}	8.0×10^{-4}
BBO	2	2	3.3×10^{-3}	2.6×10^{-3}	2.7×10^{-4}	5.0×10^{-3}	4.5×10^{-3}	3.9×10^{-4}
		3	3.0×10^{-3}	2.2×10^{-3}	3.1×10^{-4}	5.2×10^{-3}	4.5×10^{-3}	4.0×10^{-4}
		4	3.0×10^{-3}	2.4×10^{-3}	2.5×10^{-4}	5.4×10^{-3}	4.6×10^{-3}	4.7×10^{-4}
	3	2	3.2×10^{-3}	2.5×10^{-3}	2.5×10^{-4}	5.1×10^{-3}	4.3×10^{-3}	3.8×10^{-4}
		3	$\mathbf{2.9 \times 10^{-3}}$	$\mathbf{2.1 \times 10^{-3}}$	3.6×10^{-4}	5.4×10^{-3}	4.6×10^{-3}	5.8×10^{-4}
	4	2	3.0×10^{-3}	2.4×10^{-3}	2.7×10^{-4}	5.2×10^{-3}	4.3×10^{-3}	6.8×10^{-4}
MFO	2	2	3.5×10^{-3}	2.7×10^{-3}	2.4×10^{-4}	4.8×10^{-3}	4.5×10^{-3}	2.7×10^{-4}
		3	3.4×10^{-3}	2.6×10^{-3}	2.7×10^{-4}	4.9×10^{-3}	4.5×10^{-3}	2.8×10^{-4}
		4	3.3×10^{-3}	2.6×10^{-3}	2.4×10^{-4}	5.0×10^{-3}	4.5×10^{-3}	3.1×10^{-4}
	3	2	3.4×10^{-3}	2.6×10^{-3}	2.7×10^{-4}	$\mathbf{4.7 \times 10^{-3}}$	4.4×10^{-3}	3.2×10^{-4}
		3	3.2×10^{-3}	2.5×10^{-3}	2.6×10^{-4}	5.0×10^{-3}	4.4×10^{-3}	4.3×10^{-4}
	4	2	3.3×10^{-3}	2.6×10^{-3}	2.4×10^{-4}	5.4×10^{-3}	4.5×10^{-3}	1.8×10^{-3}
CS	2	2	3.5×10^{-3}	3.3×10^{-3}	5.2×10^{-5}	5.2×10^{-3}	4.5×10^{-3}	1.3×10^{-3}
		3	3.4×10^{-3}	3.3×10^{-3}	4.4×10^{-5}	5.0×10^{-3}	4.5×10^{-3}	4.3×10^{-4}
		4	3.4×10^{-3}	3.3×10^{-3}	5.5×10^{-5}	5.2×10^{-3}	4.54×10^{-3}	4.9×10^{-4}
	3	2	3.5×10^{-3}	3.4×10^{-3}	5.2×10^{-5}	5.1×10^{-3}	4.3×10^{-3}	4.8×10^{-4}
		3	3.5×10^{-3}	3.4×10^{-3}	3.3×10^{-5}	5.4×10^{-3}	4.5×10^{-3}	4.7×10^{-4}
	4	2	3.5×10^{-3}	3.4×10^{-3}	8.9×10^{-5}	6.3×10^{-3}	4.6×10^{-3}	1.7×10^{-3}
MPA	2	2	3.1×10^{-3}	2.5×10^{-3}	3.0×10^{-4}	5.0×10^{-3}	4.5×10^{-3}	3.5×10^{-4}
		3	3.2×10^{-3}	2.7×10^{-3}	2.4×10^{-4}	5.1×10^{-3}	4.5×10^{-3}	4.8×10^{-4}
		4	3.1×10^{-3}	2.5×10^{-3}	2.4×10^{-4}	5.3×10^{-3}	4.5×10^{-3}	5.2×10^{-4}
	3	2	3.0×10^{-3}	2.4×10^{-3}	2.9×10^{-4}	4.9×10^{-3}	4.3×10^{-3}	3.1×10^{-4}
		3	3.1×10^{-3}	2.5×10^{-3}	2.7×10^{-4}	5.4×10^{-3}	4.5×10^{-3}	5.4×10^{-4}
	4	2	3.0×10^{-3}	2.3×10^{-3}	3.2×10^{-4}	5.6×10^{-3}	4.5×10^{-3}	9.0×10^{-4}
MVO	2	2	3.4×10^{-3}	2.8×10^{-3}	1.6×10^{-4}	4.8×10^{-3}	4.4×10^{-3}	3.7×10^{-4}
		3	3.4×10^{-3}	3.0×10^{-3}	1.3×10^{-4}	5.0×10^{-3}	4.6×10^{-3}	3.0×10^{-4}
		4	3.3×10^{-3}	2.9×10^{-3}	1.7×10^{-4}	5.1×10^{-3}	4.6×10^{-3}	4.2×10^{-4}
	3	2	3.4×10^{-3}	2.8×10^{-3}	1.8×10^{-4}	4.8×10^{-3}	4.4×10^{-3}	2.5×10^{-4}
		3	3.4×10^{-3}	3.1×10^{-3}	1.1×10^{-4}	5.2×10^{-3}	4.5×10^{-3}	4.4×10^{-4}
	4	2	3.3×10^{-3}	3.0×10^{-3}	1.4×10^{-4}	5.3×10^{-3}	4.5×10^{-3}	6.0×10^{-4}
SHO	2	2	3.5×10^{-3}	3.2×10^{-3}	2.5×10^{-4}	4.9×10^{-3}	4.5×10^{-3}	3.7×10^{-4}
		3	3.5×10^{-3}	2.7×10^{-3}	3.1×10^{-4}	5.2×10^{-3}	4.4×10^{-3}	4.9×10^{-4}
		4	3.7×10^{-3}	3.0×10^{-3}	5.5×10^{-4}	5.5×10^{-3}	4.6×10^{-3}	6.4×10^{-4}
	3	2	3.8×10^{-3}	3.1×10^{-3}	4.2×10^{-4}	5.8×10^{-3}	$\mathbf{4.0 \times 10^{-3}}$	3.0×10^{-3}
		3	4.2×10^{-3}	3.4×10^{-3}	7.9×10^{-4}	6.0×10^{-3}	4.8×10^{-3}	1.0×10^{-3}
	4	2	4.3×10^{-3}	3.3×10^{-3}	7.5×10^{-4}	6.1×10^{-3}	4.8×10^{-3}	1.4×10^{-3}
TLBO	2	2	3.4×10^{-3}	2.7×10^{-3}	1.9×10^{-4}	4.8×10^{-3}	4.5×10^{-3}	2.1×10^{-4}
		3	3.3×10^{-3}	2.6×10^{-3}	1.7×10^{-4}	5.0×10^{-3}	4.6×10^{-3}	3.5×10^{-4}
		4	3.1×10^{-3}	2.4×10^{-3}	2.8×10^{-4}	5.2×10^{-3}	4.4×10^{-3}	4.4×10^{-4}
	3	2	3.1×10^{-3}	2.2×10^{-3}	3.7×10^{-4}	4.9×10^{-3}	4.4×10^{-3}	3.1×10^{-4}
		3	3.1×10^{-3}	2.3×10^{-3}	2.8×10^{-4}	5.3×10^{-3}	4.6×10^{-3}	4.0×10^{-4}
	4	2	3.0×10^{-3}	2.3×10^{-3}	3.8×10^{-4}	5.3×10^{-3}	4.5×10^{-3}	5.8×10^{-4}

Best results are given in bold.

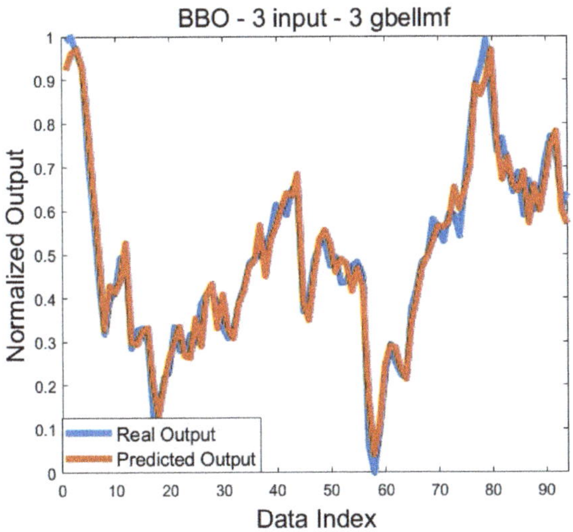

Figure 7. Comparison of graphs of real and predicted outputs plotted according to the best training error obtained for M_{Min}.

The results obtained regarding the estimation of the highest monthly price of Brent oil are given in Table 8. The increase in the number of membership functions, especially in ABC, BBO, MFO, and TLBO, improved the training mean errors. A similar situation was observed in MVO, except for one application. All mean error values are the same except for when using two gbellmf on a two-input system, which produced a different mean training error value of the MPA. The best mean error value among all applications was found using three gbellmf on a three-input system with BBO and TLBO algorithms. This value is 2.0×10^{-3}. Apart from BBO and TLBO, the best mean training error value belongs to MPA. The worst mean training error value belongs to SHO. This value is 3.1×10^{-3}. In the light of this information, it is seen that the mean error values obtained for the training process in estimating the monthly maximum value are between 2.0×10^{-3} and 3.1×10^{-3}. It has also been determined that the training mean errors in two- and three-input systems are generally better than in four-input systems, and the best mean training results are obtained in these systems. The best training error value was found to be 1.6×10^{-3} using TLBO. The best training error values found with BBO and MPA are 1.7×10^{-3} and 1.9×10^{-3}, respectively. Effective standard deviation values for the training process were reached. Standard deviation values at the 10^{-4} or 10^{-5} level were obtained. Looking at the test results, the change in the number of memberships generally affected the results differently. It was observed that the mean test error values of BBO and TLBO were not as good as the mean training error values. The best test mean error values were obtained to be 7.5×10^{-3} using MFO and MVO. The best test error value was found to be 4.9×10^{-3} with MFO. The test results show that standard deviation values were obtained at 10^{-3} and 10^{-4} levels. These values are consistent with the results obtained. Figure 8 shows the comparison of the real output and the predicted output for the best training error value. Both graphs largely overlap. This is one of the indicators demonstrating that the training process was successful.

Table 8. Comparison of the results obtained for the solution of the M_{Max} problem.

Algorithm	Number of Inputs	Number of MFs	Results					
			Train			Test		
			Mean	Best	Standard Deviation	Mean	Best	Standard Deviation
ABC	2	2	2.6×10^{-3}	2.2×10^{-3}	1.4×10^{-4}	8.6×10^{-3}	6.6×10^{-3}	1.1×10^{-3}
		3	2.4×10^{-3}	2.2×10^{-3}	9.0×10^{-5}	8.3×10^{-3}	5.4×10^{-3}	1.0×10^{-3}
		4	2.3×10^{-3}	2.1×10^{-3}	7.08×10^{-5}	8.2×10^{-3}	6.8×10^{-3}	8.9×10^{-4}
	3	2	2.5×10^{-3}	2.2×10^{-3}	1.5×10^{-4}	8.4×10^{-3}	5.2×10^{-3}	1.3×10^{-3}
		3	2.3×10^{-3}	2.1×10^{-3}	1.1×10^{-4}	8.4×10^{-3}	6.0×10^{-3}	1.2×10^{-3}
	4	2	2.4×10^{-3}	2.0×10^{-3}	1.5×10^{-4}	8.2×10^{-3}	5.6×10^{-3}	1.4×10^{-3}
FPA	2	2	2.6×10^{-3}	2.3×10^{-3}	1.1×10^{-4}	8.1×10^{-3}	7.0×10^{-3}	7.8×10^{-4}
		3	2.6×10^{-3}	2.4×10^{-3}	8.6×10^{-5}	8.3×10^{-3}	7.0×10^{-3}	1.0×10^{-3}
		4	2.5×10^{-3}	2.4×10^{-3}	7.4×10^{-5}	8.2×10^{-3}	6.6×10^{-3}	7.0×10^{-4}
	3	2	2.7×10^{-3}	2.4×10^{-3}	9.2×10^{-5}	8.0×10^{-3}	6.4×10^{-3}	8.9×10^{-4}
		3	2.6×10^{-3}	2.4×10^{-3}	1.1×10^{-4}	8.3×10^{-3}	5.8×10^{-3}	1.1×10^{-3}
	4	2	2.8×10^{-3}	2.4×10^{-3}	1.9×10^{-4}	8.5×10^{-3}	5.9×10^{-3}	1.5×10^{-3}
BBO	2	2	2.3×10^{-3}	2.0×10^{-3}	1.5×10^{-4}	7.7×10^{-3}	5.5×10^{-3}	9.4×10^{-4}
		3	2.2×10^{-3}	2.0×10^{-3}	1.4×10^{-4}	7.7×10^{-3}	6.2×10^{-3}	9.4×10^{-4}
		4	2.1×10^{-3}	2.0×10^{-3}	1.2×10^{-4}	7.9×10^{-3}	6.2×10^{-3}	1.1×10^{-3}
	3	2	2.2×10^{-3}	1.9×10^{-3}	1.8×10^{-4}	8.7×10^{-3}	6.6×10^{-3}	1.1×10^{-3}
		3	**2.0×10^{-3}**	1.7×10^{-3}	1.7×10^{-4}	8.8×10^{-3}	5.9×10^{-3}	2.7×10^{-3}
	4	2	2.2×10^{-3}	1.9×10^{-3}	2.0×10^{-4}	8.1×10^{-3}	6.2×10^{-3}	1.4×10^{-3}
MFO	2	2	2.5×10^{-3}	2.1×10^{-3}	2.5×10^{-4}	**7.5×10^{-3}**	6.1×10^{-3}	6.9×10^{-4}
		3	2.4×10^{-3}	2.0×10^{-3}	2.1×10^{-4}	7.8×10^{-3}	6.4×10^{-3}	7.5×10^{-4}
		4	2.3×10^{-3}	2.1×10^{-3}	1.6×10^{-4}	**7.5×10^{-3}**	6.4×10^{-3}	7.2×10^{-4}
	3	2	2.5×10^{-3}	2.1×10^{-3}	2.2×10^{-4}	8.2×10^{-3}	6.5×10^{-3}	7.9×10^{-4}
		3	2.4×10^{-3}	2.0×10^{-3}	1.8×10^{-4}	8.3×10^{-3}	6.5×10^{-3}	7.4×10^{-4}
	4	2	2.4×10^{-3}	2.1×10^{-3}	2.3×10^{-4}	8.2×10^{-3}	**4.9×10^{-3}**	1.1×10^{-3}
CS	2	2	2.5×10^{-3}	2.4×10^{-3}	7.4×10^{-5}	7.9×10^{-3}	6.5×10^{-3}	7.1×10^{-4}
		3	2.5×10^{-3}	2.4×10^{-3}	6.7×10^{-5}	7.8×10^{-3}	5.6×10^{-3}	9.2×10^{-4}
		4	2.5×10^{-3}	2.4×10^{-3}	4.2×10^{-5}	8.1×10^{-3}	6.1×10^{-3}	1.0×10^{-3}
	3	2	2.6×10^{-3}	2.4×10^{-3}	8.7×10^{-5}	8.8×10^{-3}	6.4×10^{-3}	2.5×10^{-3}
		3	2.5×10^{-3}	2.3×10^{-3}	1.0×10^{-4}	8.5×10^{-3}	6.2×10^{-3}	1.3×10^{-3}
	4	2	2.7×10^{-3}	2.5×10^{-3}	1.2×10^{-4}	8.1×10^{-3}	5.6×10^{-3}	1.3×10^{-3}
MPA	2	2	2.3×10^{-3}	2.1×10^{-3}	9.3×10^{-5}	7.8×10^{-3}	6.2×10^{-3}	9.4×10^{-4}
		3	2.2×10^{-3}	2.1×10^{-3}	9.7×10^{-5}	8.3×10^{-3}	5.9×10^{-3}	1.1×10^{-3}
		4	2.2×10^{-3}	2.0×10^{-3}	1.1×10^{-4}	8.0×10^{-3}	6.0×10^{-3}	9.5×10^{-4}
	3	2	2.2×10^{-3}	1.9×10^{-3}	1.4×10^{-4}	8.4×10^{-3}	6.5×10^{-3}	1.4×10^{-3}
		3	2.2×10^{-3}	1.9×10^{-3}	1.3×10^{-4}	8.6×10^{-3}	6.4×10^{-3}	9.0×10^{-4}
	4	2	2.2×10^{-3}	1.9×10^{-3}	2.1×10^{-4}	9.0×10^{-3}	6.4×10^{-3}	1.3×10^{-3}
MVO	2	2	2.5×10^{-3}	2.2×10^{-3}	1.8×10^{-4}	**7.5×10^{-3}**	6.2×10^{-3}	7.7×10^{-4}
		3	2.4×10^{-3}	2.2×10^{-3}	1.1×10^{-4}	7.8×10^{-3}	5.8×10^{-3}	8.9×10^{-4}
		4	2.4×10^{-3}	2.2×10^{-3}	1.2×10^{-4}	8.2×10^{-3}	6.1×10^{-3}	9.4×10^{-4}
	3	2	2.5×10^{-3}	2.1×10^{-3}	2.0×10^{-4}	8.0×10^{-3}	6.1×10^{-3}	9.1×10^{-4}
		3	2.4×10^{-3}	2.2×10^{-3}	1.4×10^{-4}	8.7×10^{-3}	6.1×10^{-3}	2.7×10^{-3}
	4	2	2.5×10^{-3}	2.1×10^{-3}	2.8×10^{-4}	7.8×10^{-3}	5.7×10^{-3}	1.3×10^{-3}
SHO	2	2	2.7×10^{-3}	2.3×10^{-3}	2.4×10^{-4}	8.2×10^{-3}	6.1×10^{-3}	8.8×10^{-4}
		3	2.6×10^{-3}	2.1×10^{-3}	3.9×10^{-4}	8.9×10^{-3}	7.1×10^{-3}	1.3×10^{-3}
		4	2.7×10^{-3}	2.1×10^{-3}	3.7×10^{-4}	8.6×10^{-3}	6.4×10^{-3}	1.1×10^{-3}
	3	2	2.9×10^{-3}	2.2×10^{-3}	4.9×10^{-4}	8.5×10^{-3}	5.9×10^{-3}	1.5×10^{-3}
		3	3.1×10^{-3}	2.4×10^{-3}	4.8×10^{-4}	9.0×10^{-3}	7.4×10^{-3}	1.2×10^{-3}
	4	2	3.1×10^{-3}	2.3×10^{-3}	4.1×10^{-4}	8.6×10^{-3}	5.9×10^{-3}	2.3×10^{-3}
TLBO	2	2	2.4×10^{-3}	2.0×10^{-3}	1.6×10^{-4}	8.0×10^{-3}	6.5×10^{-3}	1.1×10^{-3}
		3	2.3×10^{-3}	1.9×10^{-3}	1.6×10^{-4}	8.0×10^{-3}	5.7×10^{-3}	1.3×10^{-3}
		4	2.2×10^{-3}	1.8×10^{-3}	1.5×10^{-4}	7.9×10^{-3}	6.3×10^{-3}	7.7×10^{-4}
	3	2	2.3×10^{-3}	2.0×10^{-3}	1.8×10^{-4}	8.3×10^{-3}	6.7×10^{-3}	9.3×10^{-4}
		3	**2.0×10^{-3}**	**1.6×10^{-3}**	2.0×10^{-4}	9.2×10^{-3}	7.5×10^{-3}	1.1×10^{-3}
	4	2	2.1×10^{-3}	**1.6×10^{-3}**	2.4×10^{-4}	8.9×10^{-3}	6.0×10^{-3}	1.4×10^{-3}

Best results are given in bold.

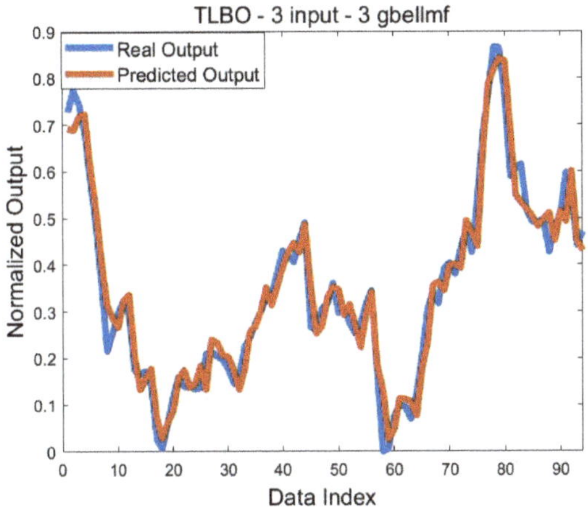

Figure 8. Comparison of graphs of real and predicted outputs plotted according to the best training error obtained for M_{Max}.

The findings obtained in this study should be interpreted within the scope of certain limitations. In particular, the number of inputs, the number and type of membership functions, population size, and the maximum number of generations are the primary constraints considered. Exploring alternative configurations beyond these parameters may lead to higher-quality solutions. However, due to the significant time and computational cost required for such evaluations, the scope of the study was intentionally limited.

The use of historical data proved to be more effective in daily and weekly forecasts. The results clearly show that daily and weekly predictions outperform monthly predictions, as demonstrated in the related tables and figures. One possible reason for this difference is the limited number of data points in the monthly dataset. Additionally, the longer time gap between the input data and the predicted output in monthly forecasts increases the likelihood of external factors influencing the outcome, which may also reduce accuracy.

When examining both training and test results for daily, weekly, and monthly predictions, it is observed that standard deviation values are generally low. This indicates that the successful outcomes obtained are consistent and repeatable. The fact that test results largely aligned with training results suggests that the training process was effectively conducted and that no overfitting occurred.

Although all algorithms yielded effective results, it can be stated that BBO and TLBO performed better than the others in solving the target problem. This does not imply that the other algorithms were unsuccessful, but rather that these two algorithms were more suitable for this specific problem and configuration. It should also be considered that the observed performance differences may be influenced by the previously mentioned limitations of the study.

Furthermore, an increase in the number of inputs and membership functions also increases the number of parameters to be optimized during training, which extends the overall training time. Considering that each algorithm was executed 30 times for statistical validity, the increase in training duration should be considered a critical factor.

In addition to the findings discussed above, the study was conducted within a methodologically symmetric framework. Each of the nine metaheuristic algorithms was applied under identical conditions, using the same datasets, ANFIS configurations, and performance metrics. The number of runs, input–output structures, and evaluation criteria were all uniformly defined across algorithms and prediction types (daily, weekly, and monthly).

This symmetric design ensured a fair comparison and enhanced the reproducibility and objectivity of the results. Such a balanced experimental structure not only strengthens the internal validity of the study but also aligns with the scientific focus of symmetry, where consistency and structured modeling approaches are emphasized.

These findings offer valuable insights into the energy market, particularly in the context of crude oil price forecasting. The results indicate that accurate short- and medium-term predictions can be achieved using ANFIS models trained with metaheuristic algorithms. The superior performance observed in daily and weekly forecasts, compared to monthly ones, highlights the potential of the proposed approach for short-term decision-making processes such as risk management, investment planning, and dynamic pricing strategies. Moreover, the consistently low standard deviation values observed across multiple runs suggest that the model is stable and reliable, which is essential for supporting data-driven decisions in volatile energy markets like crude oil trading.

5. Conclusions

In this study, an Adaptive Neuro-Fuzzy Inference System (ANFIS) was trained using nine different metaheuristic algorithms—namely SHO, BBO, MVO, TLBO, CS, MFO, MPA, FPA, and ABC—to predict short- and medium-term Brent crude oil prices. The main objective was to evaluate the performance of these training algorithms in estimating the daily, weekly, and monthly minimum and maximum price levels of Brent oil. The raw time-series data were preprocessed and transformed into ANFIS-compatible input–output structures, allowing the use of past values to predict future ones. In addition, the effects of different input sizes and varying numbers of membership functions were also systematically examined. The key findings of the study can be summarized as follows:

- All nine metaheuristic algorithms produced effective results when used to train ANFIS models for Brent oil price prediction. These findings confirm that ANFIS models enhanced with metaheuristic optimization are suitable tools for handling nonlinear and dynamic characteristics in energy market forecasting.
- A strong consistency was observed between training and test results, indicating that the models were not overfitted and maintained generalizability across different problem sets. This also highlights the robustness of the training process and the reliability of the optimized ANFIS configurations.
- Distinct mean error values were observed for daily, weekly, and monthly predictions. While some algorithms performed well in daily or weekly predictions, their effectiveness declined in monthly contexts. This observation emphasizes the need for context-specific tuning of algorithms depending on the prediction window.
- The number and type of membership functions significantly influenced the prediction performance in some cases, while in others, variations in membership function count had a negligible impact. This suggests that for certain complex problem structures, the optimization process may reach saturation, preventing further improvement regardless of parameter adjustments. Such limitations might stem from the intrinsic difficulty of the problem or insufficient input diversity.
- Across all experiments, both training and testing phases yielded low standard deviation values. This indicates that the algorithms provided stable and repeatable solutions even though each training phase started from random initial conditions. This reinforces the statistical reliability of the proposed approach.
- Although all algorithms achieved acceptable performance levels, BBO and TLBO consistently outperformed the others in most scenarios. These two algorithms demon-

strated stronger optimization capabilities in guiding ANFIS training toward more accurate predictions, especially in terms of lower error rates and faster convergence.

- The symmetric structure of the evaluation process—equal iterations, consistent datasets, and identical parameter settings—strengthens the objectivity and reliability of the findings.

Overall, this study provides evidence that combining ANFIS with metaheuristic optimization offers a powerful framework for short- and medium-term energy price forecasting. The models developed here are particularly useful for stakeholders in the energy market who require reliable, interpretable, and adaptable prediction tools. These results are not only relevant in the context of Brent oil price forecasting but also offer broader insights into the use of adaptive hybrid AI systems in energy economics. The methodology demonstrated here can be adapted to other commodities and financial markets where nonlinear patterns dominate, and high prediction reliability is required. Future research may focus on exploring hybrid training strategies, incorporating additional economic indicators, or evaluating the models under real-time constraints to enhance practical applicability.

Author Contributions: E.K.: conceptualization, methodology, validation, software, review and editing, original draft preparation, supervision; A.K.: methodology, software, writing, data curation, original draft preparation; C.B.K.: software, writing, data curation, example analysis, visualization, original draft preparation. All authors have read and agreed to the published version of the manuscript.

Funding: This research was produced from the project supported by TUBITAK—TEYDEB (The Scientific and Technological Research Council of Türkiye—Technology and Innovation Funding Programmes Directorate) (Project No. 3230705).

Data Availability Statement: The raw data supporting the conclusions of this article will be made available by the authors on request.

Conflicts of Interest: Author Ebubekir KAYA is primarily affiliated with Nevşehir Hacı Bektaş Veli University and is also employed part-time at CEKA Software R&D Co, Ltd., the remaining authors declare that the research was conducted in the absence of any commercial or financial relationships that could be construed as a potential conflict of interest. No financial support was received from CEKA Software R&D Co. Ltd. The company solely contributed to the provision of a productive working environment. CEKA Software R&D Co. Ltd. was not involved in the study design, data collection, analysis, analysis, interpretation, writing of the manuscript, or the decision to submit the article for publication.

References

1. Gupta, N.; Nigam, S. Crude oil price prediction using artificial neural network. *Procedia Comput. Sci.* **2020**, *170*, 642–647. [CrossRef]
2. Kulkarni, S.; Haidar, I. Forecasting model for crude oil price using artificial neural networks and commodity futures prices. *arXiv* **2009**, arXiv:0906.4838.
3. Amin, F.; Fahmi, A.; Abdullah, S. Dealer using a new trapezoidal cubic hesitant fuzzy TOPSIS method and application to group decision-making program. *Soft Comput.* **2019**, *23*, 5353–5366. [CrossRef]
4. Fahmi, A.; Abdullah, S.; Amin, F.; Khan, M.S.A. Trapezoidal cubic fuzzy number Einstein hybrid weighted averaging operators and its application to decision making. *Soft Comput.* **2019**, *23*, 5753–5783. [CrossRef]
5. Karaboga, D.; Kaya, E. Estimation of number of foreign visitors with ANFIS by using ABC algorithm. *Soft Comput.* **2020**, *24*, 7579–7591. [CrossRef]
6. Ata, R.; Koçyigit, Y. An adaptive neuro-fuzzy inference system approach for prediction of tip speed ratio in wind turbines. *Expert Syst. Appl.* **2010**, *37*, 5454–5460. [CrossRef]
7. Bisht, D.C.; Jangid, A. Discharge modelling using adaptive neuro-fuzzy inference system. *Int. J. Adv. Sci. Technol.* **2011**, *31*, 99–114.

8. Okwu, M.O.; Tartibu, L.K.; Ojo, E.; Adume, S.; Gidiagba, J.; Fadeyi, J. ANFIS model for cost analysis in a dual source multi-destination system. *Procedia Comput. Sci.* **2023**, *217*, 1266–1279. [CrossRef]
9. Jang, J.-S. ANFIS: Adaptive-network-based fuzzy inference system. *IEEE Trans. Syst. Man Cybern.* **1993**, *23*, 665–685. [CrossRef]
10. Yu, L.; Wang, S.; Lai, K.K. Forecasting crude oil price with an EMD-based neural network ensemble learning paradigm. *Energy Econ.* **2008**, *30*, 2623–2635. [CrossRef]
11. Lang, K.; Auer, B.R. The economic and financial properties of crude oil: A review. *N. Am. J. Econ. Financ.* **2020**, *52*, 100914. [CrossRef]
12. Amano, A. A small forecasting model of the world oil market. *J. Policy Model.* **1987**, *9*, 615–635. [CrossRef]
13. Huntington, H.G. Oil price forecasting in the 1980s: What went wrong? *Energy J.* **1994**, *15*, 1–22. [CrossRef]
14. Abramson, B.; Finizza, A. Probabilistic forecasts from probabilistic models: A case study in the oil market. *Int. J. Forecast.* **1995**, *11*, 63–72. [CrossRef]
15. Hamdi, M.; Aloui, C. Forecasting crude oil price using artificial neural networks: A literature survey. *Econ. Bull* **2015**, *35*, 1339–1359.
16. Wang, S.; Yu, L.; Lai, K.K. A novel hybrid AI system framework for crude oil price forecasting. In Proceedings of the Chinese Academy of Sciences Symposium on Data Mining and Knowledge Management, Beijing, China, 12–14 July 2004; pp. 233–242.
17. Mirmirani, S.; Cheng Li, H. A comparison of VAR and neural networks with genetic algorithm in forecasting price of oil. In *Applications of Artificial Intelligence in Finance and Economics*; Emerald Group Publishing Limited: Leeds, England, 2004; pp. 203–223.
18. Gori, F.; Ludovisi, D.; Cerritelli, P. Forecast of oil price and consumption in the short term under three scenarios: Parabolic, linear and chaotic behaviour. *Energy* **2007**, *32*, 1291–1296. [CrossRef]
19. Chiroma, H.; Abdulkareem, S.; Abubakar, A.; Zeki, A.; Gital, A.Y.u.; Usman, M.J. Co—Active neuro-fuzzy inference systems model for predicting crude oil price based on OECD inventories. In Proceedings of the 2013 International Conference on Research and Innovation in Information Systems (ICRIIS), Kuala Lumpur, Malaysia, 27–28 November 2013; pp. 232–235.
20. Mombeini, H.; Yazdani-Chamzini, A. Developing a new approach for forecasting the trends of oil price. *Bus. Manag. Rev.* **2014**, *4*, 120.
21. Abdollahi, H.; Ebrahimi, S.B. A new hybrid model for forecasting Brent crude oil price. *Energy* **2020**, *200*, 117520. [CrossRef]
22. Abd Elaziz, M.; Ewees, A.A.; Alameer, Z. Improving adaptive neuro-fuzzy inference system based on a modified salp swarm algorithm using genetic algorithm to forecast crude oil price. *Nat. Resour. Res.* **2020**, *29*, 2671–2686. [CrossRef]
23. Anshori, M.Y.; Rahmalia, D.; Herlambang, T.; Karya, D.F. Optimizing Adaptive Neuro Fuzzy Inference System (ANFIS) parameters using Cuckoo Search (Case study of world crude oil price estimation). *J. Phys. Conf. Ser.* **2021**, *1836*, 012041. [CrossRef]
24. Eliwa, E.H.I.; El Koshiry, A.M.; Abd El-Hafeez, T.; Omar, A. Optimal gasoline price predictions: Leveraging the ANFIS regression model. *Int. J. Intell. Syst.* **2024**, *1*, 8462056. [CrossRef]
25. Awijen, H.; Ben Ameur, H.; Ftiti, Z.; Louhichi, W. Forecasting oil price in times of crisis: A new evidence from machine learning versus deep learning models. *Ann. Oper. Res.* **2025**, *345*, 979–1002. [CrossRef]
26. Jabeur, S.B.; Khalfaoui, R.; Arfi, W.B. The effect of green energy, global environmental indexes, and stock markets in predicting oil price crashes: Evidence from explainable machine learning. *J. Environ. Manag.* **2021**, *298*, 113511. [CrossRef] [PubMed]
27. Jiang, Z.; Zhang, L.; Zhang, L.; Wen, B. Investor sentiment and machine learning: Predicting the price of China's crude oil futures market. *Energy* **2022**, *247*, 123471. [CrossRef]
28. Hasan, M.; Abedin, M.Z.; Hajek, P.; Coussement, K.; Sultan, M.N.; Lucey, B. A blending ensemble learning model for crude oil price forecasting. *Ann. Oper. Res.* **2024**, 1–31. [CrossRef]
29. Sezer, O.B.; Gudelek, M.U.; Ozbayoglu, A.M. Financial time series forecasting with deep learning: A systematic literature review: 2005–2019. *Appl. Soft Comput.* **2020**, *90*, 106181. [CrossRef]
30. Iftikhar, H.; Zafar, A.; Turpo-Chaparro, J.E.; Canas Rodrigues, P.; López-Gonzales, J.L. Forecasting day-ahead brent crude oil prices using hybrid combinations of time series models. *Mathematics* **2023**, *11*, 3548. [CrossRef]
31. Zhao, Y.; Hu, B.; Wang, S. Prediction of brent crude oil price based on lstm model under the background of low-carbon transition. *arXiv* **2024**, arXiv:2409.12376.
32. Dong, Y.; Jiang, H.; Guo, Y.; Wang, J. A novel crude oil price forecasting model using decomposition and deep learning networks. *Eng. Appl. Artif. Intell.* **2024**, *133*, 108111. [CrossRef]
33. Naeem, M.; Aamir, M.; Yu, J.; Albalawi, O. A novel approach for reconstruction of IMFs of decomposition and ensemble model for forecasting of crude oil prices. *IEEE Access* **2024**, *12*, 34192–34207. [CrossRef]
34. Xu, Y.; Liu, T.; Fang, Q.; Du, P.; Wang, J. Crude oil price forecasting with multivariate selection, machine learning, and a nonlinear combination strategy. *Eng. Appl. Artif. Intell.* **2025**, *139*, 109510. [CrossRef]

35. Sen, A.; Choudhury, K.D. Forecasting the Crude Oil prices for last four decades using deep learning approach. *Resour. Policy* **2024**, *88*, 104438. [CrossRef]
36. Jin, B.; Xu, X. Price forecasting through neural networks for crude oil, heating oil, and natural gas. *Meas. Energy* **2024**, *1*, 100001. [CrossRef]
37. Fausto, F.; Cuevas, E.; Valdivia, A.; González, A. A global optimization algorithm inspired in the behavior of selfish herds. *Biosystems* **2017**, *160*, 39–55. [CrossRef]
38. Saraçoğlu, B.; Güvenç, U.; Dursun, M.; Poyraz, G.; Duman, S. Biyocağrafya Tabanlı Optimizasyon Metodu Kullanarak Asenkron Motor Parametre Tahmini. *İleri Teknol. Bilim. Derg.* **2013**, *2*, 46–54.
39. Simon, D. Biogeography-based optimization. *IEEE Trans. Evol. Comput.* **2008**, *12*, 702–713. [CrossRef]
40. Mirjalili, S.; Mirjalili, S.M.; Hatamlou, A. Multi-verse optimizer: A nature-inspired algorithm for global optimization. *Neural Comput. Appl.* **2016**, *27*, 495–513. [CrossRef]
41. Rosales Muñoz, A.A.; Grisales-Noreña, L.F.; Montano, J.; Montoya, O.D.; Perea-Moreno, A.-J. Application of the multiverse optimization method to solve the optimal power flow problem in alternating current networks. *Electronics* **2022**, *11*, 1287. [CrossRef]
42. Rao, R.V.; Savsani, V.J.; Vakharia, D.P. Teaching–learning-based optimization: A novel method for constrained mechanical design optimization problems. *Comput.-Aided design* **2011**, *43*, 303–315. [CrossRef]
43. Yang, X.-S.; Deb, S. Engineering optimisation by cuckoo search. *Int. J. Math. Model. Numer. Optim.* **2010**, *1*, 330–343. [CrossRef]
44. Mirjalili, S. Moth-flame optimization algorithm: A novel nature-inspired heuristic paradigm. *Knowl.-Based Syst.* **2015**, *89*, 228–249. [CrossRef]
45. Faramarzi, A.; Heidarinejad, M.; Mirjalili, S.; Gandomi, A.H. Marine Predators Algorithm: A nature-inspired metaheuristic. *Expert Syst. Appl.* **2020**, *152*, 113377. [CrossRef]
46. Mugemanyi, S.; Qu, Z.; Rugema, F.X.; Dong, Y.; Wang, L.; Bananeza, C.; Nshimiyimana, A.; Mutabazi, E. Marine predators algorithm: A comprehensive review. *Mach. Learn. Appl.* **2023**, *12*, 100471. [CrossRef]
47. Yang, X.-S. Flower pollination algorithm for global optimization. In Proceedings of the International Conference on Unconventional Computing and Natural Computation, Orléan, France, 3–7 September 2012; pp. 240–249.
48. Kaya, E. Adaptif ağ tabanlı bulanık çıkarım sistemleri (anfis)\'nin yapay arı koloni algoritması ile eğitilmesi (Adaptive network based fuzzy inference system (anfis) training by using artificial bee colony algorithm). Ph.D. Thesis, Erciyes University, Talas, Turkey, 2017.
49. Karaboga, D. Artificial bee colony algorithm. *Scholarpedia* **2010**, *5*, 6915. [CrossRef]
50. Karaboga, D.; Kaya, E. Adaptive network based fuzzy inference system (ANFIS) training approaches: A comprehensive survey. *Artif. Intell. Rev.* **2019**, *52*, 2263–2293. [CrossRef]

symmetry

MDPI

Article

High-Efficiency and Ultrawideband Polarization Conversion Metasurface Based on Topology and Shape Optimizaiton Design Method

Chuan Liu [1,*], Yi Tang [2] and Jian Wang [1]

[1] School of Information Science and Engineering, Ningbo University, Ningbo 315211, China; wangjian1@nbu.edu.cn
[2] School of Electromechanical and Automotive Engineering, Yantai University, Yantai 264005, China; tangyi0319@126.com
* Correspondence: liuchuan@nbu.edu.cn

Abstract: This study introduces a two-stage optimization method for designing an ultrawideband polarization conversion metasurface. By integrating topology and shape optimization techniques, the proposed method expands the design space to achieve enhanced polarization conversion bandwidth. The first stage employs genetic-algorithm-based topology optimization to establish the initial structural configuration through binary coding. Subsequently, the second stage refines the design through shape optimization by extracting and modifying the boundaries of the topology-optimized structure. The optimized design demonstrates high polarization conversion efficiency (>90%) across 4.08–14.39 GHz, yielding a relative bandwidth of 111.64%, which represents a 4.88% improvement compared to topology-only optimization. This enhancement demonstrates the effectiveness of our combined optimization method in ultrawideband polarization conversion metasurface design, offering a promising method for developing high-performance electromagnetic devices.

Keywords: metasurface; polarization conversion; ultrawideband; topology optimization; shape optimization; genetic algorithm

1. Introduction

The emergence of metamaterials [1,2] has revolutionized electromagnetic wave manipulation through their engineered subwavelength structures that enable unprecedented control over electromagnetic properties. Their two-dimensional equivalents, metasurfaces [3], have attracted particular interest due to their reduced fabrication complexity, superior integrability, and compact form factor. Among the diverse functionalities of metasurfaces, polarization state manipulation has received significant interest for its fundamental importance in electromagnetic applications. Specifically, polarization conversion metasurfaces [4] have demonstrated exceptional capabilities across multiple frequency regimes, from microwave [5] to terahertz [6] and optical domains [7]. These advances have catalyzed innovations in communications [8], electromagnetic sensing [9], and radar technology [10], making polarization conversion metasurfaces critical components in modern electromagnetic systems.

Recent research on polarization conversion metasurfaces has primarily focused on expanding operational bandwidth. Gao et al. [11] designed a double V-shaped architecture with relative bandwidth 77% (12.4–27.96 GHz) that utilizes multi-resonance mechanism to achieve broadband polarization conversion. Jia et al. [12] developed a dual-patch configuration incorporating both square and L-shaped resonators, where the strategic coupling between these patches effectively expands the operational bandwidth (6.03–17.78 GHz, 98% bandwidth). In [13], Xu et al. introduced an H-shaped structural design; the wideband polarization conversion depends on four resonances generated in the simple-geometry unit (7–19.52 GHz, 94% bandwidth). Additional geometries [14–21] achieving wideband polarization conversion include the W-shaped structure (82.3% bandwidth) [14], square split ring structure (94.8% bandwidth) [15], and strip-based fractal structure (96.8% bandwidth) [16], each contributing unique methods to bandwidth enhancement. Despite these achievements, conventional design methods face several limitations. The reliance on predefined geometric shapes inherently limits the exploration of potential optimal configurations, constraining the available design space. Moreover, the trial-and-error nature of empirical design methods further compounds these challenges, resulting in a time-consuming design process. These limitations underscore the need for a more systematic design method that can overcome the constraints of conventional methods and potentially discover novel geometric configurations for enhanced performance.

Topology optimization, an established technique for automated material distribution, has proven effective in structural design, particularly in mechanical engineering [22–26]. Recently, this method has been successfully adapted to electromagnetic design challenges [27–31], including polarization conversion metasurfaces [32–35]. The fundamental nature of topology optimization involves solving a binary (0–1) optimization problem to determine material presence in discrete design domains. The computational complexity of topology optimization typically relates to the mesh elements in the design domain. This becomes particularly challenging in electromagnetic applications, where fine mesh resolutions are often required for accurate wave solutions. The overall computational complexity of the topology optimization process, considering I iterations, mesh elements N_{mesh}, and the cost of a single simulation M, is given by $O(I \cdot N_{mesh} \cdot M)$ [36–38]. As mesh density increases to improve solution accuracy, both N_{mesh} and the computational cost M grow significantly, making it challenging to balance accuracy with computational resources. Achieving higher design freedom through refined meshing often incurs substantial computational costs, while coarser meshes may compromise optimal performance. These limitations have prompted the need for an optimization method that can balance design freedom with computational efficiency.

Current research in the polarization conversion metasurfaces faces two gaps: the limited exploration of design space due to conventional design methods, and the computational inefficiency of pure topology optimization methods. To address these gaps, we propose a two-stage optimization method that combines both topology and shape optimization techniques. Our method specifically targets these limitations by first employing topology optimization to explore the full design space and generate an initial conceptual configuration of the unit cell, unrestricted by predetermined geometries. This is followed by a shape optimization phase utilizing Bezier curve parameterization for boundary regularization and refinement, which significantly reduces computational complexity while maintaining design freedom. By integrating these optimization techniques, our method achieves both design efficiency and bandwidth expansion. The effectiveness of this optimization method is demonstrated through the design of polarization conversion metasurfaces with ultrawideband characteristics. Compared to conventional design methods, our method offers a more efficient pathway for designing ultrawideband polarization conversion metasurfaces. The proposed method can also be extended to various electromagnetic devices, including antennas, metamaterials, and other wave manipulation devices.

2. Design Method

2.1. Theoretical Analysis and Unit Cell Design

The fundamental operating principle of polarization conversion metasurfaces relies on differential phase responses between orthogonal directions [4], as illustrated in Figure 1. When y-polarized electromagnetic waves interact with an anisotropic unit cell structure (Figure 1b), the incident electric field $\vec{E}_i$ decomposes into two orthogonal components along the u- and v-axes, which are oriented at 45° counterclockwise relative to the x-y coordinate system. The anisotropic unit cell generates distinct reflection coefficients for these orthogonally polarized components. We can mathematically express the incident and reflected electric fields as [39]:

$$\vec{E}_i = E_{iu}e^{j\varphi}\hat{u} + E_{iv}e^{j\varphi}\hat{v} \tag{1}$$

$$\vec{E}_r = r_u E_{iu}e^{j(\varphi+\varphi_u)}\hat{u} + r_v E_{iv}e^{j(\varphi+\varphi_v)}\hat{v} \tag{2}$$

where E_{iu} and E_{iv} represent the incident field amplitudes along the u- and v-directions, respectively; φ denotes the incident wave phase; r_u and r_v are reflection coefficient amplitudes; and φ_u and φ_v correspond to the reflection coefficient phases. The polarization conversion from y- to x-polarization occurs when two conditions are satisfied: equal reflection coefficient amplitudes ($|r_u| = |r_v|$) and a phase difference of 180° between orthogonal components ($|\varphi_u - \varphi_v| = 180°$). This fundamental anisotropic characteristic forms the basis for the unit cell design. The coding scheme of the structure design relies heavily on this anisotropic characteristic.

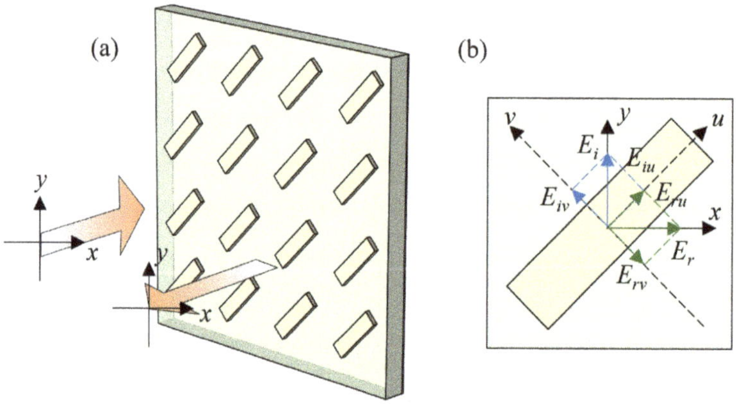

Figure 1. (**a**) Conceptual illustration of cross-polarization conversion. (**b**) Working principle of the polarization conversion metasurface.

Figure 2a illustrates the unit cell of the proposed metasurface. The unit cell comprises four layers: the top layer is the metallic structure to be designed, followed by a dielectric substrate layer, an air gap, and a bottom metallic layer. The thicknesses of the dielectric substrate and air layer are denoted as d and h, respectively, while the periodicity is p. The metallic layers comprise 18-μm-thick copper ($\sigma = 5.8 \times 10^7$ S/m) on both top and bottom surfaces. The structure features $d = 1$ mm, $h = 5$ mm, and $p = 12$ mm, with F4B (dielectric constant 2.65 and loss tangent 0.001) serving as the dielectric substrate. Based on the preceding analysis, to achieve polarization conversion functionality, the designed metasurface must possess anisotropic properties. Therefore, the design region is set as the dashed area shown in Figure 2b, with the remaining parts of the structure determined by symmetry.

Based on the above theoretical analysis, achieving broadband polarization conversion requires the careful design of the metallic pattern to maintain the required amplitude and phase conditions across a wide frequency range. To systematically explore the vast design space and find an optimal structure that satisfies these conditions, we employ a two-stage optimization method. The first stage uses topology optimization to establish the initial structural configuration, which we describe in detail below.

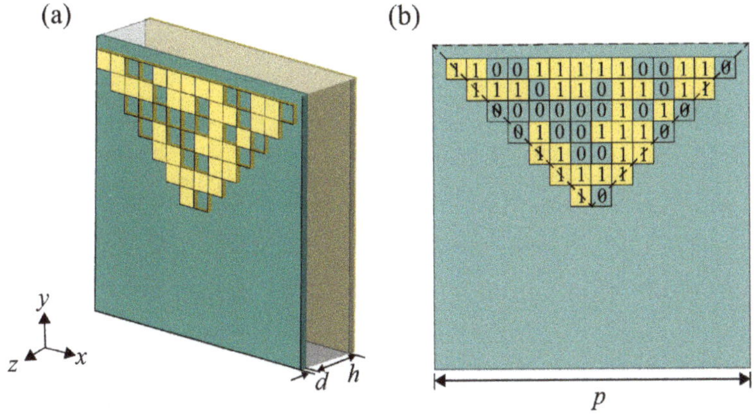

Figure 2. (**a**) Unit cell of the proposed design. (**b**) Schematic of the binary encoding method for topology optimization.

2.2. Topology Optimizaiton

In the first design stage, topology optimization is implemented to determine the intial unit cell conceptual configuration. The top metallic pattern is represented by a binary topology code sequence where metallized regions are indicated by 1 and non-metallized regions by 0. In the topology optimization process, the genetic algorithm (GA) is employed. Unlike gradient-based methods, GA is less likely to be trapped in local optima, making it particularly suitable for the design of metasurfaces. Moreover, the ability of GA to explore a broad design space enables it to identify innovative and efficient configurations. The study combines MATLAB and CST Microwave Studio (CST), where MATLAB handles the GA-based optimization and CST provides electromagnetic simulation for evaluating the fitness function. This hybrid framework ensures accurate electromagnetic analysis and efficient optimization.

The workflow begins with the initialization of the population in MATLAB, where random unit cell designs are generated according to the coding scheme. The electromagnetic performance of each design is then evaluated through full-wave simulation in CST. The frequency domain solver is employed with tetrahedral mesh type. The mesh density is set to 10 cells per wavelength at the highest frequency of interest. The adaptive mesh refinement is enabled with a convergence criterion of 0.02 for S-parameters. The electromagnetic response is analyzed using a single unit cell with periodic boundaries along the x- and y-axes. The polarization conversion characteristics of the metasurface are quantified through co-polarized (r_{yy}, r_{xx}) and cross-polarized (r_{xy}, r_{yx}) reflection coefficients, corresponding to the preserved and transformed polarization components, respectively. Considering the symmetry and for simplicity, the analysis of the polarization conversion metasurface in this work only considers the case of y-polarized incidence.

The simulation results are further processed in MATLAB to calculate the fitness value. If the optimization criteria are not met, the algorithm proceeds with the selection of superior individuals based on their fitness values, followed by crossover and mutation operations to generate new populations. The fitness function is defined based on the polarization conversion ratio [$\mathrm{PCR} = r_{xy}^2/(r_{xy}^2 + r_{yy}^2)$], where the optimization objective is to maximize the frequency range where the polarization conversion efficiency exceeds 90%. This threshold of 90% is consistent with the established standard in the field for defining high-efficiency polarization conversion [13,15]. Consequently, the fitness function can be formulated accordingly:

$$FIT = -\frac{2(f_{max} - f_{min})}{(f_{max} + f_{min})} \tag{3}$$

where f_{max} and f_{min} denote the upper and lower frequency bounds of the operating band (PCR > 0.9), respectively. The topology optimization problem is formulated as a non-linear binary programming problem. The design variable $\chi = \{\chi_1, \chi_2, \cdots, \chi_n\}$ represents the material distribution in the design domain, where $\chi_i \in \{0,1\}$ indicates the absence or presence of metallic material in the i-th element of the mesh. The objective is to maximize the bandwidth while maintaining high polarization conversion efficiency. Thus, the FIT is minimized, which is inversely related to the bandwidth. The optimization problem is expressed as:

$$\begin{aligned} &\text{find} \quad \chi \\ &\text{min} \quad FIT \\ &\text{s.t.} \quad \sum_{i=1}^{N_e} \chi_i s_i \le S_f \sum_{i=1}^{N_e} s_i \\ &\qquad i = 1, \ldots, N_e \\ &\qquad \text{PCR}(f, \chi) = \frac{r_{xy}^2(f, \chi)}{[r_{xy}^2(f, \chi) + r_{yy}^2(f, \chi)]} \ge P_m, \forall f \in [fl, fu] \end{aligned} \tag{4}$$

where $\text{PCR}(f, \chi)$ is the polarization conversion ratio at frequency f, $[fl, fu]$ defines the frequency range of interest, s_i represents the area of each element, S_f is the maximum allowable metal fill ratio, N_e is the number of design variables, and P_m is the minimum required PCR threshold (set to 0.9 based on established standards in the field). The inequality constraint on PCR ensures that the conversion efficiency meets or exceeds the required threshold across the operating bandwidth. Through iterative selection, crossover, and mutation operations, the algorithm progressively evolves toward improved designs until either the optimization goal (relative bandwidth > 120) is achieved or the maximum iteration (60) is reached. Figure 3 presents the framework of our topology optimization process.

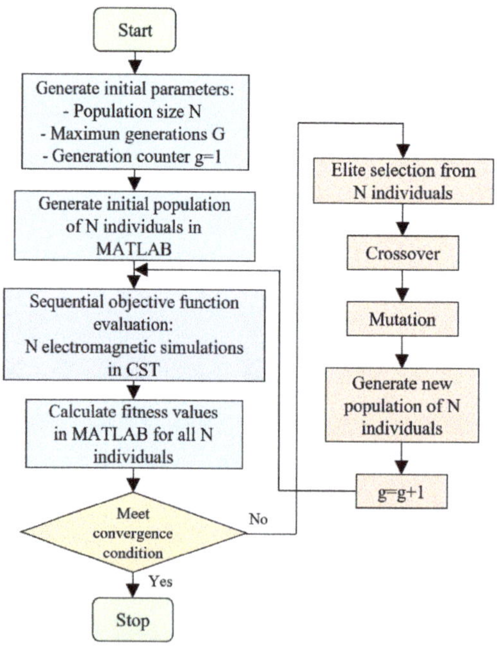

Figure 3. Computational workflow for topology-based metasurface design.

The topology-optimized structure is depicted in Figure 4a; it demonstrates the successful implementation of the optimization method, resulting in a unique arrangement of metallic patches in a diagonally symmetric pattern. The mesh element size was carefully selected to balance computational efficiency and design accuracy. The optimization process was conducted on a total of 56 binary design variables, with the following parameters: a population size of 14, mutation rate of 0.3, and maximum iteration number of 60. The algorithm was running on a workstation with an Intel Core i7-10700K processor (manufactured by Intel Corporation in Santa Clara, CA, USA) and 32 GB RAM. Convergence was achieved after 24 iterations, with a total computation time of approximately 120 h. The final fitness value reached -106.45. The polarization conversion performance is shown in Figure 4b,c. Figure 4b presents the reflection coefficients of the structure. At normal incidence, between 4.17 GHz and 13.66 GHz, the cross-polarized reflection coefficient r_{xy} (green dashed curve) approaches 0 dB, while the co-polarized reflection coefficient r_{yy} (blue solid curve) remains below -10 dB, indicating predominant reflection with orthogonal polarization relative to the incident waves. The high polarization conversion efficiency within this frequency range demonstrates that the topology-optimized design achieves effective polarization conversion. Furthermore, three adjacent resonances can be observed at frequencies of 4.55 GHz, 7.52 GHz, and 12.83 GHz, where the polarization conversion efficiency peaks at nearly 100%, and the superposition of these three resonances forms a wideband polarization conversion. Figure 4c shows the calculated PCR as a function of frequency, revealing PCR values consistently above 0.9 from 4.17 GHz to 13.66 GHz, demonstrating that more than 90% of y-polarized incident waves are successfully converted to x-polarized reflected waves. The design achieves a polarization conversion bandwidth of 9.49 GHz, equivalent to a relative bandwidth of 106.45%. It is evident that through the first step of topology optimization, the fundamental structure of the unit cell is established, already achieving significant polarization conversion bandwidth. This initial configuration serves as the basis for further shape optimization in the next design stage.

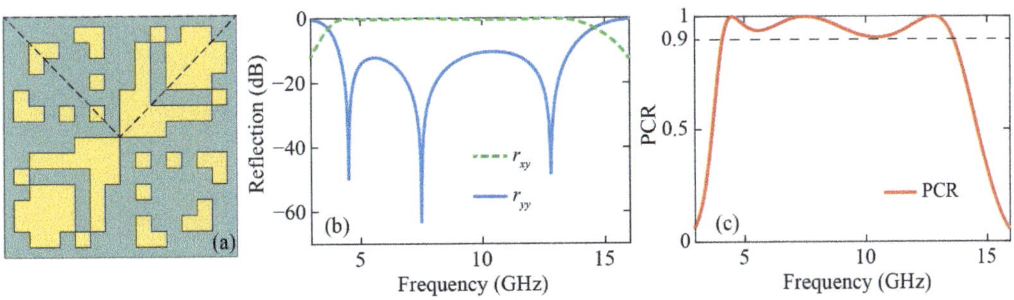

Figure 4. (**a**) Binary structural pattern obtained through genetic algorithm-based topology optimization, where yellow regions represent the presence of metallic patches. Electromagnetic performance of the topology-optimized structure: (**b**) frequency-dependent co-polarization (r_{yy}) and cross-polarization (r_{xy}) reflection coefficients, demonstrating the conversion between orthogonal polarization states; (**c**) PCR, showing the efficiency of polarization conversion across the operating frequency band with a bandwidth of 106.45% (PCR > 0.9).

2.3. Shape Optimizaiton

Following the topology optimization, a shape optimization stage is conducted to further refine the structural configuration. This optimization stage addresses the challenge of refining complex boundaries while maintaining electromagnetic performance, with the objective of optimizing the boundary shape of the topology-optimized structure while preserving its topological characteristics. The boundary optimization problem is mathematically formulated using Bezier curve parameterization, where each boundary segment is described by $B(t) = \sum_{i=0}^{n} \binom{n}{i} P_i (1-t)^{n-i} t^i, t \in [0,1]$, with the binomial coefficient $\binom{n}{i}$ calculated as $\frac{n!}{i!(n-i)!}$, and P_i representing control points. The optimization process begins with the boundary extraction of the topology-optimized design, where the structural contours are represented by coordinate points. As shown in Figure 5a, the boundaries of the metallic pattern (indicated by blue lines) are extracted through image processing techniques in MATLAB using the bwboundaries function, which enables the precise description of the topological boundaries. The extracted boundaries serve as the foundation for subsequent Bezier curve fitting and optimization, providing a discrete set of boundary points that accurately represent the topology-optimized structure.

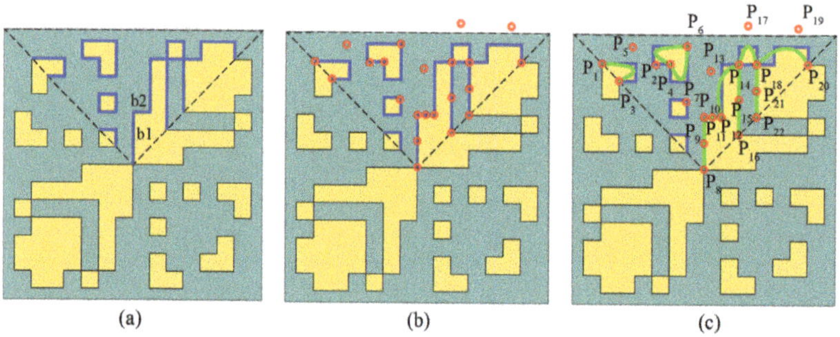

Figure 5. (**a**) Extraction of boundary points from the topology optimization result. (**b**) Control point placement. (**c**) Boundary fitting for the topology optimization result.

Control points for the Bezier curves are placed based on two main factors: (1) geometric features and (2) electromagnetic characteristics. As illustrated in Figure 5b, control points are first positioned at locations with prominent geometric variations, such as sharp turns and corners. Additional control points are then added based on the surface current distribution analysis shown in Figure 6, which presents the current distributions at three resonant frequencies: 4.55 GHz, 7.52 GHz, and 12.83 GHz. The analysis reveals strong current concentrations near the central region across all resonant frequencies, with particularly intense currents along boundary b1 and b2 (labelled in Figure 5a) at the lowest and highest resonant frequencies. Small structural features exhibiting weak surface currents are identified and removed to make the designed structure simplified. The final control point distribution and the resulting boundary fitting are shown in Figure 5c.

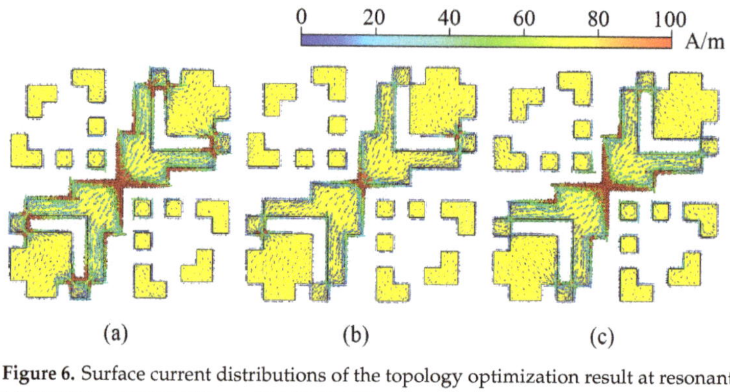

Figure 6. Surface current distributions of the topology optimization result at resonant frequencies: (**a**) 4.55 GHz; (**b**) 7.52 GHz; and (**c**) 12.83 GHz.

The shape optimization was also solved using GA, with the optimization formulation as follows:

$$\begin{aligned}
\text{find} \quad & x_i, y_i \quad i = 1, \ldots, N_n \\
\min \quad & FIT \\
\text{s.t.} \quad & a_i \le x_i \le b_i, \\
& c_i \le y_i \le d_i, \\
& \text{PCR} = \frac{r_{xy}^2(x_i, y_i)}{\left[r_{xy}^2(x_i, y_i) + r_{yy}^2(x_i, y_i)\right]} > P_m
\end{aligned} \tag{5}$$

where x_i and y_i represent the coordinates of the control point i, and a_i, b_i, c_i, and d_i denote the upper and lower bound of control point i.

Based on the obtained control points, the unit cell was reconstructed in the software, as shown in Figure 7a. The objective function remains consistent with the topology optimization stage, aiming to maximize the polarization conversion bandwidth. The optimization primarily adjusts the positions of critical control points while preserving the key features of the topology-optimized design, resulting in a refined structure with an expanded polarization conversion bandwidth. Table 1 presents the initial coordinates of the control points along with their upper and lower bounds. The optimization process utilizes a population size of 10 and a mutation rate of 0.3, continuing until either the optimization goal is achieved or the maximum iteration count is reached. The optimization process follows a similar procedure as in the topology optimization phase.

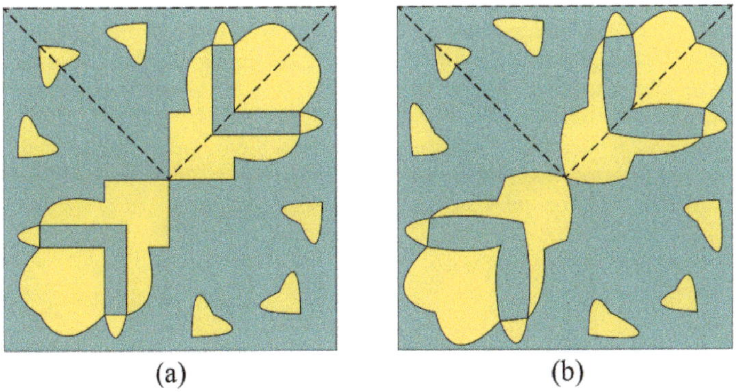

Figure 7. (**a**) Reconstructed model derived from the topology optimization result, where the boundaries of metallic patches are extracted and parameterized for subsequent optimization; (**b**) final optimized structure after shape optimization, showing refined boundary shapes of the unit cell.

Table 1. Initial coordinates of control points and their upper and lower bounds.

	P_1	P_2	P_3	P_4	P_5	P_6	P_7	P_8	P_9
x/mm	−4.706	−2.228	−3.938	−1.569	−3.288	−0.801	−0.833	0	0
y/mm	4.706	4.662	3.938	4.706	5.448	5.495	3.036	0	1.185
a/mm	−4.706	−3.000	−3.938	−1.569	−4.000	−0.801	−1.200	0	−0.500
b/mm	−4.706	−1.700	−3.938	−1.569	−3.000	−0.801	0.600	0	0.500
c/mm	4.706	3.800	3.938	4.706	5.000	5.495	2.500	0	0.800
d/mm	4.706	5.000	3.938	4.706	6.000	5.495	4.000	0	1.300
	P_{10}	P_{11}	P_{12}	P_{13}	P_{14}	P_{15}	P_{16}	P_{17}	P_{18}
x/mm	0	0.376	0.778	0.296	1.569	1.569	1.569	1.963	2.358
y/mm	2.358	2.358	2.358	4.410	4.706	3.137	1.569	6.315	4.706
a/mm	−0.300	0.100	0.600	−0.100	1.200	1.200	1.569	1.500	2.000
b/mm	0.200	0.500	0.900	0.700	1.700	1.700	1.569	2.200	3.000
c/mm	2.000	2.000	2.000	3.800	4.200	2.800	1.569	5.800	4.200
d/mm	2.600	2.600	2.600	5.500	5.500	3.600	1.569	6.800	5.000

Table 1. *Cont.*

	P_{19}	P_{20}	P_{21}	P_{22}
x/mm	3.885	4.706	2.358	2.358
y/mm	6.183	4.706	3.532	2.358
a/mm	3.200	4.706	2.000	2.358
b/mm	4.300	4.706	2.800	2.358
c/mm	5.800	4.706	3.000	2.358
d/mm	6.800	4.706	3.800	2.358

3. Results and Discussion

3.1. Results

The final optimized structure is shown in Figure 7b, and the coordinates of all control points are listed in Table 2. The polarizaton conversion performance of the metasurface designed through the combined topology and shape optimization method is presented in Figure 8. For comparison, the results from the topology-only optimization (dash-dotted curves) are plotted alongside those from the complete two-stage optimization process (solid curves). The reflection coefficients plotted in Figure 8a reveal three distinct resonances in both cases, demonstrating the fundamental characteristics of the polarization conversion mechanism. Notably, the proposed two-stage optimization method achieves a wider frequency range by shifting the second and third resonances toward higher frequencies while maintaining high cross-polarization conversion efficiency. The PCR comparison in Figure 8b clearly illustrates the expanded bandwidth achieved through the combined optimization method. The metasurface exhibits high-efficiency polarization conversion (PCR > 0.9) over a wider frequency range of 4.08–14.39 GHz, corresponding to an operational bandwidth of 10.31 GHz. This translates to a remarkable relative bandwidth of 111.64%, representing a 4.88% improvement over the topology-only optimization result. This enhancement can be attributed to the additional design flexibility provided by the shape optimization stage, which enables the fine-tuning of the critical structural features.

Table 2. Optimized coordinates of control points.

	P_1	P_2	P_3	P_4	P_5	P_6	P_7	P_8	P_9
x/mm	−4.706	−2.600	−3.938	−1.569	−4.000	−0.801	−0.800	0	−0.400
y/mm	4.706	4.600	3.938	4.706	5.900	5.495	3.500	0	1.100
	P_{10}	P_{11}	P_{12}	P_{13}	P_{14}	P_{15}	P_{16}	P_{17}	P_{18}
x/mm	0	0.400	0.800	0.700	1.400	1.200	1.569	1.700	2.400
y/mm	2.200	2.300	2.500	4.200	4.900	3.200	1.569	6.600	5.000
	P_{19}	P_{20}	P_{21}	P_{22}					
x/mm	4.200	4.706	2.700	2.358					
y/mm	6.800	4.706	3.300	2.358					

The polarization conversion performance at varying angles of incidence of the final design is further examined. As shown in Figure 9a, with an increasing incidence angle, the second resonance of the co-polarization reflection coefficient shifts to higher frequencies, while the third resonance shifts to lower frequencies. Additionally, the reflection coefficient values increase across the frequency range. Consequently, as illustrated in Figure 9b, the PCR gradually decreases, resulting in a reduced bandwidth for efficient polarization conversion. Despite this reduction, the metasurface maintains a PCR above 0.8 across a broad frequency range for incident angles less than 30°. Even at an incident angle of 40°, the metasurface demonstrates high-efficiency operation within the 4.12–11.83 GHz frequency range. This indicates that the proposed design performs well across a wide range of incident angles, making it a promising candidate for applications requiring robust polarization conversion under oblique incidence. Further analysis at larger oblique incidence angles reveals that the performance deteriorates more significantly for angles beyond 40°, with the PCR dropping below 0.6 at 50° incidence. This represents a common limitation in polarization conversion metasurface designs, while our proposed structure maintains reasonable performance for most practical applications where incident angles typically remain below 40°.

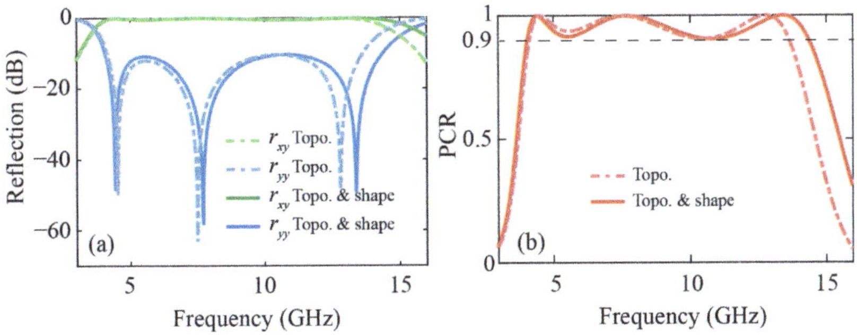

Figure 8. Performance comparison between topology-optimized and shape-optimized designs: (**a**) frequency-dependent co-polarization (r_{yy}) and cross-polarization (r_{xy}) reflection coefficients for both designs; (**b**) PCR exceeding 0.9 over 4.17–13.66 GHz for topology optimization and 4.08–14.39 GHz for combined optimization, demonstrating bandwidth enhancement from 106.45% to 111.64% through the two-stage optimization method.

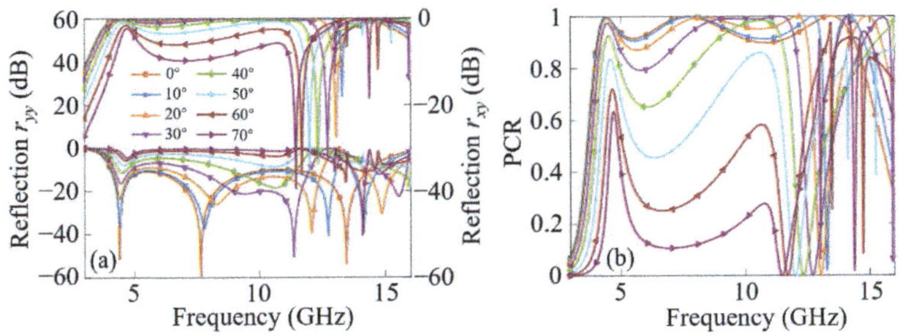

Figure 9. (**a**) Simulated co- and cross-polarization reflection coefficients, and (**b**) PCRs under oblique incidence.

To demonstrate the effectiveness of our two-stage optimization method, we have compared the performance metrics with previous works, as summarized in Table 3. The comparison reveals that our combined topology and shape optimization method achieves superior bandwidth performance.

3.2. Discussion

These results demonstrate the effectiveness of the proposed two-stage optimization method in expanding the design space and enhancing flexibility. The shape optimization stage successfully refines the topology-optimized configuration by adjusting the boundary curves through control point, ultimately expanding the bandwidth to 111.64%, representing a 4.88% improvement. This enhancement can be attributed to the shape optimization stage's ability to fine-tune the boundary curves through control point manipulation, which allows for the more precise adjustment of the resonant characteristics. Compared to existing methods in the literature, our method shows competitive performance. The superior bandwidth can be attributed to the complementary roles of topology and shape optimization, where topology optimization establishes the fundamental structure through binary coding, and shape optimization enables fine geometric adjustments for performance enhancement. The optimized structure can be conveniently manufactured using standard printed circuit board (PCB) technology.

Table 3. Performance comparison with previous works.

Works	Design Technique (Resonators)	Operating Bandwidth (GHz)	Bandwidth (PCR > 0.9) (GHz)	Relative Bandwidth (%)
[40]	asymmetric double ring	6.67–17.09	10.42	87.7
[41]	cut wire	5.10–12.10	7.0	78.6
[20]	modified double square ring	6.30–20.50	14.3	105.9
[32]	topology design	8.00–30.00	<22	<115.7
Our work	topology and shape design	4.08–14.39	10.31	111.64

The practical implementation of metasurfaces demands careful consideration of manufacturing constraints. At lower frequencies, conventional PCB fabrication methods have demonstrated their effectiveness and cost-efficiency in metasurface manufacturing. However, as operational frequencies extend from microwave through terahertz to optical regimes, two significant challenges emerge: the necessity for higher fabrication precision due to reduced structural dimensions, and the complexity of achieving large-area manufacturing [42]. Although various advanced fabrication techniques have been developed to address these challenges [43,44], the development of manufacturing methods continues to pursue the simultaneous achievement of low cost, large-area, and high resolution. Manufacturing feasibility must be incorporated into the metasurface design phase to ensure that fabricated structures achieve their intended performance. Specifically, the minimum feature size must comply with fabrication limitations. Furthermore, smooth boundaries in metasurface structures enhance manufacturability without compromising performance, a characteristic naturally achieved through our shape optimization stage. These design considerations, together with appropriate material selection, facilitate reliable fabrication while preserving the desired performance. Our future work will focus on experimental validation to optimize the design for practical applications and evaluate the impact of fabrication constraints on performance.

4. Conclusions

In this work, we introduced a two-stage optimization method that integrates GA-based topology optimization with subsequent shape refinement using Bezier curve fitting. Compared to conventional topology-only method, this combined strategy offers enhanced flexibility in the structural design process and enables the more efficient exploration of the metasurface parameter space. Through this method, we achieved an ultrawideband polarization conversion metasurface with a polarization conversion ratio exceeding 0.9 across a wide frequency range (4.08–14.39 GHz), corresponding to a relative bandwidth of 111.64%. This performance represents a meaningful improvement (approximately 4.88%) over results derived from topology-only optimization. Furthermore, our metasurface demonstrated robustness under oblique incidence up to 40°, showing robustness under oblique incidence. Compared to other metasurface designs, our integrated method leverages the strengths of both global and local optimization: topology optimization provides a global structural framework, while shape refinement introduces precise geometric tuning. This combined method facilitates the more effective navigation of the complex parameter space than a single method alone. As a result, the proposed method can be readily applied or adapted to a wide range of electromagnetic devices. While our numerical simulations demonstrate promising results, several factors should be considered in practical implementations. The two-stage optimization method may increase computational complexity, potentially limiting its scalability for more intricate or higher-dimensional problems. The actual performance may be influenced by fabrication tolerances and material property variations. These limitations suggest opportunities for future research, including the integration of advanced optimization algorithms and development of optimization strategies that consider fabrication constraints.

Author Contributions: Conceptualization, C.L.; methodology, C.L.; software, C.L. and Y.T.; validation, C.L., Y.T. and J.W.; formal analysis, C.L. and J.W.; writing—original draft preparation, C.L.; writing—review and editing, C.L., Y.T. and J.W.; and funding acquisition, C.L. All authors have read and agreed to the published version of the manuscript.

Funding: This research was funded by the National Natural Science Foundation of China (Grant number 12202214).

Data Availability Statement: Data are contained within the article.

Conflicts of Interest: The authors declare no conflicts of interest.

References

1. Shalaev, V.M. Optical negative-index metamaterials. *Nat. Photonics* **2007**, *1*, 41–48. [CrossRef]
2. Zheludev, N.I.; Kivshar, Y.S. From metamaterials to metadevices. *Nat. Mater.* **2012**, *11*, 917–924. [CrossRef] [PubMed]
3. Yu, N.; Capasso, F. Flat optics with designer metasurfaces. *Nat. Mater.* **2014**, *13*, 139–150. [CrossRef] [PubMed]
4. Hao, J.; Yuan, Y.; Ran, L.; Jiang, T.; Kong, J.A.; Chan, C.T.; Zhou, L. Manipulating electromagnetic wave polarizations by anisotropic metamaterials. *Phys. Rev. Lett.* **2007**, *99*, 063908. [CrossRef] [PubMed]
5. Khan, M.I.; Tahir, F.A. An angularly stable dual-broadband anisotropic cross polarization conversion metasurface. *J. Appl. Phys.* **2017**, *122*, 053103. [CrossRef]
6. Jin, G.; Ren, Y.; Tang, B. Numerical simulations of circular dichroism and polarization conversion in VO_2-based terahertz metamaterials. *Crystals* **2023**, *13*, 437. [CrossRef]
7. Ding, F.; Wang, Z.; He, S.; Shalaev, V.M.; Kildishev, A.V. Broadband high-efficiency half-wave plate: A supercell-based plasmonic metasurface approach. *ACS Nano* **2015**, *9*, 4111–4119. [CrossRef] [PubMed]
8. Chuang, H.R.; Kuo, L.C. 3-D FDTD design analysis of a 2.4-GHz polarization-diversity printed dipole antenna with integrated balun and polarization-switching circuit for WLAN and wireless communication applications. *IEEE Trans. Microw. Theory Technol.* **2003**, *51*, 374–381. [CrossRef]
9. Heydari, S.; Bazgir, M.; Zarrabi, F.B.; Gandji, N.P.; Rastan, I. Novel optical polarizer design based on metasurface nano aperture for biological sensing in mid-infrared regime. *Opt. Quantum. Electron.* **2017**, *49*, 83. [CrossRef]
10. Barry, C. A smart radar absorber. *Smart Mater. Struct.* **1999**, *8*, 64.
11. Gao, X.; Han, X.; Cao, W.P.; Li, H.O.; Ma, H.F.; Cui, T.J. Ultrawideband and high-efficiency linear polarization converter based on double V-shaped metasurface. *IEEE Trans. Antennas Propag.* **2015**, *63*, 3522–3530. [CrossRef]
12. Jia, Y.; Liu, Y.; Guo, Y.J.; Li, K.; Gong, S. A dual-patch polarization rotation reflective surface and its application to ultra-wideband RCS reduction. *IEEE Trans. Antennas Propag.* **2017**, *65*, 3291–3295. [CrossRef]
13. Xu, J.; Li, R.; Qin, J.; Wang, S.; Han, T. Ultra-broadband wide-angle linear polarization converter based on H-shaped metasurface. *Opt. Express* **2018**, *26*, 20913–20919. [CrossRef] [PubMed]
14. Zheng, Q.; Guo, C.; Yuan, P.; Ren, Y.H.; Ding, J. Wideband and high-efficiency reflective polarization conversion metasurface based on anisotropic metamaterials. *J. Electron. Mater.* **2018**, *47*, 2658–2666. [CrossRef]
15. Li, F.; Chen, H.; Zhang, L.; Zhou, Y.; Xie, J.; Deng, L.; Harris, V.G. Compact high-efficiency broadband metamaterial polarizing reflector at microwave frequencies. *IEEE Trans. Microw. Theory Technol.* **2019**, *67*, 606–614. [CrossRef]
16. Zheng, Q.; Guo, C.; Vandenbosch, G.A.E.; Yuan, P.; Ding, J. Ultra-broadband and high-efficiency reflective polarization rotator based on fractal metasurface with multiple plasmon resonances. *Opt. Commun.* **2019**, *449*, 73–78. [CrossRef]
17. Omar, A.A.; Hong, W.; Al-Awamry, A.; Mahmoud, A. A single-layer via-less wideband reflective polarization rotator utilizing perforated holes. *IEEE Antennas Wirel. Propag. Lett.* **2020**, *19*, 2053–2056. [CrossRef]
18. Couto, M.M.; Silva, M.W.B.; Campos, A. A novel ultra-wideband reflective cross-polarization converter based on anisotropic metasurface. *J. Electromagn. Waves Appl.* **2021**, *35*, 1652–1662. [CrossRef]
19. Kamal, B.; Chen, J.D.; Ying, Y.Z.; Jian, R.; Ullah, S.; Khan, W.U.R. High efficiency and ultra-wideband polarization converter based on an I-shaped metasurface. *Opt. Mater. Express* **2021**, *11*, 1343–1352. [CrossRef]
20. Chatterjee, J.; Mohan, A.; Dixit, V. Ultrawideband RCS reduction of planar and conformal surfaces using ultrathin polarization conversion metasurface. *IEEE Access* **2022**, *10*, 36563–36575. [CrossRef]
21. Khan, H.A.; Rafique, U.; Abbas, S.M.; Ahmed, F.; Huang, Y.F.; Uqaili, J.A.; Mahmoud, A. Polarization-independent ultra wideband RCS reduction conformal coding metasurface based on integrated polarization conversion-diffusion-absorption mechanism. *Photonics* **2023**, *10*, 281. [CrossRef]
22. Sigmund, O.; Maute, K. Topology optimization approaches. *Struct. Multidiscip. Optim.* **2013**, *48*, 1031–1055. [CrossRef]

23. Deaton, J.D.; Grandhi, R.V. A survey of structural and multidisciplinary continuum topology optimization: Post 2000. *Struct. Multidiscip. Optim.* **2014**, *49*, 1–38. [CrossRef]
24. Zhu, J.H.; Zhang, W.H.; Xia, L. Topology optimization in aircraft and aerospace structures design. *Arch. Comput. Methods Eng.* **2016**, *23*, 595–622. [CrossRef]
25. Latifi Rostami, S.A.; Ghoddosian, A. Topology Optimization Under Uncertainty by Using the New Collocation Method. *Period Polytech-civ* **2019**, *63*, 278–287. [CrossRef]
26. Latifi Rostami, S.A.; Li, M.; Kolahdooz, A.; Chung, H.; Zhang, J. Robust Topology Optimization of Continuum Structures Under the Hybrid Uncertainties: A Comparative Study. *Period. Polytech. Civ. Eng.* **2023**, *67*, 637–645. [CrossRef]
27. Diaz, A.R.; Sigmund, O. A topology optimization method for design of negative permeability metamaterials. *Struct. Multidiscip. Optim.* **2010**, *41*, 163–177. [CrossRef]
28. Hassan, E.; Wadbro, E.; Berggren, M. Topology optimization of metallic antennas. *IEEE Trans. Antennas Propag.* **2014**, *62*, 2488–2500.
29. Molesky, S.; Lin, Z.; Piggott, A.Y.; Jin, W.; Vucković, J.; Rodriguez, A.W. Inverse design in nanophotonics. *Nat. Photonics* **2018**, *12*, 659–670. [CrossRef]
30. Zhu, S.H.; Yang, X.S.; Wang, J.; Wang, B.Z. Design of mimo antenna isolation structure based on a hybrid topology optimization method. *IEEE Trans. Antennas Propag.* **2019**, *67*, 6298–6307. [CrossRef]
31. Chen, F.; Zhu, J.; Zhang, W. Topology optimization for the layout design of radar absorbing coatings in cavities. *Struct. Multidiscip. Optim.* **2022**, *65*, 250. [CrossRef]
32. Sui, S.; Ma, H.; Wang, J.; Feng, M.; Pang, Y.; Xia, S.; Xu, Z.; Qu, S. Symmetry-based coding method and synthesis topology optimization design of ultra-wideband polarization conversion metasurfaces. *Appl. Phys. Lett.* **2016**, *109*, 014104. [CrossRef]
33. Yuan, Q.; Ma, H.; Sui, S.; Wang, J.F.; Zheng, L.; Meng, Y.Y.; Qu, S.B. Centrosymmetric topology optimization design achieves ultra-broadband polarization conversion and its further application. *J. Phys. D Appl. Phys.* **2020**, *53*, 335001. [CrossRef]
34. Wang, J.; Zhao, X.C.; Jiang, Y.N.; Gu, W.Q.; Xu, K.D. Optimal design of broadband linear-to-circular polarization conversion metasurface. *Mater. Des.* **2024**, *242*, 113004. [CrossRef]
35. Zhang, Y.J.; Li, C.L.; Luan, J.Q.; Zhao, M.; Gao, D.S.; Li, P.L. Ultra-broadband and wide-angle reflective terahertz polarization conversion metasurface based on topological optimization. *Chin. Phys. B* **2024**, *33*, 104210. [CrossRef]
36. Huang, X.; Xie, M. *Evolutionary Topology Optimization of Continuum Structures: Methods and Applications*; John Wiley & Sons: Hoboken, NJ, USA, 2010.
37. Bendsoe, M.P.; Sigmund, O. *Topology Optimization: Theory, Methods, and Applications*; Springer Science & Business Media: Berlin/Heidelberg, Germany, 2013.
38. Maksum, Y.; Amirli, A.; Amangeldi, A.; Inkarbekov, M.; Ding, Y.; Romagnoli, A.; Rustamov, S.; Akhmetov, B. Computational acceleration of topology optimization using parallel computing and machine learning methods–analysis of research trends. *J. Ind. Inf. Integr.* **2022**, *28*, 100352. [CrossRef]
39. Liu, C.; Gao, R.; Wang, Q.; Liu, S. A design of ultra-wideband linear cross-polarization conversion metasurface with high efficiency and ultra-thin thickness. *J. Appl. Phys.* **2020**, *127*, 153103. [CrossRef]
40. Xu, J.; Li, R.; Wang, S.; Han, T. Ultra-broadband linear polarization converter based on anisotropic metasurface. *Opt. Express* **2018**, *26*, 26235–26241. [CrossRef] [PubMed]
41. Zhao, J.C.; Cheng, Y.Z. Ultra-broadband and high-efficiency reflective linear polarization convertor based on planar anisotropic metamaterial in microwave region. *Optik* **2017**, *136*, 52–57. [CrossRef]
42. Yoon, G.; Tanaka, T.; Zentgraf, T.; Rho, J. Recent progress on metasurfaces: Applications and fabrication. *J. Phys. D Appl. Phys.* **2021**, *54*, 383002. [CrossRef]
43. Su, V.C.; Chu, C.H.; Sun, G.; Tsai, D.P. Advances in optical metasurfaces: Fabrication and applications [Invited]. *Opt. Express* **2018**, *26*, 13148–13182. [CrossRef]
44. Ako, R.T.; Upadhyay, A.; Withayachumnankul, W.; Bhaskaran, M.; Sriram, S. Dielectrics for terahertz metasurfaces: Material selection and fabrication techniques. *Adv. Opt. Mater.* **2020**, *8*, 1900750. [CrossRef]

symmetry

MDPI

Article

An Improved NSGA-III with a Comprehensive Adaptive Penalty Scheme for Many-Objective Optimization

Xinghang Xu [1], Du Cheng [2], Dan Wang [1], Qingliang Li [3] and Fanhua Yu [3,*]

[1] College of Computer Science and Technology, Beihua University, Jilin 132013, China; qixiangxxh123@gmail.com (X.X.); wangdanjl_jl@163.com (D.W.)
[2] School of Artificial Intelligence, Jilin University, Changchun 130012, China; chengdu23@mails.jlu.edu.cn
[3] College of Computer Science and Technology, Changchun Normal University, Changchun 130032, China; liqingliang@ccsfu.edu.cn
* Correspondence: yufanhua@beihua.edu.cn

Abstract: Pareto dominance-based algorithms face a significant challenge in handling many-objective optimization problems. As the number of objectives increases, the sharp rise in non-dominated individuals makes it challenging for the algorithm to differentiate their quality, resulting in a loss of selection pressure. The application of the penalty-based boundary intersection (PBI) method can balance convergence and diversity in algorithms. The PBI method guides the evolution of individuals by integrating the parallel and perpendicular distances between individuals and reference vectors, where the penalty factor is crucial for balancing these two distances and significantly affects algorithm performance. Therefore, a comprehensive adaptive penalty scheme was proposed and applied to NSGA-III, named caps-NSGA-III, to achieve balance and symmetry between convergence and diversity. Initially, each reference vector's penalty factor is computed based on its own characteristic. Then, during the iteration process, the penalty factor is adaptively adjusted according to the evolutionary state of the individuals associated with the corresponding reference vector. Finally, a monitoring strategy is designed to oversee the penalty factor, ensuring that adaptive adjustments align with the algorithm's needs at different stages. Through a comparison involving benchmark experiments and two real-world problems, the competitiveness of caps-NSGA-III was demonstrated.

Keywords: many-objective optimization; penalty-based boundary intersection; comprehensive adaptive penalty scheme; NSGA-III

1. Introduction

Many real-world optimization problems often involve multiple conflicting objectives to be optimized simultaneously, which are referred to as multi-objective optimization problems (MOPs). Multi-objective evolutionary algorithms (MOEAs) are powerful tools for addressing MOPs as they can extensively explore the decision space and evaluate and select individuals to achieve the optimization of multiple objectives. MOEAs can be broadly categorized into three categories: Pareto dominance-based approaches [1–3], decomposition-based approaches [4–6], and indicator-based approaches [7–9]. Among these, Pareto dominance-based algorithms, such as NSGA-II and SPEA2, have been widely applied to various engineering and real-world problems, such as path decision [10], flight optimization [11], and distributed generation system planning [12]. However, these algorithms encounter considerable difficulties when addressing many-objective optimization problems (MaOPs) involving more than three objectives. The primary challenge arises from the sharp increase in the proportion of non-dominated individuals within the population as the dimensionality of objectives increases. This results in the Pareto dominance relationship becoming ineffective, making the algorithm's convergence not guaranteed.

To address the aforementioned issues, extensive research has been conducted, which can be primarily categorized into three approaches. The first approach is improvements to the Pareto dominance relationship, such as ϵ-dominance [13], hpaEA [14], and PeEA [15]. Specifically, ϵ-dominance is a novel dominance relation that divides the objective space into multiple hyperboxes, each containing at most one solution, thereby maintaining a balance between convergence and diversity. The hpaEA identifies non-dominated solutions with significant Pareto front tendencies as prominent and then refines these non-dominated solutions using hyperplanes formed by them and their neighbors, thereby relaxing the Pareto dominance relationship. PeEA is a method for estimating the shape of the Pareto front (PF) by guiding the search process with a curvature-based approach, which handles the issue of selection pressure loss in problems with varying PF shapes. The second approach is to define new diversity criteria. Deb and Jain [3] proposed NSGA-III, which uses a reference point-based method to increase selection pressure and maintain solution diversity. The third approach is the adoption of collaborative strategies, such as θ-NSGA-III [16] and SSCEA [17]. θ-NSGA-III builds on NSGA-III by incorporating the θ-dominance relationship to balance the algorithm's convergence and diversity. SSCEA is a coevolutionary method that combines indicator-based and Pareto dominance-based approaches.

Notably, the θ-dominance relationship in θ-NSGA-III makes use of the PBI method [4]. The PBI method effectively balances algorithm convergence and diversity, with its performance primarily dependent on the penalty factor θ. A smaller θ promotes convergence, while a larger θ promotes diversity. However, setting a fixed penalty factor based on empirical knowledge does not guarantee the performance of PBI when dealing with Pareto fronts (PFs) of different shapes. An excessively large penalty factor may result in a uniformly distributed PF, which may not represent the true PF. Conversely, an excessively small penalty factor could lead to the loss of boundary individuals. Therefore, adaptive adjustment of the penalty factor is necessary. Yang et al. [18] proposed two penalty schemes: the adaptive penalty scheme (APS) and the subproblem-based penalty scheme (SPS). In APS, all subproblems have the same θ, which progressively increases as the iterations proceed, gradually shifting the focus from convergence to diversity. In SPS, penalty values are calculated based on the subproblems. To prevent the loss of boundary individuals during iterations, larger penalty values are assigned to boundary subproblems to emphasize diversity, while smaller penalty values are set for intermediate subproblems to emphasize convergence. Additionally, based on population and weight vector distribution information, Han et al. [19] proposed a dynamic penalty scheme. Specifically, when a subproblem is farther from the associated individuals and neighboring subproblems, the penalty factor is increased to enhance diversity. Conversely, the penalty factor is decreased to enhance convergence.

The adaptive penalty schemes enhance the algorithm's performance in handling MaOPs. Different penalty schemes involve the algorithm's needs at different stages, characteristics of subproblems, and the state of population evolution. However, existing works do not comprehensively consider these factors, which could be more beneficial for designing penalty schemes. In summary, we proposed a comprehensive adaptive penalty scheme and applied it to NSGA-III (caps-NSGA-III) to balance the convergence and diversity of the algorithm. The main contributions of this paper are as follows:

1. An adaptive penalty scheme is proposed. Each penalty factor is initially calculated based on its reference vector and is then adaptively adjusted according to the evolutionary state of the individuals associated with that reference vector during the iteration process.
2. A monitoring strategy is proposed, in which the adaptive penalty scheme is monitored and adjusted to meet the algorithm's needs at different stages. For example, if diversity adjustment is performed during the algorithm's early stage (convergence phase), this is considered a violation. Once the violation handling criterion is met, a convergence operation is performed.

3. Through comparisons with five state-of-the-art many-objective evolutionary algorithms on benchmark function experiments and two real-world applications, the competitiveness of caps-NSGA-III is demonstrated.

The rest of the paper is structured as follows: Basic definitions and improvement motivations are introduced in Section 2. The proposed caps-NSGA-III algorithm is presented in Section 3. The experimental setup and results are described in Section 4. Finally, Section 5 concludes this paper and discusses some future work.

2. Related Work

2.1. Basic Definitions

A multi-objective optimization problem (MOP) is typically considered as a minimization problem and can be mathematically defined as follows [20]:

$$\begin{aligned} &\min F(x) = (f_1(x), f_2(x), \cdots, f_m(x))^T \\ &\text{subject to} \quad x \in \Omega \end{aligned} \tag{1}$$

where $x = (x_1, x_2, \cdots, x_n)^T$ is an n-dimensional decision variable vector from the decision space Ω and m is the number of objectives. $F : \Omega \rightarrow R^m$ is the vector of m objective function values, and R^m represents the objective space. When $m > 3$, the problem is termed a many-objective optimization problem (MaOP).

Pareto dominance

For two solutions $x_1, x_2 \in \Omega$, x_1 is said to Pareto dominate x_2 ($x_1 \prec x_2$), if $f_i(x_1) \le f_i(x_2)$, for every $i \in \{1, 2, \cdots, m\}$, and $f_j(x_1) < f_j(x_2)$, for at least one index $j \in \{1, 2, \cdots, m\}$.

Pareto optimal

For a decision vector $x^* \in \Omega$, if there does not exist another vector $x \in \Omega$ such that $x \prec x^*$, then x^* is Pareto optimal.

Pareto set

The Pareto set (PS) is defined as

$$PS = \{x \in \Omega \mid x \text{ is Pareto optimal}\}$$

Pareto front

The Pareto front (PF) is defined as

$$PF = \{f(x) \in R^m \mid x \in PS\}$$

2.2. NSGA-III

The Non-dominated Sorting Genetic Algorithm III (NSGA-III) is one of the most outstanding many-objective evolutionary algorithms available today. It has proven effective in addressing various engineering optimization problems, leading to significant outcomes [21–23]. However, as a Pareto dominance-based algorithm, it has a significant limitation. With increasing dimensionality of objectives, the Pareto non-dominance relation gradually fails, making the algorithm's convergence not guaranteed. Additionally, in the selection process of NSGA-III, only those individuals closest to the reference vectors are considered. While this approach can achieve good diversity, the convergence is unsatisfactory. Therefore, there is a need to enhance the consideration of convergence.

2.3. PBI and SPS

The penalty-based boundary intersection (PBI) method can balance convergence and diversity, and its computation is as follows:

$$g^{pbi}(x \mid \omega, Z^*) = d_1 + \theta d_2 \tag{2}$$

where x is the decision vector, ω is the reference vector, Z^* is the ideal point in the objective space, θ is penalty factor, d_1 is the projection of $F(x)$ onto ω, and d_2 is the perpendicular distance from $F(x)$ to ω. The calculations for d_1 and d_2 are as follows:

$$d_1 = \frac{\| (F(x) - Z^*)^T w \|}{\| w \|} \tag{3}$$

$$d_2 = \| F(x) - Z^* - d_1 \frac{w}{\| w \|} \| \tag{4}$$

where $F(x)$ is the objective vector for the individual x. d_1 and d_2 are illustrated in Figure 1.

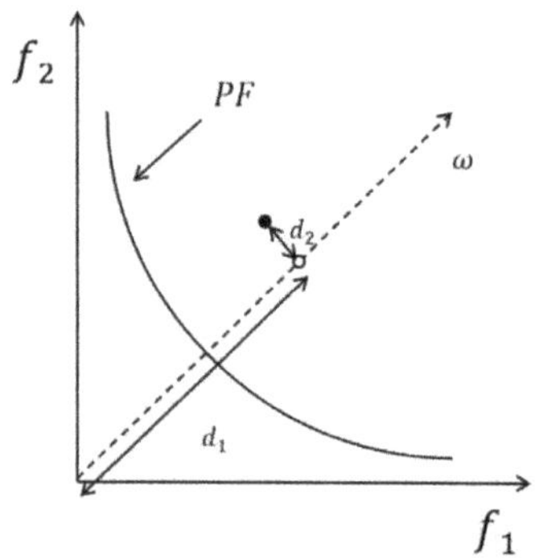

Figure 1. Illustration of distances d_1 and d_2.

The penalty factor in PBI significantly impacts its performance. The subproblem-based penalty scheme (SPS) is a method for calculating penalty factors as follows:

$$\theta_i = e^{\alpha \beta_i}$$
$$\beta_i = \max_{1 \le j \le m} \omega_i^j - \min_{1 \le j \le m} \omega_i^j \tag{5}$$

where i is the ith reference vector, α is a control parameter for the magnitude of the penalty, and β_i is the difference between the maximum and minimum component of i.

Within SPS, boundary weight vectors and intermediate weight vectors have different penalty factors θ. For boundary weight vectors, especially near the coordinate axes, β_i approaches 1 and θ_i takes a higher value, which emphasizes diversity. For the intermediate weight vectors, where all components are nearly equal, β_i approaches 0 and θ_i approaches 1, emphasizing convergence. It is worth noting that after initialization, θ values remain constant during the iteration, which could potentially lead to the abandonment of valuable solutions.

In Figure 2, $\omega = (0.1, 0.9)^T$ is a boundary weight vector, and segment $A - B$ is part of the true PF. As seen in Figure 2, for ω and the associated individuals a and b, it is evident that individual b is closer to the expected PF segment than individual a. However, due to g^{pbi} of b being greater than that of a, individual b is not selected. This indicates that an excessive focus on the weight vectors themselves, while neglecting the algorithm's need for individuals with strong convergence in the early stage, and a blind pursuit of diversity, may impair the algorithm's convergence performance.

In Figure 3, $\omega = (0.5, 0.5)^T$ is an intermediate weight vector. Individuals a and b are two points associated with ω, located near the segment $A - B$ of the true PF. As seen in Figure 3, for ω and the associated individuals a and b, it is evident that individual b is closer to ω. However, because the g^{pbi} of a is less than that of b, the more diverse individual b is abandoned. This indicates that an excessive focus on the weight vectors themselves, while neglecting the algorithm's need for individuals with strong diversity in the late stage, and a blind pursuit of convergence, could result in a decrease in solution diversity.

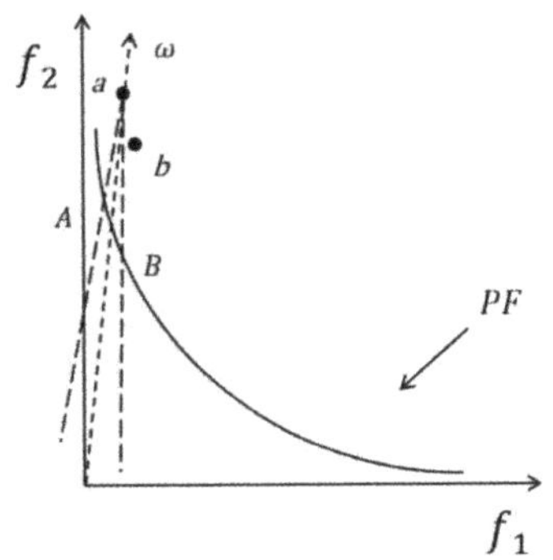

Figure 2. Illustration of the limitation of the fixed θ value in SPS using boundary weight vector.

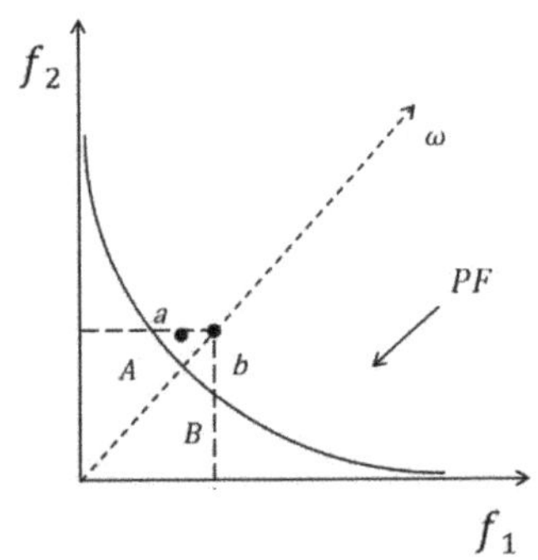

Figure 3. Illustration of the limitation of the fixed θ value in SPS using intermediate reference vector.

2.4. Motivation

Pareto-based methods have limitations in addressing many-objective optimization problems (MaOPs). Researchers have extensively explored improvements by improving the Pareto dominance relationship, defining new diversity criteria, and adopting collaborative approaches. In fact, collaborative approaches essentially combine the Pareto dominance relationship with additional convergence metrics. Solutions are initially ranked based on Pareto dominance and further selected according to convergence metrics. For example, the knee point proposed by Zhang et al. [24] and the grid dominance measure proposed by Yang et al. [25] are both additional convergence metrics. Additionally, the PBI method used in θ-NSGA-III is also a convergence-related metric. It calculates the parallel distance (measuring convergence) and the perpendicular distance (measuring diversity) between solutions and reference vectors, adjusting the importance of both through a penalty factor. Notably, the penalty factor significantly affects the algorithm's performance, and a fixed value based on experience may not be suitable for all types of problems. To address this issue, Yang et al. [18] proposed two adaptive penalty schemes: APS and SPS. APS adjusts the penalty factor based on the algorithm's needs at different stages. In the early stage, it focuses on convergence, and as the iterations progress, the penalty factor gradually increases to emphasize diversity. SPS sets the penalty factors based on the characteristics of each subproblem, with central subproblems focusing on convergence and boundary subproblems emphasizing diversity. Additionally, Han et al. [19] proposed an adaptive penalty scheme that adjusts the penalty factor based on the evolutionary state of the population. However, existing methods do not comprehensively consider these aspects. Therefore, we propose a comprehensive penalty scheme. Based on the limitations of the SPS method described in Section 2.3 and the adaptive adjustment strategy for the penalty factor based on the population's evolutionary state, we propose an adaptive penalty scheme to improve the performance of the algorithm in handling MaOPs, as detailed in Section 3.2. Additionally, there is a key threshold in the adaptive penalty scheme that determines the algorithm's convergence and diversity behavior. This threshold should not be fixed but should be adjusted throughout the entire evolutionary process. Therefore, we propose a monitoring strategy to adjust the threshold, allowing the adaptive penalty scheme to meet the algorithm's varying requirements for convergence and diversity at different stages, thus improving its ability to handle MaOPs, as detailed in Section 3.3.

3. Proposed Algorithm

The main framework of caps-NSGA-III is shown in Algorithm 1. First, the reference vectors are generated and the initial penalty factors are calculated. Next, the population is initialized using chaotic mapping, after which the iteration process begins. First, the offspring population Q_t is generated using NSGA-III's genetic operators and then combined with P_t to form the population R_t. After, non-dominated sorting is utilized to divide R_t into various Pareto-based non-domination levels, with the final layer denoted as layer l. Next, starting from F_1, each Pareto layer is added to the set S_t until the number of individuals in S_t is greater than or equal to N. If the number equals N, the next iteration begins. Otherwise, individuals from the first l layers are stored, and a PBI distance-based NSGA-III selection procedure (replacing the perpendicular distance with the PBI distance (PBI value)) is executed in layer l to select the remaining required individuals. After generating the population P_{t+1}, each penalty factor is adaptively adjusted, and the monitoring strategy is then executed.

Algorithm 1 General framework of caps-NSGA-III

Input: N (Population size), M (Number of objectives), V (Number of decision variables), ub (Upper bounds of decision variables), lb (Lower bounds of decision variables), $MFEs$ (Maximum number of fitness evaluations), ε (Threshold of convergence metric), VF (Violation factor)
Output: population P

$Z \leftarrow$ Generate Reference Vectors()
$\theta_0 \leftarrow$ Calculate the initial penalty factor //SPS
$P_0 \leftarrow$ Chaotic mapping population initialization(N, V, ub, lb) //Algorithm 2
while termination condition is not met **do**
  $Q_t \leftarrow$ Genetic Operator(P_t)
  $R_t = P_t \cup Q_t$
  $(F_1, F_2, \cdots)$ = Non-dominated-sort(R_t)
  repeat
  $S_t = S_t \cup F_i$ and $i = i + 1$
  until $|S_t| \geqslant N$
  Last front to be included: $F_l = F_i$
  if $|S_t| = N$ **then**
    $P_{t+1} = S_t$, **break**
  else
    $P_{t+1} = \cup_{j=1}^{l-1} F_j$
    $P_{t+1} \leftarrow$ The selection process of NSGA-III based on PBI distance.
  end if
  $\theta_{t+1} \leftarrow$ Adaptive penalty factor$(P_t, P_{t+1}, \theta_t, t, MFEs, N, Z, \varepsilon)$ //Algorithm 3
  $[\varepsilon, \theta_{t+1}, VF] \leftarrow$ Monitoring strategy$(P_t, P_{t+1}, \theta_t, \theta_{t+1}, VF, \varepsilon)$ //Algorithm 4
end while

3.1. *Chaotic Mapping Population Initialization*

With increasing objective dimensions, the initial population may exhibit duplication or clustering, leading to reduced diversity. Therefore, we introduced a widely used chaotic mapping method [26] to initialize the population [27,28]. The Logistic equation is a typical chaotic mapping system [29] and is calculated as follows:

$$xl = \mu x(1 - x) \quad (6)$$

where x is a random number in [0, 1], and μ is a logistic control parameter, a random floating-point number in the range [0, 4].

The specific process for chaotic mapping initialization of the population is detailed in Algorithm 2.

Algorithm 2 Chaotic mapping population initialization (N, V, ub, lb)

Input: N, V, ub, lb
Output: P_0

```
P_0 = ∅
for i = 1 : | N | do
    for j = 1 : | V | do
        x_j = rand(0, 1)
        xl_j = μ x_j (1 − x_j)
        x_{i,j} = lb_j + (ub_j − lb_j) xl_j
    end for
    P_0 = P_0 ∪ x_i
end for
```

3.2. *Adaptive Penalty Factor*

In the SPS method, after initializing the penalty factor (θ) it remains fixed, which may lead to the abandonment of some excellent individuals and affect the algorithm's performance. Therefore, we proposed an adaptive method based on SPS. Initially, each reference vector's penalty factor is computed based on its own characteristic. Then, during the iteration process, the penalty factor is adaptively adjusted according to the evolutionary state of the individuals associated with the corresponding reference vector. Specifically, for reference vector i, the PBI of the centroid of the individuals associated with i is calculated in P_t and P_{t+1}, respectively. The d_1 of PBI is used as a convergence indicator: a smaller d_1 means the next-generation centroid is closer to the true PF, suggesting that individuals associated with i are converging. When d_1 changes relatively significantly, the θ value is reduced to emphasize convergence. Conversely, the θ value is increased to emphasize diversity. The detailed process is outlined in Algorithm 3.

Algorithm 3 Adaptive penalty factor $(P_t, P_{t+1}, \theta_t, t, MFEs, N, Z, \varepsilon)$

Input: $P_t, P_{t+1}, \theta_t, t, MFEs, N, Z, \varepsilon$
Output: θ_{t+1}

```
CP = P_t ∪ P_{t+1}
Perform associated operation on CP.
for i = 1 : | Z | do
    AS_t ← Find the set of individuals in P_t associated with Z(i)
    AS_{t+1} ← Find the set of individuals in P_{t+1} associated with Z(i)
    Calculate the centroids c_t and c_{t+1} of AS_t and AS_{t+1}, respectively.
    Calculate d_1, d_2, and PBI for c_t and c_{t+1}, respectively.
    if d_{1,c_t} − d_{1,c_{t+1}} / d_{1,c_t} > ε then
        θ_{t+1} = θ_t − (t*N / MFEs) × |PBI_{c_{t+1}} − PBI_{c_t}| / PBI_{c_t}
    else
        θ_{t+1} = θ_t + (t*N / MFEs) × |PBI_{c_{t+1}} − PBI_{c_t}| / PBI_{c_t}
    end if
end for
```

3.3. Monitoring Strategy

Algorithms have varying requirements at different stages. The adaptive adjustment of the penalty factor should align with the algorithm's needs, with controlling the threshold for increasing or decreasing θ being crucial, as it directly impacts the algorithm's convergence and diversity behavior. To achieve symmetry between convergence and diversity, we proposed a monitoring strategy. Specifically, if a diversity adjustment is performed during the convergence phase, it is considered a violation. When the predefined violation factor is exceeded, convergence adjustment is then performed. Similarly, during the diversity phase, if the number of convergence adjustments exceeds the violation factor, a diversity adjustment is then performed. The specific process is detailed in Algorithm 4.

Algorithm 4 Monitoring strategy($P_t, P_{t+1}, \theta_t, \theta_{t+1}, VF, \varepsilon$)

Input: P_t , P_{t+1} , θ_t , θ_{t+1} , VF , ε
Output: ε, θ_{t+1}, VF

Phase = 0 //Phase = 0 represents the early stage of the algorithm.
$[d_{1,t}, d_{1,t+1}]$ = Calculate the sum of d_1 for individuals' PBI in P_t and P_{t+1}.
if $t > T/2$ **then**
  if $d_{1,t}$ - $d_{1,t+1}/d_{1,t} < 10^{-3}$ **then**
    Phase = 1 // Phase = 1 represents the late stage of the algorithm.
  end if
end if
if Phase = 0 **then**
  if $\theta_{t+1} - \theta_t > 0$ **then**
    $VF = VF - 1$ //Violation
  end if
  if $VF = 0$ **then**
    $\varepsilon = \varepsilon - \mid cr_d \mid *$ rand(0, 1) //cr_d is the rate of change of d_1 in the centroid's PBI at the first violation.
    $\theta_{t+1} = \theta_{t+1} - \mid cr_{pbi} \mid *$ rand(0, 1) //cr_{pbi} is the sum of the rate of change of the PBI of the centroid for the three violations.
  end if
else
  if $\theta_{t+1} - \theta_t < 0$ **then**
    $VF = VF - 1$ //Violation
  end if
  if $VF = 0$ **then**
    $\varepsilon = \varepsilon + \mid cr_d \mid *$ rand(0, 1)
    $\theta_{t+1} = \theta_{t+1} + \mid cr_{pbi} \mid *$ rand(0, 1)
  end if
end if

3.4. Complexity Analysis

The time complexity calculation for caps-NSGA-III primarily includes chaotic mapping population initialization (Algorithm 2), non-dominated sorting (line 7), environmental selection (line 16), adaptive penalty factor (Algorithm 3), and monitoring strategy (Algorithm 4). Assuming the population size is N, the number of objectives is M, the number of decision variables is V, and the number of reference vectors is K. Consequently, the time complexity of chaotic mapping population initialization is $O(NV)$ and the time complexity of non-dominated sorting is $O(MN^2)$. The main components of environmental selection include normalization, PBI calculation, and niche selection. The time complexity for normalization is $O(MN^2)$, for PBI calculation is $O(MNK)$, and for niche selection is $O(N^2)$ (in the worst case, selecting N individuals). Since $K \leq N$, the time complexity of environmental selection is $O(MN^2)$. Additionally, the time complexity of the adaptive penalty factor (Algorithm 3) is $O(NK)$ and that of the monitoring strategy (Algorithm 4) is O(K). In summary, the overall time complexity of caps-NSGA-III is $O(MN^2)$.

4. Experimental Studies

4.1. Benchmark Function and Algorithm Parameter Settings

4.1.1. Benchmark Function Settings

The experiments utilize the widely used DTLZ [30] and WFG [31] test suites. For DTLZ, we focus only on the DTLZ1 to DTLZ4 problems, similar to NSGA-III. The decision variable V is defined as $V = M + r - 1$, where the objective dimension M ranges from 3 to 15 and the parameter r is 10 (or 5 for DTLZ1). For WFG, we consider all problems and define the decision variable V as $V = k + l$, where the position-related variable $k = 2(M - 1)$ and the distance-related variable $l = 20$.

4.1.2. Algorithm Parameter Settings

The experiment compared five many-objective evolutionary algorithms: SSCEA, PeEA, hpaEA, θ-NSGA-III, and NSGA-III. These five algorithms were all designed to address the limitations of the traditional Pareto dominance method in handling many-objective optimization problems, covering the three approaches mentioned in Section 1. Among them, SSCEA and θ-NSGA-III, like caps-NSGA-III, belong to the third approach; NSGA-III belongs to the second approach; and PeEA and hpaEA belong to the first approach. Our aim is to validate the effectiveness of caps-NSGA-III by comparing it with similar methods as well as those from the other two approaches. The algorithms' parameter settings involved in this study are as follows:

1. Population size settings: The population size is determined by the parameter H and the objective dimension M, with specific settings detailed in Table 1. We use the method of Das and Dennis [32] to generate reference vectors. When M exceeds 3, the method of Deb and Jain [3] is employed.
2. Runs and termination criteria: The number of runs is 20 for each instance, with the termination criteria for the algorithms defined as the maximum number of fitness evaluations, as detailed in Table 2.
3. Crossover and mutation operator settings: The crossover probability is 1, with the distribution index set to 30 (20 for SSCEA, PeEA, and hpaEA). The mutation probability is $1/V$, with a distribution index of 20.
4. Parameter Settings: All algorithms use the parameter settings from the original studies. In caps-NSGA-III, $\mu = 4$ for the Logistic equation and $\alpha = 4$ for SPS. The initial threshold is defined as $cd * rand$, where cd is the initial rate of change of d_1 of the centroid associated with the reference vector, and the violation factor is set to 3.

Table 1. Settings of population size.

M	H	Population Size
3	12	91
5	6	210
8	$H_1 = 3, H_2 = 2$	156
10	$H_1 = 3, H_2 = 2$	275
15	$H_1 = 3, H_2 = 1$	135

H_1 and H_2 represent the number of divisions for the boundary layer and the inner layer, respectively.

Table 2. Settings of termination condition.

Test Instance	M = 3	M = 5	M = 8	M = 10	M = 15
DTLZ1-DTLZ4	18,200	42,000	31,200	55,000	27,000
WFG1-WFG9	36,400	157,500	234,000	550,000	405,000

4.2. *Performance Metrics*

4.2.1. Inverted Generational Distance (IGD)

Let P represent the set of points on the final obtained PF and P^* represent a set of points uniformly spread over the true PF. The IGD [33] is then calculated as follows:

$$\text{IGD}(P, P^*) = \frac{\sum_{i=1}^{|P|} d(P_i, P^*)}{|P^*|} \tag{7}$$

where $|P|$ is the number of individuals in set P, $d(P_i, P^*)$ is the minimum Euclidean distance from the solution P_i to P^*, and $|P^*|$ is the number of individuals in set P^*.

4.2.2. Hypervolume (HV)

Let P represent the set of points on the final obtained PF and $Z = (z_1, z_2, \cdots, z_m)^T$ represent an m-dimensional reference point in the objective space that is dominated by all Pareto optimal points. The HV [34] is then calculated as follows:

$$\text{HV}(P, Z) = Volume(\cup_{F \in P}[f_1, z_1] * \cdots * [f_m, z_m]) \tag{8}$$

4.3. *Results and Discussion*

4.3.1. Results on DTLZ Suite

The IGD values obtained by the six algorithms under different DTLZ1-4 instances are shown in Table 3, with the best results highlighted. According to Table 3, caps-NSGA-III excels in 10 out of 20 tests on DTLZ1-4. Especially on DTLZ3, caps-NSGA-III outperforms other algorithms in tests with all objectives except for the 10-objective instance. Additionally, SSCEA works well on the eight-objective and ten-objective DTLZ1 instances, the 10-objective DTLZ2 instance, and the 10-objective DTLZ3 instance. PeEA excels on the 10-objective DTLZ4 instance. The hpaEA demonstrates superior performance on the three-objective DTLZ2 instance and on the three-objective and five-objective DTLZ4 instances. θ-NSGA-III excels on the 15-objective DTLZ2 instance. NSGA-III performs well on the three-objective DTLZ1 instance.

Figure 4 presents the final PFs generated by six algorithms on the 15-objective DTLZ4 instance. As seen in Figure 4, caps-NSGA-III's overall performance surpasses other algorithms. The diversity performance of θ-NSGA-III and NSGA-III is slightly inferior. Notably, hpaEA exhibits poor convergence, with the maximum function values for all objectives exceeding 1.

4.3.2. Results on WFG Suite

Table 4 presents the HV values obtained by the six algorithms on the WFG suite, with the best results highlighted. According to Table 4, caps-NSGA-III excels in 24 out of 45 tests. Notably, it outperforms other algorithms across all objectives on the WFG3 and WFG8 test problems. Additionally, SSCEA, hpaEA, θ-NSGA-III, and NSGA-III achieve the best performance in nine, two, eight, and two instances, respectively. Among them, SSCEA performs well on WFG2 and WFG4. Additionally, it also demonstrates superior results on the eight-objective and fifteen-objective WFG1 instances. The hpaEA performs excellently only on the three-objective and five-objective WFG9 instances. θ-NSGA-III demonstrates excellent performance on WFG6 and achieves superior results in high-dimensional (10- and 15-objective) tests on WFG5 and WFG7. Additionally, it also attains superior performance on the 10-objective WFG9 instance. Finally, NSGA-III shows excellent performance only on the 10-objective WFG6 instance and the 15-objective WFG9 instance. Notably, PeEA does not show any advantages in the comparisons.

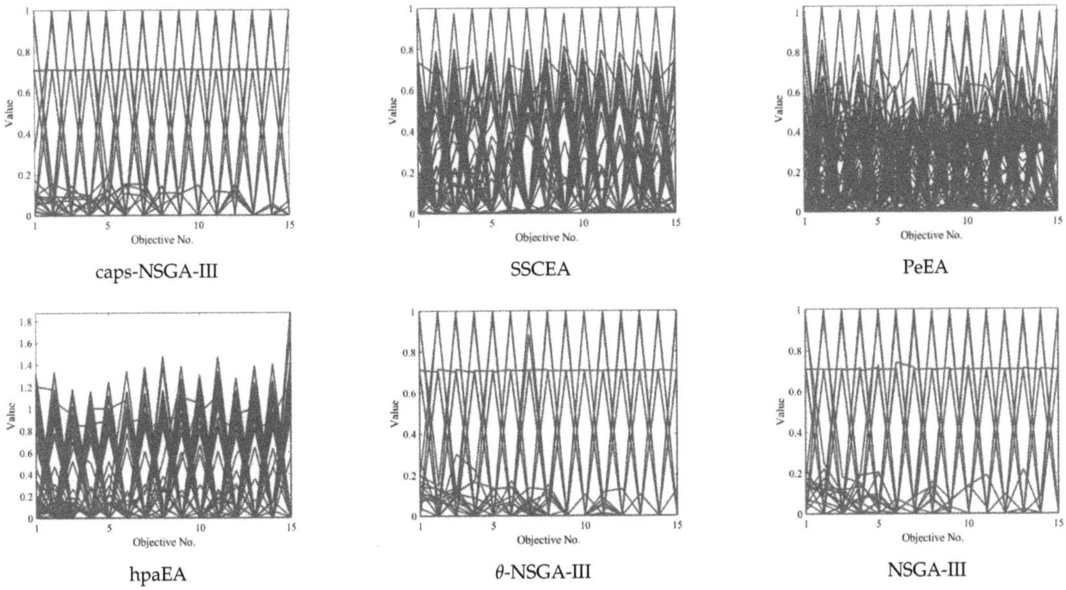

Figure 4. Parallel coordinates of the non-dominated fronts obtained by the six algorithms on the 15-objective DTLZ4 instance.

Figure 5 presents the final PFs generated by six algorithms on the 15-objective WFG4 instance. As seen in Figure 5, caps-NSGA-III's overall performance surpasses the other algorithms. θ-NSGA-III and NSGA-III exhibit marginally lower performance compared to caps-NSGA-III. Notably, hpaEA shows poor diversity, as does PeEA for objectives 2–8.

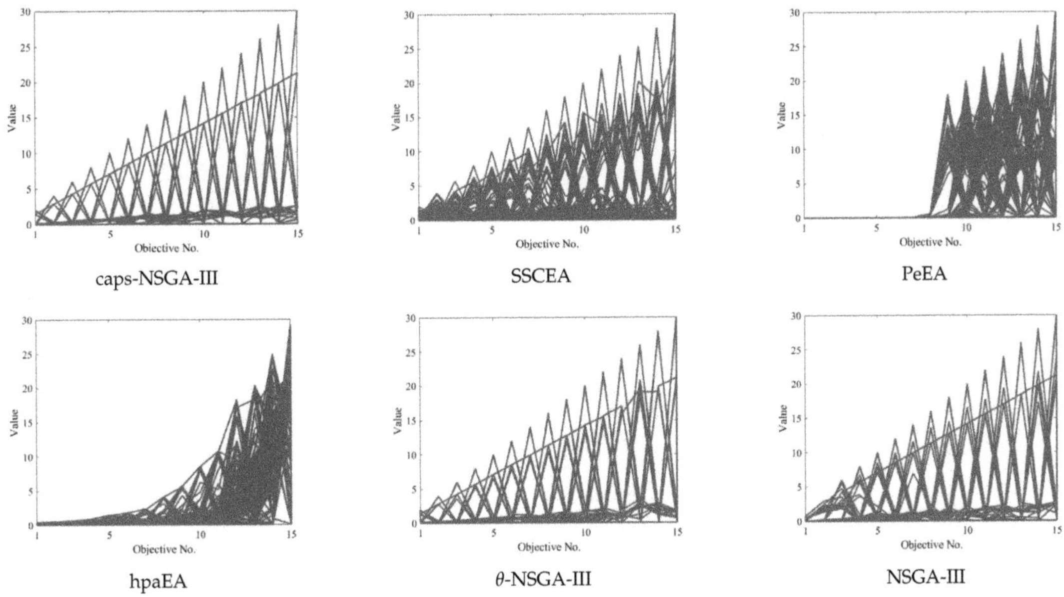

Figure 5. Parallel coordinates of the non-dominated fronts obtained by the six algorithms on the 15-objective WFG4 instance.

Table 3. The IGD values (mean and standard deviation) obtained by caps-NSGA-III and other algorithms on the DTLZ test suite.

Problem	M	NSGA-III	θ-NSGA-III	hpaEA	PeEA	SSCEA	caps-NSGA-III
DTLZ1	3	$1.464 \times 10^{-1} (1.63 \times 10^{-1})$	$2.360 \times 10^{-1} (3.12 \times 10^{-1})$	$1.989 \times 10^{-1} (1.78 \times 10^{-1})$	$2.046 \times 10^{-1} (2.26 \times 10^{-1})$	$2.705 \times 10^{-1} (2.68 \times 10^{-1})$	$3.515 \times 10^{-1} (1.02 \times 10^{-4})$
	5	$2.084 \times 10^{-1} (1.73 \times 10^{-1})$	$1.145 \times 10^{-1} (1.39 \times 10^{-1})$	$2.180 \times 10^{-1} (1.79 \times 10^{-1})$	$7.526 \times 10^{-2} (5.66 \times 10^{-2})$	$7.342 \times 10^{-2} (5.84 \times 10^{-2})$	$5.592 \times 10^{-2} (5.34 \times 10^{-3})$
	8	$9.122 \times 10^{-1} (3.31 \times 10^{-3})$	$4.305 \times 10^{-1} (3.29 \times 10^{-1})$	$1.277 \times 10^{0} (7.22 \times 10^{-1})$	$1.937 \times 10^{-1} (1.21 \times 10^{-1})$	$1.162 \times 10^{-1} (4.63 \times 10^{-2})$	$4.199 \times 10^{-1} (2.14 \times 10^{-1})$
	10	$2.996 \times 10^{-1} (1.99 \times 10^{-1})$	$2.458 \times 10^{-1} (1.98 \times 10^{-1})$	$3.023 \times 10^{0} (1.15 \times 10^{0})$	$1.443 \times 10^{-1} (6.18 \times 10^{-2})$	$1.070 \times 10^{-1} (4.45 \times 10^{-3})$	$1.855 \times 10^{-1} (4.61 \times 10^{-2})$
	15	$8.530 \times 10^{-1} (5.76 \times 10^{-1})$	$5.601 \times 10^{-1} (2.78 \times 10^{-1})$	$3.703 \times 10^{0} (9.28 \times 10^{-1})$	$3.380 \times 10^{-1} (1.79 \times 10^{-1})$	$3.411 \times 10^{-1} (1.86 \times 10^{-1})$	$3.357 \times 10^{-1} (1.54 \times 10^{-1})$
DTLZ2	3	$5.449 \times 10^{-2} (2.41 \times 10^{-5})$	$5.448 \times 10^{-2} (1.59 \times 10^{-5})$	$5.361 \times 10^{-2} (1.78 \times 10^{-1})$	$6.471 \times 10^{-2} (4.45 \times 10^{-3})$	$5.795 \times 10^{-2} (1.05 \times 10^{-3})$	$8.223 \times 10^{-1} (8.50 \times 10^{-2})$
	5	$1.651 \times 10^{-1} (1.01 \times 10^{-4})$	$1.651 \times 10^{-1} (8.64 \times 10^{-4})$	$1.674 \times 10^{-1} (2.00 \times 10^{-2})$	$1.763 \times 10^{-1} (3.24 \times 10^{-3})$	$1.652 \times 10^{-1} (8.64 \times 10^{-4})$	$1.651 \times 10^{-1} (4.99 \times 10^{-5})$
	8	$4.017 \times 10^{-1} (8.92 \times 10^{-2})$	$3.235 \times 10^{-1} (2.50 \times 10^{-3})$	$5.267 \times 10^{-1} (5.52 \times 10^{-2})$	$3.670 \times 10^{-1} (4.28 \times 10^{-3})$	$3.477 \times 10^{-1} (6.92 \times 10^{-3})$	$3.217 \times 10^{-1} (5.15 \times 10^{-3})$
	10	$4.655 \times 10^{-1} (4.49 \times 10^{-2})$	$4.266 \times 10^{-1} (2.39 \times 10^{-3})$	$6.238 \times 10^{-1} (4.50 \times 10^{-2})$	$4.214 \times 10^{-1} (2.35 \times 10^{-2})$	$3.870 \times 10^{-1} (4.82 \times 10^{-3})$	$4.319 \times 10^{-1} (1.50 \times 10^{-2})$
	15	$6.527 \times 10^{-1} (2.14 \times 10^{-2})$	$6.172 \times 10^{-1} (1.01 \times 10^{-2})$	$9.358 \times 10^{-1} (3.55 \times 10^{-2})$	$7.521 \times 10^{-1} (5.69 \times 10^{-2})$	$6.432 \times 10^{-1} (5.64 \times 10^{-2})$	$6.393 \times 10^{-1} (1.65 \times 10^{-2})$
DTLZ3	3	$1.302 \times 10^{1} (5.49 \times 10^{0})$	$8.846 \times 10^{0} (4.42 \times 10^{0})$	$1.534 \times 10^{1} (9.83 \times 10^{0})$	$5.328 \times 10^{0} (2.97 \times 10^{0})$	$1.742 \times 10^{1} (1.32 \times 10^{1})$	$9.933 \times 10^{-1} (2.10 \times 10^{-4})$
	5	$4.914 \times 10^{0} (4.09 \times 10^{0})$	$5.605 \times 10^{0} (3.04 \times 10^{0})$	$5.359 \times 10^{0} (3.03 \times 10^{0})$	$3.833 \times 10^{0} (3.20 \times 10^{0})$	$3.242 \times 10^{0} (2.08 \times 10^{0})$	$1.020 \times 10^{0} (8.38 \times 10^{-1})$
	8	$1.360 \times 10^{1} (6.24 \times 10^{0})$	$1.281 \times 10^{1} (9.54 \times 10^{0})$	$3.358 \times 10^{1} (5.52 \times 10^{-2})$	$1.202 \times 10^{1} (8.69 \times 10^{0})$	$7.162 \times 10^{0} (4.01 \times 10^{0})$	$7.148 \times 10^{0} (4.64 \times 10^{0})$
	10	$9.363 \times 10^{0} (5.06 \times 10^{0})$	$6.361 \times 10^{0} (5.17 \times 10^{0})$	$5.414 \times 10^{1} (1.83 \times 10^{1})$	$3.762 \times 10^{0} (3.26 \times 10^{0})$	$2.846 \times 10^{0} (2.72 \times 10^{0})$	$6.693 \times 10^{0} (6.93 \times 10^{0})$
	15	$2.385 \times 10^{1} (9.98 \times 10^{0})$	$1.421 \times 10^{1} (5.60 \times 10^{0})$	$8.530 \times 10^{1} (2.28 \times 10^{1})$	$9.575 \times 10^{0} (6.39 \times 10^{0})$	$9.853 \times 10^{0} (6.53 \times 10^{0})$	$9.567 \times 10^{0} (4.62 \times 10^{0})$
DTLZ4	3	$5.449 \times 10^{-2} (1.82 \times 10^{-5})$	$5.449 \times 10^{-2} (1.17 \times 10^{-5})$	$5.352 \times 10^{-2} (3.59 \times 10^{-4})$	$6.149 \times 10^{-2} (1.10 \times 10^{-3})$	$5.765 \times 10^{-2} (7.68 \times 10^{-4})$	$8.135 \times 10^{-1} (9.64 \times 10^{-2})$
	5	$1.651 \times 10^{-1} (1.21 \times 10^{-4})$	$1.650 \times 10^{-1} (6.17 \times 10^{-5})$	$1.612 \times 10^{-1} (7.55 \times 10^{-4})$	$1.729 \times 10^{-1} (2.05 \times 10^{-3})$	$1.674 \times 10^{-1} (1.24 \times 10^{-3})$	$1.651 \times 10^{-1} (5.96 \times 10^{-5})$
	8	$3.260 \times 10^{-1} (1.62 \times 10^{-3})$	$3.285 \times 10^{-1} (2.50 \times 10^{-2})$	$3.594 \times 10^{-1} (1.26 \times 10^{-2})$	$3.656 \times 10^{-1} (2.85 \times 10^{-3})$	$3.510 \times 10^{-1} (1.01 \times 10^{-3})$	$3.251 \times 10^{-1} (1.17 \times 10^{-3})$
	10	$4.351 \times 10^{-1} (3.31 \times 10^{-3})$	$4.312 \times 10^{-1} (2.58 \times 10^{-3})$	$5.156 \times 10^{-1} (1.71 \times 10^{-2})$	$4.080 \times 10^{-1} (4.42 \times 10^{-3})$	$4.081 \times 10^{-1} (8.42 \times 10^{-3})$	$4.375 \times 10^{-1} (2.63 \times 10^{-3})$
	15	$6.333 \times 10^{-1} (1.63 \times 10^{-2})$	$6.320 \times 10^{-1} (4.47 \times 10^{-3})$	$6.479 \times 10^{-1} (1.09 \times 10^{-2})$	$1.115 \times 10^{0} (8.88 \times 10^{-2})$	$8.627 \times 10^{-1} (1.01 \times 10^{-1})$	$6.317 \times 10^{-1} (1.30 \times 10^{-2})$

Table 4. The HV values (mean and standard deviation) obtained by caps-NSGA-III and other algorithms on the WFG test suite.

Problem	M	NSGA-III	θ-NSGA-III	hpaEA	PeEA	SSCEA	caps-NSGA-III
WFG1	3	$6.746 \times 10^{-1} (4.34 \times 10^{-3})$	$7.122 \times 10^{-1} (6.21 \times 10^{-4})$	$4.859 \times 10^{-1} (3.13 \times 10^{-3})$	$7.268 \times 10^{-1} (2.14 \times 10^{-3})$	$5.905 \times 10^{-1} (6.46 \times 10^{-3})$	$8.025 \times 10^{-1} (3.81 \times 10^{-2})$
	5	$8.553 \times 10^{-1} (2.47 \times 10^{-4})$	$8.708 \times 10^{-1} (5.37 \times 10^{-3})$	$8.731 \times 10^{-1} (3.08 \times 10^{-2})$	$9.199 \times 10^{-1} (3.20 \times 10^{-3})$	$8.955 \times 10^{-1} (2.78 \times 10^{-3})$	$9.313 \times 10^{-1} (4.33 \times 10^{-2})$
	8	$7.840 \times 10^{-1} (2.16 \times 10^{-3})$	$8.034 \times 10^{-1} (6.43 \times 10^{-3})$	$7.872 \times 10^{-1} (6.17 \times 10^{-3})$	$9.086 \times 10^{-1} (4.86 \times 10^{-2})$	$9.113 \times 10^{-1} (9.39 \times 10^{-2})$	$8.838 \times 10^{-1} (7.07 \times 10^{-2})$
	10	$9.340 \times 10^{-1} (7.66 \times 10^{-3})$	$9.466 \times 10^{-1} (4.35 \times 10^{-3})$	$9.142 \times 10^{-1} (6.78 \times 10^{-2})$	$9.224 \times 10^{-1} (1.95 \times 10^{-2})$	$9.773 \times 10^{-1} (9.64 \times 10^{-2})$	$9.858 \times 10^{-1} (2.45 \times 10^{-3})$
	15	$8.056 \times 10^{-1} (3.21 \times 10^{-3})$	$7.754 \times 10^{-1} (6.42 \times 10^{-3})$	$7.859 \times 10^{-1} (1.28 \times 10^{-3})$	$9.217 \times 10^{-1} (4.57 \times 10^{-3})$	$9.770 \times 10^{-1} (2.11 \times 10^{-3})$	$9.197 \times 10^{-1} (1.80 \times 10^{-1})$
WFG2	3	$8.319 \times 10^{-1} (9.62 \times 10^{-2})$	$8.153 \times 10^{-1} (5.79 \times 10^{-2})$	$7.941 \times 10^{-1} (8.36 \times 10^{-3})$	$8.112 \times 10^{-1} (8.71 \times 10^{-3})$	$8.428 \times 10^{-1} (6.33 \times 10^{-3})$	$9.046 \times 10^{-1} (8.40 \times 10^{-3})$
	5	$9.497 \times 10^{-1} (4.38 \times 10^{-3})$	$9.235 \times 10^{-1} (5.24 \times 10^{-3})$	$8.624 \times 10^{-1} (9.77 \times 10^{-2})$	$9.046 \times 10^{-1} (9.32 \times 10^{-2})$	$9.583 \times 10^{-1} (9.31 \times 10^{-2})$	$9.794 \times 10^{-1} (6.59 \times 10^{-4})$
	8	$8.961 \times 10^{-1} (8.95 \times 10^{-3})$	$3.862 \times 10^{-1} (9.31 \times 10^{-2})$	$5.058 \times 10^{-1} (1.23 \times 10^{-3})$	$9.236 \times 10^{-1} (6.64 \times 10^{-2})$	$9.571 \times 10^{-1} (6.58 \times 10^{-2})$	$9.318 \times 10^{-1} (2.11 \times 10^{-2})$
	10	$9.503 \times 10^{-1} (4.25 \times 10^{-3})$	$8.669 \times 10^{-1} (6.82 \times 10^{-2})$	$9.394 \times 10^{-1} (2.32 \times 10^{-2})$	$4.051 \times 10^{-1} (5.26 \times 10^{-3})$	$9.751 \times 10^{-1} (6.29 \times 10^{-3})$	$9.352 \times 10^{-1} (1.89 \times 10^{-2})$
	15	$8.237 \times 10^{-1} (6.82 \times 10^{-3})$	$7.129 \times 10^{-1} (8.41 \times 10^{-3})$	$8.087 \times 10^{-1} (2.19 \times 10^{-2})$	$8.865 \times 10^{-1} (2.81 \times 10^{-2})$	$9.296 \times 10^{-1} (9.02 \times 10^{-2})$	$3.027 \times 10^{-1} (9.79 \times 10^{-2})$
WFG3	3	$3.446 \times 10^{-1} (6.55 \times 10^{-3})$	$3.407 \times 10^{-1} (5.49 \times 10^{-3})$	$3.324 \times 10^{-1} (3.46 \times 10^{-3})$	$3.247 \times 10^{-1} (2.14 \times 10^{-3})$	$3.835 \times 10^{-1} (1.49 \times 10^{-3})$	$4.631 \times 10^{-1} (2.72 \times 10^{-2})$
	5	$1.086 \times 10^{-1} (3.97 \times 10^{-2})$	$1.444 \times 10^{-1} (3.18 \times 10^{-3})$	$1.149 \times 10^{-1} (5.51 \times 10^{-3})$	$1.605 \times 10^{-1} (5.76 \times 10^{-2})$	$1.610 \times 10^{-1} (5.48 \times 10^{-3})$	$6.142 \times 10^{-1} (5.04 \times 10^{-3})$
	8	$0.000 \times 10^{0} (0.00 \times 10^{0})$	$4.469 \times 10^{-4} (3.13 \times 10^{-1})$	$0.000 \times 10^{0} (0.00 \times 10^{0})$	$1.681 \times 10^{-2} (5.95 \times 10^{-2})$	$6.349 \times 10^{-3} (3.97 \times 10^{-3})$	$4.317 \times 10^{-1} (1.93 \times 10^{-2})$
	10	$0.000 \times 10^{0} (0.00 \times 10^{0})$	$0.000 \times 10^{0} (0.00 \times 10^{0})$	$0.000 \times 10^{0} (0.00 \times 10^{0})$	$5.147 \times 10^{-1} (4.72 \times 10^{-3})$	$0.000 \times 10^{0} (0.00 \times 10^{0})$	$5.335 \times 10^{-1} (2.63 \times 10^{-3})$
	15	$0.000 \times 10^{0} (0.00 \times 10^{0})$	$0.000 \times 10^{0} (0.00 \times 10^{0})$	$0.000 \times 10^{0} (0.00 \times 10^{0})$	$0.000 \times 10^{0} (0.00 \times 10^{0})$	$0.000 \times 10^{0} (0.00 \times 10^{0})$	$3.237 \times 10^{-1} (1.15 \times 10^{-1})$

Table 4. *Cont.*

Problem	M	NSGA-III	θ-NSGA-III	hpaEA	PeEA	SSCEA	caps-NSGA-III
	3	5.456×10^{-1} (2.75×10^{-2})	5.471×10^{-1} (4.57×10^{-3})	5.056×10^{-1} (3.25×10^{-3})	5.338×10^{-1} (4.66×10^{-3})	5.496×10^{-1} (1.27×10^{-3})	5.474×10^{-1} (1.87×10^{-3})
	5	7.879×10^{-1} (3.62×10^{-3})	7.898×10^{-1} (2.54×10^{-3})	6.468×10^{-1} (4.13×10^{-3})	7.693×10^{-1} (5.52×10^{-3})	7.983×10^{-1} (9.47×10^{-3})	7.858×10^{-1} (2.85×10^{-2})
WFG4	8	8.918×10^{-1} (4.33×10^{-3})	9.039×10^{-1} (6.47×10^{-3})	5.615×10^{-1} (2.39×10^{-3})	7.963×10^{-1} (3.82×10^{-3})	9.065×10^{-1} (7.16×10^{-3})	8.996×10^{-1} (4.05×10^{-3})
	10	9.327×10^{-1} (5.74×10^{-3})	9.561×10^{-1} (4.16×10^{-2})	6.008×10^{-1} (6.79×10^{-3})	6.811×10^{-1} (3.81×10^{-3})	9.570×10^{-1} (9.47×10^{-2})	9.508×10^{-1} (5.43×10^{-1})
	15	$9.596 \times 10^{-1}1$ (2.06×10^{-2})	9.779×10^{-1} (8.30×10^{-3})	4.659×10^{-1} (9.78×10^{-3})	8.226×10^{-1} (2.24×10^{-1})	9.568×10^{-1} (9.30×10^{-3})	9.843×10^{-1} (1.63×10^{-3})
	3	5.073×10^{-1} (3.95×10^{-3})	5.069×10^{-1} (2.59×10^{-3})	5.001×10^{-1} (5.29×10^{-2})	5.006×10^{-1} (5.64×10^{-3})	5.009×10^{-1} (4.43×10^{-3})	5.289×10^{-1} (3.58×10^{-3})
	5	7.517×10^{-1} (3.07×10^{-4})	7.529×10^{-1} (5.81×10^{-3})	7.330×10^{-1} (4.27×10^{-3})	7.240×10^{-1} (4.75×10^{-3})	7.200×10^{-1} (8.26×10^{-2})	7.628×10^{-1} (1.86×10^{-3})
WFG5	8	8.496×10^{-1} (5.24×10^{-2})	8.536×10^{-1} (4.16×10^{-3})	7.366×10^{-1} (2.87×10^{-2})	8.086×10^{-1} (2.01×10^{-2})	8.067×10^{-1} (5.70×10^{-1})	8.599×10^{-1} (1.06×10^{-3})
	10	8.980×10^{-1} (5.87×10^{-2})	9.020×10^{-1} (5.42×10^{-2})	7.794×10^{-1} (9.41×10^{-2})	3.546×10^{-1} (8.19×10^{-2})	8.517×10^{-1} (2.63×10^{-1})	8.942×10^{-1} (2.45×10^{-3})
	15	9.082×10^{-1} (5.29×10^{-2})	9.147×10^{-1} (5.33×10^{-2})	5.713×10^{-1} (3.89×10^{-3})	8.136×10^{-1} (1.41×10^{-3})	8.275×10^{-1} (6.59×10^{-1})	9.137×10^{-1} (6.11×10^{-2})
	3	5.137×10^{-1} (3.89×10^{-3})	5.128×10^{-1} (3.11×10^{-3})	5.060×10^{-1} (3.39×10^{-3})	4.963×10^{-1} (1.16×10^{-3})	5.141×10^{-1} (2.64×10^{-2})	5.198×10^{-1} (2.01×10^{-3})
	5	7.600×10^{-1} (6.58×10^{-2})	7.618×10^{-1} (4.33×10^{-3})	7.439×10^{-1} (5.80×10^{-3})	7.132×10^{-1} (5.01×10^{-3})	7.592×10^{-1} (2.63×10^{-3})	7.422×10^{-1} (3.49×10^{-3})
WFG6	8	8.610×10^{-1} (1.13×10^{-2})	8.661×10^{-1} (6.52×10^{-3})	7.972×10^{-1} (1.55×10^{-3})	7.190×10^{-1} (4.79×10^{-3})	8.654×10^{-1} (8.67×10^{-2})	8.384×10^{-1} (6.63×10^{-3})
	10	9.124×10^{-1} (1.38×10^{-2})	9.120×10^{-1} (1.57×10^{-2})	8.471×10^{-1} (2.72×10^{-2})	7.681×10^{-1} (1.52×10^{-2})	9.091×10^{-1} (1.19×10^{-1})	8.732×10^{-1} (5.79×10^{-3})
	15	9.171×10^{-1} (1.67×10^{-2})	9.259×10^{-1} (6.66×10^{-3})	6.445×10^{-1} (1.44×10^{-2})	8.495×10^{-1} (2.79×10^{-2})	9.130×10^{-1} (1.31×10^{-1})	8.808×10^{-1} (9.39×10^{-3})
	3	5.391×10^{-1} (1.35×10^{-3})	5.395×10^{-1} (5.71×10^{-3})	5.376×10^{-1} (1.16×10^{-2})	5.371×10^{-1} (4.55×10^{-3})	4.923×10^{-1} (7.26×10^{-3})	5.517×10^{-1} (3.93×10^{-3})
	5	8.000×10^{-1} (1.19×10^{-3})	8.011×10^{-1} (9.44×10^{-4})	7.732×10^{-1} (2.13×10^{-3})	7.721×10^{-1} (9.63×10^{-4})	7.268×10^{-1} (7.09×10^{-1})	8.020×10^{-1} (5.04×10^{-3})
WFG7	8	8.261×10^{-1} (5.41×10^{-3})	9.045×10^{-1} (7.63×10^{-4})	7.343×10^{-1} (6.05×10^{-2})	8.761×10^{-1} (4.35×10^{-3})	8.023×10^{-1} (2.19×10^{-1})	9.124×10^{-1} (3.75×10^{-3})
	10	8.754×10^{-1} (6.43×10^{-3})	9.623×10^{-1} (7.11×10^{-1})	7.757×10^{-1} (7.26×10^{-3})	9.240×10^{-1} (3.08×10^{-3})	8.762×10^{-1} (9.03×10^{-1})	9.535×10^{-1} (2.63×10^{-3})
	15	9.652×10^{-1} (8.18×10^{-3})	9.866×10^{-1} (5.81×10^{-2})	5.897×10^{-1} (6.42×10^{-2})	8.825×10^{-1} (4.57×10^{-2})	8.792×10^{-1} (7.39e+)	9.860×10^{-1} (1.10×10^{-2})
	3	4.470×10^{-1} (2.88×10^{-3})	4.533×10^{-1} (3.71×10^{-3})	4.463×10^{-1} (5.16×10^{-3})	4.367×10^{-1} (5.16×10^{-3})	4.684×10^{-1} (4.88×10^{-2})	5.068×10^{-1} (2.15×10^{-2})
	5	6.730×10^{-1} (2.19×10^{-3})	6.748×10^{-1} (3.51×10^{-2})	6.730×10^{-1} (4.42×10^{-3})	6.411×10^{-1} (6.07×10^{-3})	6.720×10^{-1} (7.46×10^{-1})	7.522×10^{-1} (2.85×10^{-2})
WFG8	8	7.529×10^{-1} (9.69×10^{-3})	7.468×10^{-1} (1.19×10^{-2})	6.789×10^{-1} (7.65×10^{-3})	7.544×10^{-1} (1.39×10^{-2})	7.533×10^{-1} (6.26×10^{-1})	8.863×10^{-1} (1.23×10^{-2})
	10	8.520×10^{-1} (8.49×10^{-3})	8.405×10^{-1} (1.75×10^{-2})	7.473×10^{-1} (9.28×10^{-3})	8.529×10^{-1} (8.73×10^{-2})	8.398×10^{-1} (2.86×10^{-1})	9.440×10^{-1} (5.43×10^{-1})
	15	8.635×10^{-1} (1.42×10^{-1})	8.852×10^{-1} (5.24×10^{-2})	6.432×10^{-1} (1.49×10^{-2})	8.744×10^{-1} (1.77×10^{-2})	8.946×10^{-1} (3.21e+)	9.769×10^{-1} (4.26×10^{-3})
	3	4.674×10^{-1} (2.05×10^{-3})	4.678×10^{-1} (1.84×10^{-2})	5.006×10^{-1} (2.28×10^{-3})	4.685×10^{-1} (5.27×10^{-3})	4.566×10^{-1} (3.02×10^{-1})	4.971×10^{-1} (9.71×10^{-4})
	5	6.667×10^{-1} (2.16×10^{-2})	6.747×10^{-1} (3.41×10^{-3})	6.814×10^{-1} (2.56×10^{-2})	6.678×10^{-1} (8.07×10^{-3})	6.196×10^{-1} (2.06×10^{-1})	6.799×10^{-1} (2.85×10^{-2})
WFG9	8	7.042×10^{-1} (1.68×10^{-2})	7.138×10^{-1} (1.93×10^{-2})	6.716×10^{-1} (2.38×10^{-2})	6.970×10^{-1} (9.09×10^{-3})	6.328×10^{-1} (3.49×10^{-1})	7.347×10^{-1} (3.04×10^{-3})
	10	7.616×10^{-1} (3.73×10^{-3})	7.860×10^{-1} (4.18×10^{-2})	7.288×10^{-1} (8.77×10^{-3})	5.620×10^{-1} (4.07×10^{-3})	6.921×10^{-1} (6.34×10^{-2})	7.627×10^{-1} (5.43×10^{-1})
	15	7.475×10^{-1} (2.78×10^{-2})	7.445×10^{-1} (4.05×10^{-2})	5.730×10^{-1} (1.87×10^{-3})	7.103×10^{-1} (5.01×10^{-2})	6.172×10^{-1} (2.77×10^{-1})	7.337×10^{-1} (5.93×10^{-3})

Overall, caps-NSGA-III performs the best in many-objective tests for DTLZ1-4 and WFG1-9, particularly in DTLZ3, WFG3, and WFG8. This demonstrates the effectiveness of the penalty scheme we proposed in tackling complex many-objective problems. The adaptive penalty scheme enhances the algorithm's performance, and the monitoring strategy further harmonizes its convergence and diversity performance across different stages.

4.4. Real-World Problem Applications

Two real-world cases were selected for experimental comparison: car side impact [35,36] and water resource planning [35,36]. Among these, water resource planning refers to the optimal planning problem for urban storm drainage systems. It involves three variables (local detention storage capacity, maximum treatment rate, and maximum allowable overflow rate) and five objective functions, which include costs (drainage network, storage facility, treatment facility, and expected flood damage) and expected economic loss due to flood. The car side impact problem involves seven variables, including the thicknesses of the B-Pillars, floor, crossmembers, door beam, roof rail, etc. It aims to achieve three objectives: minimizing the car's weight, minimizing the public force experienced by a passenger, and minimizing the average velocity of the V-Pillar responsible for withstanding impact load. As recommended by Tanabe and Ishibuchi [35], an additional objective function was added to each problem: minimizing the total constraint violation.

For both problems, the population sizes are 100 and 150, respectively, and the termination conditions are 10,000 and 21,000 fitness evaluations, respectively. Other algorithm settings remain consistent with those outlined in Section 4.1.2. Due to the unavailability of the true PF, the HV metric is employed for evaluation, with the obtained HV results presented in Table 5. According to Table 5, caps-NSGA-III exhibits the best performance for both problems. This demonstrates the algorithm's effectiveness in addressing real-world problems.

Table 5. The HV values (mean and standard deviation) obtained by caps-NSGA-III and other algorithms on real-world problems.

Problem	NSGA-III	θ-NSGA-III	SPS-NSGA-III	hpaEA	PeEA	SSCEA	caps-NSGA-III
Car side impact	2.677×10^{-2} (1.27×10^{-3})	2.537×10^{-2} (1.05×10^{-3})	2.653×10^{-2} (1.20×10^{-3})	1.795×10^{-2} (2.31×10^{-3})	1.779×10^{-2} (2.50×10^{-3})	2.323×10^{-2} (1.56×10^{-3})	2.732×10^{-2} (1.11×10^{-3})
Water resource planning	1.097×10^{-1} (2.35×10^{-2})	6.780×10^{-2} (2.69×10^{-2})	1.105×10^{-1} (2.24×10^{-2})	1.221×10^{-1} (1.68×10^{-2})	1.192×10^{-1} (2.81×10^{-2})	1.217×10^{-1} (1.73×10^{-2})	1.249×10^{-1} (2.70×10^{-2})

4.5. Parameter Sensitivity Analysis

To investigate the impact of parameters on caps-NSGA-III, we conducted a sensitivity analysis on the parameter α in the SPS method with values of 1, 2, and 4. The experimental setup is consistent with Section 4. We selected four test problems—WFG3 (linear PF), WFG8 (concave PF), WFG2 (convex PF), and WFG1 (mixed PF)—to identify the optimal value of α.

Figure 6 presents the HV line plots for different values of α across various types of PF. It can be observed from the figure that different values of α indeed affect the performance of caps-NSGA-III. Although performance differences on WFG8 are small, indicating that concave problems may be less influenced by the penalty factor θ, caps-NSGA-III overall performs best when $\alpha = 4$. On the whole, caps-NSGA-III achieves the best results when $\alpha = 4$, especially on WFG2, where the difference compared to other α values is the most significant. This may be because the boundary regions of convex problems are harder to identify, and larger values of α can lead to higher θ values for boundary vectors, thereby helping to maintain diversity.

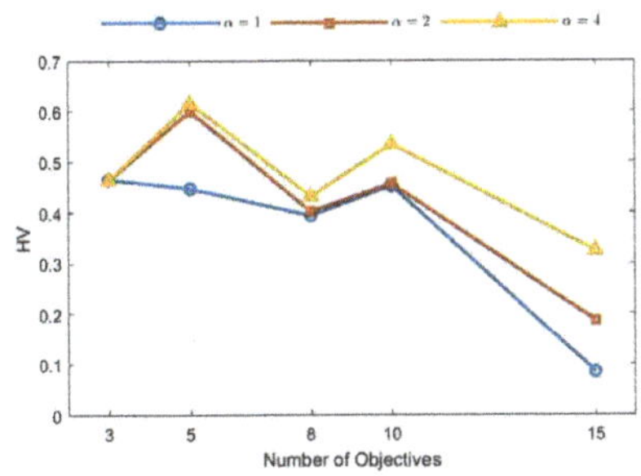

WFG3

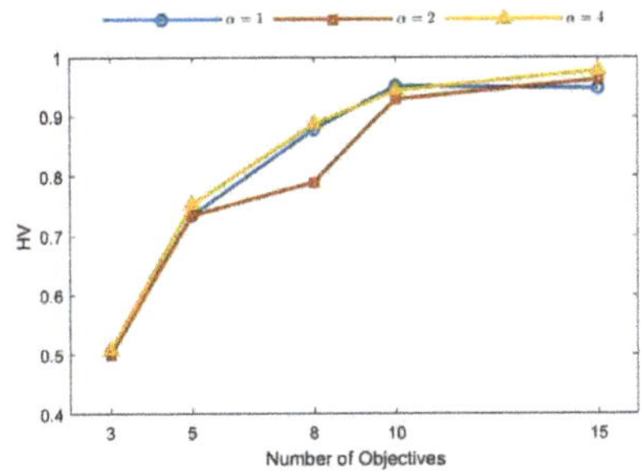

WFG8

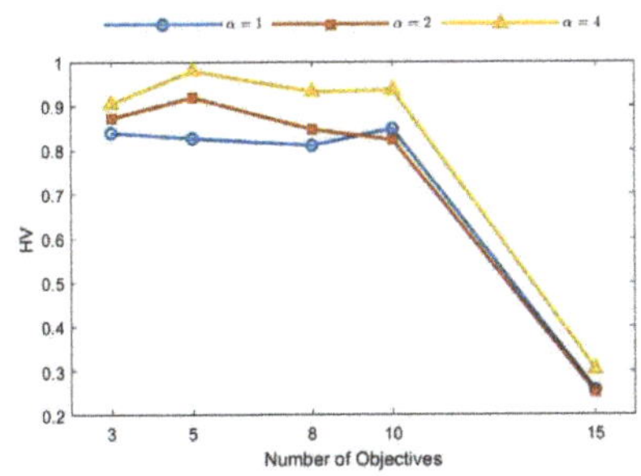

WFG2

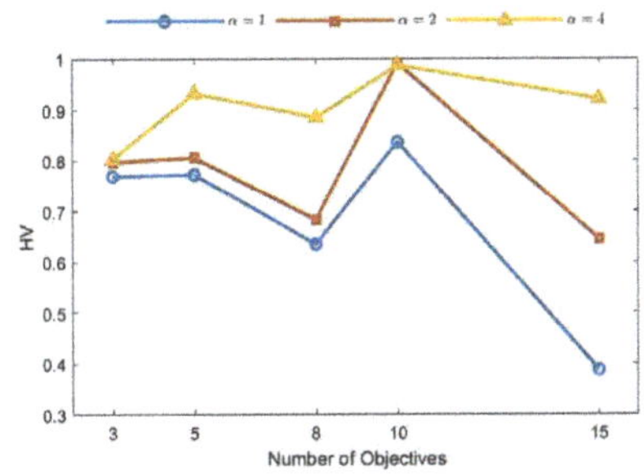

WFG1

Figure 6. Analysis of the impact of α on caps-NSGA-III for the WFG1, WFG2, WFG3, and WFG8 problems. The blue line represents $\alpha = 1$, the orange line represents $\alpha = 2$, and the yellow line represents $\alpha = 4$.

4.6. Ablation Studies

To verify the effectiveness of the adaptive penalty factor and monitoring strategy components, we conducted a series of ablation experiments on the three-, eight-, and fifteen-objective WFG test suites, with the experimental setup consistent with that described in Section 4. The algorithms compared include the original PBI-NSGA-III, SPS-NSGA-III, adaptive penalty factor-NSGA-III (AP-NSGA-III), and caps-NSGA-III, which combines the adaptive penalty factor with the monitoring strategy. Among these, PBI-NSGA-III represents the baseline algorithm, SPS-NSGA-III is used to validate the effectiveness of the SPS component, AP-NSGA-III is used to validate the effectiveness of the adaptive penalty factor component, and caps-NSGA-III is used to validate the effectiveness of the monitoring strategy component.

Table 6 presents the HV values obtained by the four algorithms on the WFG suite, with the best results highlighted. The results show that caps-NSGA-III performed the best, achieving the top performance in 20 out of 27 comparisons. It is followed by AP-NSGA-III, which achieved the best performance in four comparisons, and then SPS-NSGA-III, which achieved the best performance in three comparisons. Notably, PBI-NSGA-III did not show any advantages in the comparisons. By comparing the four algorithms both as a whole and individually, it can be observed that the introduction of each component indeed improved the performance of the algorithms.

Table 6. The HV values (mean and standard deviation) obtained by caps-NSGA-III and other algorithms on the WFG test suite.

Problem	M	PBI-NSGA-III	SPS-NSGA-III	AP-NSGA-III	caps-NSGA-III
WFG1	3	7.477×10^{-1} (4.26×10^{-2})	7.780×10^{-1} (2.67×10^{-2})	7.881×10^{-1} (3.08×10^{-2})	8.025×10^{-1} (3.81×10^{-2})
	8	7.488×10^{-1} (1.63×10^{-1})	9.174×10^{-1} (1.06×10^{-1})	9.340×10^{-1} (7.05×10^{-2})	8.838×10^{-1} (7.07×10^{-2})
	15	7.686×10^{-1} (2.48×10^{-1})	8.863×10^{-1} (1.90×10^{-1})	8.637×10^{-1} (2.15×10^{-1})	9.197×10^{-1} (1.80×10^{-1})
WFG2	3	8.001×10^{-1} (9.38×10^{-2})	8.311×10^{-1} (8.54×10^{-2})	9.018×10^{-1} (1.15×10^{-2})	9.046×10^{-1} (8.40×10^{-3})
	8	7.856×10^{-1} (6.63×10^{-2})	8.466×10^{-1} (1.14×10^{-1})	9.018×10^{-1} (2.94×10^{-2})	9.318×10^{-1} (2.11×10^{-2})
	15	3.303×10^{-1} (7.13×10^{-2})	4.540×10^{-1} (9.23×10^{-2})	4.467×10^{-1} (1.45×10^{-1})	3.027×10^{-1} (9.79×10^{-2})
WFG3	3	4.481×10^{-1} (3.28×10^{-2})	4.595×10^{-1} (2.52×10^{-2})	4.889×10^{-1} (1.79×10^{-2})	4.631×10^{-1} (2.72×10^{-2})
	8	4.141×10^{-1} (3.33×10^{-2})	4.107×10^{-1} (2.54×10^{-2})	4.116×10^{-1} (2.42×10^{-2})	4.317×10^{-1} (1.93×10^{-2})
	15	3.851×10^{-1} (4.09×10^{-2})	3.998×10^{-1} (5.18×10^{-2})	3.931×10^{-1} (5.01×10^{-2})	3.237×10^{-1} (1.15×10^{-1})
WFG4	3	5.463×10^{-1} (1.76×10^{-3})	5.471×10^{-1} (1.69×10^{-3})	5.473×10^{-1} (1.42×10^{-3})	5.474×10^{-1} (1.87×10^{-3})
	8	8.615×10^{-1} (7.47×10^{-2})	8.664×10^{-1} (6.15×10^{-2})	8.797×10^{-1} (5.39×10^{-2})	8.996×10^{-1} (4.05×10^{-3})
	15	9.720×10^{-1} (1.41×10^{-2})	9.721×10^{-1} (1.42×10^{-2})	9.517×10^{-1} (5.01×10^{-2})	9.843×10^{-1} (1.63×10^{-3})
WFG5	3	5.273×10^{-1} (3.53×10^{-3})	5.273×10^{-1} (2.97×10^{-3})	5.277×10^{-1} (3.03×10^{-3})	5.289×10^{-1} (3.58×10^{-3})
	8	8.482×10^{-1} (4.92×10^{-2})	8.449×10^{-1} (9.32×10^{-2})	8.510×10^{-1} (3.27×10^{-2})	8.599×10^{-1} (1.06×10^{-3})
	15	8.913×10^{-1} (6.73×10^{-2})	8.766×10^{-1} (8.30×10^{-2})	8.526×10^{-1} (1.05×10^{-1})	9.137×10^{-1} (6.11×10^{-2})
WFG6	3	5.194×10^{-1} (2.75×10^{-3})	5.194×10^{-1} (1.89×10^{-3})	5.202×10^{-1} (2.95×10^{-3})	5.198×10^{-1} (2.01×10^{-3})
	8	8.371×10^{-1} (6.49×10^{-3})	8.395×10^{-1} (8.29×10^{-3})	8.325×10^{-1} (4.62×10^{-3})	8.384×10^{-1} (6.63×10^{-3})
	15	8.764×10^{-1} (2.02×10^{-2})	8.762×10^{-1} (1.64×10^{-2})	8.802×10^{-1} (1.12×10^{-2})	8.808×10^{-1} (9.39×10^{-3})
WFG7	3	5.522×10^{-1} (3.62×10^{-3})	5.518×10^{-1} (2.96×10^{-3})	5.525×10^{-1} (1.46×10^{-3})	5.517×10^{-1} (3.93×10^{-3})
	8	9.045×10^{-1} (3.69×10^{-2})	8.499×10^{-1} (4.61×10^{-2})	8.700×10^{-1} (7.61×10^{-2})	9.124×10^{-1} (3.75×10^{-3})
	15	9.811×10^{-1} (4.26×10^{-3})	9.809×10^{-1} (4.52×10^{-3})	9.630×10^{-1} (3.74×10^{-2})	9.860×10^{-1} (1.10×10^{-2})
WFG8	3	4.992×10^{-1} (1.72×10^{-2})	4.989×10^{-1} (1.92×10^{-2})	4.991×10^{-1} (1.80×10^{-2})	5.068×10^{-1} (2.15×10^{-2})
	8	7.833×10^{-1} (2.17×10^{-2})	7.892×10^{-1} (2.03×10^{-2})	7.471×10^{-1} (1.77×10^{-2})	8.863×10^{-1} (1.23×10^{-2})
	15	8.837×10^{-1} (6.71×10^{-2})	9.002×10^{-1} (1.04×10^{-2})	9.424×10^{-1} (4.41×10^{-2})	9.769×10^{-1} (4.26×10^{-3})
WFG9	3	4.966×10^{-1} (1.09×10^{-3})	4.968×10^{-1} (1.62×10^{-3})	4.963×10^{-1} (1.22×10^{-3})	4.971×10^{-1} (9.71×10^{-4})
	8	7.010×10^{-1} (9.82×10^{-2})	7.247×10^{-1} (7.30×10^{-2})	7.134×10^{-1} (6.39×10^{-2})	7.347×10^{-1} (3.04×10^{-3})
	15	7.150×10^{-1} (6.20×10^{-2})	6.856×10^{-1} (8.63×10^{-2})	6.445×10^{-1} (8.38×10^{-2})	7.337×10^{-1} (5.93×10^{-3})
Best/Worse		3/24	5/22	6/21	

Best means that the algorithm's HV value is better than caps-NSGA-III, while Worse means it is worse than caps-NSGA-III.

5. Conclusions

In this paper, an improved algorithm named caps-NSGA-III is proposed. This algorithm integrates NSGA-III with a comprehensive adaptive penalty scheme to balance convergence and diversity. Specifically, chaotic mapping is used in caps-NSGA-III to initialize the population, achieving a more uniform distribution and enhanced population diversity. Additionally, in the initial stage, penalty factors are computed according to the properties of the reference vectors themselves. Then, during iterations, these penalty factors are adaptively adjusted according to the evolutionary state of the individuals associated with the corresponding reference vectors, thereby better balancing the algorithm's convergence and diversity. Simultaneously, controlling the threshold for convergence or diversity operation is crucial. To meet the algorithm's needs at different stages, we proposed a monitoring strategy. The adaptive adjustment of penalty factors is monitored during algorithm iterations to achieve adaptive threshold changes, thereby further enhancing the algorithm's performance. Caps-NSGA-III's effectiveness was demonstrated through comparisons with five many-objective evolutionary algorithms. Additionally, the capability of caps-NSGA-III to address practical issues was also validated through comparative experiments on real-world problems. Although our proposed caps-NSGA-III shows improvements in solving MaOPs, its performance on large-scale MaOPs requires further study. Therefore, future work will focus on further exploring caps-NSGA-III and delving into the following aspects: decision variable analysis (DVA [37]), cooperative coevolution (CC) frameworks (incorporating various grouping methods like random grouping [38], dynamic grouping [39], and differential grouping [40]), and problem transformation techniques (such as the Weighted Optimization Framework, WOF [41]) to enhance its performance on MaOPs involving a large number of decision variables.

Author Contributions: Conceptualization, X.X., D.C. and F.Y.; methodology, X.X., D.C. and F.Y.; software, X.X. and D.C.; validation, X.X.; formal analysis, X.X., D.C. and F.Y.; investigation, X.X.; resources, D.C. and F.Y.; data curation, D.W.; writing—original draft preparation, X.X.; writing—review and editing, X.X., D.C. and F.Y.; visualization, X.X. and Q.L.; supervision, F.Y.; project administration, F.Y.; funding acquisition, F.Y. All authors have read and agreed to the published version of the manuscript.

Funding: This work was supported by the Jilin Provincial Science and Technology Development Plan Project under grant 20220203184SF and the General Project of Graduate Innovation Program at Beihua University ([2023]051).

Data Availability Statement: All of the data are in the article, no other new data are created.

Conflicts of Interest: The authors declare no conflicts of interest.

Abbreviations

The following abbreviations are used in this manuscript:

PBI	Penalty-based boundary intersection
caps-NSGA-III	Comprehensive adaptive penalty scheme-NSGA-III
MOPs	Multi-objective optimization problems
MOEAs	Multi-objective evolutionary algorithms
MaOPs	Many-objective optimization problems
PF	Pareto front
PS	Pareto set
APS	Adaptive penalty scheme
SPS	Subproblem-based penalty scheme
cr_d	Rate of change of d_1 in the centroid's PBI at the first violation
cr_{pbi}	Sum of the rate of change of the PBI of the centroid for the three violations
IGD	Inverted generational distance
HV	Hypervolume

References

1. Deb, K.; Pratap, A.; Agarwal, S.; Meyarivan, T. A fast and elitist multiobjective genetic algorithm: NSGA-II. *IEEE Trans. Evol. Comput.* **2002**, *6*, 182–197. [CrossRef]
2. Zitzler, E.; Laumanns, M.; Thiele, L. SPEA2: Improving the strength Pareto evolutionary algorithm. *TIK Rep.* **2001**, *103*.
3. Deb, K.; Jain, H. An evolutionary many-objective optimization algorithm using reference-point-based nondominated sorting approach, part I: Solving problems with box constraints. *IEEE Trans. Evol. Comput.* **2013**, *18*, 577–601. [CrossRef]
4. Zhang, Q.; Li, H. MOEA/D: A multiobjective evolutionary algorithm based on decomposition. *IEEE Trans. Evol. Comput.* **2007**, *11*, 712–731. [CrossRef]
5. Asafuddoula, M.; Ray, T.; Sarker, R. A decomposition-based evolutionary algorithm for many objective optimization. *IEEE Trans. Evol. Comput.* **2014**, *19*, 445–460. [CrossRef]
6. Bao, C.; Gao, D.; Gu, W.; Xu, L.; Goodman, E.D. A new adaptive decomposition-based evolutionary algorithm for multi-and many-objective optimization. *Expert Syst. Appl.* **2023**, *213*, 119080. [CrossRef]
7. Bader, J.; Zitzler, E. HypE: An algorithm for fast hypervolume-based many-objective optimization. *Evol. Comput.* **2011**, *19*, 45–76. [CrossRef]
8. Sun, Y.; Yen, G.G.; Yi, Z. IGD indicator-based evolutionary algorithm for many-objective optimization problems. *IEEE Trans. Evol. Comput.* **2018**, *23*, 173–187. [CrossRef]
9. Yuan, J.; Liu, H.L.; Yang, S. An adaptive parental guidance strategy and its derived indicator-based evolutionary algorithm for multi-and many-objective optimization. *Swarm Evol. Comput.* **2024**, *84*, 101449. [CrossRef]
10. Zhu, C.; Zhu, X. Multi-objective path-decision model of multimodal transport considering uncertain conditions and carbon emission policies. *Symmetry* **2022**, *14*, 221. [CrossRef]
11. Yang, W.; Wen, X.; Wu, M.; Bi, K.; Yue, L. Three-Dimensional Conflict Resolution Strategy Based on Network Cooperative Game. *Symmetry* **2022**, *14*, 1517. [CrossRef]
12. Ney, R.; Canha, L.; Adeyanju, O.; Arend, G. Multi-objective optimal planning of distributed energy resources using SPEA2 algorithms considering multi-agent participation. In Proceedings of the 2019 54th International Universities Power Engineering Conference (UPEC), Bucharest, Romania, 3–6 September 2019; IEEE: Piscataway, NJ, USA, 2019; pp. 1–6.
13. Laumanns, M.; Thiele, L.; Deb, K.; Zitzler, E. Combining convergence and diversity in evolutionary multiobjective optimization. *Evol. Comput.* **2002**, *10*, 263–282. [CrossRef] [PubMed]
14. Chen, H.; Tian, Y.; Pedrycz, W.; Wu, G.; Wang, R.; Wang, L. Hyperplane assisted evolutionary algorithm for many-objective optimization problems. *IEEE Trans. Cybern.* **2019**, *50*, 3367–3380. [CrossRef]

15. Li, L.; Yen, G.G.; Sahoo, A.; Chang, L.; Gu, T. On the estimation of pareto front and dimensional similarity in many-objective evolutionary algorithm. *Inf. Sci.* **2021**, *563*, 375–400. [CrossRef]
16. Yuan, Y.; Xu, H.; Wang, B. An improved NSGA-III procedure for evolutionary many-objective optimization. In Proceedings of the 2014 Annual Conference on Genetic and Evolutionary Computation, Vancouver, BC, Canada, 12–16 July 2014; pp. 661–668.
17. Liu, G.; Pei, Z.; Liu, N.; Tian, Y. Subspace segmentation based co-evolutionary algorithm for balancing convergence and diversity in many-objective optimization. *Swarm Evol. Comput.* **2023**, *83*, 101410. [CrossRef]
18. Yang, S.; Jiang, S.; Jiang, Y. Improving the multiobjective evolutionary algorithm based on decomposition with new penalty schemes. *Soft Comput.* **2017**, *21*, 4677–4691. [CrossRef]
19. Han, D.; Du, W.; Du, W.; Jin, Y.; Wu, C. An adaptive decomposition-based evolutionary algorithm for many-objective optimization. *Inf. Sci.* **2019**, *491*, 204–222. [CrossRef]
20. Srinivas, N.; Deb, K. Muiltiobjective optimization using nondominated sorting in genetic algorithms. *Evol. Comput.* **1994**, *2*, 221–248. [CrossRef]
21. Wang, Y.; Chen, C.; Tao, Y.; Wen, Z.; Chen, B.; Zhang, H. A many-objective optimization of industrial environmental management using NSGA-III: A case of China's iron and steel industry. *Appl. Energy* **2019**, *242*, 46–56. [CrossRef]
22. Liu, F.; Liu, J.; Yan, X. Solving the asymmetry multi-objective optimization problem in PPPs under LPVR mechanism by Bi-level programing. *Symmetry* **2020**, *12*, 1667. [CrossRef]
23. Liu, Y.; You, K.; Jiang, Y.; Wu, Z.; Liu, Z.; Peng, G.; Zhou, C. Multi-objective optimal scheduling of automated construction equipment using non-dominated sorting genetic algorithm (NSGA-III). *Autom. Constr.* **2022**, *143*, 104587. [CrossRef]
24. Zhang, X.; Tian, Y.; Jin, Y. A knee point-driven evolutionary algorithm for many-objective optimization. *IEEE Trans. Evol. Comput.* **2014**, *19*, 761–776. [CrossRef]
25. Yang, S.; Li, M.; Liu, X.; Zheng, J. A grid-based evolutionary algorithm for many-objective optimization. *IEEE Trans. Evol. Comput.* **2013**, *17*, 721–736. [CrossRef]
26. Schuster, H.G.; Just, W. *Deterministic Chaos: An Introduction*; John Wiley & Sons: Hoboken, NJ, USA, 2006.
27. Gutiérrez, A.; Lanza, M.; Barriuso, I.; Valle, L.; Domingo, M.; Perez, J.; Basterrechea, J. Comparison of different pso initialization techniques for high dimensional search space problems: A test with fss and antenna arrays. In Proceedings of the 5th European Conference on Antennas and Propagation (EUCAP), Rome, Italy, 11–15 April 2011; IEEE: Piscataway, NJ, USA, 2011; pp. 965–969.
28. Guo, H.; Zhu, D.; Zhou, C.; Zou, C. DNA sequences design under many objective evolutionary algorithm. *Clust. Comput.* **2024**, *27*, 14167–14183. [CrossRef]
29. May, R.M. Simple mathematical models with very complicated dynamics. *Nature* **1976**, *261*, 459–467. [CrossRef]
30. Deb, K.; Thiele, L.; Laumanns, M.; Zitzler, E. Scalable test problems for evolutionary multiobjective optimization. In *Evolutionary Multiobjective Optimization: Theoretical Advances and Applications*; Springer: Berlin/Heidelberg, Germany, 2005; pp. 105–145.
31. Huband, S.; Hingston, P.; Barone, L.; While, L. A review of multiobjective test problems and a scalable test problem toolkit. *IEEE Trans. Evol. Comput.* **2006**, *10*, 477–506. [CrossRef]
32. Das, I.; Dennis, J.E. Normal-boundary intersection: A new method for generating the Pareto surface in nonlinear multicriteria optimization problems. *SIAM J. Optim.* **1998**, *8*, 631–657. [CrossRef]
33. Zitzler, E.; Thiele, L.; Laumanns, M.; Fonseca, C.M.; Da Fonseca, V.G. Performance assessment of multiobjective optimizers: An analysis and review. *IEEE Trans. Evol. Comput.* **2003**, *7*, 117–132. [CrossRef]
34. Zitzler, E.; Thiele, L. Multiobjective evolutionary algorithms: A comparative case study and the strength Pareto approach. *IEEE Trans. Evol. Comput.* **1999**, *3*, 257–271. [CrossRef]
35. Tanabe, R.; Ishibuchi, H. An easy-to-use real-world multi-objective optimization problem suite. *Appl. Soft Comput.* **2020**, *89*, 106078. [CrossRef]
36. Palakonda, V.; Kang, J.M.; Jung, H. Benchmarking Real-World Many-Objective Problems: A Problem Suite With Baseline Results. *IEEE Access* **2024**, *12*, 49275–49290. [CrossRef]
37. Trivedi, A.; Srinivasan, D.; Sanyal, K.; Ghosh, A. A survey of multiobjective evolutionary algorithms based on decomposition. *IEEE Trans. Evol. Comput.* **2016**, *21*, 440–462. [CrossRef]
38. Yang, Z.; Tang, K.; Yao, X. Large scale evolutionary optimization using cooperative coevolution. *Inf. Sci.* **2008**, *178*, 2985–2999. [CrossRef]
39. Li, X.; Yao, X. Cooperatively coevolving particle swarms for large scale optimization. *IEEE Trans. Evol. Comput.* **2011**, *16*, 210–224.
40. Mei, Y.; Omidvar, M.N.; Li, X.; Yao, X. A competitive divide-and-conquer algorithm for unconstrained large-scale black-box optimization. *ACM Trans. Math. Softw. (TOMS)* **2016**, *42*, 1–24. [CrossRef]
41. Zille, H.; Ishibuchi, H.; Mostaghim, S.; Nojima, Y. A framework for large-scale multiobjective optimization based on problem transformation. *IEEE Trans. Evol. Comput.* **2017**, *22*, 260–275. [CrossRef]

symmetry

MDPI

Article

Imperative Genetic Programming

Iztok Fajfar *, Žiga Rojec, Árpád Bűrmen, Matevž Kunaver, Tadej Tuma, Sašo Tomažič and Janez Puhan

Faculty of Electrical Engineering, University of Ljubljana, Tržaška 25, 1000 Ljubljana, Slovenia
* Correspondence: iztok.fajfar@fe.uni-lj.si; Tel.: +386-1-476-8722

Abstract: Genetic programming (GP) has a long-standing tradition in the evolution of computer programs, predominantly utilizing tree and linear paradigms, each with distinct advantages and limitations. Despite the rapid growth of the GP field, there have been disproportionately few attempts to evolve 'real' Turing-like imperative programs (as contrasted with functional programming) from the ground up. Existing research focuses mainly on specific special cases where the structure of the solution is partly known. This paper explores the potential of integrating tree and linear GP paradigms to develop an encoding scheme that universally supports genetic operators without constraints and consistently generates syntactically correct Python programs from scratch. By blending the symmetrical structure of tree-based representations with the inherent asymmetry of linear sequences, we created a versatile environment for program evolution. Our approach was rigorously tested on 35 problems characterized by varying Halstead complexity metrics, to delineate the approach's boundaries. While expected brute-force program solutions were observed, our method yielded more sophisticated strategies, such as optimizing a program by restricting the division trials to the values up to the square root of the number when counting its proper divisors. Despite the recent groundbreaking advancements in large language models, we assert that the GP field warrants continued research. GP embodies a fundamentally different computational paradigm, crucial for advancing our understanding of natural evolutionary processes.

Keywords: evolutionary algorithms; tree genetic programming; linear genetic programming; imperative programming

1. Introduction

Genetic programming (GP) is a prominent sub-field of evolutionary algorithms (EAs), simulating Darwinian processes on a computer. The GP paradigm was established by John Koza in the early 1990s [1] and had been steadily growing until recently [2]. This trend appears to have reversed with the emergence of large language models (LLMs) [3]. However, we believe that GP will continue to be a significant study area, both as a complementary approach to LLMs and an independent research topic.

Despite the rapid growth of the GP field since the 1990s, there have been disproportionately few attempts to evolve 'real' Turing-like programs. Most research focuses on less complex logical or arithmetic expressions, without incorporating iteration or memory [4]. One reason is that the original GP concept is not Turing complete, a limitation addressed by [5] through the introduction of indexed memory. Another reason is that the original GP paradigm encodes a program as a tree, necessitating viewing a computer program as a sequential application of functions and operators to arguments (so-called functional programming). While not a limitation per se, this is not the most natural way to conceptualize computer programs. Shortly after the traditional tree representation of a computer program in GP, linear and graph representations emerged [6,7]. In contrast to the functional programming language expressions encoded by trees in traditional GP, linear genetic programming evolves sequences of instructions from an imperative programming language. The difference in program representation necessitates different genetic operators, making both approaches even more distinct. Both approaches, tree and linear, have their respective advantages and disadvantages, and researchers and practitioners select one based on the specific requirements of their problem. There has been criticism that the GP concept has an intrinsic flaw in that it cannot produce real software effectively [2,4], primarily because computer code is not as robust as genetic code. It is extremely susceptible to even the smallest changes. This is one of the main reasons that the existing research focuses mainly on specific special cases where the structure of the solution is partly known [8,9]. The vast majority of studies are limited to symbolic regression and classification problems [2,10–22]. Other important domains where GP is being used include, but are not limited to, control systems [23,24], analog optimization [8,25–28], scheduling [29,30], and image processing [31,32]. To the best of our knowledge, no systematic research has been conducted to evolve general Turing-like (imperative) programs (as contrasted with functional programming) from scratch, with no a priori assumptions on the solution structure.

The contribution of this paper is twofold. First, we introduce a computer program representation that merges tree and linear representations, using trees for expressions and a linear representation for encoding the overall computer program. We use Python as a programming language for generated programs. Second, we systematically apply our approach to several well-known algorithms of varying complexities to identify the limits of the proposed method.

The structure of this paper is as follows. Sections 2 and 3 detail the encoding of programs and the methodology for generating a concrete program from this encoding. Section 4 describes the evolutionary algorithm employed, while Section 5 outlines the overall experimental setup. The final sections present and discuss the results.

2. The Proposed Program Genotype

2.1. The Basic Idea

A computer program is a linear sequence of instructions, generally asymmetrical. However, a program can contain nested conditional and loop statements, which imply an inherently symmetrical tree structure. Expressions also exhibit a tree structure. This symmetrical/asymmetrical duality of a computer program was the most important issue we had to address when devising the structure of our genotype. Another critical consideration was the possibility of a randomly created loop-controlling expression resulting in an infinite loop or a loop with an unreasonably high number of iterations. Limiting the number of loop iterations is crucial when composing and executing thousands of randomly generated programs.

We encoded the program itself as a linear set of statements. Whenever there is a control statement header, a certain number of the following lines form the statement's body. That number is stored with the header and is subject to evolutionary operations.

Most authors address the problem of non-halting programs or programs with excessive loop iterations by setting an upper limit on the number of executed instructions. We adopted a slightly different approach by limiting the number of iterations for any loop. This method prevents the potentially destructive effects of genetic operators, which could compromise the program by including parts of already functioning code in a loop. If the code is such that successive repetitions have no different effects than a single iteration, the program will continue to function correctly. Conversely, if the number of instructions is limited, parts of the code outside the loop may never execute.

We implemented the upper limit on loop iterations using a for loop combined with a break statement. For example, we encode a while loop with a control expression $expr$ and an upper limit of $maxIter$ iterations in the following manner:

for $i \leftarrow 1$ **to** $maxIter$ **do**
  if not $expr$ **then** break
  end if
  // Loop body comes here

end for

Here, the loop iterator i is a safeguard, while *expr* is the control expression of the equivalent while loop:

while *expr* **do**
// Loop body comes here
end while

2.2. The Structure of the Genotype

We composed the genotype of a program with a fixed number of consecutive lines, thus eliminating bloat and simplifying genetic operators. To make the system even simpler and more robust, every program line has the same structure, containing the necessary information to be decoded into any possible line depending on its position in the program. That way, we are always able to build a syntactically correct program. The consequence of this universality is a large amount of redundant code stored in our genotype. The redundant pieces of code are not expressed in the phenotype (an actual program) and are usually referred to as introns. This redundancy seems like a downside, but it is also believed that introns reduce search space and speed up the convergence by dynamically hiding the genotype segments not needed for the ultimate solution [33].

The structure of a single line of code is depicted in Figure 1. After the type of the line, which can be an assignment, a macro, a control statement's header, or simply the pass placeholder, the line also includes the parameter *bodyLen* (holding the control statement body length), the expression tree, the macro index, and the list of variables. The *bodyLen* parameter is only relevant when the line type is a control statement's header, and its value ranges from 2 to the maximum body length (see Table 1).

assignment/macro/for/if/else/pass
bodyLen
An expression tree
macroIndex
A list of variables (*varList*)

Figure 1. The structure of a single line of a program.

Figure 2 shows an example of an expression tree. Each node of the expression tree contains two code snippets: the first one is used when the node is terminal, while the second one is used when the node is non-terminal (see Figure 3). As seen in Figure 2, the root of the tree—a non-terminal node in our case—produces the greater-than operator, which will compare the expressions derived from the left and right subtrees. We derive the expression $\text{abs}(x_2)$ from the right subtree because the first node is non-terminal while the second is terminal. In the same way, we use the mod, − (minus), and abs from the three non-terminal nodes of the left subtree, and 2, x_3, and x_2 from the three terminal nodes. Thus, from this tree, we derive the expression $\text{mod}(2 - x_3, \text{abs}(x_2)) > \text{abs}(x_2)$.

It is probably worth mentioning at this point that we have limited ourselves to using only scalar variables. A serious consequence is that functions that can be added as prefabricated elements to our genetic material cannot return more than a single value. Note that although Python works exclusively with references, one still cannot pass a scalar variable by reference to obtain an output value from a function. This limitation does not allow us to use, for example, a function that swaps the values of two variables. For that reason, we added macros to our genotype. The parameter *macroIndex* is used to select a macro from the list of predefined macros.

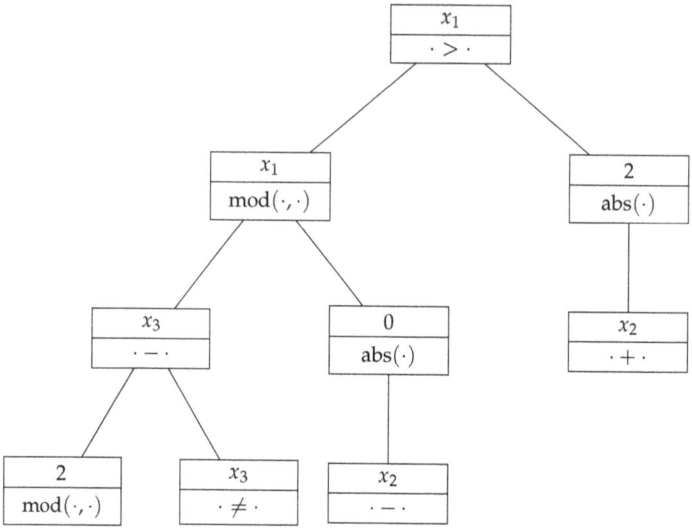

Figure 2. An example of a tree representing the expression $\mathrm{mod}(2 - x_3, \mathrm{abs}(x_2)) > \mathrm{abs}(x_2)$.

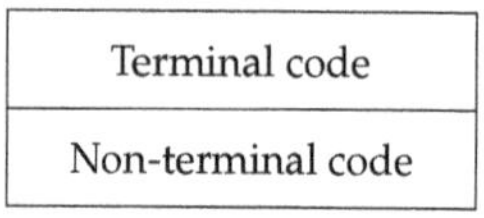

Figure 3. The structure of a single node of an expression tree.

Finally, the list of variables holds as many variables as there are placeholders to fill in the largest macro from the list. If the line type is an assignment, then the first from the variable list will be used as a left value in the assignment.

Notice that some data contained in program lines and expression trees may appear redundant in specific contexts. They are nevertheless retained to standardize crossover, mutation, and code extraction procedures. Moreover, these 'redundant' data might encapsulate hidden genetic material that was once beneficial and could prove useful again (see, e.g., [34]).

At the beginning of each evolutionary run, we need a population of randomly generated programs, which are constructed using several parameters summarized in Table 1 together with a short explanation of their meaning. The first parameter limits the number of variables used in the generated program. All the variables share the same name prefix with added numbers (e.g., $x_0, x_1, x_2, \cdots$). Next comes a list of operators and function names. The operators must be selected among the standard Python operators. At the same time, the function names can be arbitrary as long as they are defined separately and their definitions added to the list of function definitions. Following the list of macro definitions and constants is a list of probabilities indicating the likelihood of each line type being selected during the initial random genotype creation. Those probabilities also guide the random line type selection during the mutation procedure.

The limitation of the depth of control statement nestings is also important. More than a single nested loop is hardly necessary. At the same time, it would be extremely time-consuming if we allowed it. On the other hand, it is important to allow deeper nesting of a conditional statement since there are a lot of cases in which such a statement comes in handy when nested in an already nested loop. Apart from loop nesting, the maximum number of iterations should also be limited, lest the programs could unreasonably slow down the evolution.

As expressions in our programs need not be too complex, we limited the expression tree depth. Initial depth is limited to two but grows later due to bloat. We employed two mechanisms to fight bloat. The first is a limit on the depth to which a tree is evaluated, and the second is a limit on the maximum allowed depth by trimming a tree after each crossover and mutation. The first of the two limits is lower, so some hidden genetic material usually stays in a tree. Note that, technically, it is not a problem to limit the evaluation depth since every node includes a code to be used in both cases—when the node acts as a terminal or as a non-terminal. The evaluation algorithm simply selects the proper one and ignores the other.

The last three parameters in Table 1 represent three more important limits on evaluation trees' densities, the overall program length, and the maximum control statement body length. Note that the actual program length can be shorter than the given length because of possible pass statements.

Table 1. The program parameters used in our experiments. Values in parentheses are default values used in our experiments. If there is no default value (N/A), the value must be explicitly provided for each experiment by the practitioner.

Number of variables (5)	How many variables will be used in the program
Operators (N/A)	List of operators and/or function names
Function definitions (N/A)	List of function definitions
Macro definitions (N/A)	List of macro definitions
Constants (N/A)	List of constants
Line type probabilities (assignment = 0.55, for = 0.10, if = 0.15, else = 0.10, pass = 0.10)	How probable it is, during a random program generation and mutation, for a certain line type to be selected
Macro selection probability (0.15)	If at least one macro is defined, this probability is added to the above list. All the probabilities are proportionally reduced so that they sum to 1
Maximum loop nesting (1)	The maximum allowed depth of loop nesting
Maximum if nesting (2)	The maximum allowed depth of conditional statement nesting
Maximum loop iterations (100)	The maximum allowed number of iterations of a single loop
Tree generation depth (2)	The maximum initial depth of an expression tree
Tree evaluation depth (3)	The maximum depth to which an expression tree is evaluated
Maximum tree depth (5)	The depth to which trees are trimmed after crossover and mutation
Tree density (0.7)	The density of an expression tree during generation and mutation
Program length (15)	The number of lines in the program
Maximum body length (5)	Maximum number of statements within a control statement body

3. Building a Python Program

Algorithm 1 illustrates the construction of actual Python code from the genotype introduced in Section 2. To thoroughly comprehend the algorithm, one must understand the role of indentation in Python code. In Python, the body of a control statement consists of indented lines. All indented lines belong to the statement's body. Conversely, the first line with the same indentation level as the control statement's header is no longer part of that control statement but it succeeds it.

Algorithm 1 Algorithm for constructing a Python program from genotype.

```
1: procedure ComposePythonProgram
2:     indent ← 0
3:     for each line in the program do
4:         if lineType = assignment then
5:             code ← code + varList[0] + "=" + expressionFromTree()
6:         else if lineType = for then
7:             if indent < maxLoopNest then
8:                 code ← code + "for i in range(" + maxIter + ")"
9:                 indent ← indent + 1
10:                code ← code + "if " + expressionFromTree() + ": break"
11:            end if
12:        else if lineType = if then
13:            if indent < maxIfNest then
14:                code ← code + "if " + expressionFromTree() + ":"
15:                indent ← indent + 1
16:            end if
17:        else if lineType = else then
18:            if inside an if or for block then
19:                if the block contains at least one line of code then
20:                    indent ← indent − 1
21:                    code ← code + "else:"
22:                    indent ← indent + 1
23:                end if
24:            end if
25:        else if lineType = macro then
26:            selectedMacro ← macroList[macroIndex]
27:            Replace placeholders in selectedMacro with variables from varList
28:            code ← code + selectedMacro
29:        else if lineType = pass then
30:            code ← code + "pass"
31:        end if
32:        if number of statements in current block equals bodyLen then ▷ The block has
33:            indent ← indent − 1                         ▷ reached the maximum allowed length
34:        end if
35:    end for
36:    code ← code + "pass"     ▷ In case the last line of the program is if, for, or else.
37: end procedure
```

In Section 2, we saw that the genotype of an individual program consists of multiple sequential lines of code. Each line is divided into five distinct parts, with the first part specifying the line's type. This type determines how subsequent parts are utilized during code construction. Algorithm 1 operates through a loop that processes each line of the program genotype. Prior to this loop, the code indentation is initialized to zero (see Line 2). Within the loop, various line types are addressed using an if–else chain. The first type in this sequence, denoted as 'assignment' (see Line 4), builds an assignment statement. Here, $varList[0]$ (i.e., the first variable in the list) is used as the variable name on the left side of the assignment operator, while the expression derived from the corresponding expression tree forms the right side. Note that both these elements—the variable list and the expression tree—are encapsulated within the line's genotype. Note that *code* is a string, with the + symbol serving as a concatenation operator. Moreover, every line of code from Algorithm 1 starts with the correct indentation and ends with a newline character—details omitted from the algorithm for clarity.

The next line type addressed in the algorithm is the for statement (see Line 6). It is important to note that this line is bypassed once the maximum permitted loop nesting depth is reached. Otherwise, the algorithm generates a two-line code segment. The initial line forms a conventional Python loop executing *maxIter* times. Recall that *maxIter* sets the upper limit for the number of loop iterations. Following this, an indented if statement is introduced—indicating its inclusion within the loop body—which triggers an early loop exit when its expression evaluates as true. As explained in Section 2.1, this design effectively creates a while loop equipped with a safeguard against excessive iterations, crucial to prevent undue hindrance in the evolutionary process.

The if statement (Line 12) is managed similarly. It is skipped entirely when the maximum permitted nesting depth is attained. Following the addition of the control statement header, the indentation increases to ensure that the following lines fall within the statement body.

The else part, handled in Line 17, is incorporated only when nested within the body of an if or for statement that contains at least one line of code. Note that in Python, a for loop can also have an optional else segment, which is executed upon loop completion. However, it will not be executed if the loop is interrupted by a break statement. Recall, in our context, the for loop functions akin to a while loop with a capped number of iterations. Hence, the else segment only comes into play when this iteration limit is met. Such a design can prove beneficial during evolution, though it might be extraneous in final programs. When integrating the else keyword, the indent level is reduced beforehand and then increased afterward, effectively closing the current block and commencing a new one.

Line 25 processes a macro. It simply takes a macro from the list and replaces its placeholders, in order of appearance, with the variables from the variable list.

The final line type addressed is the pass statement (see Line 29), serving as a placeholder for potential subsequent code. After that (see Line 32), it is necessary to verify if the current block length is reached, and if so, conclude that block by decreasing the indentation. Upon completing the program, an additional pass statement is appended (see Line 36) to avoid an error if the program's last line is a control statement header.

4. The Evolutionary Algorithm

The evolutionary algorithm is outlined in Algorithm 2. First, some initialization procedures are carried out in Lines 2 to 4. After some preliminary runs, we settled with the genetic parameters summarized in Table 2 that we used in all our experiments. We explain the meaning of each parameter later on in the context of the algorithm. The program parameters, however (see Line 3 of Algorithm 2), are initialized differently for each run, depending on the type of program we want to evolve. Recall that the used program parameters are summarized in Table 1 at the end of Section 2.

Table 2. The genetic parameters used in our experiments.

Population size	1000
Array of training data length	20
Selection	Linear ranking with elitism
Selection pressure	1.3
Elite size	10
Number of generations	2000
Mutation probability	0.5
Line crossover probability	0.3
Number of crossover lines	4
Toggle terminal probability	0.3
Mutation depth	2
Fitness calculation method	Least squares
Premature stopping criterion 1	Fitness does not change for 600 generations
Premature stopping criterion 2	Fitness drops to zero

Line 4 of Algorithm 2 prepares the training data. This is simply an array of input/output pairs of data that our program should produce. For instance, if we wanted to evolve a program that returns the largest of three input values, we would need the array $[[[2, 7, 12], 12], [[-4, 56, 21], 56], [[6, -15, 3], 6], \cdots]$. The array is generated randomly using some preset limit values. It turned out that without them, the algorithm might not work in limited cases. For example, in multiplication, it is necessary to include training data involving ones and zeroes in different combinations. It is also important that these critical values appear as first and second parameters. It happened that the algorithm trained on the data missing multiplication with zero as the second parameter worked for multiplications of the form $0 \cdot x$ but not $x \cdot 0$. It also happened that in evolving the algorithm detecting primes, the training array contained only even non-primes. Naturally, the evolved algorithm erroneously detected even numbers instead of primes.

The last thing we need to do before entering the main program loop is generate random programs and evaluate their fitness values. As seen in Table 2, we use the least squares method to calculate the program fitness. To do that, we run the program and then calculate the sum of squared differences between actual and required outputs. The program with the smallest fitness is the best.

Algorithm 2 The evolutionary algorithm.

```
procedure EVOLVEPROGRAM
    Initialize genetic parameters
    Initialize program parameters
    Calculate training data
    Generate a population of random programs
    Calculate the fitness of each program in the population
    for generation = 1 to Number of generations do
        Selection
        for Pair of programs in selection do                      ▷ Parents
            if Random value in [0,1) < p_line crossover then
                Line crossover
            else
                Program crossover
            end if
        end for
        for program in selection do                               ▷ Children
            if Random value in [0,1) < p_mutation then
                Mutate program
            end if
            Calculate fitness
        end for
        Replacement
        if at least one of the premature stopping criteria met then
            Stop evolution
        end if
    end for
end procedure
```

4.1. Selection

In the main program loop, we first select programs to participate in genetic operations. Because the fitness landscape of a computer program's population is extremely rugged, we opted for rank selection to give less fit programs an equal chance to reproduce. We used linear ranking [35], where selection probability is linearly dependent on the rank position of the individual in the population. We calculate the probability p for rank position r_i as

$$p(r_i) = \frac{1}{n}\left(sp - (2sp - 2)\frac{i-1}{n-1}\right), \quad 1 \le i \le n, \quad 1 \le sp \le 2.$$

Here, n is the size of the population and sp is selection pressure. Notice that $sp = 1$ gives equal probabilities for all the population members, which means there is no selection pressure. On the other hand, if $sp = 2$, selection pressure is very high. As seen in Table 2, we set selection pressure to 1.3, which—combined with the elite size of 10—produced the best results.

4.2. Crossover

The next operation in the main program loop is crossover. We form random pairs of programs from the group selected for genetic operations and perform either a program or line crossover, depending on a preset probability $p_{\text{line crossover}}$.

The crossover of the whole program is straightforward. We select a random cutting point (the same for both programs in question) and then swap cutoff parts of the programs as shown in Figure 4.

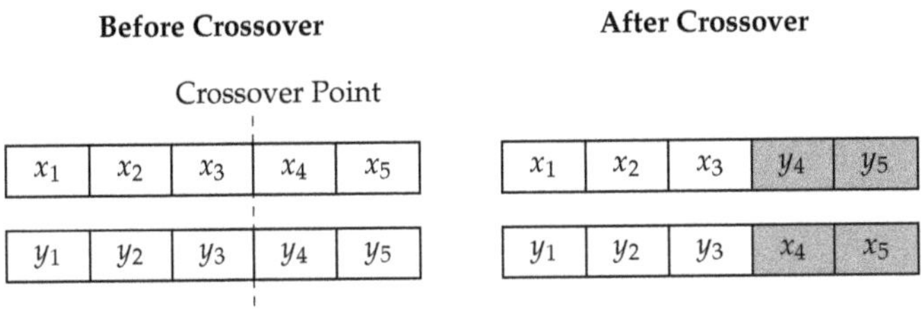

Figure 4. The crossover of two 5-line programs x and y. The crossover point lies between the 3rd and 4th lines. The operation swaps the lines x_4 and x_5 with y_4 and y_5.

The line crossover is a little more elaborate. First, we randomly select a prescribed number of lines from each program. The number is one of the genetic parameters shown in Table 2. As the line structure is universal, there is no limit on which lines to select. Figure 5 shows an example of the line crossover of two programs. On each pair of lines, we perform one of the following crossover operations:

- Exchange the first part of the line (i.e., the type of statement).
- Exchange the second part of the line (i.e., the *bodyLen* parameter).
- Perform the expression tree crossover.
- Exchange the fourth part of the line (i.e., the *macroIndex* parameter).
- Perform the list of variables crossover.

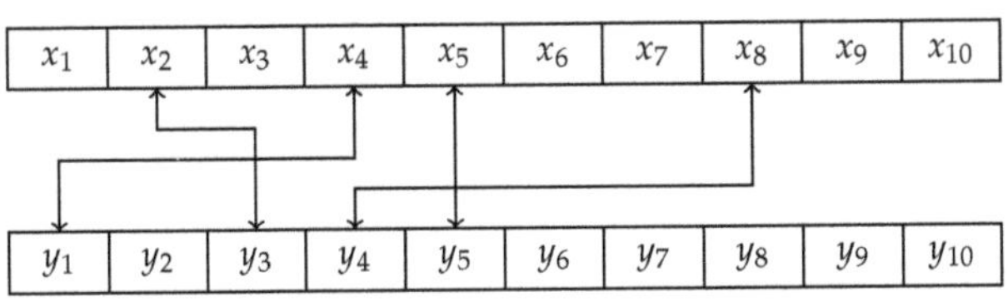

Figure 5. An example of the line crossover of two 10-line programs x and y. Lines x_2, x_4, x_5, and x_8 from the first program and lines y_1, y_3, y_4, and y_5 from the second program were selected for the crossover.

The parts of the lines that hold a single value (i.e., the type of statement and the parameters *bodyLen* and *macroIndex*) are exchanged. When the crossover is performed on expression trees, the operation follows the standard tree crossover procedure where we cut a random subtree from each tree and swap the cutoff parts. Figure 6 shows the procedure. Note that, if both cutting points are above the roots of the trees, the expression trees are merely exchanged.

In order to limit bloat—as already mentioned in Section 2.2—the trees are trimmed after the crossover not to exceed the prescribed maximum depth (see Table 1).

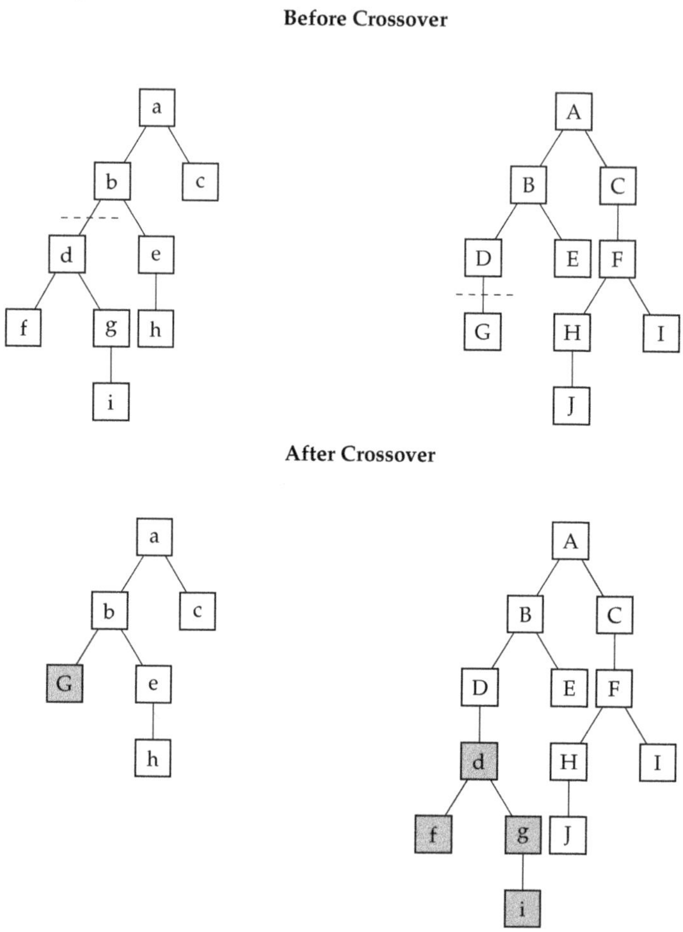

Figure 6. In tree crossover, two random subtrees are selected and swapped.

The crossover on the list of variables is carried out the same way as it is on the whole program (see Figure 4). Like in expression tree crossover, the whole lists can also be exchanged if the crossover point appears before the first element of the list.

4.3. Mutation

The children obtained as a result of the crossover are mutated with the probability p_{mutation} (see Line 16 in Algorithm 2). If the child is selected for mutation, one component of one line of its code is picked up randomly and mutated in the following manner:

- The line type is randomly replaced by one of the six possible choices.
- The parameter *bodyLen* is randomly replaced with the number between 2 and the maximum allowed number of statements within a control statement body.
- In the expression tree, a randomly selected node (not deeper than mutation depth—see Table 2) is mutated as described below.
- The parameter macro index is replaced by a randomly chosen index.
- In the list of variables, a randomly selected variable is replaced by another randomly picked up variable.

The mutation of a node in an expression tree consists of two operations. First, the terminal code is replaced by a randomly selected element from the list of variables and constants.

Second, the non-terminal code is replaced by a randomly selected element from the list of functions and operators. If the newly selected function or operator needs more arguments, additional random subtrees are generated to support them. Finally, we toggle the type of the node (i.e., terminal or non-terminal) with the toggle terminal probability (see Table 2).

4.4. Replacement and Stopping

After the genetic operations have been completed, we replace the whole population except for the elite (see Table 2) with the obtained children. If the fitness of the best individual in the population drops to zero or the fitness does not change for 600 generations (see Table 2), the evolution stops. Otherwise, the evolution continues until the maximum number of generations has been reached.

5. Experiment Setup

Given that we aim to evolve our programs from the ground up, without using any a priori knowledge about the solution structure, we conjectured that the problem set for our experiment should consist mainly of basic, with some intermediate, programming problems. We constructed the problem set using assignments from the introductory programming course at our university, selecting 35 different problems to test our approach. The selection of problems themselves including the sets of operators and functions/macros used must be diverse enough to push our approach to its limits—both lower (no success) and upper (100% success rate). At the same time, most problems should fall within the intermediate range, with success rates in between.

Table 3 summarizes all the problems with the operators, functions, macros, and constants used to evolve the programs for their solutions. The number of arguments and return values for each problem is given in parentheses after the problem name. The functions mod, idiv, mul, and bigMul are safe modulo, integer division, and multiplication operators, respectively, with their definitions listed in Appendix A. The rest of the parameters were common to all the runs and are listed in Table 1.

Table 3. The problems used in our experiments.

Problem Name (No. of Input/Output Values)	Operators	Notes	Constants
absolute (1/1)	−, <	Absolute value of a number	0, 1
absoluteDifference (2/1)	−, <	Absolute difference of two numbers	0, 1
absoluteDifferencePlus (2/1)	+, <	No minus operator	0, 1
absoluteDifferencePlusMacro (2/1)	+, <	Utilize macro `if b > a: a, b = b, a`	0, 1
absoluteDifferencePlusSorted (2/1)	+, <	First argument not less than second	0, 1
collatz (1/1)	+, −, <, =, mul, mod, idiv	Length of Collatz sequence	0, 1, 2, 3
collatzMacro (1/1)	+, <, =	Utilize macro `a = a // 2 if a % 2 == 0 else a * 3 + 1`	0, 1
collatzStep (1/1)	+, <, =, mul, mod, idiv	The next number in Collatz sequence	0, 1, 2, 3
countDigits (1/1)	+, −, <, =, idiv	Number of digits in a natural number	0, 1, 10
exactDivision (2/1)	+, −, <, =	Integer division without remainder	0, 1
exactDivisionPlus (2/1)	+, <, =	No minus operator	0, 1

Table 3. *Cont.*

Problem Name (No. of Input/Output Values)	Notes		
	Operators		Constants
exactDivisionTimes (2/1)	+, <, =, mul	Utilize multiplication operator	0, 1
factorial (1/1)	−, <, bigMul	$n!$	0, 1
fibonacci (1/1)	+, <, =	n-th number of Fibonacci sequence	0, 1
fibonacciMacro (1/1)	+, <, =	Utilize macro `a, b = b, a`	0, 1
gcd (2/1)	−, <, =	Greatest common divisor	0, 1
gcdMacro (2/1)	<, mod	Utilize macro `a, b = b, a`	0
gcdModulo (2/1)	−, <, =, ∧, mod	Utilize modulo operator	0, 1
integerDivision (2/1)	+, −, <	Floor division, dismiss remainder	0, 1
integerDivisionRem (2/2)	+, −, <	Floor division, quotient and remainder	0, 1
lcm (2/1)	+, −, <, =, idiv, mul	Least common multiple	0, 1
lcmMacro1 (2/1)	+, −, <, =, idiv, mul	Utilize macro `if a > b: a = a - b`	0, 1
lcmMacro2 (2/1)	+, −, <, =, idiv, mul	Utilize macro `a = a - b`	0, 1
lcmMacro4 (2/1)	+, −, <, =, idiv, mul	Utilize macro `a, b = b, a`	0, 1
max2 (2/1)	<	Larger of two numbers	0, 1
max3 (3/1)	<	Largest of three numbers	0, 1
multiplication (2/1)	+, −, <, =	Product of two integers	0, 1
multiplicationNonneg (2/1)	+, −, <, =	Nonnegative integers	0, 1
prime (1/1)	+, <, =, mod	Test primality of a number	0, 1, 2
primeMacro (1/1)	+, <, =, mod	Utilize macro `if mod(a, b) == 0: c = 0`	0, 1, 2
properDivisors (1/1)	+, −, <, =, mod	Count proper divisors	0, 1
properDivisorsMacro (1/1)	+, −, <, =, mod	Utilize macro `if mod(a, b) == 0: c = c + 1`	0, 1
remainder (2/1)	−, <, =	Remainder of floor division	0, 1
sort (2/2)	<	Sort two numbers	0, 1
triangularNumber (1/1)	+, <, =	Sum of natural numbers from 1 to n	0, 1

For the most part, Table 3 is self-explanatory. There are, however, some points that need further explanation. The problems with the same names but different suffixes evolved under the same conditions, the only difference being the set of used operators, functions, and macros. For instance, *absoluteDifference* and *absoluteDifferencePlus* differ only in that the first uses the subtraction and the other the addition operator. Or, `fibonacci` and `fibonacciMacro` differ in that the second uses a macro that swaps the values of two variables (for the reader unfamiliar with Python, it might be useful to know that the code `a, b = b, a` swaps the values of the variables `a` and `b`.). Whenever we use a macro as the building block for the solution, the used macro is listed in Python format in the Notes column. Notice that some macros could also be implemented as functions without affecting the results.

6. Results and Discussion

We performed 1000 evolution runs for each program from the previous section using 20 2.66 GHz Core i5 (four cores per CPU) machines, which took 3 weeks of computing time. Table 4 lists the percentages of successful evolution runs for each program, with the average number of needed generations (averaged over successful runs only) and estimated program complexity. We calculated the Halstead metrics for the hand-written programs, and we list in the table programming effort (E), program difficulty (D), and intelligence content (I). The calculated complexity measures generally agree with the evolution success rate. One notable exception is the gcdModulo (greatest common divisor) function using the modulo operator. The success rate is surprisingly high with extremely high values of the E and D measures and a relatively high I measure. When we looked deeper into the matter, we discovered an error by one of our researchers. Namely, his version was a brute force gcd algorithm trying divisions with all integers between 1 and the smaller of the two parameters, which resulted in unreasonably high complexity measures. The evolution came up with a much smarter version of the algorithm, which, after removing the statements with no effect and replacing the for and break statements with the while loop, looks like this:

```
def gcdModulo(x, y):
   while y > 0:
      tmp = x
      x = y
      y = tmp % y
   return x
```

Halstead complexity measures for the above function are $E = 640$, $D = 10.40$, and $I = 5.92$, which better agrees with the evolution success rate for that function.

Table 4 also shows that using a macro for coding a part of the solution invariably increases the success rate. That was, of course, expected, because including an appropriate building block necessarily decreases the algorithm complexity. That way, we can successfully evolve more complex algorithms that would otherwise defy evolution. For example, we could not evolve the collatz function because of the high complexity. We were, however, able to evolve collatzStep function with high probability and then use this function to evolve collatzMacro. We observed a similar situation with the functions absoluteDifferencePlus, sort, and absoluteDifferencePlusMacro. Indeed, any macro utilized in our experiments is sufficiently straightforward that we could evolve it effectively as a function. The next step in such cases would be to automatize the definition of a helper function and its use in the same evolutionary process. The idea of *automatically defined functions* (ADFs) has already been introduced in [1] as a way of reusing code in genetic programming but has not received very much attention [36,37]. The solutions are limited to tree-formed GP and impose serious constraints on the genetic operators, as different branches are not allowed to directly exchange genetic material, leaving this question an important open research issue.

We carried out additional experiments using a different set of operators not shown in Table 4. In some cases, fewer operators increased the success rate significantly. For example, removing the less than operator from the Fibonacci function increased the success rate to 27.4%, and removing the minus operator from the countDigits function increased it to 26.7%. Both results are significant with p-value $p = 0.01$. Removing the equality, minus and conjunction operators, and the constant value 1 from the gcdModulo function did not change the success rate but dropped the average number of generations to 339, which was also a statistically significant result with $p = 0.01$. In some other cases, we also observed some improvement although not statistically significant. Those improvements could be attributed to the smaller search space we created with fewer building blocks. Generally, the search space dimension increases exponentially with the number of building blocks [7]. It is difficult to say how strong the influence of certain superfluous operators is. Still, at least the operators that can be replaced by the ones already included in the set should be removed. For example, one does not need less than and greater than operators in the same set. Usually, even equality or inequality operators are extra in conjunction with the less-than operator. By the same token, we observed that often more learning samples give better results. One possible explanation is that more samples increase the resolution of the search space, making it easier to descend towards the minimum.

Table 4. Proportions of solved problems (1000 runs) with an average number of generations and Halsteas metrics. To calculate the average number of fitness evaluations, multiply the number of generations by the population size (1000). Since each fitness evaluation involves running a program on all the input/output pairs in the training data array, the actual number of program executions is 20 times larger, corresponding to the length of the training data array.

Program Name	Program Complexity E	D	I	Success Rate (%)	Avg. Number of Generations
absolute	269	8.75	3.52	100.0	6
max2	301	8.17	4.51	100.0	11
absoluteDifference	403	9.33	4.62	100.0	23
sort	484	10.50	4.39	100.0	32
max3	596	10.00	5.96	99.7	65
gcdMacro				90.0	404
collatzStep	694	10.00	6.94	87.7	259
collatzMacro				71.3	515
gcdModulo	2337	19.50	6.15	61.6	619
absoluteDifferencePlusSorted	768	10.50	6.96	36.0	562
primeMacro				26.7	571
lcmMacro1				22.0	796
remainder	637	13.50	3.50	21.0	650
absoluteDifferencePlusMacro				20.6	619
countDigits	715	11.0	5.91	19.7	853
fibonacciMacro				17.1	1186
prime	1054	12.83	6.40	16.7	801
exactDivisionTimes	781	10.83	6.65	16.0	799
triangularNumber	684	10.80	5.86	9.8	747
integerDivision	873	11.67	6.42	8.4	692
exactDivision	693	10.00	6.93	6.4	806
fibonacci	868	9.71	9.20	6.3	1584
multiplicationNonneg	873	11.67	6.42	4.6	622
properDivisorsMacro				2.4	1441
integerDivisionRem	811	10.83	6.91	2.2	1098
lcmMacro2				2.2	1043
exactDivisionPlus	856	10.29	8.09	2.1	643
factorial	880	13.00	5.21	1.3	1947
gcd	2346	26.67	3.27	1.6	895
lcm	2166	20.00	5.42	0.9	714
absoluteDifferencePlus	1848	16.67	6.65	0.0	N/A
collatz	3164	24.29	5.37	0.0	N/A
multiplication	2667	20.58	6.29	0.0	N/A
properDivisors	1636	16.50	6.01	0.0	N/A

Another noteworthy observation is that some of the evolutions appear to have huge jumps in fitness value, while the majority exhibit a more or less steady drop. Figure 7 shows the convergence of Fibonacci and factorial functions in which significant drops can be observed. Interestingly, these drops happen in different runs at approximately the same levels as the graphs show (notice the suggested horizontal lines formed by the alignment of graphs). On the other hand, functions in Figure 8 show more steady convergence, although here, one also observes lots of sudden drops that stem from the highly nonlinear nature of the search process caused by the destructive nature of genetic operators in linear GP [2,4]. The more severe fitness drops in Figure 7 are caused by a coarse fitness landscape. Namely, Fibonacci and factorial values are positioned far apart, while values obtained from, for instance, multiplication cover the space more evenly.

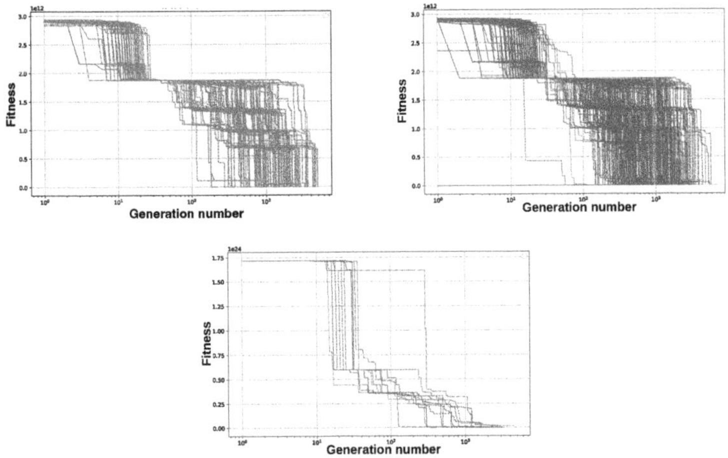

Figure 7. Convergence of functions fibonacci, FibonacciMacro, and factorial.

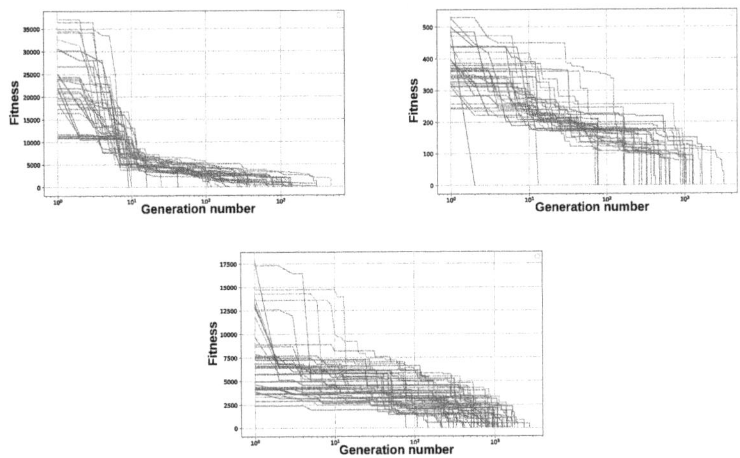

Figure 8. Convergence of functions multiplication, exactDivisionPlus, and gcd.

We already looked at a specific evolved program (for finding the greatest common divisor) at the beginning of this section where the evolution came up with quite a cunning solution. Of course, we discovered more similarly interesting solutions. The following one is the program that counts the number of proper divisors.

```
def properDivisorsMacro(n):
   count = 0
   div = 1
   x1 = 0
   x2 = 1
   x2 += 1
   while x2 <= n:
      if n % div == 0: count += 1
      if x1 % 2 == 0: div += 1
      x2 += div
      x1 += 1
   return count
```

We removed from the original program all the statements with no side effects, renamed the variables, and made some other minor changes so the program is more human-readable. We retained, however, the basic idea behind the solution, which is quite fascinating. Namely, if one wants to count all proper divisors of n, one does not need to try divisions by numbers greater than $\sqrt{n}$. And that is exactly what the above program is doing—instead of trying divisions with numbers greater than $\sqrt{n}$, it counts each division with numbers in the (left–closed and right–open) interval $[2, \sqrt{n})$ twice. Of course, the program would not have to try each division twice but only count them. It is, nevertheless, an interesting solution.

It is easy to see in the above program that each division with numbers greater than one is carried out twice. But does the process stop at $\sqrt{n}$? Notice that variable $x2$, responsible for halting the program, starts with 2 $(= 1 + 1)$. Then, we have

$$x2 = 2\sum_{k=1}^{n-1} + n = n^2.$$

We made some more similar observations. For example, in a program that detects primes, the division was first tried by two, then only with odd numbers smaller than the number tested. Certainly, all these observations took some serious looking because evolved programs are generally quite obscure and often follow confusing logic with many redundant operations, but they are by no means wrong. One possible direct application of these programs would be software obfuscation. Let us conclude this section with an example of an unedited function returning the $x0$th number of a Fibonacci sequence:

```
def fibonacci(x0):
   x1=x2=x3=x4=0
   x4=x2==x1
   x2=x4+x1
   for i in range(100):
      if x0+x3<x0<x0: break
      x4=x4
      x3=x3==x4==x0+x2
   x3=x2==x3
   for i in range(100):
      if x3==x0: break
      x4=x4
      x1=x2
      x2=x4+x2
      x3=1+x3
      x4=x1
      pass
   return x4
```

7. Conclusions

In this paper, we studied the possibility of evolving imperative computer programs that are not purely expression-oriented but allow for the linear sequence of statements. Specifically, we evolved Python programs. The basis for our work is a special gene-encoding approach combining linear sequences of statements and trees encoding expressions. Because the program population is spawned randomly, it is important to prevent infinite loops. Therefore, we encoded the while statement as the for loop with a break. The iterator of the for loop serves as a safety net setting the upper limit on the number of iterations, while the break statement contains the actual loop condition. We tried in our experiments to evolve different simple programs for which we also calculated Halstead metrics. As expected, we had less success with programs with higher complexity measures, or at least the evolution lasted more generations. We observed that increasing the number of used operators or decreasing the number of training samples could hinder the evolution, often with statistical significance. Whenever we added a useful prefabricated building block (in the form of a macro) to genetic material, the evolution results were better. Specifically, the success rates for the next number of the Collatz sequence calculation and the sequence length counting using a macro were quite high. In contrast, the evolution of the sequence length counting alone was unsuccessful. That leads to the possibility of augmenting the fitness function to support automatically defined functions in the same evolution for more complex tasks, which we feel is an important open research question. Last, we observed some smart solutions evolved by our approach that went beyond a simple brute force approach. It is important to point out that those solutions appeared without being explicitly enforced by the fitness function. We believe that with additional fitness criteria that would favor more efficient solutions, we could obtain more optimal programs. There is also room for improvement in several other directions. For example, incorporating array processing would be an enormous step towards more useful programs.

In conclusion, we believe our paper is an important step that will hopefully motivate further research in this direction. Although the advent of large language models may make the GP approach seem outdated, it is important to emphasize that the pure evolutionary approach operates at a fundamentally different level of computation. While it is lower in abstraction than higher-level computational methods, it is by no means inferior in significance.

Author Contributions: Conceptualization, I.F. and Ž.R.; methodology, J.P.; software, Ž.R. and M.K.; validation, J.P., Á.B. and T.T.; formal analysis, Á.B.; investigation, M.K. and J.P.; resources, S.T.; data curation, I.F., M.K. and Ž.R.; writing—original draft preparation, I.F.; writing—review and editing, Ž.R.; visualization, I.F.; supervision, T.T. and Á.B.; project administration, T.T. and S.T.; funding acquisition, S.T. All authors have read and agreed to the published version of the manuscript.

Funding: This research was funded by the Slovenian Research and Innovation Agency (Javna agencija za znanstvenoraziskovalno in inovacijsko dejavnost Republike Slovenije) through the program P2-0246 (ICT4QoL—Information and Communications Technologies for Quality of Life).

Data Availability Statement: Data are contained within the article.

Conflicts of Interest: The authors declare no conflicts of interest. The funders had no role in the design of the study; in the collection, analyses, or interpretation of data; in the writing of the manuscript; or in the decision to publish the results.

Appendix A. Functions Used in Evolution

This appendix lists all the functions that we used as building blocks for the programs to be evolved. The functions implement basic mathematical operators with built-in safety mechanisms that guard against undesired scenarios like division by zero or multiplication overflow.

```
def mod(x, y):            #Safe modulo
    if y == 0: return 1   #Prevent division by zero
    return x % y

def idiv(x, y):           #Safe floor division
    if y == 0: return 0   #Prevent division by zero
    return x // y

def mul(x, y):            #Limited multiplication
    if x * y > 10000: return 10000
    if x * y < -10000: return -10000
    else: return x * y

def bigMul(x, y):         #Limited multiplication
    if x * y > 100000000000000: return 100000000000000
    if x * y < -100000000000000: return -100000000000000
    else: return x * y
```

References

1. Koza, J.R. *Genetic Programming: On the Programming of Computers by Means of Natural Selection*; MIT Press: Cambridge, MA, USA, 1992.
2. Yampolskiy, R.V. Why We Do Not Evolve Software? Analysis of Evolutionary Algorithms. *Evol. Bioinform.* **2018**, *14*, 1176934318815906. [CrossRef]
3. Romera-Paredes, B.; Barekatain, M.; Novikov, A.; Balog, M.; Kumar, M.P.; Dupont, E.; Ruiz, F.J.R.; Ellenberg, J.S.; Wang, P.; Fawzi, O.; et al. Mathematical discoveries from program search with large language models. *Nature* **2023**, *625*, 468–475. [CrossRef] [PubMed]
4. Woodward, J.; Bai, R. Why evolution is not a good paradigm for program induction: A critique of genetic programming. In Proceedings of the first ACM/SIGEVO Summit on Genetic and Evolutionary Computation, Shanghai, China, 12–14 June 2009; pp. 593–600. [CrossRef]
5. Teller, A. Turing completeness in the language of genetic programming with indexed memory. In Proceedings of the First IEEE Conference on Evolutionary Computation. IEEE World Congress on Computational Intelligence, Orlando, FL, USA, 27–29 June 1994; Volume 1, pp. 136–141. [CrossRef]
6. Banzhaf, W.; Francone, F.D.; Keller, R.E.; Nordin, P. *Genetic Programming: An Introduction: On the Automatic Evolution of Computer Programs and Its Applications*; Morgan Kaufmann Publishers Inc.: San Francisco, CA, USA, 1998.
7. Brameier, M.F.; Banzhaf, W. *Linear Genetic Programming*; Springer: New York, NY, USA, 2007. [CrossRef]
8. Fajfar, I.; Puhan, J.; Bűrmen, Á. Evolving a Nelder-Mead Algorithm for Optimization with Genetic Programming. *Evol. Comput.* **2016**, *25*, 351–373. [CrossRef] [PubMed]
9. Cramer, N.L. A representation for the adaptive generation of simple sequential programs. In Proceedings of the First International Conference on Genetic Algorithms and Their Applications, Pittsburgh, PA, USA, 24–26 July 1985; Psychology Press: London, UK, 1985; Volume 183, p. 187.
10. Augusto, D.A.; Barbosa, H.J.C. Symbolic regression via genetic programming. In Proceedings of the Sixth Brazilian Symposium on Neural Networks, Rio de Janeiro, Brazil, 25 November 2000; Volume 1, pp. 173–178. [CrossRef]
11. Icke, I.; Bongard, J.C. Improving genetic programming based symbolic regression using deterministic machine learning. In Proceedings of the 2013 IEEE Congress on Evolutionary Computation, Cancun, Mexico, 20–23 June 2013; pp. 1763–1770. [CrossRef]
12. Evans, B.; Al-Sahaf, H.; Xue, B.; Zhang, M. Evolutionary Deep Learning: A Genetic Programming Approach to Image Classification. In Proceedings of the 2018 IEEE Congress on Evolutionary Computation (CEC), Rio de Janeiro, Brazil, 8–13 July 2018; pp. 1–6. [CrossRef]
13. Bi, Y.; Xue, B.; Zhang, M. *Genetic Programming for Image Classification: An Automated Approach to Feature Learning*; Springer: Berlin/Heidelberg, Germany, 2021. [CrossRef]
14. Najaran, M.H.T. A genetic programming-based convolutional deep learning algorithm for identifying COVID-19 cases via X-ray images. *Artif. Intell. Med.* **2023**, *142*, 102571. [CrossRef]
15. Bakurov, I.; Castelli, M.; Scotto di Freca, A.; Vanneschi, L.; Fontanella, F. A novel binary classification approach based on geometric semantic genetic programming. *Swarm Evol. Comput.* **2021**, *69*, 101028. [CrossRef]
16. Espejo, P.G.; Ventura, S.; Herrera, F. A Survey on the Application of Genetic Programming to Classification. *IEEE Trans. Syst. Man Cybern. Part C Appl. Rev.* **2010**, *40*, 121–144. [CrossRef]
17. Dara, O.A.; Lopez-Guede, J.M.; Raheem, H.I.; Rahebi, J.; Zulueta, E.; Fernandez-Gamiz, U. Alzheimer's Disease Diagnosis Using Machine Learning: A Survey. *Appl. Sci.* **2023**, *13*, 8298. [CrossRef]

18. Rovito, L.; Bonin, L.; Manzoni, L.; De Lorenzo, A. An Evolutionary Computation Approach for Twitter Bot Detection. *Appl. Sci.* **2022**, *12*, 5915. [CrossRef]
19. Muni, D.; Pal, N.; Das, J. Genetic programming for simultaneous feature selection and classifier design. *IEEE Trans. Syst. Man Cybern. Part B Cybern.* **2006**, *36*, 106–117. [CrossRef]
20. Oğuz, K.; Bor, A. Prediction of Local Scour around Bridge Piers Using Hierarchical Clustering and Adaptive Genetic Programming. *Appl. Artif. Intell.* **2022**, *36*, 2001734. [CrossRef]
21. Alturky, S.; Toma, G. A Metaheuristic Optimization Algorithm for Solving Higher-Order Boundary Value Problems. *Int. J. Appl. Metaheuristic Comput.* **2022**, *13*, 1–17. [CrossRef]
22. Sobania, D.; Schmitt, J.; Köstler, H.; Rothlauf, F. Genetic programming for iterative numerical methods. *Genet. Program. Evolvable Mach.* **2022**, *23*, 253–278. [CrossRef]
23. Brablc, M.; Žegklitz, J.; Grepl, R.; Babuska, R. Control of Magnetic Manipulator Using Reinforcement Learning Based on Incrementally Adapted Local Linear Models. *Complexity* **2021**, *2021*, 6617309. [CrossRef]
24. García, C.A.; Velasco, M.; Angulo, C.; Marti, P.; Camacho, A. Revisiting Classical Controller Design and Tuning with Genetic Programming. *Sensors* **2023**, *23*, 9731. [CrossRef] [PubMed]
25. Beşkirli, A.; Dağ, İ. An efficient tree seed inspired algorithm for parameter estimation of Photovoltaic models. *Energy Rep.* **2022**, *8*, 291–298. [CrossRef]
26. Beşkirli, A.; Dağ, İ. A new binary variant with transfer functions of Harris Hawks Optimization for binary wind turbine micrositing. *Energy Rep.* **2020**, *6*, 668–673. [CrossRef]
27. Beşkirli, A.; Dağ, İ. Parameter extraction for photovoltaic models with tree seed algorithm. *Energy Rep.* **2023**, *9*, 174–185. [CrossRef]
28. Beskirli, A.; Özdemir, D.; Temurtas, H. A comparison of modified tree–seed algorithm for high-dimensional numerical functions. *Neural Comput. Appl.* **2020**, *32*, 6877–6911. [CrossRef]
29. Zhan, R.; Zhang, J.; Cui, Z.; Peng, J.; Li, D. An Automatic Heuristic Design Approach for Seru Scheduling Problem with Resource Conflicts. *Discret. Dyn. Nat. Soc.* **2021**, *2021*, 8166343. [CrossRef]
30. Xu, M.; Mei, Y.; Zhang, F.; Zhang, M. Genetic Programming and Reinforcement Learning on Learning Heuristics for Dynamic Scheduling: A Preliminary Comparison. *IEEE Comput. Intell. Mag.* **2024**, *19*, 18–33. [CrossRef]
31. Mahmood, M.T. Defocus Blur Segmentation Using Genetic Programming and Adaptive Threshold. *Comput. Mater. Contin.* **2022**, *70*, 4867–4882. [CrossRef]
32. Correia, J.; Rodriguez-Fernandez, N.; Vieira, L.; Romero, J.; Machado, P. Towards Automatic Image Enhancement with Genetic Programming and Machine Learning. *Appl. Sci.* **2022**, *12*, 2212. [CrossRef]
33. Wineberg, M.; Oppacher, F. The Benefits of Computing with Introns. In Proceedings of the First Annual Conference, Stanford, CA, USA, 28–31 July 1996; Koza, J.R., Goldberg, D.E., Fogel, D.B., Riolo, R.L., Eds.; Stanford University: Stanford, CA, USA, 1996; pp. 410–415. [CrossRef]
34. Abdelkhalik, O. Hidden Genes Genetic Optimization for Variable-Size Design Space Problems. *J. Optim. Theory Appl.* **2013**, *156*, 450–468. [CrossRef]
35. Baker, J.E. Adaptive Selection Methods for Genetic Algorithms. In Proceedings of the 1st International Conference on Genetic Algorithms, Pittsburgh, PA, USA, 24–26 July 1985; pp. 101–111.
36. Ferreira, C. Automatically Defined Functions in Problem Solving. In *Gene Expression Programming: Mathematical Modeling by an Artificial Intelligence*; Springer: Berlin/Heidelberg, Germany, 2006; pp. 233–273. [CrossRef]
37. Ferreira, C. Automatically Defined Functions in Gene Expression Programming. In *Genetic Systems Programming: Theory and Experiences*; Nedjah, N., Abraham, A., Macedo Mourelle, L.D., Eds.; Springer: Berlin/Heidelberg, Germany, 2006; Volume 13, pp. 21–56. [CrossRef]

symmetry

MDPI

Article

Enhancing NSGA-II Algorithm through Hybrid Strategy for Optimizing Maize Water and Fertilizer Irrigation Simulation

Jinyang Du [1], Renyun Liu [1,*], Du Cheng [2], Xu Wang [1], Tong Zhang [1] and Fanhua Yu [3]

[1] Department of Mathematics, Changchun Normal University, Changchun 130032, China; QX202200197@stu.ccsfu.edu.cn (J.D.); QX202200217@stu.ccsfu.edu.cn (X.W.); QX202200207@stu.ccsfu.edu.cn (T.Z.)
[2] School of Artificial Intelligence, Jilin University, Changchun 130012, China; DUGOCD@126.com
[3] Jilin Communications Polytechnic, Changchun 130015, China; yufanhua@163.com
* Correspondence: liurenyun@ccsfu.edu.cn

Abstract: In optimization problems, the principle of symmetry provides important guidance. This article introduces an enhanced NSGA-II algorithm, termed NDE-NSGA-II, designed for addressing multi-objective optimization problems. The approach employs Tent mapping for population initialization, thereby augmenting its search capability. During the offspring generation process, a hybrid local search strategy is implemented to augment the population's exploration capabilities. It is crucial to highlight that in elite selection, norm selection and average distance elimination strategies are adopted to strengthen the selection mechanism of the population. This not only enhances diversity but also ensures convergence, thereby improving overall performance. The effectiveness of the proposed NDE-NSGA-II is comprehensively evaluated across various benchmark functions with distinct true Pareto frontier shapes. The results consistently demonstrate that the NDE-NSGA-II method presented in this paper surpasses the performance metrics of the other five methods. Lastly, the algorithm is integrated with the DSSAT model to optimize maize irrigation and fertilization scheduling, confirming the effectiveness of the improved algorithm.

Keywords: NSGA-II; DSSAT model; local search; optimization of irrigation and fertilization

1. Introduction

In the real world, optimization problems frequently manifest as multi-objective optimization problems (MOPs), characterized by a set of conflicting objective functions [1–4]. MOPs are pervasive across numerous application domains, rendering research on intelligent algorithms for addressing MOPs a perennially active area of investigation [5–7]. In MOPs, improving one objective often worsens another, caused by conflicting objectives. In most cases, no single solution can optimize all the objectives at the same time, so the algorithm must find a set of trade-off solutions called the Pareto front (PF) [8,9].

A common challenge in MOPs is devising methods to swiftly attain a convergent solution while also achieving a more evenly distributed solution set [10,11]. To better solve more complex problems, in recent years, various multi-objective evolutionary algorithms (MOEA) have been proposed, including NSGA-II [12], MOEA/D [13], SPEA2 [14], and other algorithms. Since their inception, these algorithms have garnered immense attention from researchers due to their impressive global search performance, high-speed operational efficiency, and straightforward algorithmic framework. These multi-objective optimization algorithms are applied to agricultural models. Zhou and Fan [15] optimized the agricultural industry structure through a genetic-algorithm-based MOP to achieve sustainable development. Llera [16] et al. optimized control settings using the NSGA-II algorithm to help growers achieve maximum yield and minimize costs under greenhouse conditions. Cheng [17] et al. optimized the irrigation and fertilization plan for winter wheat by combining the NSGA-II algorithm with the DSSAT model. Song [18] et al. optimized the spring wheat irrigation plan using the AquaCrop model and NSGA-II algorithm. Liu and Yang [19] constructed a distributed AquaCrop model and NSGA-II for simulation optimization to develop effective irrigation plans. Despite the theoretical and experimental effectiveness of these classic algorithms, they exhibit significant shortcomings in practical applications, particularly regarding convergence speed and solution consistency. Specifically, when addressing high-dimensional and complex problems, the existing algorithms often require extended periods to achieve satisfactory solutions. In practical applications, rapid convergence is essential for conserving computational resources and time. Furthermore, the solutions generated by the current algorithms can vary significantly between different runs, leading to insufficient reliability. Ensuring solution consistency is crucial for maintaining the stability and reproducibility of results.

This article proposes an improved NSGA-II algorithm to address the aforementioned issues. In initializing the population, using the Tent mapping initialization method ensures a more unified initial solution, facilitates exploration of different regions, and enhances the initial searchability. In the adaptive elite selection strategy proposed in this article, in the early stage, the solutions with good convergence and diversity are selected based on norms to enhance convergence and maintain a certain degree of diversity. In the later stage, a selection method based on the average distance elimination strategy is adopted to evenly distribute the population on the Pareto front, which is beneficial for the diversity of the algorithm. Furthermore, within the offspring generation process, a mixed local search strategy is employed. This approach facilitates random updates of the solution between the optimal individual and neighboring individuals, thereby enhancing the solution's search capabilities. Subsequently, the algorithm was combined with the DSSAT [20–22] model to optimize irrigation and fertilization management during the maize growth cycle. The main contributions of this article are summarized as follows: (1) The initialization method of the Tent chaotic mapping was employed for initializing the population. (2) An adaptive elite selection strategy grounded in norm and average distance elimination was formulated to identify superior solutions. (3) A mixed local search strategy was added during the generation of offspring. (4) The algorithm was integrated with the DSSAT model to simulate agricultural scenarios, leading to the development of a successful irrigation and fertilization strategy.

The rest of this article is organized as follows. Section 2 introduces the NSGA-II and its related works. Section 3 provides a comprehensive description of the proposed NDE-NSGA-II, including the applied strategies and a complete framework. Section 4 conducted experiments on the benchmark function, evaluated the performance of NDE-NSGA-II, and discussed the experimental results in detail. Section 6 applies NDE-NSGA-II and the original algorithm to maize yield optimization, proving the feasibility of the algorithm proposed in this paper. Afterwards, the performance of the algorithm is discussed. Finally, this article provides a summary in the sixth section.

2. Related Works

2.1. Multi-Objective Algorithm NSGA-II

NSGA-II is developed based on NSGA, incorporating the principles of nondominated sorting and an elitism strategy. The algorithm calculates the neighborhood density of individuals using the crowding distance (CD). Selection operators for both fitness and diversity are employed to enhance the overall performance of the algorithm.

According to the nondominated sorting strategy of NSGA-II, as illustrated in Figure 1, suppose the population size is N, and Population R_t (with a size of $2N$) is formed by combining the current dominated solution set P_t and the current offspring Q_t. Following the dominance relation, R_t obtains a series of nondominated Pareto solution sets denoted as $F_1, F_2, \ldots$, where F_1 is at the top level. If the quantity of F1 is less than N, all members of F1 are selected into Population P_{t+1}. The remaining members in Population P_{t+1} are chosen from F_2, F_3, and so forth, until the total number of members reaches N. Notably, the order of the first member in F_3 is less than N, while the order of the last member is greater than N. To maintain population diversity, the NSGA-II algorithm employs CD sorting on F_3. Individuals with a larger CD are given priority to enter Population P_{t+1}. The CD calculation method is expressed in Formula (1).

$$n_d = \sum_{m=1}^{M} \frac{f_m(i+1) - f_m(i-1)}{f_m^{max} - f_m^{min}} \quad (1)$$

where f_m^{max} and f_m^{min} are the maximum and minimum of objective function f_m, m is the individual of the solution set, M represents the number of targets.

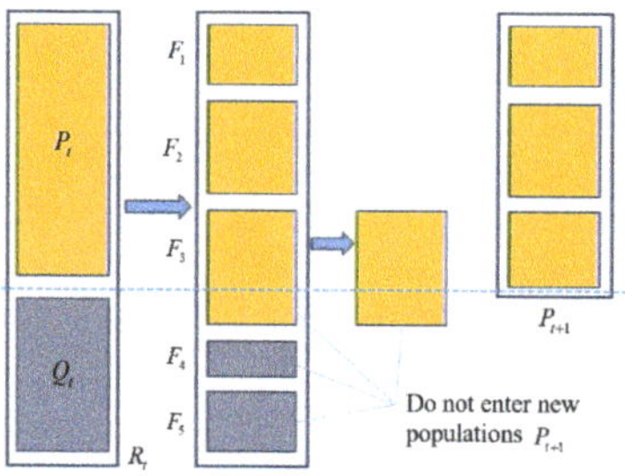

Figure 1. Nondominated sorting strategy of nondominated sorting genetic algorithm II [23] (NSGA-II).

2.2. Problems in CD Sorting of NSGA-II

Following the completion of nondominated sorting, the CD of each solution within the nondominated solution set at the same level is calculated based on the objective space. The CD of the extreme solution (either the maximum or minimum solution across all objectives within the objective space) is consistently set as infinity. For all other solutions, they are sorted based on all objectives, and their CD is defined as the average value of target distances between two adjacent solutions.

In Figure 2, considering eight nondominated solutions, five solutions were selected based on the CD. According to the CD sorting algorithm of NSGA-II, solutions 1, 2, 3, 4, and 8 are chosen. However, it is observed that after the selection, the results of Solutions 4 and 8 are deemed unreasonable due to the sparse distance between them.

Upon the preceding analysis, it is evident that the congestion distance mechanism employed by NSGA-II exhibits uneven distribution issues, potentially compromising the diversity of solutions. Consequently, we present an enhancement strategy for this mechanism in the subsequent section.

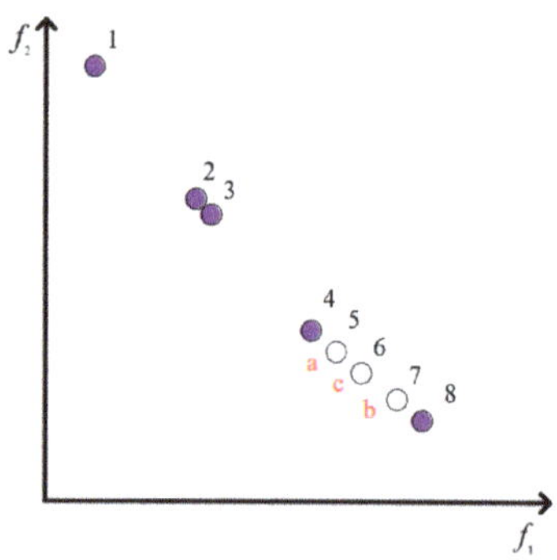

Figure 2. Screening results with NSGA-II. The numbers in the figure denote different individuals, and the letters indicate those that have been removed.

3. The Proposed NDE-NSGA-II

This section provides a comprehensive introduction to the proposed NDE-NSGA-II, with the main objective of enhancing the convergence and diversity of NSGA-II. Firstly, the initialization method of Tent mapping in chaotic mapping was adopted to generate a more uniform population during the initialization stage. Subsequently, a local search strategy and an adaptive elite selection mechanism were adopted to maintain convergence and diversity within the population, ensuring the balance of solutions. Then the overall workflow of NDE-NSGA-II was introduced, including these key enhancements to the traditional NSGA-II model. The overall framework is illustrated in Figure 3.

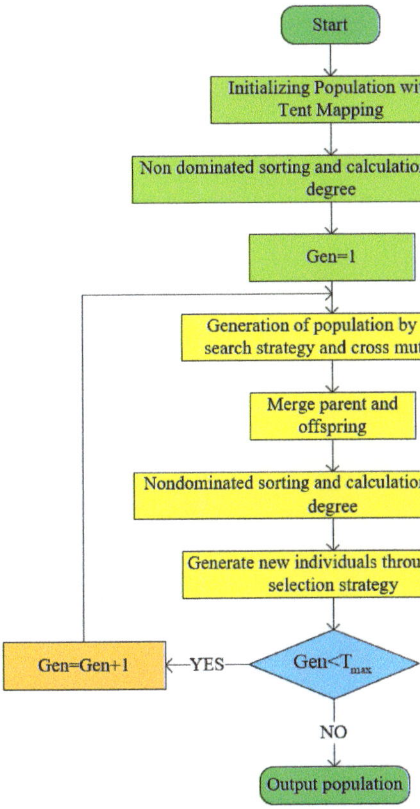

Figure 3. The flow chart of NDE-NSGA-II algorithm.

3.1. Initializing Population with Tent Mapping

Over the past few decades, chaotic mapping [24] has found extensive application across various fields, including parameter optimization, feature selection, and chaos control. The popularity of chaotic mapping arises from three distinctive properties inherent in chaotic mapping sequences: initial value sensitivity, ergodicity, and non-repeatability. Utilizing chaotic mapping in the initialization stage serves to mitigate repetition, fostering a more uniformly distributed initial population. This approach addresses challenges encountered by previous intelligent optimization algorithms during the initialization phase, consequently enhancing the diversity of the decision space. The Tent mapping in chaotic maps has been proven to be an effective initialization method [25].

This article employs the Tent mapping in chaotic mapping for initialization, and the method is outlined as follows:

$$Pop = lb + T(N, dim) \times (ub - lb) \tag{2}$$

In this context, Pop represents the initialized population, u_b and l_b denote the upper and lower bounds of the population, N signifies the number of populations, dim indicates the number of decision variables, and T represents the mapped random number. The formula for calculating T is as follows:

$$T_{n+1} = \begin{cases} \frac{T_n}{\alpha} & T_n < \alpha \\ \frac{1-T_n}{1-\alpha} & T_n \geq \alpha \end{cases} \tag{3}$$

Among them, $\alpha = 0.7$. The pseudocode for initializing the population is as shown in Algorithm 1.

Algorithm 1 Tent Chaos Initialization

Input: : population size N, decision variables dim, variable upper bound ub, variable lower bound lb
Output: : new population Pop

$\alpha = 0.7$ Tent chaos coefficient
$T = rand(N, dim)$ Random initialization population
for $i = 1 : N$ **do**
    for $j = 2 : dim$ **do**
        if $T_{i,j-1} < \alpha$ **then**
            $T_{i,j} = T_{i,j-1}/\alpha$
        else
            $T_{i,j} = (1 - T_{i,j-1})/(1 - \alpha)$
        end if
    end for
end for
$Pop = lb + T \times (ub - lb)$

3.2. Local Search Strategy

In NSGA-II, nondominated sorting is used to assign individuals to different Pareto levels. Utilizing this approach can bolster the algorithm's convergence; however, in instances where the optimization problem exhibits high complexity, it may suffer from inadequate optimization accuracy and susceptibility to local optima. Quadratic interpolation serves as a technique for locating the minimum value point of the objective function, a method previously demonstrated to enhance local exploration capabilities [26]. This paper advances the existing methods by introducing a hybrid local update strategy. In this strategy, particles undergo random updates positioned between the optimal individual and neighboring individuals. The formula for this update strategy is as follows:

$$X_i = \begin{cases} Y_i & \text{rand} < 0.3 \\ Z_i & \text{rand} > 0.3 \end{cases} \tag{4}$$

$$Y_{i,j} = 0.5 \times \frac{(X_{i,j}^2 - X_{m,j}^2) \times f_b + (X_{m,j}^2 - X_{b,j}^2) \times f_i + (X_{b,j}^2 - X_{i,j}^2) \times f_m}{(X_{i,j} - X_{m,j}) \times f_b + (X_{m,j} - X_{b,j}) \times f_i + (X_{b,j} - X_{i,j}) \times f_m} \tag{5}$$

Among these, $X_{i,j}$ represents the current particle, where $X_{m,j}$ and f_m denote the mean individual and fitness values of the j-th dimensional particle, respectively. Furthermore, f_b and $X_{b,j}$ represent random individuals and fitness values among those with Pareto level 1.

$$Z_{i,j} = \begin{cases} X_{i,j} + c_1 \times (X_{n,j} - X_{i,j}) \times (1 - \frac{t}{T})^2 & c_2 > 0.5 \\ X_{i,j} - c_1 \times (X_{n,j} - X_{i,j}) \times (1 - \frac{t}{T})^2 & c_2 < 0.5 \end{cases} \tag{6}$$

c_1 and c_2 are random numbers sampled from the interval [0,1], where t denotes the current iteration number, T represents the maximum iteration number, and $X_{n,j}$ refers to the neighboring individual of the current individual. The above two formulas demonstrate symmetry. The formula is as follows:

$$X_{n,j} = rand(1 - sin(\frac{2t}{T} \times \pi)) \times X_{i,j} \tag{7}$$

In the aforementioned update strategies, individuals constituting 0.4 N are selected for local updates. The pseudocode for a local search is as shown in Algorithm 2.

Algorithm 2 The local searching strategy

Input: : individuals at boundary and center points POp, offspring size N
Output: : population determined by local algorithm Nnf

```
for i = 1 : N do
    Randomly select an individual X from Pop
    index=rand(dim)
    x=X_index
    Conduct local updates based on Formula (4).
    X_index=x_new
end for
Nnf=Pop
```

3.3. Convergence and Diversity Measures

The NSGA-II algorithm utilizes the Pareto dominance method for solution selection, effectively maintaining convergence. However, the selection of solutions from the last layer can impact the algorithm's convergence and diversity during elite selection. To address this, the article introduces enhancements to the elite selection strategy. The convergence degree of each solution in population P is assessed using the p-norm value of the objective vector:

$$Norm(x) = \| F(x)^n \|_p = \sum_{i=1}^{M} (f_i^n(x)^p)^{(1/p)} \tag{8}$$

where $F_n(x)$ is the objective vector of solution x after the normalization and M is the number of objectives. The most commonly used norm values are $p = 1$ and $p = 2$. In this context, we opt for $p = 2$. A smaller $Norm$ value of solution x indicates its better convergence performance.

In the initial stages of population iteration, to guarantee that the algorithm can sustain both convergence and substantial diversity, the formula for selecting based on the norm and crowding distance is as follows:

$$f(x) = -Norm(x) \times \alpha + CD(x) \times \beta \tag{9}$$

Among them, $a = 0.8, b = 0.2$.

The smaller $Norm(x)$, the better, and the larger $CD(x)$, the better. Therefore, a larger $f(x)$ is better. Based on this, when selecting a solution, we choose a larger $f(x)$.

The NSGA-II algorithm ensures diversity through a crowding distance strategy. However, as previously discussed, when the distance between two individuals is very close, and the crowding distance is large, this method may struggle to effectively preserve population diversity. This article introduces a strategy based on the balance of the distance between individuals. Initially, the individual with the smaller crowding distance among two individuals with the closest distance is eliminated. This process is repeated sequentially until the desired number of populations is reached. Illustrated in Figure 4, the initial elimination includes individual 3, followed by the sequential elimination of individuals 5 and 7. The final selection comprises individuals 1, 2, 4, 6, and 8, resulting in a more uniform distance between populations and better preservation of diversity.

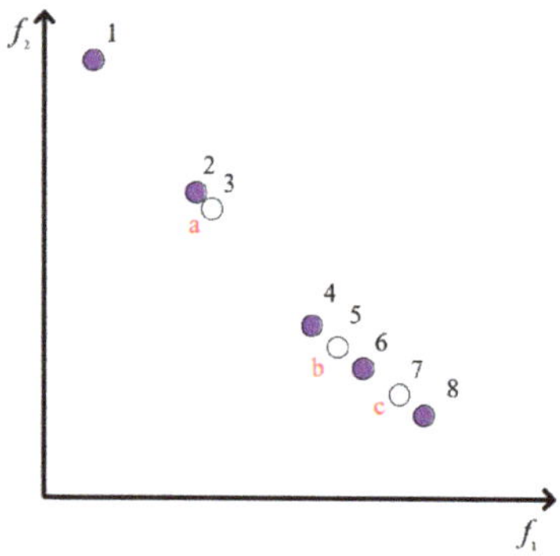

Figure 4. Screening results with average distance elimination method. The numbers in the figure denote different individuals, and the letters indicate those that have been removed.

This article employs the following formula to determine whether to conduct convergence analysis or diversity analysis:

$$P = M \times (r_a - \frac{(r_a - r_b) \times t}{T} \times \frac{n}{N}) \tag{10}$$

Among these variables, M represents the number of targets, with the values of r_a and b_a set to 0.8 and 0.3, respectively. n denotes the count of individuals with Pareto level 1 within the population, while N represents the total number of populations. The pseudocode for convergence and diversity is presented in Algorithm 3.

Algorithm 3 Elitist selection

Input: population size N, combined population *combine_X*, adaptive probability P
Output: updated population X

```
X = 0
current_N = 0
for i=1 : max_rank do
    current_N = size(combine_X_i)
    if current_N ≤ N then
        X = X + combine_X_i
    else
        remain_N = N − current_N
        if rand < P then
            Update individuals according to Equation (9)
        else
            while size(combine_X_i)! = remain_N do
                Sort(combine_X_i)    Sort based on the distance of each individual
                delete(min(combine_X_i)))
            end while
            X = X + combine_X_i
        end if
    end if
end for
```

4. Algorithm Comparison

In this section, a set of diverse benchmark tests was conducted to evaluate the performance of NDE-NSGA-II across ZDT [27] to DTLZ [28] functions. The experimental results involved a comparison with four well-established algorithms, NSGA-II, CDE-NSGA-II [23], MOEA/D, and SPEA2, alongside a novel algorithm, CMWOA [29], which incorporates a competition mechanism.

4.1. Indicators for Evaluation

Firstly, this section introduces commonly used indicators for evaluating algorithm performance. In the realm of multi-objective problems (MOPs), the Pareto front (PF) is a crucial concept. Essentially, PF reflects the quality of the Pareto set obtained by the algorithm. The properties of Pareto sets can be described in terms of convergence, diffusion, and uniformity [30], where diffusion and uniformity are denoted as diversity.

To evaluate convergence, this article adopts the indicator GD+ [31], which can be seen as an improvement on the calculation method of the change in distance of the indicator GD. It can better evaluate the convergence degree of the solution than GD. The smaller the value of GD+, the better the solution set.

In terms of diversity, the CPF [32] value is chosen as the performance indicator, with the main idea of projecting the m-dimensional solution onto the M-1 dimensional space. The Pareto set with better diversity results in a higher CPF value.

HV [33] is a comprehensive evaluation indicator for multi-objective optimization algorithms that are sensitive to advantageous relationships. Once a solution set advances in dominance, HV returns a higher value. Meanwhile, due to the important position of dominance in the Pareto set, HV also reflects other performances to a certain extent.

Beyond the aforementioned metrics, we also deliberated on the quantity of offspring discarded or generated by each algorithm within the mutation strategy.

4.2. Convergence Evaluation of Different Algorithms on ZDT and DTLZ Test Problems

Table 1 displays the average GD+ values, accompanied by standard deviations (in parentheses), for the four algorithms, with optimal values highlighted in bold font. Furthermore, a Wilcoxon rank-sum test was performed at a significance level of 0.05. Symbols such as "+", "−", and "=" in the final row denote whether the respective algorithm is significantly superior, significantly inferior, or similar to the proposed NDE-NSGA-II.

Table 1 illustrates that for GD+, NDE-NSGA-II achieved superior results in 5 instances, while NSGA-II, MOEA/D, SPEA, CDE-NSAG-II, and CMWOA secured 1, 3, 0, 0 and 3 best results, respectively. Notably, referencing the information in Table 1, it can be inferred that the proposed NDE-NSGA-II is well-suited for addressing problems with a non-uniform search space and local Pareto front, as observed in ZDT4, ZDT6, DTLZ1, and DTLZ2. However, when confronted with Pareto front problems featuring discrete features like ZDT3 and DTLZ7, NDE-NSGA-II exhibits a comparatively poorer performance. Moreover, results from Wilcoxon's rank-sum test demonstrate that NDE-NSGA-II significantly outperforms the other three methods in more than half of the 12 benchmark functions. This indicates that the NDE-NSGA-II algorithm proposed in this paper emerges as a competitive and effective solution.

Table 1. GD+ values of the proposed NDE-NSGA-II and three multi-objective algorithms.

	D	NSGA-II	MOEA/D	SPEA2	CDE-NSGA-II	CMWOA	NDE-NSGA-II
ZDT1	30	1.1801×10^{-2} $(2.56 \times 10^{-3})-$	7.5242×10^{-2} $(3.78 \times 10^{-2})-$	1.4196×10^{-2} $(2.63 \times 10^{-3})-$	8.8438×10^{-3} $(8.28 \times 10^{-4})-$	3.6228×10^{-4} $(1.09 \times 10^{-4})+$	6.5618×10^{-4} (1.92×10^{-4})
ZDT2	30	1.3028×10^{-2} $(3.38 \times 10^{-3})-$	2.1120×10^{-3} $(2.21 \times 10^{-3})-$	1.1928×10^{-2} $(4.24 \times 10^{-3})-$	1.2578×10^{-2} $(1.77 \times 10^{-3})-$	2.5870×10^{-4} $(1.12 \times 10^{-4})-$	2.2736×10^{-4} (8.81×10^{-5})
ZDT3	30	6.2900×10^{-3} $(4.67 \times 10^{-3})-$	7.5059×10^{-2} $(2.67 \times 10^{-2})-$	1.6723×10^{-3} $(9.49 \times 10^{-3})+$	6.5377×10^{-3} $(5.17 \times 10^{-4})-$	2.1435×10^{-4} $(6.90 \times 10^{-5})+$	3.0208×10^{-3} (2.86×10^{-4})
ZDT4	10	2.7336×10^{-3} $(1.39 \times 10^{-3})-$	1.9089×10^{-2} $(1.82 \times 10^{-2})-$	1.8403×10^{-1} $(1.19 \times 10^{-1})-$	7.2919×10^{-5} $(3.80 \times 10^{-5})=$	2.6171×10^{-1} $(2.05 \times 10^{-1})-$	6.6700×10^{-5} (4.22×10^{-5})
ZDT6	10	5.9099×10^{-2} $(2.59e \times 10^{-2})-$	7.6242×10^{-2} $(2.50 \times 10^{-2})-$	5.8502×10^{-2} $(2.86 \times 10^{-2})-$	1.4148×10^{-1} $(4.90 \times 10^{-2})-$	1.5845×10^{-1} $(1.67 \times 10^{-2})-$	2.4991×10^{-4} (1.47×10^{-4})
DTLZ1	7	1.5090×10^{-2} $(6.28 \times 10^{-2})-$	3.2258×10^{-3} $(1.73 \times 10^{-3})-$	1.1246×10^{-1} $(1.84 \times 10^{-1})-$	$.6833 \times 10^{-2}$ $(8.51 \times 10^{-2})-$	5.6172×10^{-1} $(5.34 \times 10^{-1})-$	2.4667×10^{-3} (1.16×10^{-3})
DTLZ2	12	1.0877×10^{-2} $(9.51 \times 10^{-4})=$	4.6049×10^{-3} $(6.05 \times 10^{-4})+$	5.4658×10^{-2} $(4.57 \times 10^{-4})-$	1.3317×10^{-2} $(1.73 \times 10^{-3})=$	3.1309×10^{-2} $(3.27 \times 10^{-3})-$	1.0645×10^{-2} (1.70×10^{-3})
DTLZ3	12	2.4541×10^{-1} $(5.12e \times 10^{-1})+$	9.8374×10^{-1} $(1.13 \times 10^{0})-$	7.5176×10^{0} $(3.57 \times 10^{0})-$	$1.9417e \times 10^{0}$ $(2.93 \times 10^{0})-$	2.4602×10^{1} $(3.41 \times 10^{1})-$	6.0531×10^{-1} $(8.26 \times 10^{-1}$
DTLZ4	12	9.2717×10^{-3} $(2.88 \times 10^{-3})=$	1.7034×10^{-3} $(2.13 \times 10^{-3})+$	2.0093×10^{-1} $(2.26 \times 10^{-1})-$	1.2253×10^{-2} $(3.76 \times 10^{-3})-$	4.0307×10^{-2} $(8.06 \times 10^{-3})-$	8.9998×10^{-3} (3.09×10^{-3})
DTLZ5	12	1.6588×10^{-3} $(3.60 \times 10^{-4})=$	2.3254×10^{-4} $(1.88 \times 10^{-4})+$	5.2708×10^{-3} $(3.00 \times 10^{-4})-$	1.6606×10^{-3} $(2.55 \times 10^{-4})=$	1.2031×10^{-2} $(2.07 \times 10^{-3})-$	1.5690×10^{-3} (3.00×10^{-4})
DTLZ6	12	2.9192×10^{-5} $(4.50 \times 10^{-5})-$	1.8013×10^{-1} $(4.84 \times 10^{-1})-$	2.8984×10^{-2} $(1.35 \times 10^{-1})-$	8.3978×10^{-5} $(3.71 \times 10^{-4})-$	2.1359×10^{-5} $(1.41 \times 10^{-6})-$	8.6511×10^{-6} (5.41×10^{-7})
DTLZ7	12	5.1449×10^{-2} $(1.10 \times 10^{-2})+$	1.6310×10^{-2} $(4.30 \times 10^{-3})+$	8.1079×10^{-2} $(1.43 \times 10^{-1})+$	1.5389×10^{-2} $(2.84 \times 10^{-2})-$	1.1640×10^{-2} $(2.09 \times 10^{-3})+$	9.6279×10^{-2} (2.51×10^{-2})
+/−/=		2/7/3	4/8/0	2/10/0	0/9/3	3/9/0	

4.3. Diversity Evaluation of Different Algorithms on ZDT and DTLZ Test Problems

Concerning diversity, as indicated by the CPF values in Table 2, the proposed NDE-NSGA-II algorithm outperforms the other five algorithms. It secures the first rank among seven benchmark tests and the second rank among two test functions.

Table 2. CPF values of the proposed NDE-NSGA-II and three multi-objective algorithms.

	D	NSGA-II	MOEA/D	SPEA2	CDE-NSGA-II	CMWOA	NDE-NSGA-II
ZDT1	30	6.8546×10^{-1} $(2.76 \times 10^{-2})-$	1.7925×10^{-1} $(8.16 \times 10^{-2})-$	8.0205×10^{-1} $(2.58 \times 10^{-2})-$	8.3221×10^{-1} $(1.95 \times 10^{-2})-$	8.7450×10^{-1} $(9.60 \times 10^{-3})=$	8.7580×10^{-1} (8.94×10^{-3})
ZDT2	30	6.4410×10^{-1} $(7.42 \times 10^{-2})-$	6.2313×10^{-3} $(8.72 \times 10^{-3})-$	7.2467×10^{-1} $(4.44 \times 10^{-2})-$	7.7441×10^{-1} $(2.79 \times 10^{-2})-$	8.7093×10^{-1} $(8.81 \times 10^{-3})=$	8.6470×10^{-1} (1.09×10^{-2})
ZDT3	30	6.6189×10^{-1} $(3.87 \times 10^{-2})+$	1.1442×10^{-1} $(5.97e \times 10^{-2})-$	7.0745×10^{-1} $(5.33 \times 10^{-2})+$	5.9863×10^{-1} $(3.30 \times 10^{-2})=$	8.9315×10^{-1} $(9.73 \times 10^{-3})+$	6.1488×10^{-1} (5.12×10^{-2})
ZDT4	10	6.7576×10^{-1} $(2.98 \times 10^{-2})-$	4.7501×10^{-1} $(1.59 \times 10^{-1})-$	3.1359×10^{-1} $(9.78 \times 10^{-2})-$	7.6621×10^{-1} $(1.94 \times 10^{-2})-$	4.6558×10^{-1} $(2.16 \times 10^{-1})-$	8.7401×10^{-1} (8.41×10^{-3})
ZDT6	10	5.1181×10^{-1} $(5.75 \times 10^{-2})-$	2.7228×10^{-1} $(1.13 \times 10^{-1})-$	5.0701×10^{-1} $(4.77 \times 10^{-2})-$	5.5266×10^{-1} $(6.90 \times 10^{-2})-$	8.4110×10^{-1} $(2.95 \times 10^{-2})-$	8.7239×10^{-1} (9.44×10^{-3})
DTLZ1	7	2.9803×10^{-1} $(4.97 \times 10^{-2})-$	7.0126×10^{-1} $(4.40 \times 10^{-3})+$	3.5206×10^{-1} $(2.17 \times 10^{-1})-$	3.0072×10^{-1} $(6.34 \times 10^{-2})-$	2.9647×10^{-1} $(2.33 \times 10^{-1})-$	5.9606×10^{-1} (2.68×10^{-2})
DTLZ2	12	3.2695×10^{-1} $(3.54 \times 10^{-2})-$	7.0787×10^{-1} $(6.26 \times 10^{-3})+$	7.1574×10^{-1} $(2.83 \times 10^{-2})+$	$3.4783e \times 10^{-1}$ $(3.56 \times 10^{-2})-$	6.6517×10^{-1} $(2.38 \times 10^{-2})+$	6.1444×10^{-1} (3.06×10^{-2})
DTLZ3	12	2.8899×10^{-1} $(7.70 \times 10^{-2})-$	4.3226×10^{-1} $(1.71 \times 10^{-1})-$	1.0824×10^{-1} $(5.32 \times 10^{-2})-$	3.1697×10^{-1} $(1.28 \times 10^{-1})-$	4.6823×10^{-1} $(1.63 \times 10^{-1})-$	4.8327×10^{-1} (1.75×10^{-1})
DTLZ4	12	3.1499×10^{-1} $(1.11 \times 10^{-1})-$	2.0613×10^{-1} $(3.01 \times 10^{-1})-$	4.9790×10^{-1} $(3.20 \times 10^{-1})-$	3.3847×10^{-1} $(8.73 \times 10^{-2})-$	6.2879×10^{-1} $(2.83 \times 10^{-2})=$	6.3433×10^{-1} (2.97×10^{-2})
DTLZ5	12	7.8294×10^{-1} $(3.54 \times 10^{-2})-$	8.1416×10^{-2} $(3.69 \times 10^{-2})-$	9.4421×10^{-1} $(1.32 \times 10^{-2})-$	9.1363×10^{-1} $(1.24 \times 10^{-2})-$	9.0961×10^{-1} $(2.74 \times 10^{-2})-$	9.5135×10^{-1} (7.11×10^{-3})
DTLZ6	12	6.7924×10^{-1} $(6.48 \times 10^{-2})-$	1.5450×10^{-1} $(1.80 \times 10^{-1})-$	9.2164×10^{-1} $(4.13 \times 10^{-2})-$	8.9498×10^{-1} $(1.54 \times 10^{-2})-$	9.1266×10^{-1} $(8.00 \times 10^{-3})-$	9.5063×10^{-1} (6.60×10^{-3})
DTLZ7	12	4.4126×10^{-1} $(4.01 \times 10^{-2})+$	2.6965×10^{-1} $(3.39 \times 10^{-2})=$	6.2981×10^{-1} $(1.13 \times 10^{-1})+$	1.8519×10^{-1} $(5.49e \times 10^{-2})-$	8.0188×10^{-1} $(8.17 \times 10^{-2})+$	2.4661×10^{-1} (6.78×10^{-2})
+/−/=		2/10/0	2/9/1	3/9/0	0/11/1	3/6/3	

An examination of the results from the rank-sum test indicates that the NDE-NSGA-II proposed in this article significantly surpasses NSGA-II, MOEA/D, SPEA2, CDE-NSGA-II, and CMWOA on 10, 9, 9, 11, and 6 benchmarks, respectively. Notably, in most test functions, the NDE-NSGA-II algorithm demonstrates both high convergence and high diversity. This further substantiates that NDE-NSGA-II can achieve commendable convergence while concurrently maintaining high diversity. Moreover, it is crucial to highlight that the CPF index effectively neutralizes the impact of convergence, providing a reliable assessment of diversity. This suggests that the adopted strategy has indeed played a pivotal role in enhancing population diversity and convergence.

4.4. Comprehensive Evaluation of Different Algorithms on ZDT and DTLZ Test Problems

As previously discussed, the HV value functions as a comprehensive indicator that reflects the overall performance of multi-objective algorithms. The algorithm's overall performance improves with an increase in the value of HV.

Table 3 presents the experimental results of HV values. It is evident from the table that the proposed NDE-NSGA-II surpasses NSGA-II in ten instances, MOEA/D in nine instances, SPEA2 in ten instances, CDE-NSGA-II in eleven instances, and CMWOA's HV value in nine instances. It is noteworthy that among the twelve examples, the proposed NDE-NSGA-II secures the top rank in six test functions.

Table 3. HV values of the proposed NDE-NSGA-II and three multi-objective algorithms.

	D	NSGA-II	MOEA/D	SPEA2	CDE-NSGA-II	CMWOA	NDE-NSGA-II
ZDT1	30	7.0524×10^{-1} $(3.16 \times 10^{-3})-$	5.4399×10^{-1} $(6.02 \times 10^{-2})-$	7.0400×10^{-1} $(3.56 \times 10^{-3})-$	7.0929×10^{-1} $(1.27 \times 10^{-3})-$	7.2012×10^{-1} $(1.43 \times 10^{-4})=$	7.1989×10^{-1} (1.99×10^{-4})
ZDT2	30	4.1906×10^{-1} $(2.54 \times 10^{-2})-$	1.0257×10^{-1} $(1.35 \times 10^{-2})-$	4.2034×10^{-1} $(6.61 \times 10^{-3})-$	4.2709×10^{-1} $(6.21 \times 10^{-3})-$	4.4480×10^{-1} $(1.47 \times 10^{-4})=$	4.4488×10^{-1} (9.95×10^{-5})
ZDT3	30	5.7787×10^{-1} $(1.93 \times 10^{-2})=$	5.6843×10^{-1} $(6.44 \times 10^{-2})-$	5.9423×10^{-1} $(2.45 \times 10^{-2})+$	5.7400×10^{-1} $(8.99 \times 10^{-4})=$	5.8321×10^{-1} $(1.28 \times 10^{-4})+$	5.7821×10^{-1} (6.09×10^{-3})
ZDT4	10	7.1643×10^{-1} $(1.76 \times 10^{-3})-$	6.8649×10^{-1} $(2.59 \times 10^{-2})-$	5.1044×10^{-1} $(1.29 \times 10^{-1})-$	7.1913×10^{-1} $(3.84 \times 10^{-5})=$	4.4701×10^{-1} $(1.66 \times 10^{-1})-$	7.2048×10^{-1} (5.05×10^{-5})
ZDT6	10	3.1969×10^{-1} $(2.98 \times 10^{-2})-$	2.7870×10^{-1} $(2.95 \times 10^{-2})-$	3.1472×10^{-1} $(3.49 \times 10^{-2})-$	2.5339×10^{-1} $(4.50 \times 10^{-2})-$	3.8867×10^{-1} $(1.87 \times 10^{-4})=$	3.8870×10^{-1} (1.79×10^{-4})
DTLZ1	7	8.0353×10^{-1} $(9.10 \times 10^{-1})-$	8.3780×10^{-1} $(2.96 \times 10^{-3})=$	6.5584×10^{-1} $(2.51 \times 10^{-1})-$	7.9397×10^{-1} $(1.20 \times 10^{-1})-$	3.1433×10^{-1} $(3.76 \times 10^{-1})-$	8.3594×10^{-1} (2.39×10^{-3})
DTLZ2	12	5.2846×10^{-1} $(4.17 \times 10^{-3})-$	5.5490×10^{-1} $(8.96 \times 10^{-4})+$	5.4292×10^{-1} $(1.44 \times 10^{-3})=$	5.2397×10^{-1} $(4.39 \times 10^{-3})-$	5.2613×10^{-1} $(4.52 \times 10^{-3})-$	5.4495×10^{-1} (2.35×10^{-3})
DTLZ3	12	4.1495×10^{-1} $(1.64 \times 10^{-1})+$	2.0737×10^{-1} $(2.31 \times 10^{-1})-$	0.0000×10^{0} $(0.00 \times 10^{0})-$	2.4195×10^{-1} $(2.17 \times 10^{-1})-$	6.9750×10^{-2} $(1.81 \times 10^{-1})-$	3.3573×10^{-1} (2.12×10^{-1})
DTLZ4	12	5.1554×10^{-1} $(5.78 \times 10^{-2})-$	3.6056×10^{-1} $(1.66 \times 10^{-1})-$	4.9017×10^{-1} $(9.55 \times 10^{-2})-$	5.1736×10^{-1} $(3.49 \times 10^{-2})-$	5.2232×10^{-1} $(5.86 \times 10^{-3})-$	5.3118×10^{-1} (4.99×10^{-2})
DTLZ5	12	1.9844×10^{-1} $(2.71 \times 10^{-4})=$	1.8256×10^{-1} $(4.25 \times 10^{-4})-$	1.9840×10^{-1} $(3.76 \times 10^{-4})=$	1.9899×10^{-1} $(2.06 \times 10^{-4})=$	1.9399×10^{-1} $(1.43 \times 10^{-3})-$	1.9899×10^{-1} (1.81×10^{-4})
DTLZ6	12	1.9946×10^{-1} $(1.32 \times 10^{-4})-$	1.5260×10^{-1} $(6.17 \times 10^{-2})-$	1.9309×10^{-1} $(3.65 \times 10^{-2})-$	1.9921×10^{-1} $(5.51 \times 10^{-3})-$	2.0018×10^{-1} $(3.47 \times 10^{-5})=$	2.0024×10^{-1} (2.26×10^{-5})
DTLZ7	12	2.4741×10^{-1} $(5.76 \times 10^{-3})+$	2.3085×10^{-1} $(1.33 \times 10^{-2})+$	2.5446×10^{-1} $(1.27 \times 10^{-2})+$	1.5659×10^{-1} $(7.12 \times 10^{-3})-$	2.7467×10^{-1} $(6.32 \times 10^{-3})+$	1.6271×10^{-1} (6.76×10^{-3})
+/−/=		2/8/2	2/9/1	2/8/2	0/9/3	2/6/4	

4.5. Quantify the Number of Mutation Strategies across Different Algorithms and Test Functions

As illustrated in Table 4, our algorithm retains a greater number of solutions compared to other algorithms across various test functions during the mutation-based offspring generation process. This demonstrates that our algorithm effectively mitigates resource waste. Furthermore, our algorithm secured first place in 6 out of the 12 test functions, further attesting to its effectiveness.

Table 4. Number of individuals eliminated/created during mutation.

	D	NSGA-II	MOEA/D	SPEA2	CDE-NSGA-II	CMWOA	NDE-NSGA-II
ZDT1	30	127/299	291/633	161/303	134/318	122/314	98/310
ZDT2	30	129/302	315/594	152/318	133/302	137/295	125/312
ZDT3	30	163/269	388/633	142/325	145/295	147/311	120/328
ZDT4	10	82/103	216/407	76/100	89/111	89/94	105/189
ZDT6	10	58/101	121/219	53/95	54/102	41/94	65/106
DTLZ1	7	8/70	36/237	8/69	10/75	20/73	8/77
DTLZ2	12	4/132	36/382	6/123	3/115	4/102	2/121
DTLZ3	12	44/126	43/347	33/117	28/113	28/108	16/126
DTLZ4	12	14/103	26/268	7/124	16/132	11/113	2/120
DTLZ5	12	7/122	13/343	9/113	11/126	13/120	6/134
DTLZ6	12	85/115	48/339	11/133	11/115	2/106	6/132
DTLZ7	12	102/193	298/587	103/222	90/230	80/233	123/241

5. Experiments and Analysis of Results

5.1. Study Area

The research area is situated in Hulan District, Harbin City, Heilongjiang Province, China (46.340683° N 126.795502° E), as shown in Figure 5. This region, located in northeastern China, falls within the continental monsoon climate of the northern temperate zone, exhibiting distinct cold, warm, dry, and wet seasons.

Figure 5. Location of the field of study.

Fine-tuning a variety of parameters is vital for accurately simulating the local growth environment. Maize (Longdan 96) has a plant height of 280 cm and an ear height of 100 cm. 18 leaves can be seen in adult plants. The number of rows per ear is 16–18, with teeth-shaped and yellow grains, and a weight of 34 g per hundred grains. It is suitable for planting in the first accumulated temperature zone of Heilongjiang Province (data sourced from Heilongjiang Academy of Agricultural Sciences). In this experiment, field data from 2015 were gathered, and the parameters in the variety parameter file were adjusted using a trial-and-error method. Weather data spanning from 2011 to 2015 for average optimization were employed. The weather data for 2015 are shown in Figure 6. The DSSAT model can effectively use these parameters to simulate the growth of local crops.

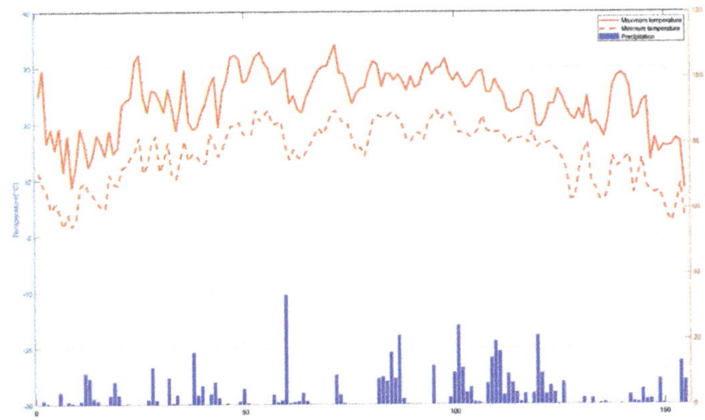

Figure 6. Precipitation and highest and lowest temperatures in 2015.

5.2. Objective Function

Multi-objective optimization problems involve maximizing or minimizing two or more objectives by adjusting one or more variables. In the context of crop production, decision-makers modify irrigation and fertilization methods to attain optimal outcomes. This study specifically addresses the timing and quantity of irrigation or fertilization in the field. The objective function is outlined as follows:

$$Max : Y = \frac{\sum_{i=0}^{N} DSSAT_i(i_{a_0}, \ldots, i_{a_j}, f_{a_0}, \ldots, f_{a_d}, D_i)}{N} \tag{11}$$

$$Min : I = \frac{\sum_{i=0}^{N} \sum_{n=0}^{j} (i_{a_n})}{N} \tag{12}$$

$$Min : F = \frac{\sum_{i=0}^{N} \sum_{m=0}^{d} (f_{a_m})}{N} \tag{13}$$

In the formula, Y is the yield, I is the total irrigation amount, F is the total nitrogen application amount, i_{a_n} is the one-time irrigation amount, f_{a_m} is the one-time nitrogen application amount, j is the irrigation amount, d is the nitrogen application amount, and N = 5 represents the number of years simulated. D_i is the time for irrigation and fertilization.

5.3. Optimization Strategies and Configuration

Symmetry also plays an important role in water and fertilizer irrigation in agriculture. Figure 7 shows the flowchart of optimizing water and fertilizer. We use the R language to drive the DSSAT model for optimization. Using the integrated method of water and fertilizer, the effect of different fertilizers on the maize yield was studied. The simulation situation is divided into two groups: rain irrigation and drip irrigation. We applied urea (N1), diammonium phosphate (N2), and ammonium nitrate (N3) separately. Maize undergoes five growth stages—seedling (VE), jointing (VJ), tasseling (VT), filling (R2), and physiological maturity (R6). Fertilization and irrigation are carried out during these stages. The dates for irrigation and fertilization are determined based on historical experience, but due to differences in weather between different years, we have set their historical experience dates to ±5 days. Considering the actual situation and based on historical experience, the sowing date of Longdan 96 is set on May 1st, and the harvest date is set on October 1st. The goal of each optimization strategy is to maximize production while minimizing resource waste. In the case of two objectives, the population is 100 with 100 iterations, and in the case of three objectives, the population is 300 with 100 iterations.

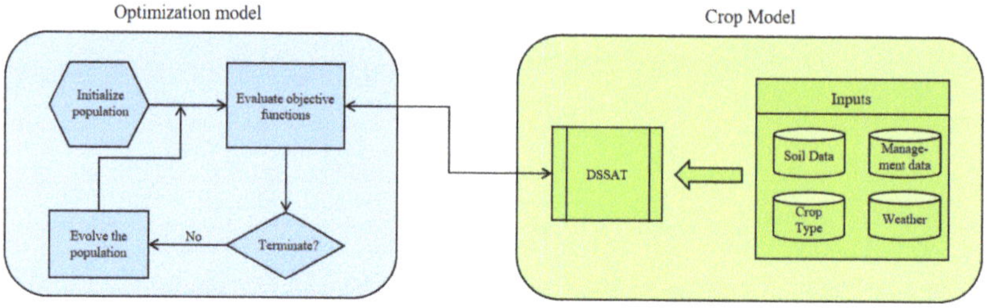

Figure 7. Flow chart of optimized water and fertilizer irrigation.

5.4. Result and Analysis

Figure 8 illustrates that in the absence of irrigation, the utilization of N1 fertilizer not only results in a higher yield (10,515 kg/ha) but also requires less fertilizer compared to the other two fertilizers. Furthermore, the enhanced algorithm identifies a more rational fertilization strategy. For instance, at the point of maximum yield (10,515 kg/ha), the original algorithm utilized 312 kg/ha of fertilizer, whereas the improved algorithm required only 264 kg/ha, reflecting a 15% reduction in fertilizer application compared to the original algorithm. This outcome substantiates the reliability and efficacy of the improved algorithm.

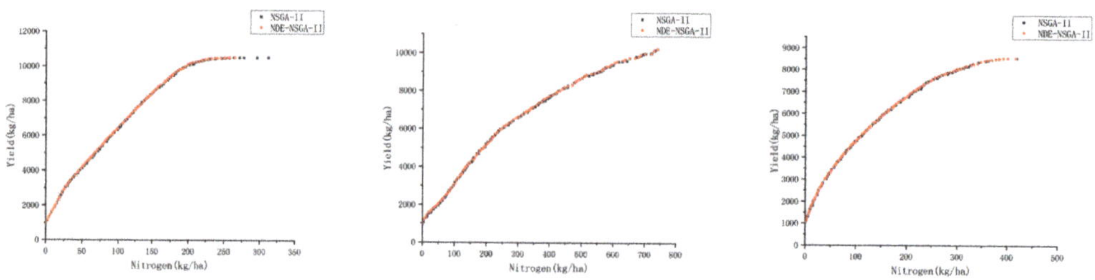

(**a**) N1 (**b**) N2 (**c**) N3

Figure 8. Comparison of fertilization strategies between NSGA-II algorithm and NDE-NSGA-II algorithm.

From Figure 9, it can be seen that under the comprehensive strategy of drip irrigation and fertilization, the highest yields of N1, N2, and N3 nitrogen fertilizers were 13,585 kg/ha, 13,589 kg/ha, and 13,587 kg/ha, respectively. This means that under irrigation conditions, all three fertilization methods can achieve higher yields. Compared with the original algorithm, the improved algorithm exhibits superior yield performance while minimizing resource waste to the greatest extent possible.

In addition, the improved algorithm provides decision-makers with more irrigation decision-making solutions and verifies its reliability. Given the relatively low resource consumption of N2 fertilizer, which has the lowest cost among the three types of fertilizers (see Table 5 for details), N2 fertilizer has become the preferred choice under irrigation strategies, improving its economic benefits. The optimal yield and resource consumption achieved by applying different fertilizers, coupled with historical experience, are detailed in Table 6, overall, applying N2 fertilizer and achieving the highest yield, with water consumption reduced by 37.5%, nitrogen application reduced by 8.3%, and yield increased by 5.9%.

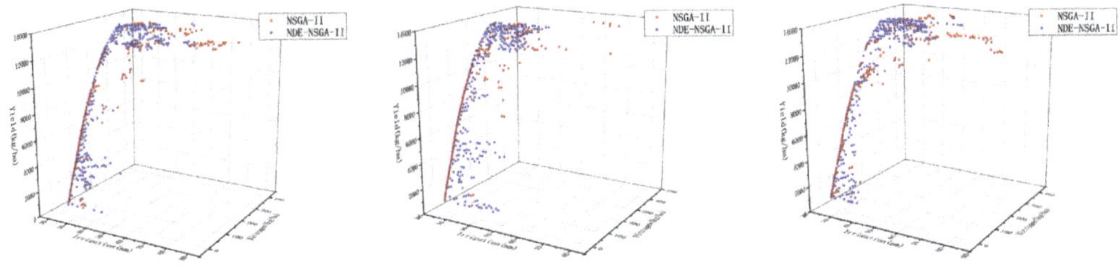

(a) N1 (b) N2 (c) N3

Figure 9. Comparison of irrigation and fertilization strategies between NSGA-II algorithm and NDE-NSGA-II algorithm.

Table 5. Different fertilizer prices.

N1 Costs (Yuan/kg)	N2 Costs (Yuan/kg)	N3 Costs (Yuan/kg)
3.98	2.65	3.82

Examining Table 6, it is evident that opting for the N2 fertilization strategy yields the highest output. However, in regions facing water scarcity, alternatives such as minimal irrigation or no irrigation strategies could be considered as viable options.

Table 6. Comparison of best-simulated irrigation and nitrogen fertilizer test results with best practices (using different fertilizers).

	Yield (kg/ha)		Yield Increase (%)	Total Irrigation (mm)		Irrigation Reduction (%)	Total Nitrogen (kg/ha)		Fertilization Reduction (%)
	Practices	Optimized Results		Practices	Optimized Results		Practices	Optimized Results	
N1	12,836	13,585	5.8%	80	55	31.3%	300	375	−25%
N2		13,589	5.9%		50	37.5%		275	8.3%
N3		13,587	5.5%		62	22.5%		277	7.7%

6. Discussion

The NDE-NSGA-II algorithm significantly outperforms traditional multi-objective optimization algorithms. It has demonstrated robust performance in test functions and excels in optimizing resource allocation strategies, such as crop irrigation and fertilization. However, the algorithm has certain limitations. Although NDE-NSGA-II improves convergence speed, its computational complexity is relatively high, particularly for large-scale optimization problems, which can lead to increased computational resource consumption. Additionally, the algorithm's performance may be sensitive to parameter settings, and improper parameter selection can affect optimization results, necessitating further research on parameter tuning and automation methods. Furthermore, this study primarily relies on simulation environments for testing, and the algorithm's performance in practical applications has not been fully validated, requiring further empirical research. In summary, the development of the NDE-NSGA-II algorithm is significant for multi-objective optimization, and its potential impact on agricultural applications underscores its practical value. However, further research is needed to address existing limitations and validate its effectiveness in real-world scenarios.

7. Conclusions

This article presents the NDE-NSGA-II algorithm as a solution for handling multi-objective problems. Specifically, chaotic mapping is utilized to enhance the initialization process. This is followed by the implementation of a point selection method based on norm and average distance elimination strategies, aiming to improve convergence and diversity within the population. The performance of the proposed NDE-NSGA-II is rigorously validated across 12 benchmark functions, each with distinct features. Comparative analyses are conducted against other state-of-the-art methods in the field of multi-objective problems (MOPs). The experimental results robustly affirm the effectiveness and reliability of the algorithm, showcasing its capability to simultaneously address multi-objective problems with high diversity and achieve commendable convergence. Finally, the NDE-NSGA-II algorithm, introduced in this paper, is applied to optimize maize-related scenarios, demonstrating superiority over the classical NSGA-II method. However, we only simulated an ideal corn water and fertilizer irrigation, which has certain limitations. In the future, we can consider using certain methods to predict weather changes and yield. These results further underscore the practical efficacy of the NDE-NSGA-II algorithm proposed in this study.

In the future, applying NDE-NSGA-II to more complex high-dimensional multi-objective problems will be a promising work. At the same time, further testing will be conducted on multi-objective problems in the real world, and the algorithm will be improved.

Author Contributions: Conceptualization, J.D. and R.L.; methodology, J.D.; software, D.C.; validation, X.W.; formal analysis, T.Z.; investigation, F.Y.; resources, J.D.; data curation, D.C.; writing—original draft preparation, R.L.; writing—review and editing, J.D.; visualization, R.L.; supervision, J.D.; project administration, X.W.; funding acquisition, D.C., R.L. and F.Y. All authors have read and agreed to the published version of the manuscript.

Funding: This research received no external funding.

Data Availability Statement: The data supporting this study's findings are available from the corresponding author upon request.

Conflicts of Interest: The authors declare no conflicts of interest.

References

1. Cai, Y.; Wang, J. Differential evolution with hybrid linkage crossover. *Inf. Sci.* **2015**, *320*, 244–287. [CrossRef]
2. Zhou, A.; Qu, B.Y.; Li, H.; Zhao, S.Z.; Suganthan, P.N.; Zhang, Q. Multiobjective evolutionary algorithms: A survey of the state of the art. *Swarm. Evol. Comput.* **2011**, *1*, 32–49. [CrossRef]
3. Pourvaziri, H.; Naderi, B. A hybrid multi-population genetic algorithm for the dynamic facility layout problem. *Appl. Soft. Comput.* **2014**, *24*, 457–469. [CrossRef]
4. Saborido, R.; Ruiz, A.B.; Luque, M. Global WASF-GA: An evolutionary algorithm in multiobjective optimization to approximate the whole pareto optimal front. *Evol. Comput.* **2017**, *25*, 309–349. [CrossRef] [PubMed]
5. Tran, K.D. An improved non-dominated sorting genetic algorithm-ii (ANSGA-II) with adaptable parameters. *Int. J. Intell. Syst. Technol. Appl.* **2009**, *7*, 347–369. [CrossRef]
6. Ahadzadeh, B.; Abdar, M.; Safara, F.; Khosravi, A.; Menhaj, M.B.; Suganthan, P.N. SFE: A simple, fast and efficient feature selection algorithm for high-dimensional data. *IEEE Trans. Evol. Comput.* **2023**, *27*, 1896–1911. [CrossRef]
7. Lin, Z.; Gao, K.; Wu, N.; Suganthan, P.N. Scheduling eight-phase urban traffic light problems via ensemble meta-heuristics and Q-learning based local search. *IEEE Trans. Intell. Transp. Syst.* **2023**, *24*, 14415–14426. [CrossRef]
8. Ma, Z.; Wu, G.; Suganthan, P.N.; Song, A.; Luo, Q. Performance assessment and exhaustive listing of 500+ nature-inspired metaheuristic algorithms. *Swarm Evol. Comput.* **2023**, *77*, 101248. [CrossRef]
9. Gad, A.G.; Houssein, E.H.; Zhou, M.C.; Suganthan, P.N.; Wazery, Y.M. Damping-assisted evolutionary swarm intelligence for industrial iot task scheduling in cloud computing. *IEEE Internet Things J.* **2023**, *11*, 1698–1710. [CrossRef]
10. Ma, H.; Zhang, Y.; Sun, S.; Liu, T.; Shan, Y. A comprehensive survey on NSGA-II for multi-objective optimization and applications. *Artif. Intell. Rev.* **2023**, *56*, 15217–15270. [CrossRef]
11. Li, W.; Zhang, T.; Wang, R.; Huang, S.; Liang, J. Multimodal multi-objective optimization: Comparative study of the state-of-the-art. *Swarm Evol. Comput.* **2023**, *77*, 101253. [CrossRef]
12. Deb, K.; Pratap, A.; Agarwal, S.; Meyarivan, T.A.M.T. A fast and elitist multiobjective genetic algorithm: NSGA-II. *IEEE Trans. Evol. Comput.* **2002**, *6*, 182–197. [CrossRef]
13. Zhang, Q.; Li, H. MOEA/D: A multiobjective evolutionary algorithm based on decomposition. *IEEE Trans. Evol. Comput.* **2007**, *11*, 712–731. [CrossRef]
14. Zitzler, E.; Laumanns, M.; Thiele, L. SPEA2: Improving the strength Pareto evolutionary algorithm. *TIK Rep.* **2001**, *103*, 10017663175.

15. Zhou, Y.; Fan, H. Research on multi objective optimization model of sustainable agriculture industrial structure based on genetic algorithm. *J. Intell. Fuzzy Syst.* **2018**, *35*, 2901–2907. [CrossRef]
16. Cheng, D.; Yao, Y.; Liu, R.; Li, X.; Guan, B.; Yu, F. Precision agriculture management based on a surrogate model assisted multiobjective algorithmic framework. *Sci. Rep.* **2023**, *13*, 1142. [CrossRef]
17. Song, J.; Li, J.; Yang, Q.H.; Mao, X.; Yang, J.; Wang, K. Multi-objective optimization and its application on irrigation scheduling based on AquaCrop and NSGA-II. *J. Hydraul. Eng.* **2018**, *49*, 1284–1295.
18. Llera, J.R.; Deb, K.; Runkle, E.; Xu, L.; Goodman, E. Evolving and comparing greenhouse control strategies using model-based multi-objective optimization. In Proceedings of the 2018 IEEE Symposium Series on Computational Intelligence (SSCI), Bangalore, India, 18–21 November 2018; pp. 1929–1936.
19. Liu, X.; Yang, D. Irrigation schedule analysis and optimization under the different combination of P and ET0 using a spatially distributed crop model. *Agric. Water Manag.* **2021**, *256*, 107084. [CrossRef]
20. White, J.W.; Alagarswamy, G.; Ottman, M.J.; Porter, C.H.; Singh, U.; Hoogenboom, G. An overview of CERES–sorghum as implemented in the crop system model version 4.5. *Agron. J.* **2015**, *107*, 1987–2002. [CrossRef]
21. Ritchie, J.T. Description and performance of CERES wheat: A user-oriented wheat yield model. *ARS Wheat Yield Proj.* **1985**, *8*, 159–175.
22. Otter-Nacke, S.; Ritchie, J.T.; Godwin, D.C.; Singh, U. *A User's Guide to CERES Barley—V2. 10*; International Fertilizer Development Center Simulation Manual: Muscle Shoals, AL, USA, 1991; IFDC-SM-3.
23. Liu, J.; Chen, X. An improved NSGA-II algorithm based on crowding distance elimination strategy. *Int. J. Comput. Intell. Syst.* **2019**, *12*, 513–518. [CrossRef]
24. Dos Santos Coelho, L.; Mariani, V.C. Use of chaotic sequences in a biologically inspired algorithm for engineering design optimization. *Expert Syst. Appl.* **2008**, *34*, 1905–1913. [CrossRef]
25. Yan, Z.; Jin, Q.; Zhang, Y.; Wang, Z.; Li, Z. An Improved Multi-Objective Harris Hawk Optimization with Blank Angle Region Enhanced Search. *Symmetry* **2022**, *14*, 967. [CrossRef]
26. Kaveh, A.; Ilchi Ghazaan, M.; Saadatmand, F. Colliding bodies optimization with Morlet wavelet mutation and quadratic interpolation for global optimization problems. *Eng. Comput.* **2022**, *38*, 2743–2767. [CrossRef]
27. Zitzler, E.; Deb, K.; Thiele, L. Comparison of multiobjective evolutionary algorithms: Empirical results. *Evol. Comput.* **2000**, *8*, 173–195. [CrossRef] [PubMed]
28. Deb, K.; Thiele, L.; Laumanns, M.; Zitzler, E. Scalable multi-objective optimization test problems. In Proceedings of the 2002 Congress on Evolutionary Computation, CEC'02 (Cat. No. 02TH8600), Honolulu, HI, USA, 12–17 May 2002; Volume 1, pp. 825–830.
29. Zeng, N.; Song, D.; Li, H.; You, Y.; Liu, Y.; Alsaadi, F.E. A competitive mechanism integrated multi-objective whale optimization algorithm with differential evolution. *Neurocomputing* **2021**, *432*, 170–182. [CrossRef]
30. Li, M.; Yao, X. Quality evaluation of solution sets in multiobjective optimisation: A survey. *ACM Comput. Surv. (CSUR)* **2019**, *52*, 26. [CrossRef]
31. Ishibuchi, H.; Masuda, H.; Tanigaki, Y.; Nojima, Y. Modified distance calculation in generational distance and inverted generational distance. In Proceedings of the Evolutionary Multi-Criterion Optimization: 8th International Conference, EMO 2015, Guimarães, Portugal, 29 March–1 April 2015; Proceedings, Part II 8; Springer International Publishing: New York, NY, USA, 2015; pp. 110–125.
32. Tian, Y.; Cheng, R.; Zhang, X.;Li, M.; Jin, Y. Diversity assessment of multi-objective evolutionary algorithms: Performance metric and benchmark problems [research frontier]. *IEEE Comput. Intell. Mag.* **2019**, *14*, 61–74. [CrossRef]
33. Zitzler, E.; Thiele, L. Multiobjective optimization using evolutionary algorithms—A comparative case study. In Proceedings of the International Conference on Parallel Problem Solving from Nature, Berlin, Heidelberg, 27–30 September 1998; Springer: Berlin/Heidelberg, Germany, 1998; pp. 292–301.

symmetry

MDPI

Article

Multi-Task Multi-Objective Evolutionary Search Based on Deep Reinforcement Learning for Multi-Objective Vehicle Routing Problems with Time Windows

Jianjun Deng [1], Junjie Wang [2], Xiaojun Wang [2], Yiqiao Cai [2,*] and Peizhong Liu [3,*]

1 Chengdu Aeronautic Polytechnic, Chengdu 610100, China; dengjianjun@cap.edu.cn
2 College of Computer Science and Technology, Huaqiao University, Xiamen 361021, China; 18816234790@163.com (J.W.); t_wxjmq@163.com (X.W.)
3 College of Engineering, Huaqiao University, Quanzhou 362000, China
* Correspondence: caiyq@hqu.edu.cn (Y.C.); pzliu@hqu.edu.cn (P.L.)

Abstract: The vehicle routing problem with time windows (VRPTW) is a widely studied combinatorial optimization problem in supply chains and logistics within the last decade. Recent research has explored the potential of deep reinforcement learning (DRL) as a promising solution for the VRPTW. However, the challenge of addressing the VRPTW with many conflicting objectives (MOVRPTW) still remains for DRL. The MOVRPTW considers five conflicting objectives simultaneously: minimizing the number of vehicles required, the total travel distance, the travel time of the longest route, the total waiting time for early arrivals, and the total delay time for late arrivals. To tackle the MOVRPTW, this study introduces the MTMO/DRP-AT, a multi-task multi-objective evolutionary search algorithm, by making full use of both DRL and the multitasking mechanism. In the MTMO/DRL-AT, a two-objective MOVRPTW is constructed as an assisted task, with the objectives being to minimize the total travel distance and the travel time of the longest route. Both the main task and the assisted task are simultaneously solved in a multitasking scenario. Each task is decomposed into scalar optimization subproblems, which are then solved by an attention model trained using DRL. The outputs of these trained models serve as the initial solutions for the MTMO/DRL-AT. Subsequently, the proposed algorithm incorporates knowledge transfer and multiple local search operators to further enhance the quality of these promising solutions. The simulation results on real-world benchmarks highlight the superior performance of the MTMO/DRL-AT compared to several other algorithms in solving the MOVRPTW.

Keywords: multiobjective vehicle routing problem with time windows; deep reinforcement learning; evolutionary multi-task optimization; knowledge transfer

1. Introduction

The vehicle routing problem with time windows (VRPTW) is a widely studied combinatorial optimization problem in logistics, encompassing areas such as supply chain management, production planning, waste collection, home healthcare, and so on [1–5]. As a crucial variant of the vehicle routing problem (VRP), the VRPTW involves servicing a set of customers with specific time windows and known demands using a fleet of vehicles [1]. The primary goal of the VRPTW is to minimize delivery costs by optimizing routes while adhering to all constraints. However, the VRPTW is computationally NP-hard [2], making it challenging to solve effectively.

Due to its practical significance in various applications in the real world, the VRPTW has emerged as a prominent research problem in the field of operations research [2,3]. Consequently, numerous optimization approaches have been developed to tackle this challenge [6–8]. Broadly, optimization approaches for the VRPTW are categorized into exact methods [6], suitable for small-scale problems, and meta-heuristic methods [7,8], preferred for large-scale problems. Meta-heuristic methods, known for their capability and potential in tackling the VRPTW, encompass various search mechanisms [3,7,8]. These methods address both the single-objective VRPTW and the multi-objective VRPTW. Previous studies [9,10] have discussed the VRPTW as an inherently multi-objective optimization problem with many conflicting objectives relevant to real-world applications. As a result, research on the multi-objective VRPTW (MOVRPTW) problem has gained significant attention and is now considered a prominent area in the field of computational intelligence [3].

However, because of the high complexity of the MOVRPTW, most existing meta-heuristic methods still face significant challenges in effectively solving it [11]. These methods often require a significant number of iterations to update the population or conduct search, especially for optimization problems with many conflicting objectives. This will lead to lengthy computational times for optimization. Furthermore, meta-heuristic methods necessitate problem-specific experience and knowledge, requiring adjustments to yield favorable results when encountering new problems or even new instances of similar problems [12]. Therefore, there yet remains much room for proposing more efficient approaches to address the challenges brought by the MOVRPTW.

With the rapid advancement of artificial intelligence technology, deep reinforcement learning (DRL) has become increasingly prevalent and successful across various fields. Notably, it has made significant contributions in areas such as computer vision [13,14] and natural language processing [15]. In the realms of operations research and combinatorial optimization, DRL has also proven its advantages in terms of autonomous feature discovery, effective accumulation of problem information, and efficient decision optimization [16–19]. However, as discussed in [20], directly applying the trained model on unseen problem instances may be considered unreliable. Furthermore, the majority of DRL-based methodologies concentrate on resolving a single MOVRPTW problem by initiating the search from scratch, disregarding the similarities between disparate tasks. Consequently, the useful knowledge gained by addressing one problem cannot be fully leveraged for optimizing other similar problems. Therefore, it is crucial to explore ways to further enhance the quality of the output results obtained by the trained model, especially in the context of DRL-based approaches.

Recently, a new paradigm called evolutionary multitask optimization (EMTO) has emerged in the field of evolutionary algorithms. EMTO aims to optimize multiple tasks simultaneously using a shared search space [21]. By leveraging the latent synergies among those tasks, EMTO has been shown to outperform single-task optimization methods, yielding superior performance in both continuous and combinatorial optimization problems [21,22]. Furthermore, the efficacy of EMTO has been demonstrated in successfully solving a wide range of combinatorial optimization problems [23,24]. It can, thus, be seen that the integration of the EMTO framework with DRL-based approaches presents a compelling proposition for addressing complex combinatorial optimization problems.

Building upon the aforementioned findings, this study introduces the MTMO/DRL-AT, a multi-task multi-objective evolutionary search algorithm for solving the MOVRPTW with five conflicting objectives. The proposed algorithm combines DRL and the multi-tasking mechanism. In the MTMO/DRL-AT, a two-objective VPRTW is constructed as an assisted task based on the characteristics of the main MOVRPTW task. Both the main task and the assisted task are decomposed into scalar optimization subproblems, each addressed by an attention model trained using DRL. The output results of these trained models serve as the initial solutions for the MTMO/DRL-AT. Subsequently, the proposed algorithm optimizes both tasks simultaneously under a multitasking framework. To further improve the quality of the solutions, multiple local search operators are employed. Experimental studies on 45 real-world instances are conducted to validate the effectiveness of the proposed algorithm. The simulation results clearly demonstrate the superiority of the MTMO/DRL-AT over other compared approaches in solving MOVRPTWs.

In summary, the main contributions of this study are as follows:

- A novel evolutionary optimization algorithm, termed the MTMO/DRL-AT, is presented for solving MOVRPTWs involving five conflicting objectives. The MTMO/DRL-AT conducts a multitasking search over both the main task and an assisted task, utilizing an attention model trained through DRL.
- The synergy between DRL-based model training and the multitasking-based search mechanism is built up. Attention models are trained using DRL for subproblems in both the main and assisted tasks, serving as the starting point for the algorithm. Knowledge transfer strategies and objectivewise local search operators are then employed to further refine the optimization of both tasks, ultimately improving the quality of solutions derived from the trained models.

The remainder of this paper is structured as follows: Section 2 describes the formulation of the MOVRPTW. Section 3 reviews related work. Section 4 shows the DRL-based modeling and training for the MOVRPTW. Section 5 presents the details of the MTMO/DRL-AT. Then, the experimental results and analysis are provided in Section 6. Finally, Section 7 gives the conclusions and future work.

2. Problem Formulation of MOVRPTW

The MOVRPTW is a complex multi-objective optimization problem with practical applications and multiple constraints. It can be mathematically represented by a complete undirected graph, denoted as G = $\{V, E\}$, where V represents the node set and E represents the edge set. The node set $V = \{v_i | i = 0, 1, \ldots, N\}$, consists of a depot, denoted as v_0, and other customer nodes, $v_1, v_2, \ldots, v_N$. The edge set $E = \{e_{i,j} | i, j \in V, i \neq j\}$, where each edge $e_{i,j}$ is linked to a travel time $t_{i,j}$ and a travel distance $d_{i,j}$. Similarly, each customer is assigned to a demand q_i, a service time window $[b_i, e_i]$, and a service time s_i.

In the MOVRPTW, each vehicle is assigned a route, $r_k = (c_0^k, c_1^k, \ldots, c_{N_k}^k, c_{N_{k+1}}^k)$, that consists of a sequence of N_k customers to be visited, denoted as r_k and $c_0^k = c_{N_k+1}^k = 0$, where c_j^k represents the jth customer to be visited in r_k and $c_0^k = c_{N_k+1}^k = 0$ (depot). Each customer is exclusively serviced by a single vehicle. Moreover, it is essential to ensure that the cumulative demand of customers assigned to each vehicle does not exceed its maximum capacity, denoted as Q. Additionally, all vehicles are obligated to depart from and return to the depot within the time window specified as $[0, e_0]$. To allow for some flexibility, a soft time window constraint is implemented, permitting a vehicle to arrive at a customer's location after the specified latest service time, e_i, within a maximum allowed delay time, denoted as md. The delay time experienced by vehicle k at the jth customer is defined as $dt_{c_j^k} = \max\{0, a_{c_j^k} - e_{c_j^k}\}$, where $a_{c_j^k}$ represents the arrival time at customer c_j^k. In case a vehicle arrives prior to the earliest service time (b_i), it is required to wait until b_i to initiate service, resulting in a waiting time. The waiting time for vehicle k at the jth customer is determined by $w_{c_j^k} = \max\{0, b_{c_j^k} - a_{c_j^k}\}$.

Figure 1 provides an example of the solution representation for the MOVRPTW. As illustrated in Figure 1, the MOVRPTW consists of one depot (i.e., 0) and nine customers to be serviced (i.e., 1 to 9). A solution comprising three routes is denoted as $x = (r_1, r_2, r_3)$, where $r_1 = (0, 5, 7, 1, 0)$, $r_2 = (0, 9, 6, 3, 0)$, and $r_3 = (0, 8, 4, 2, 0)$.

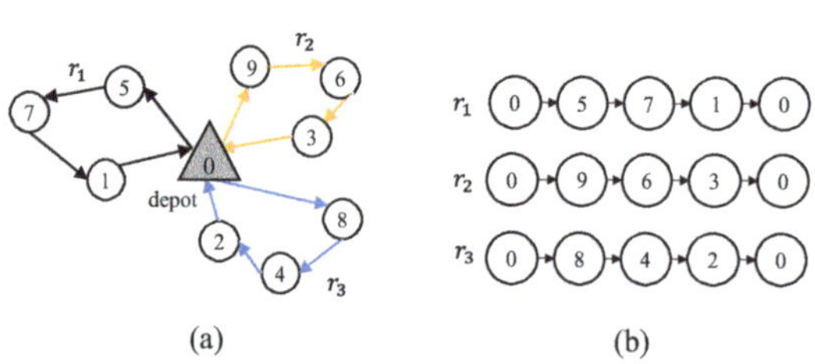

Figure 1. Solution representation for the MOVRPTW. (**a**) A solution for the MOVRTPW. (**b**) The solution representation.

To provide a clear mathematical model of the MOVRPTW, the basic notations used in this study are summarized in Table 1.

Table 1. Notations for MOVRPTW.

Notation	Description
Property sets:	
C	The set of customers: $C = \{1,2,3,\ldots,N\}$;
V	The set of vertices: $V = C \cup \{0\}$;
E	The set of edges between vertices: $E = \{e_{ij} \mid i,j \in V\}$;
D	The set of distances between customers: $D = \{d_{ij} \mid i,j \in C\}$;
T	The set of travel times between customers: $T = \{t_{ij} \mid i,j \in C\}$.;
Problem parameters:	
Q	The maximum capacity of the vehicle;
q_i	The demand of customer i;
md	The maximum allowable delay time at each customer;
$[b_i, e_i]$	The time window of customer i;
b_i	The earliest service time for customer i;
e_i	The latest service time for customer i;
s_i	The service time for customer i.
Problem variables:	
x_{ij}^k	e_{ij} is traversed by the kth vehicle (i.e., $x_{ij}^k = 1$) or not (i.e., $x_{ij}^k = 0$);
K	The number of routes in x;
r_k	The kth route consisting of a sequence of N_k customers $r_k = \{c_0^k, c_1^k, \ldots, c_{N_k}^k, c_{N_{k+1}}^k\}$;
c_j^k	The jth customer visited in the kth route;
a_i	The time the vehicle arrives at customer i;
w_i	The waiting time incurred by the vehicle at customer i;
dt_i	The delay time generated by the vehicle at customer i.

In general, the mathematical model of the MOVRPTW, which includes five objectives, is defined as follows [9,10]:

$$\min F(x) = (f_1, f_2, f_3, f_4, f_5) \tag{1}$$

$$f_1 = K \tag{2}$$

$$f_2 = \sum_{i=1}^{N} \sum_{j=0, j\neq i}^{N} \sum_{k=1}^{K} d_{ij} x_{ij}^k \tag{3}$$

$$f_3 = \max_{k=1,\ldots,K} \{\sum_{i=1}^{N} \sum_{j=0, j\neq i}^{N} x_{ij}^k (t_{ij} + w_i + s_i)\} \tag{4}$$

$$f_4 = \sum_{i=1}^{N} \sum_{j=0, j\neq i}^{N} \sum_{k=1}^{K} w_i x_{ij}^k \tag{5}$$

$$f_5 = \sum_{i=1}^{N} \sum_{j=0, j\neq i}^{N} \sum_{k=1}^{K} dt_i x_{ij}^k \tag{6}$$

The MOVRPTW mathematical model, described by Equation (1), is a multi-objective problem that encompassed five objectives. These objectives are defined as follows: In Equation (2), the first objective aims to minimize the number of vehicles required. In Equation (3), the second objective focuses on minimizing the total travel distance. In Equation (4), the third objective aims to minimize the travel time of the longest route. In Equation (5), the fourth objective seeks to minimize the total waiting time for early arrivals. In Equation (6), the fifth objective aims to minimize the total delay time for late arrivals.

The constraints of the MOVRPTW are defined as follows:

$$\sum_{i=1}^{N} x_{i0}^{k} = \sum_{j=1}^{N} x_{0j}^{k} = 1, \quad k = 1, \dots, K \tag{7}$$

$$\sum_{j=0, j\neq i}^{N} x_{ij}^{k} = \sum_{j=0, j\neq i}^{N} x_{ji}^{k} \leq 1, \quad i \in C, k = 1, \dots, K \tag{8}$$

$$\sum_{i=0, i\neq j}^{N} \sum_{k=1}^{K} x_{ij}^{k} = \sum_{j=0, j\neq i}^{N} \sum_{k=1}^{K} x_{ij}^{k} = 1, \quad i \in C, j \in C \tag{9}$$

$$\sum_{i=0}^{N} q_i \sum_{j=0, j\neq i}^{N} x_{ij}^{k} \leq Q, \quad k = 1, \dots, K \tag{10}$$

$$\sum_{j=0, j\neq i}^{N} dt_i x_{ij}^{k} \leq md, \quad i \in C, k = 1, \dots, K \tag{11}$$

$$(t_{i0} + a_i + w_i + s_i) x_{i0}^{k} \leq e_0, \quad i \in C, k = 1, \dots, K \tag{12}$$

$$x_{ij}^{k} \in \{0, 1\}, \quad i \in C, j \in C, k = 1, \dots, K \tag{13}$$

Constraints (7) and (8) ensure that each vehicle starts from the depot and then returns to the depot. Constraint (9) guarantees that each customer is served only once by one vehicle. Constraint (10) ensures that the total demand served by a vehicle does not exceed its maximum capacity Q. Constraint (11) limits the delay time for each customer to the specified value md. Constraint (12) states that each vehicle must return to the depot before it closes. Constraint (13) defines the range of the decision variable.

3. Literature Review

This section begins by providing an overview of the existing studies conducted on the VRPTW. Subsequently, it briefly examines recent DRL approaches applied to combinatorial optimization problems (COPs), with a specific focus on the VRP and its variants. Lastly, it reviews the applications of EMTO to the VRP.

3.1. Meta-Heuristic Approaches for VRPTW

Broadly, optimization approaches for the VRPTW are categorized into exact methods [6], suitable for small-scale problems, and meta-heuristic methods [7,8], preferred for large-scale problems. Meta-heuristic methods, known for their capability and potential in tackling the VRPTW, encompass various search mechanisms [3,7,8]. These methods address both the single-objective VRPTW and the multi-objective VRPTW. Previous studies [9,10] have discussed the VRPTW as an inherently multi-objective optimization problem with many conflicting objectives relevant to real-world applications. Therefore, this subsection provides only a brief overview of the related work on the MOVRPTW, which is summarized in Table 2. Other related work on the VRP and its variants can be found in [2,3,6–8].

Researchers have proposed various multi-objective optimization algorithms with various optimization frameworks and local search strategies to address the MOVRPTW. For example, Qi et al. [25] introduced a decomposition-based multi-objective evolutionary algorithm, which included a specially designed selection operator and three local searches. Moradi [26] proposed a discrete learnable evolution model for multi-objective optimization that integrated machine learning and a new priority-based representation scheme. In addition to the above evolutionary optimization methods, DRL-based methods are also used to solve the MOVRPTW. In [19], Zhang et al. introduced the MODRL/D-EL, an approach that combines the decomposition technique with attention models. They also employed evolutionary learning to further fine-tune the parameters of the trained model.

Table 2. Summary of the methods for solving the MOVRPTW.

Reference	Authors	Problem	Approach
		MOVRPTW with two objectives	
[25]	Qi et al.	MOVRPTW with f_1 and f_2	Decomposition-based EA Specially designed selection operator Three novel local searches
[26]	Moradi	MOVRPTW with f_1 and f_2	The strength Pareto evolutionary algorithm (SPEA) Discrete learnable evolution model A priority-based representation scheme
[19]	Zhang et al.	MOVRPTW with f_2 and f_3	Multiobjective DRL with evolutionary learning (MODRL/D-EL) Decomposition technique Attention models Evolutionary learning to further fine-tune the model's parameters
		MOVRPTW with many objectives	
[9]	Gutiérrez et al.	MOVRPTW with f_1–f_5	Nondominated sorting genetic algorithm (NSGA-II) New instances from real-world data
[10]	Zhou and Wang	MOVRPTW with f_1–f_5	Local-search-based multiobjective optimization algorithm (LSMOVRPTW) Objectivewise local searches
[27]	Zhang et al.	MOVRPTW with f_1–f_5	Multi-objective memetic algorithm based on adaptive local search chains (MMA-ALSC) Enhanced local search chain techniques Multi-directional local search strategy
[28]	Cai et al.	MOVRPTW with f_1–f_5	Hybrid evolutionary multitasking algorithm (HEMT) Simultaneously optimize multiple distinct instances Knowledge transfer and knowledge reuse strategies

Efforts have also been made to tackle the VRPTW with more than three objectives (also called the many-objective VRPTW [29]). To address this problem, Gutiérrez et al. [9] proposed a nondominated sorting genetic algorithm (NSGA-II) and developed new instances from real-world data to address weak dependence relationships among objectives. Followed that, Zhou and Wang [10] designed multiple objectivewise local searches for distinct objectives of the VRPTW, thereby proposing a local search-based multiobjective optimization algorithm (LSMOVRPTW). Recently, Zhang et al. [27] presented a multi-objective memetic algorithm based on adaptive local search chains (MMA-ALSC). This approach combined enhanced local search chain techniques with a multi-directional local search strategy to guide the search process. By exploiting the similarity between different MOVRPTWs, Cai et al. [28] proposed a hybrid evolutionary multitasking algorithm (HEMT). Their approach involved solving multiple different MOVRPTWs concurrently, employing an exploration stage that incorporated knowledge transfer and an exploitation stage that used a knowledge reuse strategy.

3.2. The DRL-Based Approaches for the COPs

In recent years, DRL has proven successful in addressing complex COPs across various fields. For single-objective optimization, Vinyals et al. [30] proposed a Pointer network (Ptr-Net) model based on the sequence-to-sequence (Seq2Seq) model, achieving good results on the Traveling Salesman Problem (TSP). Bello et al. [16] trained a Ptr-Net model to solve TSPs using reinforcement learning and a critic network as a baseline. Nazari et al. [31] used Ptr-Net to solve dynamic VRPs by dividing the instances into dynamic and static parts and then trained the model with reinforcement learning algorithms. Nowak et al. [32] proposed a Graph Neural Network (GNN) using supervised training and beam search. Deudon et al. [33] improved the traditional Pointer network based on a Transformer with MHA and reinforcement learning.

Kool et al. [34] introduced an attention-based approach for solving various COPs, outperforming Ptr-Net on the TSP, CVRP, PCTSP, and others. Zhao et al. [17] designed an adaptive discriminator to optimize the parameters of DRL models and a routing simulator to aid in training and evaluating the effectiveness of DRL models. Peng et al. [35] proposed a dynamic attention model for the VRP using a dynamic encoding–decoding structure with reinforcement learning. Wang et al. [18] proposed a feedback mechanism integrating an iterative greedy algorithm for flow shop scheduling problems based on DRL.

Furthermore, DRL has been applied to solve multi-objective COPs. Li et al. [12] developed the DRL-MOA, a framework using decomposition and Ptr-Net for a multi-objective TSP. Wu et al. [36] extended the DRL-MOA with the MODRL/DAM, constructing an attention model for each subproblem and training them with reinforcement learning. Similarly, Zhang et al. [19] presented the MODRL/D-EL, combining decomposition, attention models, and evolutionary algorithms for parameter fine-tuning.

3.3. The EMTO Approaches for VRP

In contrast with traditional optimization approaches that focus solely on a single optimization problem, EMTO aims to address multiple optimization tasks concurrently within a unified representation space [21,22]. By leveraging the underlying synergies among different optimization tasks, EMTO has demonstrated its potential in achieving superior performance for both continuous and combinatorial optimization problems when compared to its single-task counterparts [21,22]. The effectiveness and promising capabilities of EMTO in addressing multiple related optimization tasks have garnered significant interest from researchers, resulting in the development of various EMTO algorithms in the fields of science and engineering [22]. In the literature, EMTO has been successfully applied to solve the VRP and its variants.

In [37], a permutation-based multifactorial evolutionary algorithm (P-MFEA) was proposed to address multiple capacitated VRPs simultaneously. In the P-MFEA, a permutation-based unified representation was introduced as a replacement for the random key unified representation. Additionally, a split-based decoding operator was utilized to translate the solutions from the unified space to the problem-specific space.

In [24], an explicit EMTO (EEMTO) approach was presented to solve the capacitated VRP. EEMTO incorporates a weighted l_1-norm regularized learning process to capture the transfer mapping and uses a solution-based knowledge transfer process across different VRPs.

In [23], an EMTO was applied to address a novel variant of the VRP, called the VRP with heterogeneous capacity, time window, and occasional driver (VRPHTO). The proposed EMTO algorithm optimizes multiple VRPHTOs simultaneously and employs four operators: permutation-based common representation, split procedure, routing information exchange, and chromosome evaluation.

In [28], a hybrid evolutionary multitask algorithm (HEMT) was proposed to solve multiple MOVRPTWs in a multitasking scenario. The HEMT incorporates an exploration stage for global search with knowledge transfer, an exploitation stage for local search with knowledge reuse, and a tradeoff mechanism to balance these search processes.

The aforementioned related works highlight the advantages of using the EMTO framework in solving VRPs. However, it is worth noting that most existing EMTO approaches primarily focus on addressing VRPs with a single objective or two objectives. The application of EMTO in the context of the VRP with many objectives (more than three) is relatively limited, which motives our interest to further investigate its potential.

4. DRL-Based Modeling and Training

As reviewed above, DRL has shown its advantages in solving VRPs [36,38]. However, most of the works only focus on the extraction of node features, ignoring the fact that the distances and traveling times between customers in the real world are asymmetric. To efficiently solve the real-world MOVRPTW considered in this study, a multiobjective DRL method [36] is employed. This method uses the decomposition strategy and the attention model to enhance the optimization process.

In this section, the decomposition and parameter-transfer strategies for the MOVRPTW are firstly introduced. Then, the encoder and decoder of the attention model for each subproblem are presented. Finally, the training process for the models through DRL is given.

4.1. Decomposition and Parameter-Transfer Strategies

In this study, the MOVRPTW is decomposed into M subproblems using the weighted sum approach [39]. Specifically, a set of weight vectors W is generated for the MOVRPTW using Das and Dennis's method [40]. These weight vectors are then used to define the objective function of the jth subproblem by the weighted sum approach, as follows:

$$\min g^{ws}(\pi|\lambda_i) = \sum_{j=1}^{m} \lambda_{ij} \bar{f}_j(\pi) \tag{14}$$

where $\boldsymbol{\lambda}_i = (\lambda_{i1}, \ldots, \lambda_{iM})$ represents the weight vector of the ith subproblem, with the constraints that $\sum_{j=1}^{M} \lambda_{ij} = 1$.

After the decomposition, each scalar optimization subproblem is modeled by a neural network, which is then solved using DRL methods. Additionally, to expedite model training, a neighborhood-based parameter-transfer strategy [12] is utilized, as depicted in Figure 2. This strategy involves transferring the parameters from the model of a solved subproblem to the model of its neighboring subproblem. The neighboring subproblem's model is then trained using these transferred parameters as the initial starting point. More details of the parameter-transfer strategy can be found in [12].

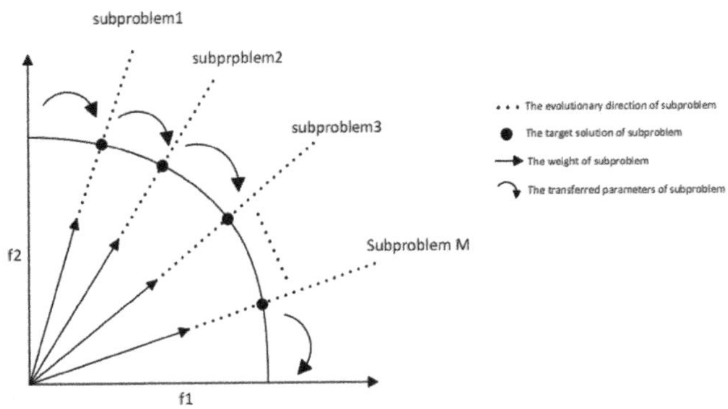

Figure 2. The neighborhood-based parameter-transfer strategy.

4.2. Encoder of Model

The encoder comprises three components. The first component uses a fully connected layer to transform the feature vectors. These vectors consist of the coordinates (x_i, y_i), time windows $[b_i, e_i]$, demands q_i, service duration w_i, travel time t_{ij}, and travel distance d_{ij} between customers, the initial embedding being h_i^0 and h_{ij}^0. The second component incorporates a multi-head attention mechanism to aggregate the information features from both node and edge embeddings. The processed data are then further updated and transformed in the last component through a combination of a residual network and a fully connected feedforward layer. This results in the generation of the final embedding h_i^N and h_{ij}^N. The structure of the encoder can be visualized in Figure 3.

As shown in Figure 3, the input data are split into two parts: node embeddings (i.e., $c_i = [(x_i, y_i), q_i, (b_i, e_i), s_i]$), which contain node-specific information, and edge embeddings (i.e., $e_{ij} = (d_{ij}, t_{ij})$), which include distance and time information between customers.

In the encoder of the model, the feature vector is transformed into the initial node embedded in the network by linear transformation as follows:

$$h_i^0 = W_N c_i + b_N \tag{15}$$

$$h_{ij}^0 = W_E e_{ij} + b_E \tag{16}$$

where $i, j \in N$, N is the No. of customers, and W_N and b_N are trainable network parameters.

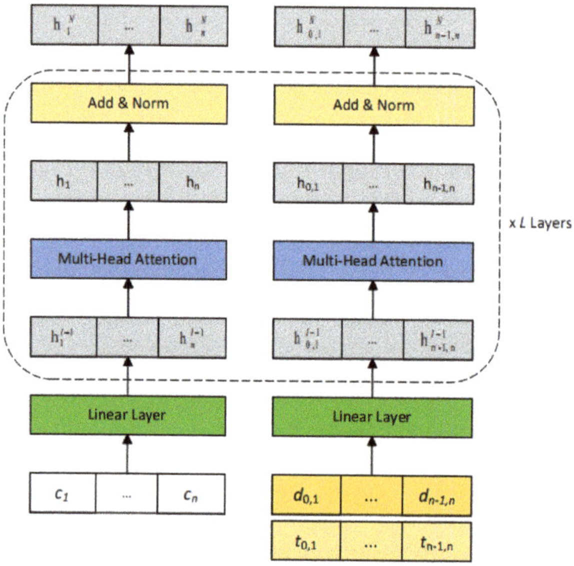

Figure 3. The structure of the encoder in the model.

Then, the node embeddings $h_0^l, \ldots, h_N^l$ and edge embeddings $h_{0,1}^l, \ldots, h_{N-1,N}^l$ are aggregated using the multi-head attention operator, as follows:

$$\widetilde{h}_i^l = BN(h_i^{l-1} + MHA^l(W_N^l h_i^{l-1})) \tag{17}$$

$$\widetilde{h}_{ij}^l = BN(MHA^l(W_E^l h_{ij}^{l-1})) \tag{18}$$

where $BN(\cdot)$ represents the batch normalized layer and $MHA(\cdot)$ refers to the multi-head attention layers. Note that the MHA is related to the three vectors q_i^l, k_i^l, and v_i^l. These vectors can be calculated as follows: $q_i^l = W_q^l h_i^{l-1}, k_i^l = W_k^l[h_i^{l-1}; h_{ij}^{l-1}], v_i^l = W_v^l[h_i^{l-1}; h_{ij}^{l-1}]$. Here, the trainable parameters W_q^l, W_k^l, and W_v^l are used to map the embeddings to the query, key, and value vectors, respectively.

After that, the embeddings of nodes and edges are combined by the residual network layer (add and norm) to update the embeddings of each node, as follows:

$$h_i^l = ReLu(h_i^{l-1} + FF^l(\hat{h}_i^l)) \tag{19}$$

$$h_{ij}^l = ReLu(h_{ij}^{l-1} + FF^l(\hat{h}_{ij}^l)) \tag{20}$$

where $FF(\cdot)$ (feedforward) is a fully connected feedforward layer, which can further improve the expression capability of the network.

Finally, the final embedding vector of each node is obtained through N attention layers, as follows:

$$\overline{h}_o^N = \frac{1}{n}\sum_{i=0}^{n} h_i^N \tag{21}$$

$$\overline{h}_e^N = \frac{1}{n}\sum_{i=0}^{n} h_{ij}^N \tag{22}$$

where $\overline{h}_o^N$ and $\overline{h}_e^N$ are the final embedding vectors of the node feature and edge feature, respectively. The node feature, the edge feature, and the final embedded vector will be output from the encoder to the decoder.

4.3. Decoder of Model

The primary function of the decoder is to estimate the probability distribution of the remaining nodes being selected based on the embedding vector of the nodes and edges that are output from the encoder. This process is repeated iteratively until all customers are served. More specifically, at each time step $t \in N$, the decoder determines the optimal decision on π_t by considering the partial tour $\pi_{1:t-1}$ and the embedding vector of the nodes and edges. Figure 4 shows the structure of the decoder.

First, a context embedding representing the relationships between contexts is needed. The initial context (i.e., $t = 1$) includes the node features ($h_o^{N'}$) and the embedding vectors of the edge features ($h_e^{N'}$), both obtained from the encoder. Additionally, the current vehicle's remaining capacity (Q_t) and the last customer served by the vehicle ($h_{\pi_{t-1}}^N$) are incorporated into the initial context. The description of the initial context is as follows:

$$h_c^{N'} = \begin{cases} [\overline{h}_o^N, \overline{h}_e^N, Q_t, h_0], & t = 1 \\ [\overline{h}_o^N, \overline{h}_e^N, Q_t, h_{\pi_{t-1}^N}], t > 1 \end{cases} \tag{23}$$

where $[\ldots]$ denotes the vector connection operator.

Then, a new context vector $h_c^{N'}$ is calculated using the MHA network layer. For each node, its key vector (q_c) and the value vector (v_c) are derived from the embedding vectors of the encoder. The transformation process is as follows:

$$\begin{aligned} q_c &= W^Q h_c^{N'}, \\ k_i &= W^K[h_i; h_{ij}] + q_c, \\ v_i &= W^V[h_i; h_{ij}] + q_c \end{aligned} \tag{24}$$

where W^Q, W^K, and W^V are the trainable parameters. Subsequently, the compatibility of each node is computed by masking the nodes that have been visited. The compatibility values are within the range of $[-1, 1]$ and are determined as follows:

$$u_{(c)i} = \begin{cases} \frac{q_c^T k_i}{\sqrt{d_k}}, i \notin \pi_t \\ -\infty, \text{otherwise} \end{cases} \tag{25}$$

where i denotes the node index and d_k is the dimension of q_c/k_i. Then, based on Equation (13), the compatibility of each node is recalculated by transforming the context vector and the embedding vectors of nodes and edges into the corresponding q, k, and v, with the range of $[-C, C]$, as follows:

$$u_{(c)i} = \begin{cases} C \cdot tanh(\frac{q_c^T k_i}{\sqrt{d_k}}), i \notin \pi_t \\ -\infty, \text{otherwise} \end{cases} \tag{26}$$

Finally, the probability of selecting node x_i as the next node to be visited is calculated as follows:

$$p_i = p_\theta(\pi_t = i|\pi_{1:t-1}, s) = \frac{e^{u_{(c)i}}}{\sum_j e^{u_{(c)j}}} \tag{27}$$

The decoder repeats the steps mentioned above, where each time, the selected node is masked. This process continues until all customers are selected.

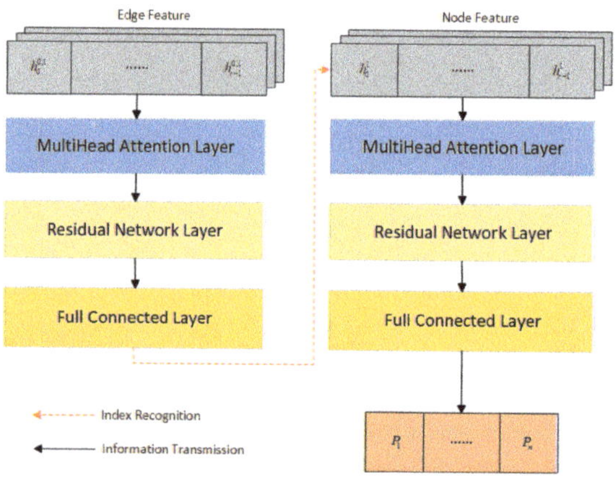

Figure 4. The structure of the decoder in the model.

4.4. Training Driven by DRL

In this section, we adopt the well-known actor–critic method [41] to train the model of each subproblem. The training process, employing the actor–critic method, is outlined in Algorithm 1. To train both the actor and critic networks, the Adam optimizer [42] is employed in this study.

In the algorithm, the actor network, which is an attention model, is responsible for learning the strategy gradient and selecting actions based on the probability distributions of nodes generated by the decoder. On the other hand, the critic network acts as a baseline to predict an estimation of the objective function for the subproblem and evaluate the results obtained from the actor network's strategy. This evaluation assists the actor in making action selections. Therefore, the training parameters of each subproblem (W_{λ_i}) include an actor network parameterized by θ and a critic network parameterized by ϕ.

Suppose that the processing sequence π generated by the actor network obeys the distribution $\pi \sim p_\theta(\cdot|X)$, where $p_\theta(\cdot|X)$ is the policy given by the actor network for an instance X. The objective $\ell(\theta|X)$ is the expected $g^{ws}(\pi|\lambda, X)$:

$$\ell(\theta|X) = \mathbb{E}_{\pi \sim p_\theta(\cdot|X)} g^{ws}(\pi|\lambda, X) \tag{28}$$

where $g^{ws}(\pi|\lambda, X)$ represents the min value calculated through the sequence π for X.

Then, the gradients of the parameters θ are calculated as follows:

$$\nabla_\theta \ell(\theta|X) = \frac{1}{B}\sum_{j=1}^{B}[(g^{ws}(\pi_i|\lambda_j, X_j) - b_\phi(X_j))\nabla_\theta log p_\theta(\pi_j|X_j)] \tag{29}$$

Here, B represents the batch size, which is the number of samples for each training iteration. X_j is a randomly selected instance of the subproblem, and π_j represents the solution for X_j obtained from the actor network. In addition, $b_\phi(X_j)$ refers to a baseline function, which is computed by the critic network. Its purpose is to estimate the expected objective value, which helps to reduce the variance of the gradients.

For the critic network, its goal is to learn how to estimate the expected objective value for a given instance X_j. Therefore, the objective function of the critic network can be defined as a mean-squared error function between the actual objective function generated by the actor network for X_j and the predicted objective value $b_\phi(X_j)$ from the critic network. This can be expressed as follows:

$$L_\phi = \frac{1}{B}\sum_{j=1}^{B}(b_\phi(X_j) - g_{\min}^{ws}(\pi_j|\lambda_i, X_j))^2 \quad (30)$$

Algorithm 1 Actor–critic training method [41]

Input: Number of problem instances T, number of iterations E, parameters of actor network θ and critic network ϕ. **Output**: Trained parameter θ, ϕ

$\theta, \phi \leftarrow$ initialized parameter as Ref. [12];
For $iteration = 1$ to E
  For $k = 1$ to T
    For $j = 1$ to B
      $\pi_j \leftarrow p_\theta(X_j)$;
      $b_j \leftarrow b_\phi(X_j)$;
    End
    $d_\theta = \frac{1}{B}\sum_{j=1}^{B}[g^{ws}(\pi_j|\lambda_i, X_j) - b_j \nabla_\theta log p_\theta(\pi_j|X_j)]$;
    $L_\phi = \frac{1}{B}\sum_{j=1}^{B}(b_j - g^{ws}(\pi_j|\lambda_i, X_j))^2$;
    $\theta \leftarrow ADAM(\theta, d_\theta)$;
    $\phi \leftarrow ADAM(\phi, \nabla_\phi L_\phi)$;
  End
End

5. MTMO/DRL-AT

In this section, a multi-task multi-objective evolutionary search algorithm based on DRL (MTMO/DRL-AT) is presented. Specifically, the general framework of the proposed algorithm is firstly outlined. Then, three main components of the MTMO/DRL-AT, i.e., the construction of the assisted task, knowledge transfer across tasks, and local search, are elaborated.

5.1. General Framework of MTMO/DRL-AT

The MTMO/DRL-AT framework is outlined in Algorithm 2. As can be seen, the MTMO/DRL-AT consists of three main phases: the initialization phase, the transfer reproduction phase, and the local search phase. In the initialization phase (Lines 3–6), the populations of the main task and the constructed assisted task are initialized using the trained DRL-based models, as described in Section 3. Specifically, n models are selected from the trained models for the main task, and thus, the population with n solutions is directly obtained by these models. Similarly, for the assisted task, its population with n solutions is produced using the selected trained models of the assisted task. In the transfer reproduction phase (Line 8), the knowledge transfer process is applied to update the solutions in the external archive A by leveraging the knowledge from both the main task and the assisted task. In the local search phase (Line 9), the objectivewise local searches [10] are employed to further refine the solutions in the archive A. Finally, when the stopping condition is met, the external archive A is returned as the approximate Pareto set for the MOVRPTW.

Algorithm 2 MTMO/DRL-AT

Input: Maximum running time of the target task T, population size $popsize$, training batch size $batch$, number of transferred solutions N_f, number of subproblems for main task N_m, number of subproblems for assisted task N_a, the trained models for the main task $Model_m$, the trained models for the assisted task $Model_a$.

Output: The external archive A.

$A = \emptyset$; //Define the external archive for the main task

$n = popsize/batch$; // Calculate the number of submodels from M

$SetIdx1 \leftarrow Random^n(1, N_m)$; // Randomly select n values from $[1, N_m]$ as the indexes of the models for the main task;

$SetIdx2 \leftarrow Random^n(1, N_a)$; // Randomly select n values from $[1, N_a]$ as the indexes of the models for the assisted task;

$Pop_m \leftarrow Model_m(SetIdx1, popsize)$; // Initialize Pop_m with the selected models for the main task

$Pop_a \leftarrow Model_a(SetIdx2, popsize)$; // Initialize Pop_a with the selected models for the assisted task

While $t < T$ **Do**

  $Transfer\_reproduction(Pop_m, Pop_a, A, N_f)$; // see Algorithm 3

  $Local\_search(Pop_m, A)$; // see Algorithm 4

End while

5.2. Construction of the Assisted Task

When solving an MOVRPTW with many objectives, most multi-objective evolutionary algorithms perform poorly due to a significant proportion of incomparable and mutually nondominated solutions [29]. To address this issue, an assisted task is constructed in a simpler search space for the MOVRPTW. This enables efficient assistance in optimizing the original problem through knowledge transfer. By leveraging the simpler task, the search process for the main task becomes more effective in finding high-quality solutions.

In the MOVRPTW, optimizing the objectives related to the total travel distance and the travel time of the longest route greatly impacts the optimization of other objectives. Therefore, the construction of the assisted task focuses on these two objectives. By selecting them as the optimization objectives for the assisted task, the aim is to effectively optimize these crucial factors, which in turn can positively influence the optimization of other related objectives in the MOVRPTW problem.

Therefore, the mathematical model of the assisted task is defined below:

$$\min H = (h_1, h_2) \tag{31}$$

$$h_1 = \sum_{k=1}^{|R|} \sum_{i=0}^{N_k} d_{c_i^k, c_{i+1}^k} \tag{32}$$

$$h_2 = \max\{t_{N_k|k=1,2,\ldots,|R|}\} \tag{33}$$

where h_1 and h_2 correspond to the f_2 and f_3, respectively, of the main task (i.e., Equation (1)). Additionally, the constraints of the assisted task are identical to those of the main task, as shown in Equation (7).

Furthermore, due to that the assisted task having a similar structure and characteristics as the main task, the DRL-based modeling and training methods described in Section 3 are also adopted for the assisted task.

5.3. Transfer Reproduction Operator

To effectively exploit the useful search experiences obtained from the constructed assisted task, a transfer reproduction operator is employed to transfer knowledge between the main and assisted tasks. The procedure of the transfer reproduction operator is shown in Algorithm 3.

Algorithm 3 Transfer reproduction

Input: Population of the main task Pop_m, population of the assisted task Pop_a, number of transferred solutions N_f, the external archive A.
Output: The updated A.

1: $C \leftarrow \emptyset$;
2: $O \leftarrow \emptyset$;
3: Use the fast nondominated sorting method [43] for the solutions in Pop_m and Pop_a, respectively;
4: $C \leftarrow$ the best N_f solutions in Pop_a;
5: $C \leftarrow C \bigcup$ the worst $popsize - N_f$ solutions in Pop_m;
6: Re-evaluate all solutions in C with the main task;
7: **For** $x_i \in C, i = 1, \ldots, popsize$
8: $\quad o_i \leftarrow Genetic\_operator(x_i)$;
9: $\quad$ Evaluate o_i with the main task;
10: $\quad O \leftarrow O \bigcup o_i$;
11: **End**
12: Update Pop_m with $C \bigcup O$;
13: Update A with $C \bigcup O$.

As shown in Algorithm 3, in Line 3, all solutions in Pop_m and Pop_a are ranked, respectively, using the fast nondominated sorting approach [43]. Subsequently, as shown in Lines 4 and 5, the best N_f solutions in Pop_a and the worst $popsize - N_f$ solutions in Pop_m are selected to form the set C. Next, in Line 6, each solution in C is re-evaluated under the main task environment. Note that the duplicate solutions are removed from the set. Afterwards, Line 8 employs the genetic operators on the solutions in C to generate offspring. In this study, the mutation strategy and the crossover operator of differential evolution (DE) [44] are adopted as the $Genetic\_operator(\cdot)$. Specifically, for each solution $x_i \in C$, a mutant vector (v_i) is first generated through the "DE/rand/1" mutation strategy, as follows:

$$v_i = x_{r1} + F \times (x_{r2} - x_{r3}) \tag{34}$$

where F is the mutation factor and $r1$, $r2$, and $r3 \in \{1, 2, \ldots, |C|\} \setminus \{i\}$ are randomly selected indices. Following that, a trial vector (u_i) is generated by using the binomial crossover operator for the pair of x_i and v_i, as follows:

$$u_{i,j} = \begin{cases} v_{i,j}, & \text{if } rand(0,1) \leq Cr \text{ or } j = j_{rand} \\ x_{i,j}, & \text{otherwise.} \end{cases} \tag{35}$$

Here, $Cr \in [0,1]$ represents the crossover rate, $rand(0,1) \in (0,1)$ denotes a randomly generated variable, and $j_{rand} \in [1, D_{\max}]$ indicates a randomly selected integer. Additionally, a random initialization will be performed if u_i exceeds the range of $[0,1]$. It is worth noting that the solution to the problem is a customer sequence vector, whereas the solution obtained by the genetic operator is a continuous vector. To convert a continuous vector into a customer sequence, a ranked order value (ROV) mapping method [45] is employed.

Once each solution in O has been evaluated with the main task, Pop_m is updated with the solutions of $C \bigcup O$ using the nondominated sorting and crowding distance, as described in Line 12, following the approach in [43]. As for updating A, the ϵ-dominance relation suggested in [10] is adopted.

5.4. Local Search Operator

To further refine the solutions in A and achieve better performance for the main task, we used the objectivewise local searches [10] in the MTMO/DRL-AT, which is presented in Algorithm 4.

First, in Line 2, an initial solution x is randomly selected from A for the subsequent local searches. After that, in Line 4, the objectivewise local searches are conducted on

x. Following the approach in [10], the local search is independently performed for each objective, denoted as $LS_{f_i}(x)$ $(i = 1, \ldots, 5)$, to enhance the quality of x with respect to the corresponding objective (f_i). Additionally, three neighborhood operators are integrated into the local searches for $f_2(x) - f_5(x)$. Specifically, in each search step, a random neighborhood operator is conducted on x to produce a new solution x'. If $f_i(x')$ is superior to $f_i(x)$, x is substituted by x'. Concurrently, x' is immediately used to update A through the ϵ-dominance relation in Line 5. For more details of the objectivewise local searches, please refer to [10]. Finally, in Line 8, the solutions in C are used to update Pop_m by directly replacing its inferior solutions.

Algorithm 4 Local search

Input: Population of the main task Pop_m, the external archive A.
Output: The updated A, the updated Pop_m.
1: $C \leftarrow \emptyset$;
2: $x \leftarrow Rndselect(A)$;
3: **For** $i = 1$ to 5
4: Perform $LS_{f_i}(x)$;
5: Update A with the obtained solutions;
6: Add the best solution in LS_{f_i} to C;
7: **End**
8: Replace the worst five solutions in Pop_m with the solutions in C.

6. Experiment

To assess the effectiveness of the MTMO/DRL-AT, a series of experiments was performed on a set of 45 real-world MOVRPTW instances. This section begins with a brief description of the MOVRPTW instances. Subsequently, the experimental setup is outlined, detailing the procedures and methodologies employed. Following that, a comprehensive comparison between the MTMO/DRL-AT and the representative algorithms is conducted. Finally, an in-depth analysis is presented to examine the influence of the main components of the MTMO/DRL-AT on its overall performance.

6.1. MOVRPTW Instances

To evaluate the effectiveness of the proposed algorithm, a set of 45 real-world instances of the MOVRPTW was adopted in this study. These instances, as described in [9], were derived from data obtained from an actual distribution company. Consequently, they reflect the complex and challenging nature of real-world MOVRPTW scenarios.

Table 3 provides an overview of the properties of these 45 MOVRPTW instances. As the table shows, these instances were generated by combining various features, including the number of customers (CN), the profile of time windows (PT), and the capacity of each vehicle (Q). The number of customers can be set to 50, 150, or 250, while the time window profile can range from 1 to 5. The capacity of each vehicle is determined using a formula that incorporates the lower and upper bounds ($\underline{D}$ and $\overline{D}$) and a modulation factor δ. Each MOVRPTW instance is labeled as "$a - b - c$", where a represents NC, b represents the index of the δ type, and c represents the index of the TW profile. For further details, please refer to [9,10].

Table 3. The real-world MOVRPTW instances.

Instance	CN	Q	PT	Instance	CN	Q	PT	Instance	CN	Q	PT
50-0-0	50	690	1	150-0-0	150	1854	1	250-0-0	250	3078	1
50-0-1	50	690	2	150-0-1	150	1854	2	250-0-1	250	3078	2
50-0-2	50	690	3	150-0-2	150	1854	3	250-0-2	250	3078	3
50-0-3	50	690	4	150-0-3	150	1854	4	250-0-3	250	3078	4
50-0-4	50	690	5	150-0-4	150	1854	5	250-0-4	250	3078	5

Table 3. *Cont.*

Instance	CN	Q	PT	Instance	CN	Q	PT	Instance	CN	Q	PT
50-1-0	50	250	1	150-1-0	150	638	1	250-1-0	250	1046	1
50-1-1	50	250	2	150-1-1	150	638	2	250-1-1	250	1046	2
50-1-2	50	250	3	150-1-2	150	638	3	250-1-2	250	1046	3
50-1-3	50	250	4	150-1-3	150	638	4	250-1-3	250	1046	4
50-1-4	50	250	5	150-1-4	150	638	5	250-1-4	250	1046	5
50-2-0	50	85	1	150-2-0	150	182	1	250-2-0	250	284	1
50-2-1	50	85	2	150-2-1	150	182	2	250-2-1	250	284	2
50-2-2	50	85	3	150-2-2	150	182	3	250-2-2	250	284	3
50-2-3	50	85	4	150-2-3	150	182	4	250-2-3	250	284	4
50-2-4	50	85	5	150-2-4	150	182	5	250-2-4	250	284	5

6.2. Experimental Setup

To train the models of the MTMO/DRL-AT, training instances of different sizes for the MOVRPTW were generated using a data simulator. The process involves randomly generating the coordinates of the depot and customer within the range $[0,1] \times [0,1]$. The distance and time matrices for travel between customers were randomly generated within the range of [0, 1]. For each customer, the demand was randomly generated within the range of [1, 9], the time window was randomly set as $b_i \in [0,5]$ and $e_i \in [0,5]$, and the service time was randomly selected from the set $\{1,5,2\}$. In addition, the maximum capacity of vehicles (Q) was set as follows: $Q = 20$ if $CN = 10$, $Q = 30$ if $CN = 20$, and $Q = 50$ if $CN = 40$. During the model-training process, problem instances with 40 nodes were used, and the dataset was generated based on the aforementioned process, with asymmetric distance and time matrices.

The parameter settings for the model and training were mostly similar to those described in [12,36], which are shown in Table 4. In addition, the parameter settings for the evolutionary search are also summarized in Table 4.

It is important to acknowledge that these parameter settings may not be optimal for the proposed algorithm, as finding the optimal settings can be challenging and often problem-specific. However, the effectiveness of these parameter settings has been demonstrated in the following experiments. In future work, the impact of these parameters on the performance of the MTMO/DRL-AT will be further investigated.

In the experiments, all the algorithms were implemented using Python, and the maximum running times of different instances were set according to the suggestions in [10]. Additionally, all the test experiments were conducted in the same configuration environment, as outlined in Table 5.

To evaluate the performance of the compared algorithms, two measures were employed: the inverted generational distance (IGD) [46] and hypervolume (HV) [47]. The IGD metric assesses both the convergence and diversity of the obtained nondominated solutions, while the HV metric evaluates the volume of the union of hypercubes determined by each nondominated solution and the reference point. A smaller value of the IGD or a larger value of the HV suggests better performance achieved by the corresponding algorithm in the approximation of the true Pareto front. For more detailed information on the IGD and HV metrics, please refer to [46,47].

To further demonstrate the significant differences between the compared algorithms, the KEEL software [48] was employed to conduct single-problem and multiple-problem analysis using the Wilcoxon test [49,50]. The results of single-problem analysis are summarized as "$w/t/l$", indicating that the considered algorithm is significantly better and performs equally to or performs worse than the competitor on the w, t, and l instances, respectively, at the 0.05 significance level. In the multiple-problem analysis, $R+$ and $R-$ represent the sum of ranks where the considered algorithm is significantly better than and worse than the competitor for all the instances, respectively. Additionally, the average ranking values of the considered algorithms for all instances were analyzed using

Friedman's test [49,50]. For brevity, this paper only presents the statistical results of the comparisons. For those interested in the detailed numerical values, please contact the corresponding author.

Table 4. Parameter settings.

Parameter	Value
For the model and training	
Input dimension	7
Node-embedding dimension	128
Batch size during training	500
Size of problem instances	5×10^6
Number of epochs for training the model for the first subproblem	5
Number of epochs for training the model for each remaining subproblem	1
Critic network architecture	four 1D convolutional layers with the following channels (7, 128), (128, 20), (20, 20), and (20, 1) $kernelsize = 1, stride = 1$
Number of attention layers	1
Number of heads	8
Dimension of the query vector and value vector	16
Learning rate for the Adam optimizer	0.0001
Number of decomposed subproblems for the main task	100
Number of decomposed subproblems for the assisted task	70
For the evolutionary search	
Population size (*popsize*)	50 for each task
Number of transferred solutions (TN)	15
Crossover rate (Cr)	0.9
Mutation factor (F)	0.5
Number of independent runs for each instance	30

Table 5. Experimental configuration.

Operating Environment	Version
Server	
System	Ubuntu 7.5.0
CPU	Intel Xeon Processor
GPU	GeForce RTX 2080 (8 G)
Memory	12 GB
CUDA	11.0
Local host	
System	Windows 10
CPU	Intel Xeon W-2223 (3.60 GHz)
Memory	16 GB

6.3. Performance Comparison

6.3.1. Comparison with LSMOVRPTW

In this section, we aim to demonstrate the effectiveness of the MTMO/DRL-AT for solving the MOVRPTW by comparing it with the LSMOVRPTW [10]. To provide a comprehensive overview of the performance comparisons, Table 6 presents the statistics summarizing these comparisons on all the instances.

As depicted in Table 6, the MTMO/DRL-AT demonstrates a significant improvement over the LSMOVRPTW in terms of both the IGD and HV. Specifically, based on the single-problem analysis conducted using the Wilcoxon test, the MTMO/DRL-AT significantly outperforms the LSMOVRPTW on 41 instances in terms of the IGD and on all 45 instances in terms of the HV. In the multiple-problem analysis carried out with the Wilcoxon test, the MTMO/DRL-AT achieves a higher $R+$ than $R-$ for both the IGD and HV. Additionally, based on the p-value, significant differences between the MTMO/DRL-AT and LSMOVRPTW are observed at both $\alpha = 0.05$ and $\alpha = 0.1$, indicating that the MTMO/DRL-AT outperforms the LSMOVRPTW overall.

Moreover, to visually illustrate the distinct characteristics of the competing algorithms, the approximate Pareto fronts of several representative instances obtained by the MTMO/DRL-AT and LSMOVRPTW are projected at the $f_1 - f_3$ and $f_2 - f_3$ planes, as shown in Figure 5. As the figure shows, the superiority of the MTMO/DRL-AT in achieving better Pareto fronts than the LSMOVRPTW for the selected instances is evident. The solutions generated by the MTMO/DRL-AT more accurately approximate the Pareto front and demonstrate a wider distribution along it. This further validates the superior convergence and diversity properties of the MTMO/DRL-AT in comparison to the LSMOVRPTW.

Table 6. Results of the single- and multiple-problem analysis by the Wilcoxon test between the MTMO/DRL-AT and LSMOVRPTW.

Algorithm	Metric	$w/t/l$	$R+$	$R-$	p-Value	$\alpha = 0.05$	$\alpha = 0.1$
MTMO/DRL-AT	IGD	41/4/0	1035.0	0.0	0.0	Yes	Yes
vs. LSMOVRPTW	HV	45/0/0	1035.0	0.0	0.0	Yes	Yes

Based on the aforementioned results, it is evident that the MTMO/DRL-AT outperforms the LSMOVRPTW on the majority of instances. This performance difference can be attributed to several factors that contribute to their varying performances: (1) The MTMO/DRL-AT incorporates attention models specifically designed for the subproblems of the MOVRPTW using DRL. These attention models are capable of adapting to MOVRPTW instances of varying scales. By leveraging the advantages of DRL, the attention models can learn to focus on critical aspects of the MOVRPTW and make more informed decisions during the optimization process. Furthermore, the output of the attention models in the MTMO/DRL-AT serves as high-quality initial solutions for the subsequent evolutionary process. These initial solutions provide a strong starting point for the algorithm, which can lead to faster convergence and better overall performance. (2) Unlike the MSMOVRPTW, which focuses solely on solving a single MOVRPTW formulation, the MTMO/DRL-AT introduces multitasking optimization. This means that the MTMO/DRL-AT can simultaneously solve multiple related optimization tasks, including the assisted task of the MOVRPTW. By incorporating multitasking optimization, valuable knowledge and insights gained from solving one task can be shared and utilized to improve the performance on other related tasks. This knowledge transfer and sharing contribute to the enhanced performance of the MTMO/DRL-AT compared to the LSMOVRPTW. (3) By combining attention models through DRL and multitasking optimization, the MTMO/DRL-AT offers a more robust and adaptive approach to solving the MOVRPTW. The attention models provide a finer grained focus on problem-specific details, while the multitasking optimization allows for the utilization of shared knowledge and insights across related tasks.

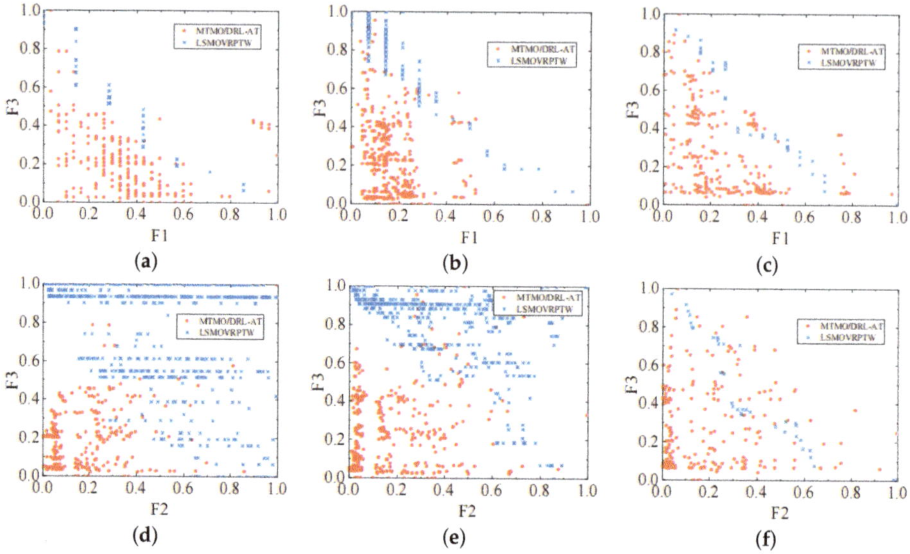

Figure 5. Distributions of the approximate Pareto fronts obtained by the MTMO/DRL-AT and LSMOVRPTW on the representative real-world instances: (**a**) 50-1-2 at f1-f3 plane; (**b**) 150-1-1 at f1-f3 plane; (**c**) 250-2-2 at f1-f3 plane; (**d**) 50-1-2 at f2-f3 plane; (**e**) 150-1-1 at f2-f3 plane; (**f**) 250-2-2 at f2-f3 plane.

6.3.2. Comparison with MMA-ALSC and HEMT

Two advanced approaches have recently been proposed to address the challenges of the MOVRPTW: the multiobjective memetic algorithm based on adaptive local search chains (MMA-ALSC) [27] and the hybrid evolutionary multitask algorithm (HEMT) [28]. The MMA-ALSC combines a multi-directional local search strategy with an enhanced local search chain technique. This allows for the search to be conducted in multiple directions in a chain-based way [27]. On the other hand, the HEMT takes a different approach by simultaneously considering multiple distinct MOVRPTWs within an evolutionary multitasking framework [28]. For this experiment, only the HEMT-hm5t variant is considered due to its promising performance. The comparisons between the MTMO/DRL-AT and MMA-ALSC (or HEMT) were conducted, and the results of the statistical tests are shown in Table 7.

Table 7. Results of the single- and multiple-problem analysis by the Wilcoxon test between the MTMO/DRL-AT and two recently proposed algorithms.

Algorithm	Metric	$w/t/l$	$R+$	$R-$	p-Value	$\alpha = 0.05$	$\alpha = 0.1$
MTMO/DRL-AT	IGD	35/9/1	1014.0	21.0	0.0	Yes	Yes
vs. MMA-ALSC	HV	45/0/0	1035.0	0.0	0.0	Yes	Yes
MTMO/DRL-AT	IGD	40/5/0	990.0	0.0	0.0	Yes	Yes
vs. HEMT	HV	45/0/0	1035.0	0.0	0.0	Yes	Yes

According to the results presented in Table 7, the MTMO/DRL-AT demonstrates superior performance compared to both the MMA-ALSC and HEMT across all instances. These findings provide a deeper understanding of the comparative performance of the algorithms: (1) In terms of the IGD, the MTMO/DRL-AT outperforms the MMA-ALSC on 35 instances and performs worse on only 1 instance. This indicates that the MTMO/DRL-AT consistently achieves better convergence and diversity in the obtained Pareto front solutions compared to the MMA-ALSC. The superior performance on the majority of instances suggests the effectiveness of the MTMO/DRL-AT in capturing a more diverse and high-quality set of solutions. (2) In terms of the HV, the MTMO/DRL-AT significantly surpasses the MMA-ALSC on all 45 instances. The consistent superiority of the MTMO/DRL-AT over the MMA-ALSC in the HV demonstrates that the MTMO/DRL-AT can generate solutions that are both close to the true Pareto front and well-distributed across the problem space. (3) The results of the Wilcoxon test in the multiple-problem analysis indicate that the MTMO/DRL-AT outperforms the MMA-ALSC significantly in terms of both the IGD and HV. This statistical analysis strengthens the claim of the superior performance of the MTMO/DRL-AT compared to the MMA-ALSC. The significance of the difference further reinforces the effectiveness of the MTMO/DRL-AT in solving the MOVRPTW. (4) When compared to the HEMT, the MTMO/DRL-AT consistently exhibits strong performance on the majority of instances. The consistent strong performance suggests that the MTMO/DRL-AT outperforms the HEMT in terms of both the IGD and HV. This indicates that the MTMO/DRL-AT can generate a more diverse set of high-quality solutions compared to the HEMT.

Overall, the observations from these comparisons provide strong evidence that the MTMO/DRL-AT is a highly effective approach for solving the MOVRPTW. The superior performance over the MMA-ALSC and HEMT, as indicated by both the quantitative metrics and statistical analysis, highlights the advantage of the MTMO/DRL-AT in achieving better convergence, diversity, and solution quality.

6.3.3. Overall Comparisons

To assess the overall performance of the proposed algorithm, a comparison was conducted between the MTMO/DRl-AT and the above competing algorithms. The results of Friedman's test are summarized in Table 8.

Based on the results in Table 8, the MTMO/DRl-AT emerges as the top algorithm for both the IGD and HV, outperforming all other algorithms. The HEMT achieves the second-best ranking for the IGD, followed by the MMA-ALSC. In terms of the HV, the LSMOVRPTW achieves the second-best ranking, followed by the MMA-ALSC.

Moreover, when considering the characteristics of various MOVRPTW instances, several observations can be derived from the detailed numerical values presented in the Supplementary File. Firstly, it is evident that the MTMO/DRL-AT outperforms its competitors in terms of both the HV and IGD values for the instances with different customer sizes. This showcases the algorithm's strengths in terms of convergence and diversity. Secondly, the performance improvement achieved by the proposed algorithm is more significant in large-scale instances compared to small-scale ones. This can be attributed to the favorable initial solution provided by DRL.

In general, these results emphasize the competitive and exceptional performance of the proposed algorithm when compared to other state-of-the-art algorithms for the MOVRPTW.

Table 8. Average ranking values of the compared algorithms on all the instances.

	IGD		HV	
Algorithm	**Average Ranking**	**Final Ranking**	**Average Ranking**	**Final Ranking**
MTMO/DRL-AT	1.00	1	1.09	1
LSMOVRPTW	3.49	4	2.63	2
MMA-ALSC	2.81	3	3.00	3
HEMT	2.70	2	3.28	4

6.4. Impact of Main Components in MTMO/DRL-AT

In this section, we conducted additional experiments to address the following issues:

- Are the solutions generated by the trained models as initial solutions better for solving the MOVRPTW compared to randomly generated initial solutions?
- Can the knowledge transfer between the main and assisted tasks effectively enhance the performance of the MTMO/DRL-AT for the MOVRPTW?

- Can the local search phase further improve the performance of the MTMO/DRL-AT?

Each of the above issues will be explored and discussed in the subsequent subsections.

6.4.1. Effect Analysis of Initializing Population Using the Trained Models

To verify the effectiveness of initializing the population with the trained models, a variant of the MTMO/DRL-AT with a random initial population, denoted as the MTMO-AT, was considered for comparison. In the MTMO-AT, the population for both the main task and assisted task is initialized in a random manner, replacing the generated solutions by the trained models. The statistical comparison results between the MTMO/DRL-AT and MTMO-AT are given in Table 9.

From Table 9, we can find that the MTMO/DRL-AT outperforms the MTMO-AT significantly overall. Specifically, the MTMO/DRL-AT shows significant improvements over the MTMO-AT on 40 and 31 instances in terms of the IGD and HV, respectively, based on single-problem analysis using the Wilcoxon test. Moreover, the results of the multiple-problem analysis reveal that the MTMO/DRL-AT achieves a higher $R+$ than $R-$ with the p-values below 0.05 in both cases, indicating significant differences between the MTMO/DRL-AT and MTMO-AT for all the instances.

In general, the superior performance of the MTMO/DRL-AT compared to the MTMO-AT highlights the promising potential of DRL-based approaches in addressing multi-objective optimization problems. The results clearly indicate that leveraging deep reinforcement learning techniques can lead to significant improvements in solving complex multi-objective optimization tasks.

Table 9. Results of the single- and multiple-problem analysis by the Wilcoxon test between the MTMO/DRL-AT and MTMO-AT.

Algorithm	Metric	$w/t/l$	$R+$	$R-$	p-Value	$\alpha = 0.05$	$\alpha = 0.1$
MTMO/DRL-AT	IGD	40/5/0	1035.0	0.0	0.0	Yes	Yes
vs. MTMO-AT	HV	31/5/9	923.0	112.0	5.0×10^{-5}	Yes	Yes

6.4.2. Effect Analysis of Knowledge-Transfer Strategy

To evaluate the influence of the knowledge-transfer strategy on the performance of the MTMO/DRL-AT, a comparison was made between the MTMO/DRL-AT and its variant, the MTMO/DRL-AT_ST, which does not include the knowledge-transfer strategy. Unlike the proposed algorithm, the MTMO/DRL-AT_ST does not generate an assisted task for the main task, and there is no knowledge sharing between the main and assisted tasks during the transfer reproduction phase. Table 10 provides a statistical summary of the performance comparisons between the MTMO/DRL-AT and MTMO/DRL-AT_ST.

According to the results shown in Table 10, the MTMO/DRL-AT consistently exhibits better performance than the MTMO/DRL-AT_ST in terms of both the IGD and HV. To be specific, in terms of the IGD, the MTMO/DRL-AT achieves significant improvement over the MTMO/DRL-AT_ST on 17 instances, while it performs worse on 13 instances. In terms of the HV, the MTMO/DRL-AT outperforms the MTMO/DRL-AT_ST on 24 instances, but is outperformed by it on 7 instances. Additionally, the multiple-problem analysis reveals that the MTMO/DRL-AT obtains a higher $R+$ value than the $R-$ value in both the IGD and HV measures. Notably, the p-values indicate that the MTMO/DRL-AT performs significantly better than the MTMO/DRL-AT_ST in terms of the HV, at both α levels of 0.05 and 0.1.

Overall, these findings clearly demonstrate the efficacy of the knowledge-transfer strategy in improving the performance of the MTMO/DRL-AT. Additionally, the advantages of constructing an assisted task with a simpler search space are also validated. In general, these results highlight the benefits and effectiveness of integrating a knowledge-transfer strategy and utilizing a simplified search space in the MTMO/DRL-AT.

Table 10. Results of the single- and multiple-problem analysis by the Wilcoxon test between the MTMO/DRL-AT and MTMO/DRL-AT_ST.

Algorithm	Metric	$w/t/l$	$R+$	$R-$	p-Value	$\alpha = 0.05$	$\alpha = 0.1$
MTMO/DRL-AT	IGD	17/15/13	705.0	330.0	3.38×10^{-2}	No	Yes
vs. MTMO/DRL-AT_ST	HV	24/14/7	745.0	155.0	4.20×10^{-5}	Yes	Yes

6.4.3. Effect Analysis of Local Search Operators

To further evaluate the effectiveness of local searches for the proposed algorithm, a comparison was conducted between the MTMO/DRL-AT and its variant without local search phase, referred to as the MTMO/DRL-ATw/oLS. Unlike the proposed algorithm, the MTMO/DRL-ATw/oLS does not utilize the local search for additional optimization after the transfer reproduction phase. The comparison results between the MTMO/DRL-AT and its variant are presented in Table 11.

Table 11 clearly indicates that the MTMO/DRL-AT exhibits a significant advantage over the MTMO/DRL-ATw/oLS in overall performance. Specifically, based on the single-problem statistical analysis, the MTMO/DRL-AT significantly outperforms the MTMO/DRL-ATw/oLS on 27 instances for the IGD and 45 instances for the HV. The multiple-problem statistical analysis also reveals that the MTMO/DRL-AT obtains a higher $R+$ value than the $R-$ value compared to its variant. Furthermore, significant differences between these two variants are observed at both $\alpha = 0.05$ and $\alpha = 0.1$. Therefore, these results convincingly demonstrate the positive impact of the local searches in further enhancing the performance of the MTMO/DRL-AT when tackling the MOVRPTW.

Table 11. Results of the single- and multiple-problem analysis by the Wilcoxon test between the MTMO/DRL-AT and MTMO/DRL-ATw/oLS.

Algorithm	Metric	$w/t/l$	$R+$	$R-$	p-Value	$\alpha = 0.05$	$\alpha = 0.1$
MTMO/DRL-AT	IGD	27/7/11	903.0	232.0	1.25×10^{-3}	Yes	Yes
vs. MTMO/DRL-ATw/oLS	HV	45/0/0	1035.0	0.0	0.0	Yes	Yes

7. Conclusions and Future Work

In this study, we have proposed the MTMO/DRL-AT, a multi-task multi-objective evolutionary search algorithm based on deep reinforcement learning (DRL), for solving the MOVRPTW. Unlike traditional evolutionary algorithms, the MTMO/DRL-AT constructs an assisted task for the MOVRPTW with a simpler search space and simultaneously optimizes both the main and assisted tasks in a multitasking scenario. Additionally, attention models specifically designed for the subproblems of the MOVRPTW are incorporated, allowing for adaptation to instances of varying scales and providing high-quality initial solutions. Experimental studies on 45 real-world MOVRPTW instances have demonstrated the outstanding and competitive performance of the proposed algorithm.

In future work, our main focus will be on enhancing the DRL-based modeling and training process by incorporating more informative structural information extracted from problem instances. We also aim to explore effective strategies for leveraging the knowledge acquired from the assisted tasks to further improve the performance of the proposed algorithm. Additionally, we intend to conduct a thorough investigation into the impact of key parameters on the performance of the MTMO/DRL-AT. Lastly, we plan to extend the application of the MTMO/DRL-AT to solve other multi-objective combinatorial optimization problems.

Supplementary Materials: The following Supporting Information can be downloaded at https://www.mdpi.com/article/10.3390/sym16081030/s1.

Author Contributions: Conceptualization, Y.C. and P.L.; methodology, J.D. and X.W.; software, J.W. and X.W.; validation, J.D. and Y.C.; writing—original draft preparation, J.D. and J.W.; writing—review and editing, Y.C.; visualization, J.W.; supervision, P.L. All authors have read and agreed to the published version of the manuscript.

Funding: This research was funded in part by the Natural Science Foundation of Fujian Province of China (No. 2021J01318), the Fujian Provincial Science and Technology Major Project (No. 2020HZ02014), and the Quanzhou Science and Technology Major Project (No. 2021GZ1).

Data Availability Statement: Data are contained with the article.

Conflicts of Interest: The authors declare no conflicts of interest. The funders had no role in the design of the study; in the collection, analyses, or interpretation of the data; in the writing of the manuscript; nor in the decision to publish the results.

References

1. Kallehauge, B.; Larsen, J.; Madsen, O.B.; Solomon, M.M. Vehicle routing problem with time windows. In *Column Generation*; Springer: Boston, MA, USA, 2005; pp. 67–98.
2. Braekers, K.; Ramaekers, K.; Nieuwenhuyse, I.V. The vehicle routing problem: State of the art classification and review. *Comput. Ind. Eng.* **2016**, *99*, 300–313. [CrossRef]
3. Mańdziuk, J. New Shades of the Vehicle Routing Problem: Emerging Problem Formulations and Computational Intelligence Solution Methods. *IEEE Trans. Emerg. Top. Comput. Intell.* **2019**, *3*, 230–244. [CrossRef]
4. Fathollahi-Fard, A.M.; Ahmadi, A.; Karimi, B. Multi-objective optimization of home healthcare with working-time balancing and care continuity. *Sustainability* **2021**, *13*, 12431. [CrossRef]
5. Mojtahedi, M.; Fathollahi-Fard, A.M.; Tavakkoli-Moghaddam, R.; Newton, S. Sustainable vehicle routing problem for coordinated solid waste management. *J. Ind. Inf. Integr.* **2021**, *23*, 100220. [CrossRef]
6. Baldacci, R.; Mingozzi, A.; Roberti, R. Recent exact algorithms for solving the vehicle routing problem under capacity and time window constraints. *Eur. J. Oper. Res.* **2012**, *218*, 1–6. [CrossRef]
7. Braeysy, O.; Gendreau, M. Vehicle Routing Problem with Time Windows, Part II: Metaheuristics. *Transp. Sci.* **2005**, *39*, 119–139. [CrossRef]
8. Dixit, A.; Mishra, A.; Shukla, A. Vehicle Routing Problem with Time Windows Using Meta-Heuristic Algorithms: A Survey. In *Harmony Search and Nature Inspired Optimization Algorithms*; Advances in Intelligent Systems and Computing; Springer: Singapore, 2019; Volume 741, pp. 539–546.
9. Gutiérrez, J.; Landa-Silva, D.; Moreno-Pérez, J. Nature of real-world multi-objective vehicle routing with evolutionary algorithms. In Proceedings of the IEEE International Conference on Systems, Man, and Cybernetics, Anchorage, AK, USA, 9–12 October 2011; pp. 257–264.
10. Zhou, Y.; Wang, J. A Local Search-Based Multiobjective Optimization Algorithm for Multiobjective Vehicle Routing Problem with Time Windows. *IEEE Syst. J.* **2017**, *9*, 1100–1113. [CrossRef]
11. Sun, Y.; Yen, G.G.; Yi, Z. IGD indicator-based evolutionary algorithm for many-objective optimization problems. *IEEE Trans. Evol. Comput.* **2019**, *23*, 173–187. [CrossRef]
12. Li, K.; Zhang, T.; Wang, R. Deep reinforcement learning for multiobjective optimization. *IEEE Trans. Cybern.* **2020**, *51*, 3103–3114. [CrossRef] [PubMed]
13. Krizhevsky, A.; Sutskever, I.; Hinton, G.E. Imagenet classification with deep convolutional neural networks. *Adv. Neural Inf. Process. Syst.* **2012**, *25*, 1–9. [CrossRef]
14. Simonyan, K.; Zisserman, A. Very deep convolutional networks for large-scale image recognition. *arXiv* **2014**, arXiv:1409.1556.
15. Li, J.; Monroe, W.; Ritter, A.; Galley, M.; Gao, J.; Jurafsky, D. Deep reinforcement learning for dialogue generation. *arXiv* **2016**, arXiv:1606.01541.
16. Bello, I.; Pham, H.; Le, Q.V.; Norouzi, M.; Bengio, S. Neural combinatorial optimization with reinforcement learning. *arXiv* **2016**, arXiv:1611.09940.
17. Zhao, J.; Mao, M.; Zhao, X.; Zou, J. A hybrid of deep reinforcement learning and local search for the vehicle routing problems. *IEEE Trans. Intell. Transp. Syst.* **2021**, *22*, 7208–7218. [CrossRef]
18. Wang, L.; Pan, Z. Scheduling optimization for flow-shop based on deep reinforcement learning and iterative greedy method. *Control Decis.* **2021**, *36*, 2609–2617.
19. Zhang, Y.; Wang, J.; Zhang, Z.; Zhou, Y. MODRL/D-EL: Multiobjective deep reinforcement learning with evolutionary learning for multiobjective optimization. In Proceedings of the 2021 International Joint Conference on Neural Networks (IJCNN), Shenzhen, China, 18–22 July 2021; pp. 1–8.
20. Tang, K.; Yao, X. Learn to Optimize-A Brief Overview. *Natl. Sci. Rev.* **2024**, *11*, nwae132. [CrossRef] [PubMed]

21. Gupta, A.; Ong, Y.S.; Feng, L. Multifactorial evolution: Toward evolutionary multitasking. *IEEE Trans. Evol. Comput.* **2015**, *20*, 343–357. [CrossRef]
22. Ong, Y.S. Towards evolutionary multitasking: A new paradigm in evolutionary computation. In *Computational Intelligence, Cyber Security and Computational Models*; Springer: Singapore, 2016; pp. 25–26.
23. Feng, L.; Zhou, L.; Gupta, A.; Zhong, J.; Zhu, Z.; Tan, K.; Qin, K. Solving Generalized Vehicle Routing Problem with Occasional Drivers via Evolutionary Multitasking. *IEEE Trans. Cybern.* **2021**, *51*, 3171–3184. [CrossRef] [PubMed]
24. Feng, L.; Huang, Y.; Zhou, L.; Zhong, J.; Gupta, A.; Tang, K.; Tan, K.C. Explicit Evolutionary Multitasking for Combinatorial Optimization: A Case Study on Capacitated Vehicle Routing Problem. *IEEE Trans. Cybern.* **2021**, *51*, 3143–3156. [CrossRef]
25. Qi, Y.; Hou, Z.; Li, H.; Huang, J.; Li, X. A decomposition based memetic algorithm for multi-objective vehicle routing problem with time windows. *Comput. Oper. Res.* **2015**, *62*, 61–77. [CrossRef]
26. Moradi, B. The new optimization algorithm for the vehicle routing problem with time windows using multi-objective discrete learnable evolution model. *Soft Comput.* **2020**, *24*, 6741–6769. [CrossRef]
27. Zhang, K.; Cai, Y.; Fu, S.; Zhang, H. Multiobjective memetic algorithm based on adaptive local search chains for vehicle routing problem with time windows. *Evol. Intell.* **2022**, *15*, 2283–2294. [CrossRef]
28. Cai, Y.; Cheng, M.; Zhou, Y.; Liu, P.; Guo, J.M. A hybrid evolutionary multitask algorithm for the multiobjective vehicle routing problem with time windows. *Inf. Sci.* **2022**, *612*, 168–187. [CrossRef]
29. Li, B.; Li, J.; Tang, K.; Yao, X. Many-objective evolutionary algorithms: A survey. *ACM Comput. Surv. (CSUR)* **2015**, *48*, 1–35. [CrossRef]
30. Vinyals, O.; Fortunato, M.; Jaitly, N. Pointer networks. *Adv. Neural Inf. Process. Syst.* **2015**, *28*, 1–9.
31. Nazari, M.; Oroojlooy, A.; Snyder, L.; Takác, M. Reinforcement learning for solving the vehicle routing problem. *Adv. Neural Inf. Process. Syst.* **2018**, *31*, 1–13.
32. Nowak, A.; Villar, S.; Bandeira, A.S.; Bruna, J. A note on learning algorithms for quadratic assignment with graph neural networks. *Stat* **2017**, *1050*, 22.
33. Deudon, M.; Cournut, P.; Lacoste, A.; Adulyasak, Y.; Rousseau, L.M. Learning heuristics for the tsp by policy gradient. In *Integration of Constraint Programming, Artificial Intelligence, and Operations Research: 15th International Conference, CPAIOR 2018, Delft, The Netherlands, 26–29 June 2018, Proceedings*; Springer: Cham, Switzerland, 2018; pp. 170–181.
34. Kool, W.; Van Hoof, H.; Welling, M. Attention, learn to solve routing problems! *arXiv* **2018**, arXiv:1803.08475.
35. Peng, B.; Wang, J.; Zhang, Z. A deep reinforcement learning algorithm using dynamic attention model for vehicle routing problems. In *Artificial Intelligence Algorithms and Applications: 11th International Symposium, ISICA 2019, Guangzhou, China, 16–17 November 2019, Revised Selected Papers*; Springer: Singapore, 2020; pp. 636–650.
36. Wu, H.; Wang, J.; Zhang, Z. MODRL/D-AM: Multiobjective deep reinforcement learning algorithm using decomposition and attention model for multiobjective optimization. In *Artificial Intelligence Algorithms and Applications: 11th International Symposium, ISICA 2019, Guangzhou, China, 16–17 November 2019, Revised Selected Papers*; Springer: Singapore, 2020; pp. 575–589.
37. Zhou, L.; Feng, L.; Zhong, J.; Ong, Y.S.; Zhu, Z.; Sha, E. Evolutionary multitasking in combinatorial search spaces: A case study in capacitated vehicle routing problem. In Proceedings of the 2016 IEEE Symposium Series on Computational Intelligence (SSCI), Athens, Greece, 6–9 December 2016; pp. 1–8.
38. Liu, M.; Wang, Z.; Li, J. A deep reinforcement learning algorithm for large-scale vehicle routing problems. In Proceedings of the International Conference on Electronic Information Technology (EIT 2022), Chengdu, China, 18–20 March 2022; Volume 12254, pp. 824–829.
39. Zhang, Q.; Hui, L. MOEA/D: A Multiobjective Evolutionary Algorithm Based on Decomposition. *IEEE Trans. Evol. Comput.* **2008**, *11*, 712–731. [CrossRef]
40. Das, I.; Dennis, J.E. Normal-boundary intersection: A new method for generating the Pareto surface in nonlinear multicriteria optimization problems. *SIAM J. Optim.* **1998**, *8*, 631–657. [CrossRef]
41. Grondman, I.; Busoniu, L.; Lopes, G.A.; Babuska, R. A survey of actor-critic reinforcement learning: Standard and natural policy gradients. *IEEE Trans. Syst. Man Cybern. Part C (Appl. Rev.)* **2012**, *42*, 1291–1307. [CrossRef]
42. Kingma, D.P.; Ba, J. Adam: A method for stochastic optimization. *arXiv* **2014**, arXiv:1412.6980.
43. Deb, K.; Pratap, A.; Agarwal, S.; Meyarivan, T. A fast and elitist multiobjective genetic algorithm: NSGA-II. *IEEE Trans. Evol. Comput.* **2002**, *6*, 182–197. [CrossRef]
44. Storn, R.; Price, K. Differential evolution–A simple and efficient heuristic for global optimization over continuous spaces. *J. Glob. Optim.* **1997**, *11*, 341–359. [CrossRef]
45. Liu, B.; Wang, L.; Jin, Y.H. An effective PSO-based memetic algorithm for flow shop scheduling. *IEEE Trans. Syst. Man Cybern. Part B (Cybern.)* **2007**, *37*, 18–27. [CrossRef] [PubMed]
46. Coello, C.A.C.; Sierra, M.R. A study of the parallelization of a coevolutionary multi-objective evolutionary algorithm. In Proceedings of the Mexican International Conference on Artificial Intelligence, Mexico City, Mexico, 26–30 April 2004; Springer: Berlin/Heidelberg, Germany, 2004; pp. 688–697.
47. Zitzler, E.; Thiele, L. Multiobjective optimization using evolutionary algorithms—A comparative case study. In Proceedings of the International Conference on Parallel Problem Solving from Nature, Amsterdam, The Netherlands, 27–30 September 1998; Springer: Berlin/Heidelberg, Germany, 1998; pp. 292–301.

48. Alcalá-Fdez, J.; Sanchez, L.; Garcia, S.; del Jesus, M.J.; Ventura, S.; Garrell, J.M.; Otero, J.; Romero, C.; Bacardit, J.; Rivas, V.M.; et al. KEEL: A software tool to assess evolutionary algorithms for data mining problems. *Soft Comput.* **2009**, *13*, 307–318. [CrossRef]
49. García, S.; Fernández, A.; Luengo, J.; Herrera, F. A study of statistical techniques and performance measures for genetics-based machine learning: Accuracy and interpretability. *Soft Comput.* **2009**, *13*, 959–977. [CrossRef]
50. Derrac, J.; García, S.; Molina, D.; Herrera, F. A practical tutorial on the use of nonparametric statistical tests as a methodology for comparing evolutionary and swarm intelligence algorithms. *Swarm Evol. Comput.* **2011**, *1*, 3–18. [CrossRef]

symmetry

MDPI

Article

Short-Term Electrical Load Forecasting Using an Enhanced Extreme Learning Machine Based on the Improved Dwarf Mongoose Optimization Algorithm

Haocheng Wang, Yu Zhang * and Lixin Mu

College of Computer and Control Engineering, Northeast Forestry University, Harbin 150040, China; wanghaocheng@nefu.edu.cn (H.W.); mulixin@nefu.edu.cn (L.M.)
* Correspondence: zhangyu0902@163.com; Tel.: +86-13804614102

Abstract: Accurate short-term electrical load forecasting is crucial for the stable operation of power systems. Given the nonlinear, periodic, and rapidly changing characteristics of short-term power load forecasts, this paper introduces a novel forecasting method employing an Extreme Learning Machine (ELM) enhanced by an improved Dwarf Mongoose Optimization Algorithm (Local escape Dwarf Mongoose Optimization Algorithm, LDMOA). This method addresses the significant prediction errors of conventional ELM models and enhances prediction accuracy. The enhancements to the Dwarf Mongoose Optimization Algorithm include three key modifications: initially, a dynamic backward learning strategy is integrated at the early stages of the algorithm to augment its global search capabilities. Subsequently, a cosine algorithm is employed to locate new food sources, thereby expanding the search scope and avoiding local optima. Lastly, a "madness factor" is added when identifying new sleeping burrows to further widen the search area and effectively circumvent local optima. Comparative analyses using benchmark functions demonstrate the improved algorithm's superior convergence and stability. In this study, the LDMOA algorithm optimizes the weights and thresholds of the ELM to establish the LDMOA-ELM prediction model. Experimental forecasts utilizing data from China's 2016 "The Electrician Mathematical Contest in Modeling" demonstrate that the LDMOA-ELM model significantly outperforms the original ELM model in terms of prediction error and accuracy.

Keywords: electrical load forecasting; machine learning; extreme learning machine; dynamic backward learning; madness factor operator

1. Introduction

Accurate electric load forecasting is crucial for the planning and reliable economic operation of power systems. It not only ensures the normal electricity usage of consumers but also reduces costs and guarantees the safety of power systems [1]. However, challenges in predicting electric load demand have increased sharply due to factors such as global climate change, energy supply constraints, increasing numbers of electricity users, and the integration of new energy device loads into the grid [2].

In the realm of electric load forecasting, researchers have employed time series regression models [3] and fuzzy linear regression models [4] to predict load, focusing on the temporal characteristics of load data and providing strong interpretability of the models. However, these methods have limitations in forecasting non-linear load data. In recent years, with the development of intelligent optimization algorithms, an increasing number of researchers have started incorporating these algorithms into electric load forecasting. Han M. C. enhanced the capability and prediction accuracy of capturing characteristics in load data by optimizing LSTM hyperparameters through a sparrow optimization algorithm that integrates Cauchy mutation and inverse learning strategies [5]. Zhang Z. C. quantified the behavior of dragonflies in the dragonfly algorithm to boost the search capability, and utilized an adaptive noise complete empirical mode decomposition method for preprocessing raw data, thereby improving the prediction accuracy of SVR in load forecasting [6]. Ge Q. B. employed K-means clustering to categorize data and then used a combined predictive algorithm of reinforcement learning and particle swarm optimization along with the least squares support vector machine to predict different types of data [7]. Fan G. F. developed a new model combining the random forest model and mean-generating function model, significantly enhancing the prediction accuracy of peaks and troughs in highly volatile data [8]. Additionally, Xu R. [9] noted that extreme learning machines offer faster learning speeds and less human intervention, and are easier to implement. Deng B. [10] argued that compared to support vector machines, extreme learning machines have milder optimization constraints and quicker learning speeds. Some researchers have also applied optimized ELMs to electric load forecasting. For instance, Wang Tong utilized an improved artificial hummingbird algorithm for optimizing parameters in Extreme Learning Machines (ELM), significantly enhancing prediction accuracy [11]. Long Gan and others have used an improved multiverse algorithm to optimize the input layer weights and thresholds of ELMs, thereby improving their prediction accuracy [12]. Wang Z-X. employed an adaptive evolutionary ELM for data prediction, integrating a chaos-adapted whale optimization algorithm based on a firefly perturbation strategy and a chaotic sparrow search algorithm, which exhibited outstanding performance [13]. Additionally, Zhang S. proposed an ELM model under a moth flame optimization algorithm based on Tsne dimensionality reduction and visualization analysis, which achieved higher prediction accuracy than the original ELM model [14].

Accurate electric load forecasting can impact related decisions in power systems, such as generation control, economic dispatch, and maintenance scheduling. Therefore, to achieve high-precision short-term electric load forecasting, this paper proposes an ELM prediction model based on the improved Dwarf Mongoose Optimization Algorithm. Applied to short-term electric load forecasting, experimental results demonstrate that this model achieves higher accuracy compared to other ELM models.

2. Extreme Learning Machine

The Extreme Learning Machine (ELM) is a type of Single-hidden Layer Feedforward Neural Network (SLFN) algorithm, introduced by Professor Guang-Bin Huang and others based on the theory of the Moore–Penrose pseudoinverse [15]. This algorithm was developed to address several issues inherent in SLFNs, such as slow learning rates, long iteration times, and the traditional need to preset learning rates and step sizes. Unlike conventional neural network learning algorithms, the ELM requires only the appropriate setting of hidden layer node numbers. It autonomously generates all necessary parameters for the hidden layer and determines the final output layer weights through the least squares method. Due to its superior learning and nonlinear approximation capabilities compared to traditional machine learning algorithms, researchers have applied the ELM across a broad range of fields, including fault diagnosis [16], load forecasting [17], and feature recognition [18].

The ELM algorithm operates with a single hidden layer, where each layer from input to output comprises independent neurons, all interconnected in a fully connected manner. The network structure of the ELM is illustrated in Figure 1.

Assuming there are N arbitrary samples (x_i, t_i), $x_i = \left[x_{i1}, x_{i2} \ldots, x_{in}\right]^T \in R^n$ and $t_i = \left[t_{i1}, t_{i2}, \cdots, t_{im}\right]^t \in R^m$. This can be represented by a single hidden layer neural network with L hidden nodes, as illustrated in Figure 1 and described by Equation (1).

$$o_j = \sum_{j=1}^{L} \beta_i g(w_i \cdot x_i + b_i) \qquad j = 1, 2, \cdots, N \tag{1}$$

Here, $g(x)$ is the activation function, $w_i = [w_{i1}, w_{i2}, \cdots, w_{in}]^T$ are the input weights, $\beta_i = [\beta_{i1}, \beta_{i2}, \cdots, \beta_{im}]^T \in R^m$ are the output weights, and b_i is the bias of the ith hidden layer unit, with $w_i \cdot x_i$ being the dot product between them.

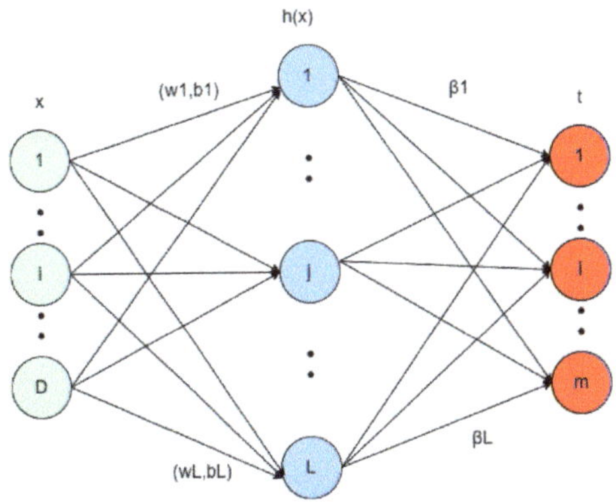

Figure 1. Extreme learning machine network structure.

Extreme Learning Machines, as a type of single hidden layer neural network, have an output error that asymptotically approaches zero, as shown in Equation (2).

$$\sum_{j=1}^{L} ||o_j - t_i|| = 0 \tag{2}$$

Equation (2) can be represented using matrices, as shown in Equation (3):

$$H\beta = T \tag{3}$$

Here, H denotes the hidden layer output matrix, β represents the output weights, and T is the target output. The matrix H can be expressed by Equation (4).

$$H = \begin{bmatrix} h_1(x_1) \cdots h_L(x_1) \\ \vdots \\ h_1(x_D) \cdots h_L(x_D) \end{bmatrix}, \ T = [t_1, \cdots t_D] \tag{4}$$

According to Equation (3), Equation (5) can be derived.

$$\beta = H^T T \tag{5}$$

In Equation (5), H^T represents the Moore–Penrose pseudoinverse of the matrix H.

3. Dwarf Mongoose Algorithm

The Dwarf Mongoose Algorithm is an intelligent optimization algorithm inspired by the social behavior of dwarf mongoose groups. This algorithm consists of three parts: the Alpha Group, the Scout Group, and the Babysitter Group. The Alpha Group produces a female leader to guide the group in foraging. The Scout Group is responsible for finding new locations for sleeping mounds, while the Babysitter Group influences the performance of the algorithm through its numbers.

3.1. Alpha Group

The population is initialized as shown in Equation (6),

$$x_{i,j} = unifrnd(LB, UB, Dim) \tag{6}$$

where $x_{i,j}$ represents the initial position, LB and UB denote the lower and upper bounds of the solution space, Dim represents the dimension of decision variables, and $unifrnd$ is a uniformly distributed random number.

Furthermore, a female leader emerges within the dwarf mongoose population, as depicted in Equation (7).

$$\alpha = \frac{fit_i}{\sum_{i=1}^{N} fit_i} \tag{7}$$

Here, fit_i represents the fitness value of the ith individual, and N is the number of individuals in the population. The number of individuals in the Alpha Group is the total population N minus the number of individuals in the Babysitter Group, i.e., $n = N - bs$.

The female leader in the Alpha Group guides the other members to the food source location via calls, as shown in Equation (8):

$$X_{new} = X_i + peep \times phi \times (X_i - X_k) \tag{8}$$

Here, X_{new} is the new position of the dwarf mongoose, $peep$ is the calling coefficient, set at $peep = 2$ in this study, and phi is a uniformly distributed random number within [0, 1]. X_i is the current position of the female leader, and X_k is the position of another random individual in the Alpha Group distinct from the leader. Subsequently, the new position X_{new} undergoes a fitness evaluation to obtain fit_{i+1}, and the value of the sleeping mound is determined according to Equation (9).

$$sm_i = \frac{fit_{i+1} - fit_i}{\max\{|fit_{i+1}, fit_i|\}} \tag{9}$$

Here, sm_i represents the value of the sleeping mound, and the average value of the sleeping mound can be calculated according to Equation (10).

$$\varphi = \frac{\sum_{i=1}^{N} sm_i}{n} \tag{10}$$

3.2. Scout Group

The primary responsibility of the Scout Group is to locate new positions for sleeping mounds, as described by the movement formula in Equation (11).

$$X_{i+1} = \begin{cases} x_i - CF \times phi \times r \times \left[x_i - \vec{M}\right], & if\ \varphi_{i+1} > \varphi_i \\ x_i + CF \times phi \times r \times \left[x_i - \vec{M}\right], & else \end{cases} \tag{11}$$

Here, r is a random number within [0, 1], CF is a mobility parameter for the dwarf mongoose population, and $\vec{M}$ is the direction vector determining the mongoose's movement direction. The formulas for calculating CF and $\vec{M}$ are given in Equations (12) and (13), respectively.

$$CF = \left(1 - \frac{Iter}{MaxIt}\right)^{\left(2\frac{Iter}{MaxIt}\right)} \tag{12}$$

$$\vec{M} = \sum_{i=1}^{N} \frac{x_i \times sm_i}{x_i} \tag{13}$$

Here, $Iter$ is the current iteration number, and $MaxIt$ is the maximum number of iterations. The movement parameter CF linearly decreases as the number of iterations increases.

3.3. Babysitter Group

When the timing parameter is greater than or equal to the exchange parameter, i.e., $C \geq L$, the Babysitter Group assumes that the Alpha Group's foraging capability is weak.

At this point, the Babysitter Group will swap roles with the Alpha Group, and the dwarf mongoose community will begin searching for a new sleeping mound.

4. Enhancements to the Dwarf Mongoose Algorithm

To address the Dwarf Mongoose Algorithm's tendency to fall into local optima and its weak global search performance, this paper proposes the incorporation of a reverse learning strategy to enhance the algorithm's exploratory capability, thereby improving its global search performance. Additionally, the inclusion of a craziness operator factor and the sine–cosine algorithm expands the local search range of the algorithm, helping to circumvent issues of local optima.

4.1. Dynamic Reverse Learning Strategy

The reverse learning strategy [19] is a common perturbation tactic that expands the algorithm's exploration range to find better solutions. In the reversed learning strategy, the new position generated is symmetrical to the original position at the point $\frac{X_i+x_i}{2}$. This measure enhances the exploratory nature of the algorithm, allowing it to search in the opposite direction for improved population individual positions. Moreover, the new position is compared with the original in terms of fitness, and the individual with the optimal fitness is selected as the population individual position. The reverse learning strategy is depicted in Equation (14).

$$X_i = LB + UB - x_i \tag{14}$$

In the formula, X_i represents the population individual after reverse learning, with LB and UB denoting the lower and upper limits of the solution space, and x_i indicating the original position of the individual within the population. To enhance the search for optimal solutions within the solution space, a random factor is included in the reverse learning strategy, further diversifying the population within the solution space. The dynamic reverse learning strategy introduced in the early stages of the algorithm iteration is shown in Equation (15).

$$X_i = r \times (LB + UB) - x_i \tag{15}$$

Here, r is a random number within (0, 1).

4.2. Sine–Cosine Algorithm

During the search process, the sine–cosine algorithm [20] conducts searches in the form of sine and cosine waveforms. This method enhances the search capabilities of the algorithm, enabling it to avoid becoming trapped in local optima. Additionally, the search process of the algorithm exhibits point symmetry characteristics typical of sine and cosine functions. While the Alpha Group, led by the female leader, is searching for new food sources, this process can easily become trapped in local optima. To avoid such outcomes, this study incorporates the sine–cosine algorithm to expand the search range of the algorithm. The formula for searching new food sources, updated with the sine–cosine algorithm, is shown in Equation (16).

$$X_{new} = \begin{cases} X_i + phi \times r_1 \times sin(r_2) \times (X_i - X_k), & if\, r < 0.5 \\ X_i + phi \times r_1 \times cos(r_2) \times (X_i - X_k), & else \end{cases} \tag{16}$$

In Equation (16), r and r_1 are random numbers within (0, 1), r_2 is a random number within (0, 2π), X_i is the position of the female leader, and X_k is the position of another individual distinct from the leader.

4.3. Craziness Factor

In the later stages of the algorithm, when dwarf mongoose individuals seek a sleeping mound, the group tends to converge on this mound, which could lead to local optima. This paper introduces a craziness operator factor, which perturbs the position of the optimal individual to prevent the algorithm from becoming trapped in local optima in its later iterations. The position of the optimal individual after incorporating the craziness operator factor is illustrated in Equation (17).

$$X_i = x_i \times (1 + Pc \times xcraze \times sign) \tag{17}$$

In Equation (17), x_i represents the original optimal individual position, and Pc and $xcraze$ are disturbance factors within the craziness operator factor, with $xcraze$ set at 0.0001. Pc and $xcraze$ are described by Equations (18) and (19), respectively.

$$Pc = \begin{cases} 1, c < P_r \\ 0, \ else \end{cases} \tag{18}$$

$$sign = \begin{cases} -1, c > 0.5 \\ 1, \ else \end{cases} \tag{19}$$

In the craziness factor, the $sign$ is determined as either 1 or -1 based on the magnitude of c, exhibiting a kind of symmetry in its values. This method of value assignment can perturb the algorithm, expanding its search range and helping to avoid local optima. In Equation (19), c is a random number within (0, 1), and P_r is the preset craziness probability, set at 0.4 in this study.

4.4. LDMOA Steps and Process

In the enhanced DMOA, the reverse learning strategy is utilized to expand the algorithm's exploratory capacity and search range, thereby enhancing its global search capabilities. Simultaneously, the introduction of the sine–cosine algorithm and the craziness operator factor enhance the local search capability of the algorithm, effectively avoiding situations of local optima. Figure 2 shows the workflow diagram of the LDMOA, and below is the operational process of the LDMOA.

Step 1: Set the initial parameters of the algorithm, such as population parameters, dimensions of the solution space and its limits, and maximum iteration parameters, and utilize the dynamic reverse learning strategy to expand the search range.

Step 2: Select the female leader according to Equation (7) and set the related coefficients. During the process of searching for new food sources by the dwarf mongoose group, incorporate the sine–cosine algorithm to further expand the search for new food source positions.

Step 3: The sleeping mound position is influenced by the optimal position; introduce the craziness operator factor to perturb it, and then determine the sleeping mound position and calculate its average value.

Step 4: Assess whether $C \geq L$; when this condition is met, swap the Alpha Group and Babysitter Group, and proceed with the formula to search for new sleeping mounds and forage.

Step 5: Determine whether the algorithm has reached the maximum iteration count; if not, repeat the above steps, and otherwise output the optimal results.

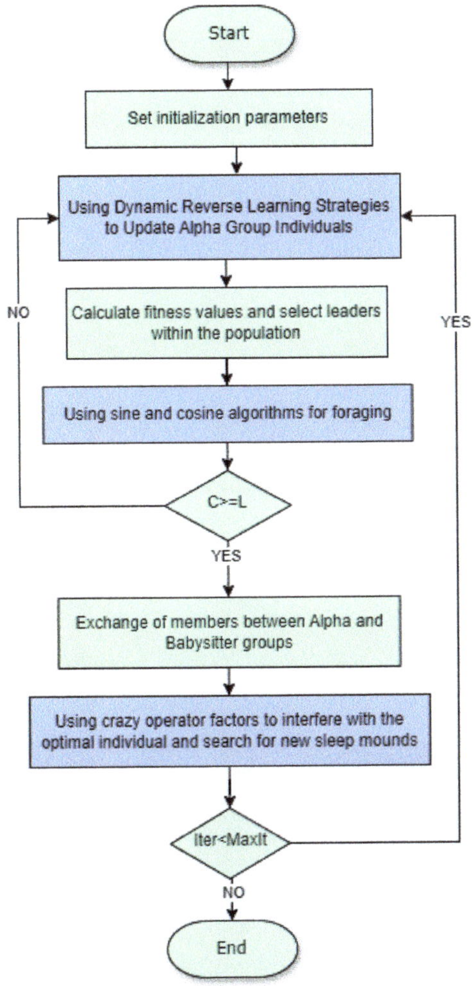

Figure 2. LDMOA Flowchart.

4.5. Benchmark Function Testing

To ensure that the enhanced strategy provides positive improvements over the original Dwarf Mongoose Optimization Algorithm (DMOA), we conducted benchmark function tests comparing the modified algorithm with the original. The selected benchmark functions are shown in Table 1.

Functions f_1 to f_2 are unimodal functions, which test the algorithm's convergence capability. Functions f_3 to f_6 are multimodal functions, evaluating the algorithm's ability to escape local optima. Functions f_7 to f_{11} are hybrid functions, and f_{12} to f_{15} are composite functions, with both sets testing the optimization performance in complex scenarios.

The enhanced and original algorithms were tested using the benchmark functions listed in the table. To ensure the accuracy of the benchmark tests, the algorithms were configured with parameters as shown in Table 2, including population initialization size ($nPop$) and solution space dimensions (Dim). The results are presented in Section 4.6 and Table 3.

Table 1. Benchmark function.

Function	Function Name	Optimal Value
f_1	Shifted and Rotated Bent Cigar Function	100
f_2	Shifted and Rotated Zakharov Function	300
f_3	Shifted and Rotated Rosenbrock's Function	400
f_4	Shifted and Rotated Lunacek Bi_Rastrigin Function	700
f_5	Shifted and Rotated Non-Continuous Rastrigin's Function	800
f_6	Shifted and Rotated Levy Function	900
f_7	Hybrid Function 2 (N = 3)	1200
f_8	Hybrid Function 3 (N = 3)	1300
f_9	Hybrid Function 4 (N = 4)	1400
f_{10}	Hybrid Function 6 (N = 4)	1600
f_{11}	Hybrid Function 6 (N = 5)	1900
f_{12}	Composition Function 1 (N = 3)	2100
f_{13}	Composition Function 3 (N = 4)	2300
f_{14}	Composition Function 5 (N = 5)	2500
f_{15}	Composition Function 9 (N = 3)	2900

Table 2. Parameter settings.

Algorithm	nPop	Dim.	Number of Runs	Number of Iterations
DMOA	50	30	30	500
LDMOA	50	30	30	500

Table 3. Function test result.

Function	Algorithm	Average Value	Standard Deviation
f_1	DMOA	2.2380×10^8	1.5191×10^8
	LDMOA	$\mathbf{4.5751 \times 10^6}$	$\mathbf{4.7176 \times 10^6}$
f_2	DMOA	3.8921×10^5	1.4859×10^5
	LDMOA	$\mathbf{1.9088 \times 10^5}$	$\mathbf{3.0369 \times 10^4}$
f_3	DMOA	6.4582×10^2	59.71001
	LDMOA	$\mathbf{4.7798 \times 10^2}$	**25.6402**
f_4	DMOA	9.8498×10^2	16.6132
	LDMOA	$\mathbf{8.7634 \times 10^2}$	**16.2196**
f_5	DMOA	1.050×10^3	15.3858
	LDMOA	$\mathbf{9.4086 \times 10^2}$	**11.9651**
f_6	DMOA	4.8974×10^3	1.1978×10^3
	LDMOA	$\mathbf{2.5027 \times 10^3}$	$\mathbf{5.5686 \times 10^2}$
f_7	DMOA	3.7911×10^8	1.5928×10^8
	LDMOA	$\mathbf{2.1834 \times 10^7}$	$\mathbf{6.8054 \times 10^6}$
f_8	DMOA	7.4329×10^6	5.6933×10^6
	LDMOA	$\mathbf{4.0444 \times 10^5}$	$\mathbf{3.4691 \times 10^5}$
f_9	DMOA	2.7983×10^5	1.1979×10^5
	LDMOA	$\mathbf{2.8142 \times 10^4}$	$\mathbf{1.4802 \times 10^4}$
f_{10}	DMOA	3.9829×10^3	2.3781×10^2
	LDMOA	$\mathbf{2.9550 \times 10^3}$	$\mathbf{1.8911 \times 10^2}$
f_{11}	DMOA	8.9163×10^4	8.4653×10^4
	LDMOA	$\mathbf{2.5640 \times 10^4}$	$\mathbf{1.8000 \times 10^4}$
f_{12}	DMOA	2.5562×10^3	18.1339
	LDMOA	$\mathbf{2.4442 \times 10^3}$	**12.3400**
f_{13}	DMOA	2.9142×10^3	17.9570
	LDMOA	$\mathbf{2.8032 \times 10^3}$	**17.5984**
f_{14}	DMOA	2.9628×10^3	20.6205
	LDMOA	$\mathbf{2.8955 \times 10^3}$	**5.5951**
f_{15}	DMOA	5.0032×10^3	1.9213×10^2
	LDMOA	$\mathbf{3.7782 \times 10^3}$	$\mathbf{1.5826 \times 10^2}$

4.6. Results of Benchmark Function Testing

In the benchmark function test results, the mean and standard deviation reflect the convergence performance and stability of the algorithms, respectively, with the best values highlighted in bold. The enhanced algorithm shows superior convergence performance and stability compared to the original algorithm. As demonstrated in Table 3, the enhanced algorithm outperforms the original in unimodal functions f_1 to f_2, multimodal functions f_3 to f_6, hybrid functions f_7 to f_{11}, and composite functions f_{12} to f_{15}. Based on the analyses in Section 4.5, the enhanced algorithm surpasses the original in convergence, avoiding local optima, and handling complex optimization problems. Figure 3 includes graphical representations of some function iterations: (a) unimodal function, (b) multimodal function, (c) hybrid function, and (d) composite function, all showing improved iterative convergence results for the enhanced algorithm.

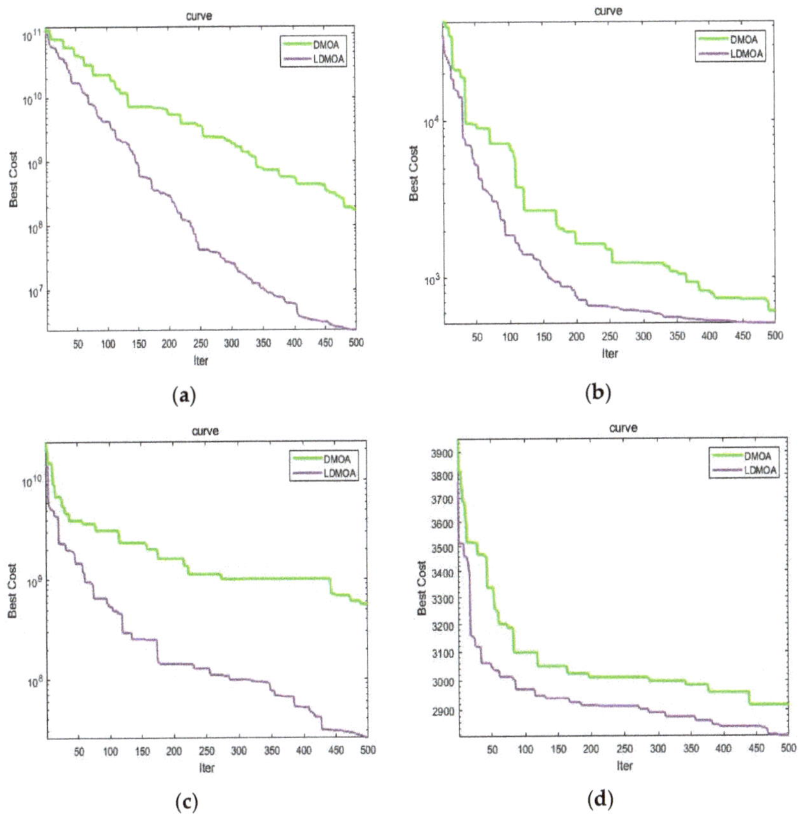

Figure 3. Images of selected test functions: (**a**) f_1, (**b**) f_3, (**c**) f_7, (**d**) f_{13}.

5. Establishing the LDMOA-ELM Model

In the Extreme Learning Machine (ELM) algorithm, the weights w and biases b significantly influence prediction outcomes. Given that these parameters are randomly generated in ELM, their randomness can significantly affect the model's prediction accuracy. This study uses the LDMOA algorithm to optimize the weights w and biases b in the ELM algorithm, leading to notable improvements in prediction error reduction and accuracy enhancement. The LDMOA-ELM model development process is outlined as follows:

Step 1: Import original load data, normalize it, and split it into training and test sets.

Step 2: Initialize DMOA parameters and use Equations (15)–(17) to optimize the initial population, the Alpha Group's foraging process, and the process of finding new sleeping mounds, respectively, resulting in the LDMOA.
Step 3: Compute the fitness function, using the MAPE of the ELM training set as the fitness measure.
Step 4: Exit the loop if the maximum number of iterations is reached or accuracy requirements are met; otherwise, repeat Steps 2 and 3.
Step 5: Use the optimized parameters as the input weights and biases for the ELM model, and then perform numerical predictions and output the model evaluation metrics.

The steps for establishing the LDMOA-ELM model are depicted in Figure 4.

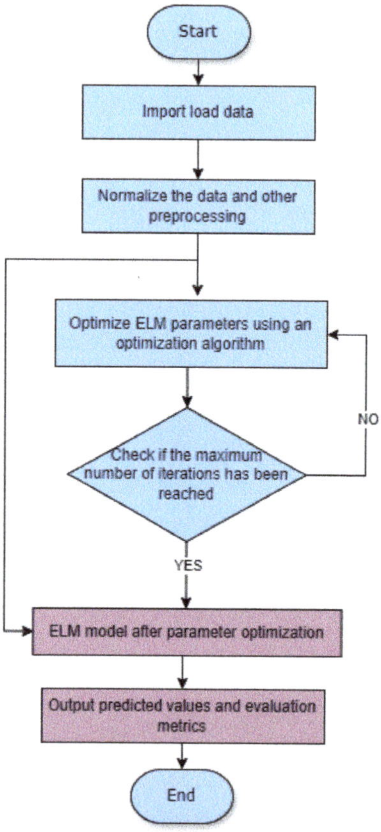

Figure 4. Establishment of the LDMOA-ELM model.

6. Simulation Experiment

In conducting electric load forecasting experiments for comparison, to ensure the efficacy of the improved algorithm, this study pits the proposed LDMOA-ELM algorithm against both the original ELM algorithm and the ELM algorithm optimized by the original Dwarf Mongoose Algorithm. The parameter settings for both the original and the enhanced Dwarf Mongoose Algorithms are detailed in Table 4, where $nPop$ is the population initialization size, Dim is the dimension of the solution space, LB is the lower bound, and UB is the upper bound of the solution space.

Table 4. Parameter settings.

Algorithm	nPop	Dim.	LB	UB	Number of Iterations
DMOA	50	30	−2	2	500
LDMOA	50	30	−2	2	500

6.1. Evaluation Metrics

The electric load forecasting evaluation standards include MAE (Mean Absolute Error), $RMSE$ (Root Mean Square Error), MSE (Mean Square Error), and R^2 (R-Squared, the coefficient of determination) [21]. The formulas for these metrics are shown in Equations (20), (21), (22), and (23), respectively.

$$MSE = \frac{1}{n}\sum_{i=1}^{n}\left(\widehat{y}_i - y_i\right)^2 \tag{20}$$

$$RMSE = \sqrt{\frac{1}{n}\sum_{i=1}^{n}(\widehat{y}_i - y_i)^2} \tag{21}$$

$$MAE = \frac{1}{n}\sum_{i=1}^{n}|\widehat{y}_i - y_i| \tag{22}$$

$$R^2 = 1 - \frac{\sum_{i=1}^{n}(\widehat{y}_i - y_i)^2}{\sum_{i=1}^{n}(y_i - \overline{y})^2} \tag{23}$$

Here, $\widehat{y}_i$ represents the hourly forecasted electric load; $\overline{y}_i$ is the average of the hourly electric load data; y_i is the actual hourly electric load data; and n is the number of data points.

In these metrics, MSE and $RMSE$ values are within '[0, +∞)', where a value closer to 0 indicates perfect model prediction and, conversely, a higher value indicates greater prediction error. The MAE follows the same range and interpretation. An R^2 value closer to 1 indicates a better fit, whereas a lower value indicates a poorer fit.

6.2. Forecasting Results Comparison

The paper utilizes the standard dataset provided by the 2016 "The Electrician Mathematical Contest in Modeling" in China, with sampling every 15 min, resulting in 96 samples per day and a total of 35,040 samples. To ensure consistency in experimental results, the number of hidden nodes in the prediction model is uniformly set to 85, with the sample configuration using data from the previous seven days to predict the eighth day, set across 100 sample groups. In this paper, we optimized the ELM model for multi-step-ahead forecasting by dividing 100 sample sets into 99 training sets and one test set. The statistical data of the three methods' predictions are shown in Table 5. Section 6.1 demonstrates that a higher R^2 value indicates better prediction results, and smaller values for other metrics indicate better performance. Here, the LDMOA-ELM model's MAE, MAPE, MSE, and RMSE values were 61.62, 0.0080845, 5953.4, and 77.158, respectively, all of which were significantly reduced compared to the ELM model. Integrating these five evaluation metrics, it is evident that the LDMOA-ELM used in this study exhibits superior performance across all indicators, with a prediction accuracy of 99.80%, which is an improvement of 15% over the ELM model. This demonstrates that the LDMOA-ELM model achieves lower prediction errors and higher prediction accuracy. The results indicate that the improved predictive model enhances the accuracy of forecasts for the experimental data used in this study.

Table 5. Evaluation metrics.

	MAE	MAPE	MSE	RMSE	R^2
ELM	527.35	0.069746	3.5048×10^5	592.02	0.86538
SSA-ELM	76.713	0.0097348	10,163	100.81	0.99659
DMOA-ELM	72.311	0.009243	9627.1	98.118	0.99689
LDMOA-ELM	61.62	0.0080845	5953.4	77.158	0.99802

As illustrated in Figure 5, LDMOA is more adept at escaping local optima and finding optimal values compared to the original Dwarf Mongoose Algorithm. Figure 6 shows the prediction results graph, indicating that the LDMOA-ELM model's prediction curve best fits the actual value curve. Figure 7 displays the relative prediction errors, revealing that the relative error between the predicted values of the LDMOA-ELM model and the actual values is significantly lower than that of the ELM model. Additionally, by integrating the statistical data from Table 5, it is evident that the LDMOA-ELM model exhibits lower prediction errors and improved accuracy compared to the original ELM model. Particularly in terms of relative prediction errors, as shown in Figure 7, there is a significant difference between the two, with the LDMOA-ELM model outperforming the original ELM model.

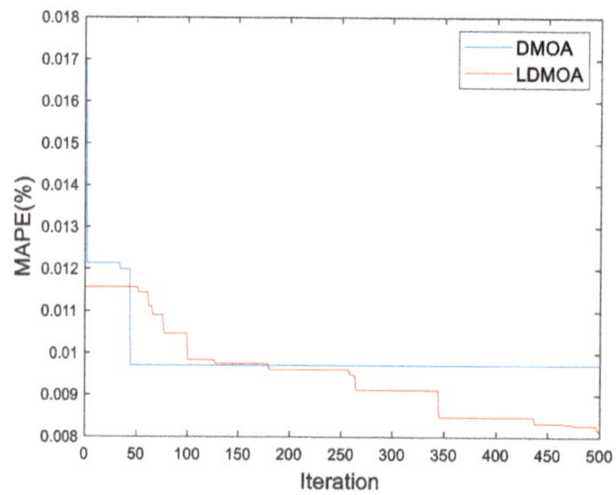

Figure 5. Iterative optimization.

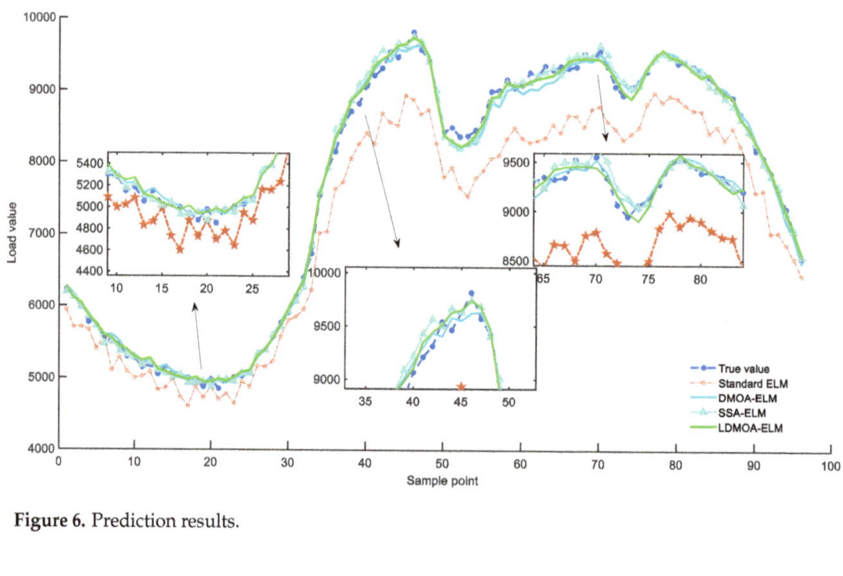

Figure 6. Prediction results.

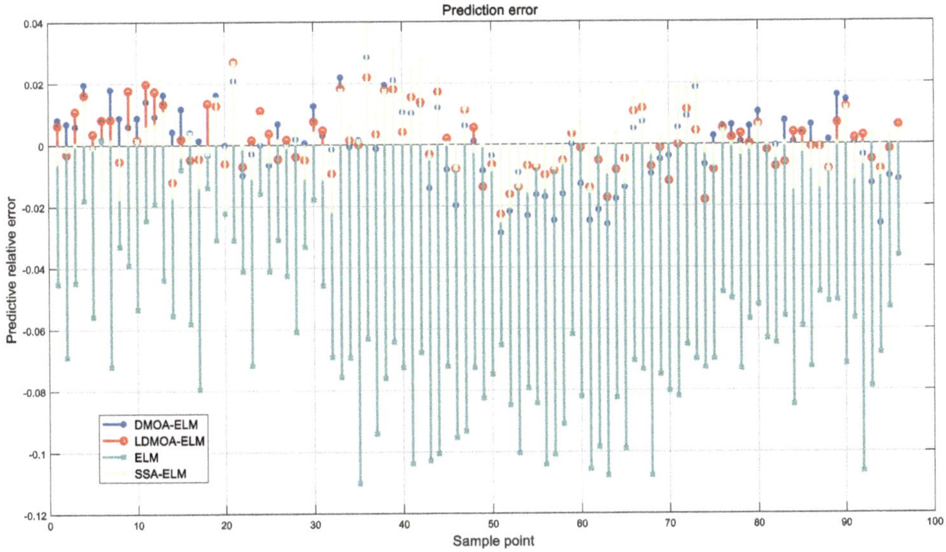

Figure 7. Relative error between predicted and actual load.

Figure 8, the prediction evaluation metrics graph, shows that the ELM model results in the highest error values, while the LDMOA-ELM model yields the smallest error values. Integrating data from Table 5 and Figures 5–8, it is evident that the LDMOA-ELM algorithm, in comparison to both the ELM and DMOA-ELM algorithms, achieves the smallest prediction errors and the highest prediction accuracy, with the LDMOA-ELM algorithm achieving a prediction accuracy of 99.80%. Figure 9 presents the statistical graph for the Mean Absolute Percentage Error (MAPE). It is evident that the original ELM model exhibits significantly higher MAPE values compared to the LDMOA-ELM model. This demonstrates that the LDMOA-ELM model achieves lower prediction errors.

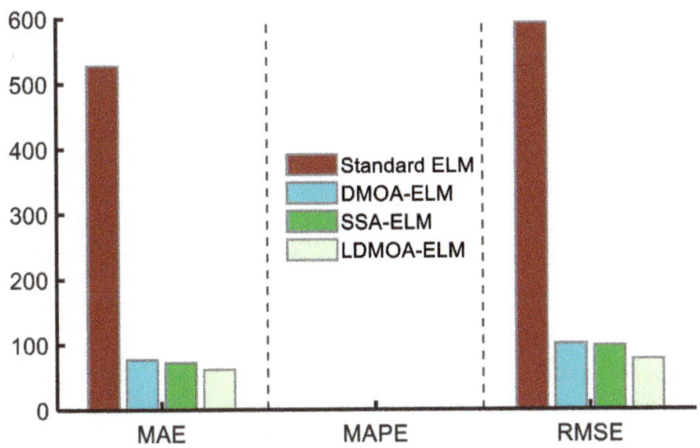

Figure 8. Evaluation metrics.

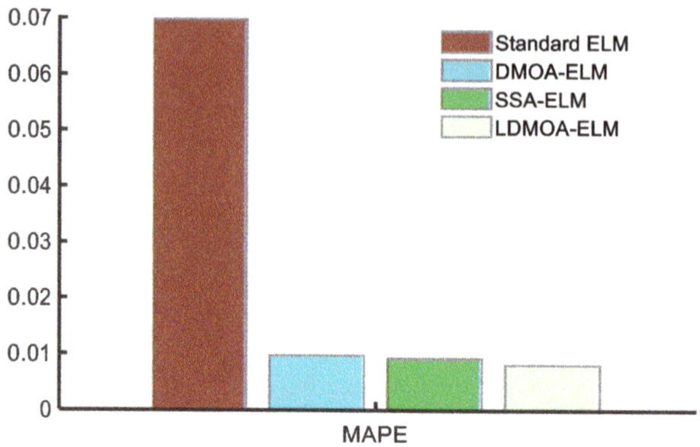

Figure 9. Mean absolute percentage error.

7. Conclusions

In response to the challenges of high randomness and low prediction accuracy in short-term electric load forecasting, this paper introduces a short-term electric load forecasting model that utilizes an enhanced Dwarf Mongoose Algorithm-based ELM. Initially, the Dwarf Mongoose Algorithm was modified by incorporating reverse learning strategies, sine–cosine strategies, and a craziness operator factor, which improved the algorithm's exploratory capabilities, enhanced its global search ability, and enabled it to escape from local optima more effectively. Subsequently, combining the LDMOA with an Extreme Learning Machine, this model was applied to forecast the relevant experimental data and subjected to experimental analysis. The results demonstrate that, compared to the original ELM and DMOA-ELM models, the LDMOA-ELM model exhibits significantly higher accuracy in predicting short-term electric loads.

The LDMOA-ELM model proposed in this paper exhibits a Mean Absolute Error (MAE) of 61.62, which is significantly lower than that of other models, thereby reducing the prediction error of the Extreme Learning Machine to a certain extent. Although the accuracy of the LDMOA-ELM model surpasses that of the original ELM model, the improvement in predictive accuracy is not markedly evident when compared with other models. Future research should focus on further refining the optimization algorithms and selecting more appropriate predictive data to verify the accuracy and applicability of the predictive model. At the same time, subsequent research projects should consider the processing of raw data and comparisons between different methodologies.

Furthermore, future research in load forecasting could consider incorporating methods such as Variational Mode Decomposition for preprocessing the raw data and compare it with other machine learning prediction methods to highlight the advanced nature of the optimized model. It could also be beneficial to explore the impact of varying the number of nodes in the prediction algorithm on the precision of the forecasts, aiming to achieve better load prediction outcomes.

Author Contributions: Conceptualization, H.W., Y.Z. and L.M.; methodology, H.W.; software, H.W.; validation, H.W., Y.Z. and L.M.; resources, Y.Z.; data curation, H.W.; writing—original draft preparation, H.W.; writing—review and editing, Y.Z.; visualization, H.W.; supervision, Y.Z. and L.M.; project administration, Y.Z.; funding acquisition, Y.Z. All authors have read and agreed to the published version of the manuscript.

Funding: This research received no external funding.

Data Availability Statement: This article does not contain new data; the results of the experimental data are presented within the article.

Conflicts of Interest: The authors declare no conflicts of interest.

References

1. Wang, L.; Lin, Y.; Tong, H.; Li, H.; Zhang, T. Short-term load forecasting based on improved Apriori correlation analysis and an MFOLSTM algorithm. *Power Syst. Prot. Control* **2021**, *49*, 74–81.
2. Xie, X.; Zhou, J.; Zhang, Y.; Wang, J.; Su, J. W-BiLSTM Based Ultra-short-term Generation Power Prediction Method of Renewable Energy. *Autom. Electr. Power Syst.* **2021**, *45*, 175–184.
3. Behmiri, N.B.; Fezzi, C.; Ravazzolo, F. Incorporating air temperature into mid-term electricity load forecasting models using time-series regressions and neural networks. *Energy* **2023**, *278*, 127831. [CrossRef]
4. Al-Kandari, A.M.; Soliman, S.A.; El-Hawary, M.E. Fuzzy short-term electric load forecasting. *Int. J. Electr. Power Energy Syst.* **2004**, *26*, 111–122. [CrossRef]
5. Han, M.C.; Zhong, J.W.; Sang, P.; Liao, H.H.; Tan, A.G. A Combined Model Incorporating Improved SSA and LSTM Algorithms for Short-Term Load Forecasting. *Electronics* **2022**, *11*, 1835. [CrossRef]
6. Zhang, Z.; Hong, W.-C. Electric load forecasting by complete ensemble empirical mode decomposition adaptive noise and support vector regression with quantum-based dragonfly algorithm. *Nonlinear Dyn.* **2019**, *98*, 1107–1136. [CrossRef]
7. Ge, Q.B.; Guo, C.; Jiang, H.Y.; Lu, Z.Y.; Yao, G.; Zhang, J.M.; Hua, Q. Industrial Power Load Forecasting Method Based on Reinforcement Learning and PSO-LSSVM. *IEEE Trans. Cybern.* **2022**, *52*, 1112–1124. [CrossRef] [PubMed]
8. Fan, G.F.; Zhang, L.Z.; Yu, M.; Hong, W.C.; Dong, S.Q. Applications of random forest in multivariable response surface for short-term load forecasting. *Int. J. Electr. Power Energy Syst.* **2022**, *139*, 108073. [CrossRef]
9. Xu, R.; Liang, X.; Qi, J.-S.; Li, Z.-Y.; Zhang, S.-S. Advances and Trends in Extreme Learning Machine. *Jisuanji Xuebao/Chin. J. Comput.* **2019**, *42*, 1640–1670. [CrossRef]
10. Deng, B.; Zhang, X.; Gong, W.; Shang, D. An overview of extreme learning machine. In Proceedings of the 4th International Conference on Control, Robotics and Cybernetics, CRC 2019, Tokyo, Japan, 2–30 September 2019; pp. 189–195.
11. Tong, W. Electric load forecasting based on improved Artificial Hummingbird Algorithm optimized ELM. *Comput. Era* **2023**, *6*, 43–47. [CrossRef]
12. Gan, L.; Mei, H.; Liqian, F.; Chongyin, J.; Yongjun, Z. Short-term power load forecasting based on an improved multi-verse optimizer algorithmoptimized extreme learning machine. *Power Syst. Prot. Control* **2022**, *50*, 99–106. [CrossRef]
13. Wang, Z.X.; Ku, Y.Y.; Liu, J. The Power Load Forecasting Model of Combined SaDE-ELM and FA-CAWOA-SVM Based on CSSA. *IEEE Access* **2024**, *12*, 41870–41882. [CrossRef]
14. Zhang, S.; Duan, X.; Zhang, L.; Jiang, A.; Yao, Y.; Liu, Y.; Mu, Y. Tsne Dimension Reduction Visualization Analysis and Moth Flame Optimized ELM Algorithm Applied in Power Load Forecasting. *Proc. Chin. Soc. Electr. Eng.* **2021**, *41*, 3120–3129.
15. Huang, G.-B.; Wang, D.H.; Lan, Y. Extreme learning machines: A survey. *Int. J. Mach. Learn. Cybern.* **2011**, *2*, 107–122. [CrossRef]
16. Wu, Z.; Lu, X. Microgrid Fault Diagnosis Based on Whale Algorithm Optimizing Extreme Learning Machine. *J. Electr. Eng. Technol.* **2024**, *19*, 1827–1836. [CrossRef]
17. Nayak, J.R.; Shaw, B.; Sahu, B.K. A fuzzy adaptive symbiotic organism search based hybrid wavelet transform-extreme learning machine model for load forecasting of power system: A case study. *J. Ambient Intell. Humaniz. Comput.* **2023**, *14*, 10833–10847. [CrossRef]
18. Pan, B.; Hirota, K.; Jia, Z.; Zhao, L.; Jin, X.; Dai, Y. Multimodal emotion recognition based on feature selection and extreme learning machine in video clips. *J. Ambient Intell. Humaniz. Comput.* **2023**, *14*, 1903–1917. [CrossRef]
19. Tizhoosh, H.R. Opposition-Based Learning: A New Scheme for Machine Intelligence. In Proceedings of the International Conference on Computational Intelligence for Modelling, Control and Automation and International Conference on Intelligent Agents, Web Technologies and Internet Commerce (CIMCA-IAWTIC'06), Vienna, Austria, 28–30 November 2005; pp. 695–701.
20. Mirjalili, S. SCA: A Sine Cosine Algorithm for solving optimization problems. *Knowl.-Based Syst.* **2016**, *96*, 120–133. [CrossRef]
21. Yuan, F.; Che, J. An ensemble multi-step M-RMLSSVR model based on VMD and two-group strategy for day-ahead short-term load forecasting. *Knowl.-Based Syst.* **2022**, *252*, 109440. [CrossRef]